LEARNING
DISABILITIES

Educational Principles and Practices

LEARNING

DISABILITIES

Educational Principles and Practices

DORIS J. JOHNSON
and
HELMER R. MYKLEBUST

Institute for Language Disorders
Northwestern University

GRUNE & STRATTON ·

A Subsidiary of Harcourt Brace Jovanovich, Publishers
New York   San Francisco   London

GRUNE & STRATTON, INC.
111 Fifth Avenue, New York, New York 10003

Library of Congress Catalog Card Number, 66-28287
International Standard Book Number, 0-8089-0219-9

Printed in the United States of America

Contents

List of Illustrations

Preface

Research and training in the area of Learning Disabilities have been in progress at the Institute for Language Disorders for more than fifteen years. During this time a wide variety of children have been enrolled in our remediation program. Some had deficiencies in learning to read, some in learning to spell or in acquiring the written word. Many were aphasic or dyscalculic. Most had deficits affecting academic learning although some were deficient in social perception, in ability to tell time, in distinguishing between right and left, in orientation and direction. Others could not judge distance, size, and speed or learn to use maps—though otherwise there was no impairment of intellect.

This volume presents the frame of reference, the principles and practices, that we have evolved in working with these children. The emphasis is psychoneurological, entailing concepts from biomedical engineering, psychology, neurology, psychiatry, education, and language pathology. The purpose throughout is to outline an approach to remediation which we have designated *Clinical Teaching*.

We have intended that this volume fill a need as a textbook for courses aimed at training teachers, as well as other educators and specialists concerned with the intriguing problem of learning disabilities. Underlying this objective is the hope that the concepts and materials might be a contribution to better understanding of learning as a process and thereby enhance this vital experience for all children.

It is with gratitude that we acknowledge the contributions of Regina Cicci as a clinical teacher, of Noriko Akiyoshi and Sue Sordon for preparing the drawings, and of Louise Wilson for her assistance with the manuscript. We are indebted also to our students, graduate and undergraduate, who, perhaps more than they realize, have stimulated our efforts and contributed to the exploration of better ways in which to more successfully meet the needs of those with learning disabilities. For encouragement and for freedom of opportunity we express appreciation to James H. McBurney, Dean of the School of Speech.

Northwestern University
January 1967

Doris J. Johnson
Helmer R. Myklebust

CHAPTER I

Learning Disabilities

Education and psychology have long been concerned with how a child learns, especially as to how he acquires the spoken, read, and written word. The history of special education reveals that often it is through study of the abnormal—mentally retarded, blind, deaf, and emotionally disturbed—that new insights have been gained regarding the intriguing problem of how any child, normal or abnormal, achieves success in learning.

Gradually, a new type of handicapped child has emerged. Presumably, this child existed in the past, but only since refined techniques for determining success in learning became available has it been possible to differentiate him from those who learn normally, to identify him with confidence and accuracy. The handicapped child of this new type has a learning disability of neurogenic origin. Study of these children already has given impetus and challenge to the educator and psychologist, specifically in relation to the question of how the child learns. Perhaps never before has the study of learning, per se, been brought so directly into the psychologist's laboratory or into the teacher's classroom. In this chapter it is our purpose to define a learning disability.

INTEGRITIES FOR LEARNING

Children learn normally only when certain basic integrities are present and when proper opportunities for learning are provided. A disadvantaged child, a child deprived of opportunity, will be deficient in various kinds of learning despite even excellent potentialities. Hence, when appraising deficiencies it is essential that opportunity be considered and evaluated. However, in this discussion our primary concern is the integrities that must be present for learning to ensue normally when opportunities are optimum or at least average. These integrities can be categorized into three types: psychodynamic factors, peripheral nervous system functions, and central nervous system functions.

Psychodynamic Factors

In the past it was assumed that a child would learn without difficulty if he had adequate vision and hearing and all of his mental capacities. Then came the era when childhood autism, childhood schizophrenia, psychogenic deafness, emotional mutism, and psychogenic reading disabilities were recognized (Goldfarb, 1961; Kanner, 1957; Kaplan, 1955; Myklebust,

1

1954). A reconsideration of learning processes became necessary and, as a result, deficiencies in learning must be appraised in terms of possible psychogenic involvement. We first consider the basic patterns of motivation and adjustment.

The processes whereby spoken language is acquired illustrate the significance of the integrity of psychodynamic factors in learning. Through the work of Mowrer (1960) and Piaget (1951) we have begun to understand the importance of factors such as identification. Mowrer demonstrated that talking birds do not talk until they first become pets and moreover that after they begin to talk, they give up some of their natural habits. He interprets these results as an indication that the bird *identified* with his trainer and that, similarly, to develop spoken language the human infant identifies with his parents, especially with his mother. These studies are highly relevant, particularly in reference to babbling. Only humans babble; thus, there is a psychology of this unique function, and accordingly, babbling may be the first distinctly expressive human act (Myklebust, 1954). The infant babbles *because* he is identifying, *because* psychological processes are developing normally. In this connection our evidence suggests that congenitally deaf children do not babble. Presumably for babbling to derive as a psychic process, it must be experienced as an auditory feedback. Otherwise it loses its emotional significance. Also, from parents we learn that autistic children do not babble. One way in which to view this severe emotional illness is that it results when there are marked disturbances in identification processes.

Study of language development indicates further that *imitation* is essential (Brown and Bellugi, 1964). Perhaps the most basic step is identification and when this occurs normally the infant begins to imitate. Through imitation he achieves ability to *internalize*. As internalization proceeds he begins to assimilate his world. Therefore, it appears that there is a hierarchy of psychic processes requisite to learning normally. Although these processes have been observed in children more than in adults, they seem basic to the well-being and understanding of all persons, irrespective of age and other factors. They are fundamental to study and evaluation of all deviations in learning. For learning to be most effective, integrity of emotional-psychic processes must be assumed.

Peripheral Nervous System Functions

Another requisite for normal learning is intactness of the peripheral nervous system. The child learns by receiving information through his senses, through his input systems. Even though all sensory functioning is involved, our discussion is limited to hearing and vision inasmuch as these are the principal channels for symbolic learning.

Many years ago educators recognized that integrity of hearing and vision was essential to normal learning. As a result, special education was provided to meet the detrimental effects deriving from these deficiencies. Gradually, as knowledge accrued concerning the ways in which sensory deprivation modified learning processes as found in normal children, a psychology of deafness and blindness developed (Myklebust, 1964; Revesz, 1950; Zahl, 1950). Through these developments progress has been made in understanding the role of the senses in learning. Moreover, this understanding has served as a background for gaining insights into neurogenic learning disabilities because peripheral and central nervous system disorders represent related but antithetic problems organismically.

As we will see in later discussion, children with dysfunctions of the brain often suffer from *overloading*; the senses deliver more information than the central nervous system is capable of integrating. In contrast, sensory deprivation results in *underloading*; the organism (the brain) is deprived of needed stimulation, of normal input, so the child lacks basic information necessary for growth and for normal maturation of psychological processes. Consequently, special education faces the task of assisting the child in circumventing this fundamental lack of experience. The role of the psychologist is to explore and describe the ways in which the sensory deprivation modifies the principles whereby hearing and visually impaired children learn. The teacher of the future will have more scientifically defined procedures for assisting deaf and hard of hearing, blind and partially sighted children in both learning and adjustment.

That children with peripheral nervous system deficiencies differ in learning processes from hearing and seeing children is becoming increasingly clear (Myklebust, 1964). This point should be stressed because there are educators who oversimplify the handicaps of deafness and blindness by reflecting an attitude of "these children can be taught just like any other child." Serious consequences accrue to those with sensory handicaps because lack of information basic for learning is not easily overcome even through the methods devised by special education.

Another reason for emphasizing the effects of peripheral nervous system defects is that these are readily confused with the effects of dysfunctions in the central nervous system. Although the psychology of deafness and blindness is relevant, it is different from the psychology of those with learning disabilities. In fact, as noted above, the similarity of these psychologies is primarily that in one case we are dealing with the *deprivation* of information and in the other with the *inability* to utilize information normally. Perhaps these psychologies are not comparable and should not be referred to as being similar because one is in a way the inverse of the other. For deeper appreciation it is necessary to view them as being dissimilar; see the definition below of a psychoneurological learning disability. Only when understood as separate and unlike entities can the needs of either group be met most advantageously. It is because they are basically different that each requires its own special education. In fact, the specific detriment on learning—emotional disturbance, peripheral nervous system defects, dysfunctions of the central nervous system—affects the organism in a manner necessitating a unique understanding. It is in this sense that the homogeneity of the groups varies, with the individual condition having a psychology of its own.

Central Nervous System Functions

The third requisite for learning normally is integrity of the central nervous system. It is the psychoeducational effect of dysfunctions in this system with which we are concerned in this volume. Though terminology for description and classification has been difficult to evolve, there is need medically, psychologically, and educationally to recognize that many children have disturbances of learning because they lack integrity of the central nervous system.

Until recent years children who presented problems in learning and adjustment were categorized as being mentally retarded, sensorially impaired, emotionally disturbed, or as having motor disorders. Gradually, workers became aware that there were children who were unable to learn to comprehend, speak, read, write, tell time, play, calculate, distinguish between right and left, or relate well with others and yet who were not mentally retarded, had no sensory impairments, were not primarily emotionally disturbed, and did not present problems of motor disability.

Through the need to find a new, more appropriate and meaningful designation for these children, the concept of minimal brain damage and learning disabilities arose. In addition to distinguishing between children who could hear and see normally and those who could not, between those who had normal motor abilities and those who did not, it became essential to differentiate those with an incapacity to learn from those who, despite integrity of emotional, mental, sensory, and motor functioning, could not learn normally. It became necessary to define a group of children as having a dysfunction in the brain which was not manifested in gross neurological abnormalities but which caused serious deficits in learning, in actualization of what might be high or even very high intellectual potential. We have become aware that many children cannot be beneficially categorized either diagnostically or educationally by groupings and classifications as used in the past, and that learning *incapacities* should not be confused with learning *disabilities*. Special education now is well on the way toward meeting this need, as it has met the needs of other handicapped children.

TERMINOLOGY

Evolving terminology has been arduous and often confusing, but this is not surprising in view of the complexity of the involvements deriving from dysfunctions in the brain. Many types of disturbances in learning and adjustment can result so that originating terms which properly and adequately reflect these involvements is a complicated process. Moreover, a number of disciplines share the obligation for proper diagnosis and classification and each is concerned that its contribution be revealed in the terminology. Perhaps never before have so many disciplines cooperated in attempting to properly diagnose, treat, and educate a particular group of children. Eventually the solution may be for each specialty—education, psychology, medicine—to adopt terminology of its own, as has so often been necessary in the past. In any event, we wish to review the major terms and classifications that have been suggested and then to present terminology which has proved to be scientifically advantageous as well as practical.

Minimal Brain Damage

One of the early terms for designating children with neurogenic learning and adjustment problems was *brain damage*. Most workers found this term unsatisfactory for at least two reasons. It seemed unusually stigmatizing for both the child and his parents; moreover, of considerable consequence scientifically, it might be inaccurate, hence inappropriate and misleading.

Dysfunctions in the brain causing learning disabilities are *not* necessarily due to damage. They may be developmental or they may occur on an endogenous basis and be hereditary in nature (Hermann, 1959; Knobloch and Pasamanick, 1959; Myklebust and Johnson, 1962). The term *damage* assumes that normalcy persisted up to a given point in the life span and that through disease or accident some type of injury was sustained. It is unsuitable for children in whom such circumstances do not pertain; the etiology is neither illness nor accident. Applying the term *minimal* only complicates the problem, as indicated by Birch (1964) and Myklebust (1964). Use of this term arose in attempting to distinguish between children whose involvement was minimal as compared with diffuse. Criteria for verifying this distinction have been difficult to establish, albeit certain children sometimes must be viewed in this manner. How much brain damage constitutes minimal and how much constitutes diffuse remains an open question. For education especially, these designations seem unwieldy and the trend is to interpret them as referring to behavioral manifestations, not to the degree of the involvement in the brain.

Strauss Syndrome

Stevens and Birch (1957) proposed *Strauss Syndrome* as a way for designating children with learning disabilities, reference being to the significant work of Strauss and Lehtinen (1947) which served as an impetus for many investigators, past and present. Despite the importance of this work, it is now apparent that the classic description of the *brain-injured* child provided by them pertains only to a segment, to a certain portion of the total group having neurogenic disorders of learning. In other words, many of these children cannot be described as being disinhibited, perseverative, or distractible—the characteristics constituting the syndrome first highlighted by these investigators. As a classification, therefore, it is often inappropriate. Other terminology is needed.

Neurophrenia

A more adequate term, *neurophrenia*, suggested by Doll (1951) is used to mean the "behavior symptoms ensuing from central nervous system impairment." Perhaps its primary limitation is in being too inclusive. In addition, it lacks specific reference to the fact that in learning disabilities it is the neurology of learning that is disturbed, that remedial education is required, and that capacity for learning is average or even greater.

Perceptually Handicapped

This designation too is an outgrowth of the work of Strauss which stressed the importance of perceptual disturbances. As with the Strauss Syndrome, it is not the initial observations that are in question but rather it is their application. If the brain dysfunction disturbs perception, the consequences in terms of learning can be great. However, to infer that all children with neurogenic learning disabilities have perceptual disturbances is to be in error and to grossly oversimplify. Often the effect is not on perception, per se, but on symbolic processes or on conceptualization. In other words, the brain dysfunction might impede learning at any level of experience, not only one, perception. In fact, because of the specific nature of the behavioral involvement, the psychological-educational problem in some children is how to prevent overdevelopment of perceptual functions to the detriment of other basic processes psychodynamically. The classification *perceptually handicapped*, therefore, is erroneous for many children with learning disabilities.

Another disadvantage of this term should be cited. Perception can be disturbed for a number of reasons, not only as a result of a dysfunction in the brain. Children having certain types and degrees of emotional disturbance, deafness, blindness, or mental retardation can be shown to have disorders of the type commonly referred to as perceptual. The designation of perceptually handicapped does not necessarily identify a child as having a learning disability of neurogenic origin. Thus we find that this classification is both unduly specific and unduly general, referring only to one type of disturbance that results from dysfunctions in the brain and including all disorders of perception irrespective of their nature and causation.

Minimal Cerebral Dysfunction Syndrome

More recently it has been suggested that children with learning disabilities be categorized as having a minimal cerebral dysfunction syndrome (Bax and MacKeith, 1963). Besides being laborious and awkward, this classification includes the disadvantages of the term *minimal,* as discussed above, and is confounded by use of the term *cerebral,* referring specifically to the area of the brain encompassed by the term *cortex.* Functionally or anatomically the brain is comprised of cortical and subcortical structures. As a term, cerebral usually is combined with cortex to specify one of these areas, the cerebral cortex. It is evident that many children have a neurogenic learning disability because of cortical dysfunctions. It is apparent also that many have subcortical, rather than cortical, dysfunctions, localized in the thalamic, hypothalamic region. These could not be included accurately under the term cerebral. Therefore, though *minimal cerebral dysfunction syndrome* may at times be useful, it has limitations for general applicability. For some children it is inaccurate and it lacks suitability for needed legislation and for educational classification.

Specific Dyslexia

Among others, Orton (1937) proposed *specific dyslexia* or *specific reading disability* to refer to children with a disability in learning to read as a result of neurological involvement. This designation has diagnostic and educational value but it cannot be applied to those who have learning disabilities other than dyslexia. For example, it is erroneous and hence inappropriate when applied to those whose disturbance is in spoken or written word usage. Its predominant limitation, therefore, is that it pertains only to deficiencies in reading and it inaccurately implies that all children with deficits in learning have a reading disability.

Psychoneurological Learning Disability

Perhaps we should not anticipate the development of ideal terminology; rarely is this possible for any area of endeavor. Yet certain terms are more suitable and acceptable than others. In education and psychology, the most poignant need is for a classification which clearly indicates that learning processes have been altered and that this modification is due to neurological dysfunction, that it is the neurology of learning which has been impaired and that the result is a *disability*, not an *incapacity*, in learning.

Another important consideration is that initially the manifestations most often are behavioral, not neurological; the more observable symptoms are psychological in nature. The central feature of the condition is the learning disability. Therefore, it is logical and warranted that this feature be specifically identified by the classification. *It is the learning disability that constitutes the basis of the homogeneity of this group of handicapped children* (see the definition below). The second most salient requirement of the terminology is that it specify that the condition is neurological in origin. A learning disability, as noted previously, can result from various conditions so the designation must indicate the type of imposition that prevails, which in this case is a dysfunction in the brain.

In seeking a term that might fulfill our needs, we encountered *psychoneurological* (Benton, 1959; Luria, 1961). The root of the term, *neurological*, clearly discloses that the basic condition is organic and involves the central nervous system. The prefix *psycho* appropriately emphasizes that an important concomitant is behavioral. The designation *psychoneurological*, therefore, indicates that the disorder is in behavior and that causation is neurological. Because it seemed more suitable than other terminology, we suggested its use and a number of workers have found it advantageous (Myklebust and Boshes, 1960).

Conceivably, in the future *psychoneurology* will designate the areas of study concerned with the behavioral disorders associated with brain dysfunctions in human beings. This would distinguish it from neuropsychology, which concerns the relationships between behavior and the nervous system in normal organisms and is usually associated with experimental work in lower animals (Beach et al., 1960). Psychoneurological, unlike terms such as brain-damage, is applicable to all aberrations of behavior having a neurological basis, irrespective of age of onset or etiology. It is in this sense that we refer to children as having a *psychoneurological learning disability*, meaning that behavior has been disturbed as a result of a dysfunction in the brain and that the problem is one of altered processes, not of a generalized incapacity to learn.

DEFINITION AND CRITERIA

Although terms have inherent meanings and implications for definition and for the criteria to be applied, it is necessary to consider these aspects in greater detail. Besides those who have psychoneurological learning disabilities, the total population of children having dysfunctions and disorders of the brain includes the cerebral palsied, the mentally retarded, and perhaps others. Consequently, criteria must be established so that the basic homogeneity of each group is logically and advantageously preserved.

Criteria for definitive differentiation have not yet been finally determined and a degree of overlap is inevitable, but progress has been made scientifically, clinically, and educationally. The crux and focus of the definition and the criteria must be those features, symptoms, and characteristics that designate, circumscribe, and point out the group's homogeneity. In the cerebral palsied it is the motor involvement rather than the difficulty in learning that constitutes the common denominator, the homogeneity of the group. In the mentally retarded it is the generalized intellectual inferiority that brings about homogeneity. In the hearing and the visually impaired it is the sensory impairment which predominates and forms the basis for their homogeneous grouping. Likewise, in the emotionally disturbed it is the psychic maladjustment that prevails and is basic to their being designated as a group within the framework of special education.

This concept of the criteria that serve as the focus for distinguishing among handicapped children by groups is fundamental to this discussion because *in those having a psychoneurological learning disability, it is the fact of adequate motor ability, average to high intelligence, adequate hearing and vision, and adequate emotional adjustment together with a deficiency in learning that constitutes the basis for homogeneity.* This group of children is homogeneous in that they have integrity emotionally, motorically, sensorially, and intellectually, but, despite these integrities, they cannot learn in the usual or normal manner, Definition, therefore, includes two fundamental presumptions: generalized integrity and a deficiency in learning. It is these which are cardinal to the homogeneity of the group and must be established when making a differential diagnosis or when classifying for educational purposes.

Specifics remain to be clarified. Children with learning disabilities might also have minor motor incoordinations as well as a degree of emotional disturbance. We cannot expect that even the best of criteria will permit dichotomous grouping for every child. To some extent each group of handicapped children overlaps with each of the other groups, and the group having neurogenic learning disabilities is no exception. For example, a child may have a learning disability superimposed on deafness, mental retardation, or on any one or more *other* handicaps. This is the well known phenomenon of multiple involvements that always must be considered diagnostically and remedially. On the other hand, the fact that multiple involvement occurs does not preclude the need for developing and applying as definitive and objective criteria as possible. Only through such effort can the classification be most efficacious and beneficial to those whom we are attempting to serve.

We have indicated that in addition to the neurological involvement, the definition of a psychoneurological learning disability presumes certain integrities as well as deficiencies in learning. It follows that the diagnostician and the educator are confronted with the question of how intact a function or an ability must be; integrity assumes what degree of intactness or competence—how much integrity must be present in order to be considered adequate. Stated differently, there is the question of how much of a deficiency in learning must be demonstrated, and on what functions and measures, before it falls within the definition of a learning disability. Each of these questions must be considered.

INTEGRITY LIMITS

Sensory Capacities

Possibly the most objective criteria have been evolved for those who have sensory impairments. It has long been known that a hearing loss of 35 to 40 decibels significantly interferes with communication. More specifically, our concern is how minimal the hearing loss might be without being detrimental to learning. Experientally, and especially in terms of psychological considerations, this limit seems to be approximately 30 to 35 decibels, computed as an average for the speech range on the better ear. A greater loss might result in a detriment to certain types of learning and should not be included within the limits of our definition.

Comparatively, more impairment of vision can be tolerated without a noticeable effect on learning. However, distinction between normal vision and partial sightedness (an impairment of 20/70) is greater than should be accepted. During the past several years we have gathered data on the relationships between ophthalmological status and learning disabilities. That such an association exists has been demonstrated; these findings are presented elsewhere (Lawson, 1967). On the basis of these results a visual impairment of 20/40 or greater should be considered consequential to normal learning. However, this cut-off point pertains only when glasses are worn. Correction through the wearing of glasses is permitted on the presumption that normal vision can be gained. In comparison, this is not true for the use of a hearing aid on the presumption that normal hearing is not attained.

To view an impairment of hearing or vision only in terms of certain cut-off points, however, is to oversimplify the problem and create confusion. By objective definition, quantitative points or limits must be followed as guidelines, but the diagnostician and educator should be aware that the *type* of impairment also is critical for learning. *To be able to hear is not necessarily to be able to listen—to be able to see is not necessarily to be able to look.* Important to the distinction between a sensory impairment and a neurogenic learning disorder is *how* the child uses his sensory capacities.

Nevertheless, our concern here is that the limits within which sensory abilities are assumed to be adequate, i.e., *not* to cause a detriment to learning, must be established as rigorously as possible if a definition is to be applied to those who have learning disabilities as a result of a dysfunction in the brain. Only then can we differentiate between the learning disabilities that are neurological in origin and those that are caused by sensory deprivation. When both a sensory impairment and a learning disability are present, it is incumbent upon the diagnostician and the educator to ascertain the extent to which each handicap is contributing to the total learning detriment and to apply remediation accordingly.

Intellectual Capacities

One of the most consequential differentiations is between mental retardation and neurogenic disorders of learning. In some instances this distinction is not made, or at least is minimized, with the result that terms such as brain injury are applied to all degrees of mental ability. This appears to be true in the works of Graham (1963) and Ernhart (1963). As indicated by this discussion of the definition, it is our contention that children included in the category of learning disability should have adequate intelligence so that the basis of the homogeneity is a *disability*, not an *incapacity*. The question then becomes: How much is adequate? What are the limits within which integrity of intelligence can be assumed and on what measures should these limits be based?

The interest and effort in behalf of children with neurogenic learning disabilities have aroused a greater awareness of the importance of degrees and types of intellectual capacity; some children previously considered to be educable mentally handicapped are now viewed as having a learning disability. The reverse, less expected by both psychologists and educators, also has occurred and is seen principally but not exclusively in children having relatively high verbal but low nonverbal mental ability. When this discrepancy is marked, the child might remain largely incompetent in social maturity *despite* adequacy in academic learning. It is significant also that marked deviations between verbal and nonverbal learning often indicate the area of dysfunction in the brain because such discrepancies may be suggestive of the hemisphere most involved. Verbal abilities typically are localized on the left (dominant) hemisphere and nonverbal abilities appear to be more on the right (non-dominant); Birch and Lefford (1964) suggest that nonverbal abilities may be more widely represented in the brain than are the verbal.

As in other functions, quantitative limits alone do not always serve our purposes well. Clinical judgments and experience are consequential, but quantitative demarcations as guidelines are essential. Brain dysfunctions are assumed to be present in most, if not all, of the mentally retarded; these dysfunctions may be exogenous or endogenous. The question is whether all children with central nervous system involvements can be educated most successfully if they are treated as one group or as two, those who are retarded and those who have learning disabilities but are not retarded. If the psychology of learning and the objectives for each of these groups are highly similar, it would seem that they should be treated as a homogeneous population. On the contrary, if the psychology of learning and the objectives are dissimilar, it seems logical that they do not constitute a homogeneous population and therefore can be educated most effectively only when treated as separate groups.

Though many aspects of this problem must be further clarified, there is increasing evidence to indicate that the psychology of learning for these two populations varies significantly (Myklebust, 1967). Moreover, the educational objectives are not the same. In the mentally retarded we assume a degree of incapacity that no remedial education can overcome, no matter how effective it might be. The task is to ascertain the means whereby these children learn most effectively and then to make certain that they are assisted to learn at the maximum level of their potential. In the child with a learning disability, *normal* potential is assumed and the objective is to actualize this potential through specialized remedial education. Because potential is *normal* or *above*, the problem is to ascertain the processes whereby the child learns most effectively and then to assist him accordingly.

The basic homogeneity of these two groups varies in that in the mentally retarded the psychology of learning involves the attaining of a limited result with limited potential, whereas in learning disabilities the task is to remedially circumvent the peculiarity in learning so that normal or above ability is actualized. In some instances this means attainment far above average because, though a learning disability has been sustained, intellectual potential remains excellent. It can be said that fundamentally the distinction between the mentally retarded and those who have deficits in learning rests on the presumption that the psychology of learning differs as it pertains to incapacities and to disabilities. Though somewhat more obvious, the same presumption is made in distinguishing between the sensorially impaired and those with learning disabilities, as well as among any of the other groups of handicapped children.

We have suggested that quantitative limits are helpful as guidelines and serve to make definitions more stringent. In recent years the trend has been to use 50 IQ as the determining point for the trainable versus the educable mentally handicapped. This cut-off point is useful but it has many limitations both diagnostically and educationally. However, of greater concern to this discussion is where to draw the line between the average and slow-learning mental levels. Common practice on the part of special education has been to classify as educable mentally handicapped those children falling within the range of 50 to 75 or 80 IQ; those falling above 80 IQ are not classified as needing special education. If these ranges are accepted, the limits for learning disabilities would begin with 80 IQ.

In some of our studies we have followed this demarcation and, assuming evidence of a neurogenic involvement, included the 80 to 90 IQ group in the learning disability population. Though this may be advantageous to certain children, using the remedial procedures discussed in this volume, success with this group has been more limited. This should be expected because, though moderate, a degree of mental retardation is present. Therefore, for research purposes, and perhaps also for purposes of remedial education, the definition should be more stringent. It is our practice to consider *adequate* as meaning an IQ of 90 or above. If intellectual ability is below 90 IQ and if a learning disability is present, we define the problem as one of multiple involvement. Obviously, this has much to do with the educational procedures suggested and with the results obtained. Moreover, this definition of integrity with respect to intelligence is directly related to estimates of the incidence of learning disabilities in any population.

Definition of what constitutes adequate intelligence is complicated by the fact that mental ability consists of a number of factors, all important to learning. Therefore, a single measure may be misleading or erroneous. Specifically, it is necessary that the quantitative limits be determined according to several intellectual functions, including both verbal and nonverbal mental abilities. Both types of measures should be employed when group tests are used for screening. The Wechsler Intelligence Scale for Children (1954) often is selected as an individual test because it has the advantage of comprising both verbal and nonverbal scales. However, the scores typically are combined to form a *total IQ*, with the result that significant indications of neurogenic learning disabilities are obscured.

Dubious scores are not uncommon and raise the question of how we define 90 IQ. Moreover, it is mandatory that we be explicit regarding the aspect of intelligence being measured and by what types of tests. A verbal score of 95 and a nonverbal of 80 for an 11-year-old is combined to form a total IQ of 87. The reverse circumstance is a verbal score of 80 and a nonverbal score of 96, with a total IQ of 86. If the total IQ is used, neither of these children falls within the definition of adequate intelligence and thus would not be included within the definition of those having learning disabilities. Depending on more inclusive evidence, both might be typical of such children and should be included in this population.

On the basis of experience, as well as on research evidence, we include in the learning disability group all children attaining an IQ of 90 on *either* a verbal or a nonverbal measure; we do *not* use the total IQ as the determining score. By so doing we find the limits, the definition of adequate intelligence, to be more accurate and effective as a means for differentiating between the mentally retarded and those with learning disabilities. Admittedly, in some instances this quantitative cut-off point fails. For example, one boy had a verbal score of 120 and a nonverbal score of 68, with a total IQ of 95. Despite high verbal intelligence, his ability to function in society even after six years of specialized training suggests that he might be mentally retarded.

More study and experience will be necessary before definite distinctions of this type can be made with confidence and assurance of validity. In other words, the degree of variation that can be assumed for mental abilities, within the limits of adequate intelligence, remains to be further ascertained. In the meantime, (as discussed under deficits in learning) it is highly important that we not take a composite of verbal and nonverbal abilities as the sole criterion for determining the adequacy level.

Motor Abilities

One of the basic ways in which Man matures is in his motor abilities. Our studies of this significant aspect of maturation and growth have included children with deafness, mental retardation, articulatory defects, reading disabilities, and social-emotional disturbance (Myklebust, 1954, 1964, 1967). Besides being a critical indicator of maturational processes, deviate patterns of motor ability are indicative of various diagnostic conditions. In fact, it is the motor deviation that constitutes the primary basis for homogeneity in children handicapped by cerebral palsy. This condition derives from neurological involvement and was one of the early types to be identified as presenting specialized needs resulting from dysfunctions in the brain; the other is mental retardation. Though cerebral palsy has a similar etiology (disorder of the central nervous system), like mental retardation it must be differentiated from the neurogenic learning disabilities. These groups are characterized by varying abilities and learning patterns, hence educational procedures and objectives are different.

Nevertheless, we cannot expect a dichotomous demarcation among the groups. One of the characteristics of children with learning disabilities is minor incoordination, often affecting acquisition of skills such as hopping, skipping, bicycle riding, buttoning, and tying shoe laces. Sitting and walking also may be slightly delayed. The amount of motor integrity that must be assumed for our definition of adequacy is as difficult to determine as that found for the other areas of behavior.

Precise definition is complicated by the lack of well standardized tests of motor ability. We are limited largely to the developmental norms of Gesell and Amatruda (1947), Doll (1953), and Bayley (1935), albeit the Heath Railwalking Test has proved unusually beneficial as a screening device (Myklebust, 1967). The Oseretsky Test (1931) is becoming standardized as a measure of motor behavior. The diagnostician as well as the educator necessarily must use clinical observations to note the incoordinations and disturbances of motor function that typify children with learning disabilities.

Quantitative demarcations, in the sense of scores, cannot now be used as cut-off points for indicating where cerebral palsy or other motor dysfunctions end and where the minor incoordinations associated with learning disabilities begin. Rather, the criterion is whether the child's predominant needs center around the motor problem or the learning disability. This criterion should be applied, keeping in mind that it is on this basis that the homogeneity of each of the groups originates and is maintained.

Other features are utilized when differentiating among these children. As discussed under the deficits in learning, apraxias and ataxias (nonparalytic motor involvements) often are associated with learning abilities and, in fact, apraxia constitutes the problem in expressive aphasia and dysgraphia and so must be included in the definition. However, *these conditions as seen in children typically are not crippling.* Laterality disturbances, as emphasized by Orton (1937), also are included, inasmuch as they too are associated with certain types of learning disabilities. Again, these may affect motor coordination, but they are not crippling. The generalization to be followed is that the *psychomotor* involvements commonly associated with deficiencies in learning are included *within* the category of adequate integrity of motor function, whereas those that are obviously crippling in nature are not.

Emotional Adjustment

Historically, scientific study of Man's emotional growth and development is more recent than the study of his physical and mental growth. Perhaps we should expect less knowledge, as well as fewer techniques for measurement to be available, particularly in regard to children. Though progress is being made, there can be little question that most appraisals of the emotional status of children must be made experientially, that is, on the basis of clinical judgment. Even when projective tests of personality are used, much is dependent on the diagnostician's insights and judgments because of the subjective nature of these tests.

Another limitation is that most personality tests require verbal facility, often to a high degree. With the exception of the MAPS (Shneidman, 1951), projective tests are dependent on spoken or on read language ability; there are few nonverbal tests of personality. Nevertheless, certain tests when properly used can be beneficial in determining the integrity of emotional adjustment and development (Porter and Cattell, 1963).

As in the area of motor functioning, however, quantitative cut-off points are neither advisable nor possible at this time. Final determination must be made on the basis of the total diagnostic information, including the case history and the Vineland Social Maturity Scale (Doll, 1953). The basic criterion is whether the child presents principally a problem of emotional maladjustment or one of a deficiency in learning. Characteristically, children with neurogenic learning disturbances relate well with other children and present no serious adjustment problems in the home. In school their primary difficulty usually is that of academic achievement.

Because of a high level of professional as well as parental interest in neurogenic learning disabilities, some children may be viewed as having these problems when their major involvement is one of emotional maladjustment. On the other hand, for a number of years some children, notably those with reading disabilities, have been viewed as having emotional disturbances only on the basis of their being unable to achieve normally.

Unless aggressive, acting-out behavior or undue preoccupation and withdrawal, together with evidence of poor adjustment in school, in the home, or in other social groups, are present, it should be assumed that the child has no significant emotional problem. Motivational aspects can be helpful in making this determination. When sympathetically understood and properly taught, the child with a learning disability wants to learn and presents no unusual problem of motivation. If he is not identified and provided for in terms of remedial education, he may develop emotional disturbances and then present problems of delinquency and even of mental illness. Fortunately, however, it is not uncommon to find children with learning disabilities who have gone unrecognized by the school for ten years or more without serious consequences emotionally. At least under certain circumstances they can withstand the experience of many years of school failure without developing the symptomatology commonly associated with emotional disturbances.

We see that, as a rule, integrity of emotional growth and adjustment must be determined by clinical assessment and judgment. Quantitative levels of demarcation cannot be applied at this time. Adequate emotional adjustment means that the principal problem is one of learning, not of emotional maladjustment, albeit problems of frustration and discipline may be present.

THE DEFICIT IN LEARNING

We have considered the integrities necessary for fulfilling the requirements of our definition of a deficiency in learning due to a dysfunction in the brain. It remains to specifically define the nature of the learning disability and the nature of the involvement of the brain. First, we analyze the deficiency in learning. The questions to be considered are: *A deficiency in learning what? How much of a deficit must be demonstrated?*

The most commonly recognized deficits in learning on the part of schools and parents are those that pertain to academic success. Therefore, the deficiencies in ability to comprehend the spoken word, to read, to write, and to do arithmetic have received the most attention both in children and in adults. Orton (1937) in neurology and Gates (1947), Monroe (1932) and Fernald (1943) in education did much to emphasize the importance of learning disabilities in children, although no conclusive definition seems to have been evolved regarding the nature and extent of the deficiency.

Another way of stressing the past status and the current circumstances is to state that in most instances attention has been given only to deficits in verbal learning, learning which in the broader sense pertains directly to academic success. Perhaps this is not unusual because these deficits are the most observable. However, experience has clearly demonstrated that deficits in verbal learning are not the *only* deficiencies that are sustained through disturbances of brain function. There are the nonverbal which also are highly significant to achievement and behavior (see Chapter VIII). In fact, depending on the total circumstances, at least in some children this type of learning disability appears more consequential behaviorally than those affecting verbal abilities. Therefore we come to a conclusion relative to the first question: A deficiency in learning what? The deficiency may be in learning *either* verbally or nonverbally, though at present, through observation as well as through objective tests, we most successfully recognize and identify those predominantly verbal in nature.

Together with deficits in the learning of arithmetic, deficiencies in acquiring spoken, read, and written language constitute the primary areas under the category of disabilities in verbal learning. Under the non-verbal are found disturbances in learning to tell time, directions (east and west), body orientation (right and left), meaning of facial expressions (happiness and anger), meaning of the behavior of others (learning to play games such as "cowboy"), music and rhythm, and meaning as conveyed in art.

We have referred to some of the limitations in nonverbal learning as deficiencies in *social perception*. Often they are recognized by both the parents and teachers who raise questions about the child's inability to understand his world and to relate with others, although he has good verbal proficiency and has no indication of emotional disturbance. These disabilities sometimes can be demonstrated by having the child describe what is happening in a picture clearly depicting a scene, such as father's return after a day's work. Children having these deficits usually see no relationship between the persons and the circumstances pictured, indicating a serious lack of ability to understand even common everyday happenings in his world. Despite good visual perception and high levels of intelligence (as measured by verbal tests) they are low on certain nonverbal measures of mental ability. These children present a challenge in terms of remedial education. Neurologically, their primary dysfunction appears to be on the right hemisphere of the brain.

Before further defining the nature of the deficit in learning, it is necessary to consider what constitutes a learning disability. These deficits represent a discrepancy between ability and achievement, between potential for learning and the level of learning attained. A neurogenic learning disability is a type of underachievement, but it differs from others in that it is due to a dysfunction in the brain and occurs in the presence of the integrities discussed above. The question before us then is: *How much of a discrepancy between ability and achievement must occur for the condition to be categorized as a learning disability?*

Several indices of the extent of the deficiency have been used with varying degrees of success. In practice, a common index has been whether the child is one year or more below the level of expectancy. Though useful as a quantitative guideline, it has serious limitations because one year below expectancy at eight years of age is not comparable to one year below expectancy at 16 years of age or, for that matter, at three or four years of age. A ratio would be more accurate, definitive, and predictive; this type of score remains constant irrespective of age.

Another factor must be mentioned. For the majority of children the mental and chronological ages are essentially equivalent and usually can be assumed inasmuch as those below 90 IQ are excluded by definition. However, some children with learning disabilities are far above average in intelligence. (We have worked with a number who have been remarkably bright, attaining IQ levels of 130 and above.) They may *not* fall below the level of expectancy according to chronological age but yet fall substantially below expectancy when mental age is used as an indication of the learning level that should be attained. Therefore, the most satisfactory ratio, the most accurate manifestation of relationships between attainment and level of learning expected, is obtained when achievement is related to mental age.

When the ratio of achievement to mental age is computed, the result is a Learning Quotient—a quotient exhibiting the degree of learning achieved in relation to intellectual potential for learning. Learning quotients can be computed for various types of verbal and nonverbal achievement, including reading, spelling, arithmetic, visual and auditory perception, and facility with the written word. However, in applying this procedure to large groups of school children, we ascertained that below 10 or 11 years of age the relationship between certain types of achievement and ability varies on the basis of chronological age and grade placement as well as on the basis of mental ability. It appears that *readiness*, particularly for learning to use written language and arithmetic, is dependent also on physical maturation and school experience, not on mental capacity alone. Therefore, the relationship between achievement and potential for learning, at least up to 10 or 11 years of age, must also take into consideration life age and school experience.

When opportunity for learning and chronological age are controlled, the Learning Quotient offers the advantage of providing a quantitative basis for defining the deficit in learning. As such, it has proved of considerable value and has become the means whereby the deficiencies in learning can be profiled so that the teacher has a specific outline of the child's level of function in relation to what should be expected.

Because we have taken an IQ of 90 as the lowest level of intelligence to be included in the learning disability group, we have taken a Learning Quotient of 89 or below as being indicative of a deficit in learning. Though this seems stringent, seems too inclusive, in actual practice it has been highly satisfactory. A common observation is that as the child becomes older his quotient diminishes because, although his mental age increases year by year, his achievement in learning increases only slightly. The result is that statistically there is a negative correlation between ability and achievement. In general, the Learning Quotient of a typical population of children with learning disabilities is considerably below 90.

The definition of a neurogenic learning disability thereby includes the need to set limits of how much of a deficiency must be shown before inclusion in this category is warranted. Our discussion now concerns the question of the function, abilities, and measures on which the deficit should be demonstrated.

AREAS OF DEFICIT

As stated previously, the deficit in learning can be either verbal or nonverbal. Because disabilities predominantly verbal in nature are more commonly observed and because measures of these functions are more firmly established, they are considered first and in greater detail. The verbal systems used by Man, all of which must be included in the concept of neurogenic learning disabilities, can be viewed in at least three ways: as input and output processes, as sensory modality processes (auditory-visual), and as processes involving integration.

Input-Output

A relationship can be seen between understanding the spoken word and speaking, and between reading and writing. These relationships are fundamental to learning and to the remedial procedures and principles presented in this volume. The presumption is that learning is systematic and sequential and that the order of events is for *output to follow, not to precede, input*. The child speaks only after he comprehends, only after he has learned words to speak. Likewise, he writes only after he can read, only after the read word has been learned.

This principle of learning in terms of input and output is stated primarily in terms of initial learning processes because, after a level of competence has been attained, words may be learned through usage. However, they have meaning in output only when they have become meaningful in input. The input-output concept of learning is exceedingly advantageous for understanding neurogenic learning disabilities and for the definition of this condition because, relative to the question of deficit on what functions, it is apparent that the deficiency may be for input or for output or for both.

Sensory Modality

Another consequential manner in which learning disabilities can be considered is by the sensory modality (or modalities) through which a given type of learning occurs and through which the learning processes might be deficient. Though tactual learning is relevant and important to our total concept, it is not emphasized here because data are limited for neurogenic detriments of this type. Perhaps because the verbal systems are predominantly auditory or visual, it is these modalities about which most information and knowledge have been gained. As the discussion throughout this volume illustrates, much academic learning is auditory, visual, or both. Again it is helpful to note the relationship to the processes involved in verbal behavior. The spoken word comprises auditory receptive capacities (comprehension—input) and an auditory expressive function (speech—output). Reading and writing entail visual receptive and visual expressive processes, reading being a receptive (input) and writing an expressive (output) function. It is apparent that deficiencies might be auditory and/or visual in nature. Moreover, these learning disabilities are common because the auditory and visual modalities are involved in most learning; those often occurring because of such involvements include the aphasias, dyslexias, spelling disorders, and the dysgraphias (Birch and Lefford, 1964; de Hirsch, 1966; Myklebust, 1965; Orton, 1937).

Integration

In the above discussion we noted that the deficit in learning may be principally in input, in output, or in both—in receptive or expressive functions, or in both. But failure to indicate another type of disability would be to erroneously oversimplify learning processes and the deficiencies that occur. Clinical experience, as well as research, has shown that input and output, reception and expression, can be intact in the presence of some of the most debilitating learning disabilities. A common example at the level of the spoken word is the *echolalic,* and at the level of the read word the most obvious example is the *word-caller.* The child who is echolalic repeats what is said and the word-caller identifies the words he sees in print. The remarkable feature in each of these conditions is that in neither case is *meaning* associated with the words. Though the words are received and expressed, they have no symbolic significance. The detrimental effect is on ability to acquire meaning. The echolalic does not know what he is saying, and the word-caller does not know what he is reading. Because the nature of the processes whereby meaning is acquired is highly complex psychologically and neurologically, the best we can do is to recognize the extreme forms of this condition. That there is a wide range within such deficits in learning seems apparent. Unfortunately, due to the types of tests available for measuring both intelligence and achievement, integrative learning disabilities often go undetected.

Detailed discussion of the primary psychoneurological processes involved in learning is reserved for Chapter II. At this point our intention is to emphasize that there are three basic ways in which learning may be impeded neurologically. *The detriment may be on expressive, receptive, or integrative functions.* In verbal behavior these deficits are categorized as occurring in expressive language, in receptive language, or in inner language.

Concerning the question "Deficit in learning what" we stress that the deficiencies may be in any one or in combinations of these functions. The most difficult to identify and to describe clinically is the deficit in acquiring meaning, the *significance* aspect of experience. Moreover, when the detriment concerns receptive functions, inner language (meaning) is reciprocally affected. Deficits in input *cause* a limitation in the development of meaning. This aspect of the *consequences* of learning disabilities has been inadequately emphasized and requires much attention from the educator.

MEASUREMENT OF DEFICITS

Thus far in our discussion of the definition of psychoneurological learning disabilities, we have considered the integrities required and the types of deficiencies to be demonstrated. It remains to discuss the measurement of these deficits. Using the concept of the Learning Quotient considered above, we illustrate the ways in which the deficiency in learning may be quantified. As far as possible the measures are to reveal achievement levels for expressive, receptive, and integrative processes, including various types of memory as well as levels of achievement both verbal and nonverbal.

Integrative learning functions are especially difficult to measure objectively because tests remain largely undeveloped. Our approach is to have the child demonstrate (verbally or nonverbally) that he has grasped the significance of the problem that has been presented. In both children and adults, but perhaps especially in preschool children, a type of "world test" might be administered. Objects representing the child's world of experience are placed before him and he is to arrange them in an order showing meaningfulness. (A similar approach was used with adults by Goldstein (1948).) For example, toy furniture and other objects representative of common furnishings in the home are given to him. With only an indication that he is to play with them, the child proceeds to arrange and organize according to a pattern that reveals his inner world of experience. Children who are not learning successfully from everyday experience assemble them in a random, meaningless manner. We have used this technique advantageously with many young children.

Another way to obtain information on integrative processes is to ascertain the extent to which the child has achieved an understanding of the concepts of time, size, direction, speed, length, and height. Deficiencies in these kinds of achievement are seen frequently and are associated with problems in verbal learning, i.e., dyslexia (Myklebust and Johnson, 1962). One of the common indications of deficits in integration is the child's inability to grasp the meaning of a passage, a paragraph, or a short story from having heard it or from reading it. The diagnostician is constantly alert to this type of problem. Tests of "social intelligence" and social perception also are useful (picture arrangement, etc.).

Deficiencies in the receptive aspects of learning, verbally and nonverbally, can be shown in various ways. Usually the techniques include exploration only of auditory and visual receptive processes, even though tactile reception may be pertinent. When evaluated verbally, the child is asked to follow directions or instructions given orally (auditory) or through his reading them (visually). Nonverbally, the child may be required to identify various social sounds and pictures; the identification does not require verbal expression. At the level of expressive learning, the child is asked to speak, write, draw, pantomime, or gesticulate.

When the achievement levels have been measured and the quotient computed for each type of learning, a profile is made of his various deficiencies. Depending upon chronological age and other factors as discussed above, if the quotient on any area is below 90 the child is viewed as having a learning disability, providing the other criteria established by the definition have been met. It is children with this type of deficit in learning who compose the group falling *within* this category of handicap. It is these learning deficiencies that constitute the homogeneity of this population. By definition, certain integrities and certain deficits, together with a neurogenic dysfunction, must be present. Our final consideration concerns the nature of the involvement in the brain.

THE BRAIN DYSFUNCTION

The definition of neurogenic disabilities in learning includes three basic attributes: the integrities to be demonstrated, the nature and extent of the deficiency in learning, and the dysfunction in the brain. The question of whether neurological evidence must be revealed, whether such evidence is mandatory before classification as a neurogenic learning disability is warranted, has been under much discussion and has at times been a source of controversy. Gradually, the disciplines involved have tended toward the observation, if not the conclusion, that in certain children no one type of evidence is clearly definitive; no one type of appraisal will necessarily reveal the brain dysfunction in a given child. In other words, positive neurological findings appear in children who show no behavioral symptoms, no deficits in learning.

The reverse also is true: the type of learning deficits herein defined may be obvious even though neurological findings are negative. These diverse circumstances are *not* necessarily inconsistent. With few exceptions, specialists no longer maintain that if *they can't find it, it does not exist.* Rather, they are aware and appreciative of the fact that their procedures and techniques do not reveal all dysfunctions in the brain. The neurologist may not be able to elicit evidence of such disorders in given children even though the dysfunctions exist and are of substantial consequence to behavior. After considerable experience, however, it is clear that neurological evidence revealing dysfunctions in the brain can be demonstrated, even statistically, more often than has been assumed (Boshes and Myklebust, 1964; Myklebust, 1967).

Electroencephalography too must be considered when we raise the question of neurological evidence. Essentially the same comments can be made regarding this procedure for eliciting objective findings of a disturbance in brain functioning as for the neurological examination. In some instances the EEG may show no abnormality even when behavioral findings indicate a marked mental deficiency. This is rare, but does occur. Again we must infer that electroencephalography reveals certain, but not necessarily all, types of the brain dysfunctions that might be present.

Inasmuch as no one procedure can be relied upon to provide evidence for all types of dysfunctions in the brain, by far the most satisfactory is to utilize *both* the neurological examination and the electroencephalogram, performed by those experienced with children. In this way objective evidence is increased; these approaches provide different types of information, hence using both is more inclusive and definitive. There is the additional fact that some of these children are benefitted by medical treatment and management. Only when these techniques are effectively and consistently used can this aspect be adequately explored.

Most learning disabilities of the neurogenic type are first observed by the parents or by the teacher. Usually their observations are followed by a psychological-educational evaluation. A psychologist, like a neurologist, may state that a psychoneurological learning disability is present on the basis of various tests chosen for the purpose. For completeness and to obtain as much evidence as possible, the child is also seen by the neurologist and the electroencephalographer. Should these studies not show positive findings, classification is made on the basis of properly derived behavioral evidence on the presumption of a dysfunction in the brain. Because there is not a 100 percent correlation between behavioral and neurological evidence, *either* is used to make the final classification.

To deny a child the benefits of special education because neurological evidence cannot be elicited is to deprive him of opportunities on the basis of an illogical, if not naive, point of view regarding differential diagnosis. Agreement between behavioral and neurological findings has been found in as many as 80 percent of children referred by schools on the presumption that neurogenic learning disorders were present (Myklebust and Boshes, 1960). As diagnostic procedures are developed and improved, the number in whom neurological evidence is lacking will be reduced.

SUMMARY

In this chapter it has been our purpose to review the problems of terminology, criteria, and definition. It is not our intention to imply that all of these problems have been resolved but to stress their nature and to indicate that progress is being made. No longer can we view these children simply as hyperkinetic, hyperactive, perceptually disturbed, or as synonymous with the mentally deficient. The basis of their homogeneity is not reflected by these classifications. Their homogeneity derives from the fact that there is a *deficit in learning in the presence of basic integrity.* ⇁ Some are hyperkinetic and some are perceptually disturbed, but many, possibly the majority, have deficits in acquiring the spoken word, in learning to read, to use written language, to spell, to tell time, to judge distance, size, length, and height, or to calculate, though they are not hyperactive and show no perceptual disturbances of the type often stressed in the past.

The principal criterion as seen in the discussion of the definition is that the child demonstrates a degree of integrity intellectually, emotionally, sensorially, and motorically—that he falls within a range of normal in respects other than in learning and that there is behavioral or neurological evidence of a dysfunction in the brain. We can emphasize this criterion by stating that the group of children having psychoneurological learning disabilities is homogeneous in that it consists of those who are not mentally retarded, emotionally disturbed, cerebral palsied, or sensorially impaired but who, despite gross integrity, are not able to learn normally. This group is heterogeneous in that many types and degrees of learning disabilities are present and in that various types and degrees of brain dysfunctions are demonstrated.

These children present a challenge diagnostically and educationally; it is incumbent upon the community of specialists involved to meet this challenge. Only then will this substantial number of children receive the benefits to which they are entitled. Only then will we have provided them with the means whereby they might actualize their potential and assume their rightful role in society.

CHAPTER II

The Brain and Learning

Scientists representing a number of disciplines have probed the relationships between brain functions and the ways in which Man learns. Especially relevant to the discussion in this chapter are the works of Birch (1964), Geschwind (1967), Gibson (1965), Hebb (1963), John (1961), Luria (1961), Mowrer (1960), Myklebust (1965), O'Connor and Hermelin (1963), Penfield and Roberts (1959), Pimsleur and Bonkowski (1961), Russell (1959), and Werner and Kaplan (1963). Through research and clinical effort it is possible to postulate the significance of the neurology of learning as it relates to educational remediation for children with learning disabilities.

The semi-autonomous systems concept is an important contribution. It proposes that the brain is made up of semi-independent systems, that at times a given system functions semi-independently from others, at times in a supplementary way with another, and that at times all systems function interrelatedly. Diagnostically and in terms of remedial education this concept has many implications for a psychoneurological theory of learning as well as for better understanding of neurogenic learning disabilities. It follows that each psychoneurosensory system must be appraised as it functions semi-autonomously, in coordination with another system, and as all of the systems function simultaneously. This means that as it pertains to learning and learning disabilities, the auditory system may function semi-autonomously from the visual system or the tactile system, and that each of these in turn may function semi-independently from any one of the other two. Olfaction, gustation, and proprioception are not stressed because, though to a degree all senses are involved in learning, these are less closely associated with neurogenic learning disabilities. This being the case, psychoneurologically there are three primary types of learning—the first requiring only one neurosensory system, such as the auditory; the second requiring two or more but not all of the systems; and the third requiring all of the systems functioning as a unit.

This frame of reference has significant implications for education, so we use the term *intraneurosensory* to refer to learning which entails predominantly one system in the brain, *interneurosensory* for that entailing more than one, and *integrative* for learning which utilizes all of the systems functioning simultaneously. Another way of stressing the neurology of learning is to emphasize that the brain must receive, categorize,

26

store, and integrate information. We will illustrate these processes as they pertain to learning disabilities.

INTRANEUROSENSORY LEARNING

Strictly considered there may be no learning that is *purely* intra-neurosensory and it is not our intention to infer that a given type of learning is exclusively auditory or visual. Rather, we view these processes as being at times (in certain instances of learning) *relatively* independent of other psychoneurosensory processes. An example is the spoken word; that which is received and that which is expressed are both auditory in nature. Though the speech motor system is involved, for purposes of learning the information is auditory.

On this basis it is assumed that a dysfunction in the brain can disturb auditory-neurological processes without fundamentally disturbing others. Indeed, ablation studies, as well as clinical experience, confirm that this is possible (John, 1961; Neff and Diamond, 1958). Accordingly, there are problems of auditory discrimination, comprehension, and memory *without* equivalent involvements of visual psychoneurological processes. In other words, the learning disability may impede the receiving, storing, recalling, and categorizing of auditory information without directly causing a similar detriment to other types of learning. The same can be said for disturbances of visual, tactile, and proprioceptive learning. It is in this sense that certain of these disorders are intraneurosensory in nature. There are obvious implications for differential diagnosis and, according to the purpose of this volume, for practices and procedures in remedial education.

INTERNEUROSENSORY LEARNING

Without so stating, psychologists and educators have been investigating both intra- and interneurosensory processes for decades. Gradually better understanding and greater knowledge are being achieved. Many investigators now stress that as a process learning has been seriously over-simplified in education, psychology, and neurology. One of the fortunate by-products of the scientific study of handicapped children is the insight gained concerning the nature of all learning; study of those with psycho-neurological learning disorders is no exception. One of these gains has been in relation to the disabilities we designate as being interneurosensory in nature.

According to the semi-autonomous systems concept, certain learning ensues when two or more systems function interrelatedly; much learning seems to be of this type. There are numerous ways in which this can be observed. A similar emphasis on this aspect of learning has been given by the terms *cross-modal* and *intersensory perception* (Birch, 1964; Pimsleur and Bonkowski, 1961). Biomedical engineering has assisted through its emphasis on *transducing.* Young (1964), with biomedical engineering models of the brain, defines a transducer system as "structures that change one form of energy to another"—he uses the eye as an illustration because it transduces light rays into electrical energy.

This definition serves our purpose but we must include the inner processes whereby one type of neurosensory information is converted into another within the brain itself. The act of uttering a word serves as an example. An individual may comprehend spoken language, be able to integrate and recall it, but not be able to say the word that he has in mind. He may be unable to speak because he cannot transduce the heard signals into their motor-kinesthetic equivalents. This condition is an *expressive aphasia,* a type of *apraxia.* Neurologists first recognized this condition more than a century ago, but only recently have new insights been gained relative to its true nature. Apraxias are frequently seen in children with neurogenic learning disabilities. There are apraxias which involve nonverbal functions, but expressive aphasia and dysgraphia are those most commonly observed.

Another interneurosensory learning disability is *dyslexia,* a condition which impedes learning to read. The first language system acquired is the spoken word (Myklebust, 1965). Initially, when the child learns to read he does so by converting or translating the visual word into its auditory equivalent; Gibson (1965) has presented illuminating data. In the presence of a certain type of dysfunction in the brain, this cross-modal learning may be impeded. The child learns the spoken word and what the letters look like, but he cannot associate these images with the way they sound (an auditory type of dyslexia). The reverse also can occur. He learns what letters sound like but cannot make the normal association between these auditory images and their appearances (a visual type of dyslexia). Disorders of this nature constitute a major portion of those encountered in children with psychoneurological learning disabilities. Various aspects of learning can be involved with many combinations, including input and output, verbal and nonverbal. Knowledge concerning these deficiencies is being acquired. Again, the implications for differential diagnosis and educational procedures are of unusual importance.

Scientifically and clinically, less assurance is claimed for transducing processes as defined by Young (1964), but these too offer excellent possibilities for understanding the complex learning disabilities referred to as *agnosia.* Like apraxias, this condition has been known in neurology for decades; Freud (1953) was one of the first to use this term. In diagnosis it refers to an individual who receives information through the senses (auditory, visual, tactual) but is not able to comprehend it; he cannot interpret what he hears, sees, or touches. Many variations are found in children with learning disabilities. Psychologically, this problem may be reflected as a disorder at the level of perception. Young's discussion provides an explanation in terms of psychoneurology. If light rays or frequencies of sound cannot be transduced into electrical impulses, lack of recognition would be expected. In contrast to apraxias, agnosias are input disorders. Broadly speaking, apraxias and agnosias make up a substantial portion of the psychoneurological deficiencies in learning. In other words, many of the deficits concern processes of reception and expression, of input and output. A number of these processes include interneurosensory functioning.

INTEGRATIVE LEARNING

A complex aspect of learning, one difficult to describe psychoneurologically, is that which involves integration. As in intra- and interneurosensory functioning, it is not implied that integration occurs or does not occur, or that it can be dichotomously differentiated from other aspects of learning. All types of learning assume some level of integration. However, as noted in Chapter I, conditions such as echolalia and word-calling highlight the need to distinguish among learning processes intra-, inter-, and integrative in nature, albeit there are types and degrees of each.

In Language Pathology, verbal behavior can be categorized as inner, receptive, and expressive. Inner language as a process is the transforming of experience into symbols (verbal and nonverbal) for purposes of self-awareness, thinking, and adjustment. Vygotsky (1962) did much to initiate this concept, and recently the work of Werner and Kaplan (1963) has extended it. Inner language is the result of basic integration of experience and makes meaning and significance possible. This aspect of human behavior is less well understood than that of reception and expression. Nevertheless, as a concept in learning it seems salient; it is that which gives substance to the processes of input and output.

Through investigations like those of Werner and Kaplan, and Miller, Galanter, and Pribram (1960) in psychology, and Geschwind (1967), Penfield and Roberts (1959), and Russell and Espir (1961) in neurology, clarification has been attained—not only in the definition of integrative learning, but in understanding the systems and processes that make it possible. Penfield's contribution includes designation of a subcortical area of the brain as the *centre-encephalic* system; this highlighted the fact that there is a neurology of inner language. Although broader functions are involved, Russell's contribution also is of importance. He differentiated the neurology for receptive, expressive, and inner language but he uses the term *central aphasia.*

In work with children who have psychoneurological learning disabilities, the integrative aspects of learning have taken on greater significance as more experience and research have been accomplished. There are many examples. Those primarily deficient in nonverbal learning often have difficulties in acquisition of meaning. Those reduced in ability to conceptualize, as defined by Goldstein (1948), appear unable to integrate normally. Those deficient in social perception also have problems of this nature. Those competent in both reception and expression of spoken language, who read fluently but cannot comprehend the meaning of a story, often present this type of learning problem. These children usually score higher on speed and oral reading than on reading for comprehension.

Much remains to be achieved, but integrative learning disabilities should be recognized by the diagnostician as well as by the educator. We should not assume that these children are mentally deficient. Often they fall within the normal range of intelligence on measures such as the Wechsler, so mental tests do not always disclose their problem. Deficiencies in integrative functioning are included in the definition of psychoneurological learning disabilities and the challenge which follows should be met.

THE BRAIN AND OVERLOADING

The semi-autonomous systems concept presupposes that the information being received through a given sensory avenue might impede normal integration of that received through another. This psychoneurological disturbance is illustrated clinically by the child who rejects auditory in favor of visual information, and vice versa. It is seen in the child who looks away so as not to see the face of the speaker because he comprehends better; he may disintegrate when trying to imitate speech by watching himself and the speaker in a mirror.

Another manifestation of this disturbance is the child who reads well silently but shows signs of disintegration when reading orally. Oral reading helps us to understand and describe aspects of brain function that take on unusual significance in the study of neurogenic learning disabilities. Reading silently, so far as input is concerned, involves only one type of information; transducing to the auditory may take place but the information to be dealt with is only visual. The reader, therefore, scans the printed page line by line, monitoring the speed of input and the direction of the flow (left to right) and at the same time integrates what is being read so that meaning is attained; *attention must be given to what is being read.* If the words are read while attention is directed elsewhere, the material may be "read" without knowledge of its content. In some respects, attention is the key whereby integrative processes are initiated.

The act of reading silently is complex, comprising a number of psychoneurological processes, but the act of oral reading is even more complex. The reader must monitor and integrate two types of information simultaneously. The primary information to be taken in is visual—words on the printed page. Therefore, the visual receptive and integrative functions must go on as in the act of silent reading but, in addition, the words must be spoken. The purpose of reading aloud is reception by others of the information contained in the written word. The words can be spoken properly only if they are monitored by audition. Thus while monitoring and integrating the visual input, what is being received through vision must be simultaneously transduced to its auditory equivalents, spoken and monitored by audition; what is spoken must conform to the visual and show proper inflection, stress, intonation, as well as dropping of the voice at the end of a sentence.

From the psychoneurological point of view, the act of reading aloud is an intricate process. It can be said to include intra- and interneurosensory and integrative functions simultaneously. A number of children manifest disturbances only when more than one process is required at a given time. It is in this context that the concept of *overloading* takes on value and is significant in education. The multisensory approach, if used promiscuously, can be damaging. Miller (1964), with remarkable precision, has shown that even normal systems within the brain can be overloaded; Young (1964) has added to this knowledge.

A dysfunction in the brain lowers tolerance limits for processing information. A child may deal effectively with information involving intraneurosensory processes but show symptoms of disintegration when interneurosensory and complex integrative functions are required; he then manifests confusion, poor recall, random movements, poor attention, disinhibition, and, in rare instances, seizures. The information being received through a given sensory modality impedes integration of that being received through another. Overloading can cause a generalized breakdown in neurological processes which has implications not only for reducing the ability to learn but for total well-being, including medical treatment and management.

To explore the concept of overloading in relation to learning, we are engaged in waking brain studies. While the child is engaged in intra- or interneurosensory and integrative learning tasks, EEGs are taken and analyzed by computer techniques. The presumption is that overloading can be defined as it relates to psychoneurological disturbances of learning. Fundamental too is the anticipation that educational methods, techniques, and procedures can be more scientifically oriented. It is conceivable that research will reveal that some children learn most effectively in the presence of certain well defined combinations of input and output. Such studies may become routine in differential diagnosis because of the possibility that some dysfunctions can be demonstrated *only* when the brain is engaged in a specific type of activity.

TYPES OF LEARNING DISABILITIES

Psychoneurological disturbances of learning can be described and categorized in various ways. We now consider behavioral classifications in relation to brain dysfunctions. Psychologically, processes of learning can be viewed as hierarchies of experience.

Sensation

Sensation is the lowest level of behavior inasmuch as it refers only to activation of sensorineural structures. Detriments at this level include deafness and blindness which are peripheral nervous system involvements causing a sensory deprivation. Our studies of the effects of one such deprivation (deafness) on learning have been presented elsewhere (Myklebust, 1964).

Perception

Behavioral concomitants of central nervous system functioning begin with *perception* which is markedly primitive psychologically. Studies of simple forms of animal life show that these forms perceive and can be taught to differentiate between stimuli that suggest reward versus those that do not.

The neurological condition referred to as agnosia behaviorally may be equivalent to perceptual disorders. The exact psychological and neurological nature of these disturbances is not known, but, as suggested by Young's (1964) definition of transducing, the neurological deficit may consist of inadequate converting of sensations into electrical impulses. This could explain a child being unable to perceive, auditorially or visually, the difference between *coal* and *cold, m* and *n, b* and *d,* etc. It is more difficult to explain imperception of body parts as seen in finger agnosia. There is the possibility that conversion of proprioceptive sensations into nerve impulses is necessitated also in this type of perceptual disturbance.

So far as learning is concerned, perceptual disorders constitute only one of the detriments that are neurogenic in origin and that must be distinguished from others. According to the hierarchical frame of reference, a perceptual disorder by reciprocation disturbs all of the levels of experience that fall above it. The implications for differential diagnosis and remedial education are great indeed.

Imagery

For a period of time, *imagery* as a process has been neglected in psychology and education; however, it was emphasized by Brain (1959) and by Penfield and Roberts (1959) in neurology. More recently Miller, Galanter, and Pribram (1960), Mowrer (1960), Russell (1956), and other students of behavior have highlighted this aspect of cognitive functioning. In learning disabilities it is not easy to evolve a comprehensive frame of reference without including imagery. Moreover, without the concept of imagery we are hard pressed to distinguish between the processes of perception and memory. A predominant difference is that perception concerns awareness relative to *ongoing* sensation whereas imagery pertains to sensations or information *already* received and perceived.

Imagery, therefore, can be considered as a way in which to describe some of the processes covered by the term memory. Though all types of imagery are of importance, we limit our discussion to the auditory and visual because of their significance in learning disabilities. In so doing we view the processes of auditorizing and visualizing, not only as being a type of memory function and thus not equivalent to perception, but as not being synonymous with verbal symbolic behavior. When an individual engages in imagery, he is recalling certain aspects of an experience, not necessarily the words that might be associated with it. In auditorizing, he is recalling the actual sounds that made up a part of the experience, whereas in visualizing, he is recalling ways in which the experience appeared visually. Much mental activity seems to be of this nature.

Although the most conspicuous deficiencies in auditorizing and visualizing are those associated with verbal behavior, some children cannot recall the nonverbal aspects of daily experience. This limitation often can be revealed through questions such as: How did it sound? or What did it look like? They may be seriously limited in ability to recall even obvious aspects of everyday experience. In one case the child could not recall common features of his bedroom or whether there were trees along the street where he walked to school. In another instance an adolescent girl, who had many of the characteristics of a visualization defect, could not remember whether there had been flowers at her birthday party; the parents had reported an unusual array of flowers for the occasion.

In the auditory sphere, the most consequential imagery other than words is that which pertains to social sounds. The average child has no difficulty in learning and recalling the sounds made by birds, dogs, frogs, and other animals, nor in recalling the sounds associated with motors, horns, bells, typewriters, running water, rustling leaves, musical instruments, and many others; we refer to these as social-nonverbal sounds. The extent to which children who have learning disabilities can identify such sounds and recall them in relation to everyday experiences must be determined because many have deficiencies in this important aspect of learning.

More generally, we have differentiated a type of learning disability in children who are otherwise highly intact intellectually, and classified it as a disturbance in *social perception. This aspect of behavior may be defined as the ability to immediately identify and recognize the meaning and significance of the behavior of others.* It is in this area of psychological functioning that perception and imagery overlap; we do not assume that these functions are mutually exclusive. The significance of nonverbal behavior has been discussed by various workers (Allport and Vernon, 1933; Hall, 1957). Some children lack facility to readily perceive meanings conveyed by facial expression and the actions of others; their parents often raise questions such as: Why can he not learn to play games as others do? These children tend to score low on picture tests—e.g., the Picture Arrangement test on the WISC. Typically auditory social-nonverbal tests are not included in batteries of intelligence tests, but abilities of this type are involved in social perception. Davitz (1964) reported findings on the differences among groups of handicapped and normal children on such abilities.

Throughout our discussion of remediation we refer to nonverbal disorders of learning. That these deficiences exist and that they are seriously troublesome to many children is of little question. Moreover, they can be explained as deficiencies in ability to learn from everyday experience and in ability to recall these experiences in the form of imagery. Because disabilities in verbal learning are more commonly understood, neurogenic involvements which affect social perception present unusual opportunities for research.

Symbolization

The fourth hierarchical aspect of experience, from the more primitive to the higher intellectually, is *symbolization.* To discuss all aspects of this uniquely human characteristic would necessitate a volume in itself. Our consideration is limited to those features most commonly associated with learning disabilities.

Symbolic behavior is highly inclusive, encompassing both verbal and nonverbal types of learning and recall, and refers to the ability to represent experience. Whether this ability is synonymous with the development of consciousness is not known. All forms of animal life engage in perception and some of the higher forms (other than Man) seem capable of imagery, at least at a rudimentary level. However, in the sense that this phenomenon is discussed here, representational behavior is essentially unique in the human being.

In the past, symbolization has been viewed principally in terms of *verbal* symbolic behavior. Note for example the work of Nissen (1958, p. 195) who states: "The essence of words is that they summarize many past experiences into a manageable unit; that is, they produce or represent a temporal integration of many diverse experiences. The use of words as a tool of thinking or reasoning or problem solving, therefore, means that a huge number of past experiences are being effective in determining present behavior. Language, or verbal mediating responses, represents an instance of extremely efficient central integration with which we, as educated human adults, are especially familiar." Miller, Galanter, and Pribram (1960, p. 142) state: "Almost nothing we could say about the psychological importance of language could be too extravagant, . . . " They consider language crucial to controlling psychological processes.

Verbal abilities are of utmost consequence to human behavior, but it is of singular importance to both normal and abnormal behavior that nonverbal symbolic functions not be overlooked. Symbolization as it appears in art, music, religion, and patriotism may be equally significant. Illustrative are the cross in religion and flags, the Statue of Liberty, and the hammer and sickle in patriotism. This type of symbolic behavior, the nonverbal, often is disturbed by dysfunctions in the brain. Observed most commonly are deficits in ability to learn to estimate and recall time, size, distance, volume, shape, height, speed, and other qualitative aspects of experience. Though the child has language, sometimes falling well above average on all verbal functions, he cannot form normal judgments in relation to time of the day or season of the year, large and small, far and near, full and half-full, circular and rectangular, high and low, fast and slow. These deficiencies have great relevancy in everyday life and must be considered under disorders of symbolic behavior. Differential diagnosis is critical to the child's total well-being and the importance of these conditions in remedial education is stressed throughout the remainder of this volume.

That verbal functions can be disturbed by brain disorders has been known for more than a century; however, this knowledge pertained mainly to adults. On the other hand, Binet discussed aphasia in children in 1916, and Morgan and Hinshelwood published their observations on dyslexia in children in 1896 and 1917. It is not that these conditions were unknown in children, but many authorities denied them so their incidence has gone largely unrecognized. Only in the past decade have we become fully aware of psychoneurological learning disabilities as they relate to deficiencies in the use of language by young children.

Man has three verbal systems: spoken, read, and written. Modifications appear under special circumstances—the sign language for the deaf and braille for the blind. The first verbal system acquired phylogenetically was the auditory (spoken word) and ontogenetically this is the first system acquired by the child. In infancy and throughout the life span this system remains fundamental. Perhaps one reason for the spoken word being most basic is that it is the easiest to learn. The auditory modality is excellent for language acquisition because it functions simultaneously in all directions and because it is mandatory. It cannot be "turned off," it is permissive, and it can be used while vision is being directed elsewhere. Another reason for the spoken word being acquired first is that it requires less psychoneurological maturity than the read and written word.

Inner Language. An intriguing aspect of language development is that word meaning must be acquired before words can be used as words; note the examples of echolalia and word-calling. Vygotsky (1962) emphasized this feature of language when he stated that a word without meaning was not a word; it is this aspect that we refer to as *inner language*. For a word to have meaning, it must represent a given unit of experience. Inner language processes are those that permit the transformation of experience into symbols; they may be verbal or nonverbal, as indicated above, but our concern here is with the verbal. Although the neurology of receptive and expressive language is better known, there is a neurology of inner language that is becoming more clearly understood (Geschwind, 1967; Penfield and Roberts, 1959; Russell and Espir, 1961). Admittedly, neither its psychology nor its neurology is well delineated and awaits additional investigation.

To further describe the inner language process is to state that it is the language with which one thinks. Also, it is the *native tongue*. If an individual has more than one tongue, more than one language, typically he thinks in the one native to him. This can be illustrated in various ways. When confronted with an important problem requiring a specific answer, the bilingual person, even if fluent in his second language, will regress and think in his native language. Another example, one that has been especially revealing, is presented by those with normal hearing but who are born to deaf parents. If the parents acquired the sign language as their native tongue, usually this is the first language learned by their children, whether or not they have normal hearing. Several of our graduate students with this background and experience have assisted us by studying the nature of their inner language. When confronted with mental tasks, as when writing an examination, they find themselves thinking in the sign language. Even though entirely competent in the spoken, read, and written forms, they think in their native tongue, the sign language.

From observation and from the highly revealing work of Werner and Kaplan (1963), we must assume that inner language not only exists but that it is not synonymous with receptive or expressive language. Moreover, because it is the first and most fundamental aspect of language to be acquired, it becomes remarkably rigid and fixed; most persons fluent in several languages learned more than one of them before reaching five years of age.

The child with a disorder of inner language may have difficulty in acquiring meaning itself—the norm of experience to be symbolized—or he may have a deficiency in ability to transform experience into verbal symbols. Traditionally, these disturbances have been categorized as global or central aphasia (Goldstein, 1948; Russell and Espir, 1961). We do not yet have techniques for ascertaining precise degrees and types of inner language disorders. Further study might reveal that deficiencies in ability to acquire concepts of time, size, direction, etc. are of this type. The child who reads well but who cannot grasp the meaning of paragraphs could have an inner language disorder. Children who have substantial involvement on the right hemisphere of the brain, but only slight involvement on the left, can have excellent input and output but are highly deficient in the acquisition of meaning. Usually there is a wide discrepancy between their verbal and nonverbal mental test scores, the verbal being superior. Even though not mentally retarded according to mental test criteria, they cannot develop a norm of experience and therefore have peculiar learning patterns. These children who have an inner language disorder present an exceedingly significant problem. Theirs is the most complex of the learning disabilities, especially in terms of remedial education.

Receptive Language. The second facet of language to be acquired is the auditory receptive, ability to comprehend the spoken word. When impaired, this deficiency is the second most debilitating to the individual. It must be noted, however, that receptive language also encompasses reading and therefore is of two basic types, auditory and visual. Either or both may be deficient in a given child. When involved, particularly in the case of the auditory, inner language is affected on a reciprocal basis; inner language is dependent on receptive processes for its development. This may be one of the reasons that disorders of auditory receptive functions are so debilitating. Or, too, it may be explained by the nature of the neurological involvement, which often includes the temporal lobe. In any event, children who have disabilities in auditory receptive learning commonly show behavior characterized by hyperactivity, perseveration, disinhibition, distractibility, and poor sustained attention. The more the learning disability is visual and the more it is limited to reading, the less this behavior pattern is present. Deficiencies in auditory receptive learning are more consequential to overtly observed aberrations of behavior (McGrady, 1964).

Another consideration is the reciprocal relationship between reception and expression. We have stressed the principle that input precedes output. Insofar as the spoken word is concerned, this means that comprehension precedes expression; understanding must be attained before the word can be used meaningfully in communication. In terms of the visual verbal system, it means that reading precedes writing. The read form (receptive) can be assumed when the written (expressive) is present.

These basic neurological principles do not imply that feedback is unimportant or that total ability to comprehend must be present before expression can occur. Receptive and expressive abilities mature simultaneously, learning in one phase enhancing learning in the other. But the receptive abilities predominate, as evidenced by the normal individual who has a more complete receptive vocabulary in both the spoken and read forms than he can command expressively—his receptive language exceeds his expressive.

Because auditory receptive abilities are inclusive, they can be affected in a number of ways; see examples in the following chapters. If there are deficiencies at the level of perception, the child may find the sounds in his environment bewildering. He cannot select and attend to the most relevant and purposeful sounds. He cannot structure the auditory world according to his needs. Compared with impairment of visual perception, little consideration has been given to this auditory process. Disturbances of auditory perception are of great consequence behaviorially and are of utmost importance in diagnosis and remediation.

One of the common symptoms of deficits in auditory perception is misunderstanding; the child misperceives what he hears. When grossly debilitated and when comprehension is limited, the child may shut out sound and behave as though it is non-existent. Sometimes he puts his hands over his ears. Unless he is given proper training in his pre-school years, such a child may relinquish all auditory awareness, making it necessary to educate him as a deaf child even though he has normal hearing acuity.

Deficiencies in perception should not be confused with deficits in symbolic functioning. In perceptual disturbances it is not comprehension of the word, per se, that constitutes the disorder. If the sounds can be discriminated and selected, they are comprehended. Due to perceptual disturbances, some children, unlike the normal, cannot discriminate among words that sound or look alike. In the sentence, *We see a tree,* the words *we, see,* and *tree* may all sound alike. Comprehension assumes discriminating, grouping, and patterning of words. Inflection, intonation, and rhythm are involved. Rate also plays a role in both audition and vision. Often simply reducing the rate will assist the child in perceiving, as it does the adult who is attempting to understand a foreign tongue.

Perception as a receptive process not only assumes discrimination, the ability to distinguish among sounds or visual stimuli, but also the capacity to organize all sensation into a meaningful whole, the capacity to structure incoming information. In addition, it assumes attention. The total process of perceiving is a complex facet of experience requiring attention, organization, discrimination, and selection. As such, impositions on perception should be differentiated from the aphasias and dyslexias because these are language disorders in which normal comprehension is disturbed, even though all aspects of perception are intact. Perceptual involvements also should be distinguished from disorders of memory. This can be done if we define perception as the psychological process required for manipulation of ongoing sensation.

Receptive language, spoken or read, can be deficient for other reasons. From the study of children with psychoneurological learning disabilities, we find that normal language comprehension and usage necessitates ability to blend sounds (syllables) into words, as well as the opposite, ability to divide words into syllables. One must be able to blend the syllables *yes-ter-day* into the word *yesterday,* and, likewise, divide *yesterday* into *yes-ter-day.* Blending and syllabicating seem especially critical when learning to read; initially, reading is facilitated when the auditory and visual components of words can be readily superimposed. These deficiencies are some of the most common learning disorders seen in school children. Much can be done to alleviate them.

Receptive language also presupposes adequate integrity of memory. As a psychoneurological function memory is all-encompassing, being entailed in essentially all mental functions. It is advantageous to distinguish between certain types of memory, such as span or sequence versus general or overall. Sequence means that the information received must be recalled and acted upon in the order given. This is the type of memory involved in the repetition of words, digits, or sentences as originally conceived in mental test form by Binet (1937). Memory span often is deficient in children with learning disabilities.

Less well known is the fact that sequence ability in the sense of commissions can be impaired, again as originally conceived by Binet. This disturbance may be even more bewildering than an inability to repeat numbers, words, or sentences. When asked to "go upstairs, take off your coat, get your book, and then bring it to me," the child cannot maintain the order of the events in mind so be becomes confused, irritable, and disintegrated. This disability varies from child to child but the pattern is clear and should be identified whenever possible. We have found these auditory processes to be associated with neurological status as determined by the neurologist (Boshes and Myklebust, 1964).

Expressive Language. Developmentally, when the child has acquired meaningful units of experience and when comprehension has been established, he is ready to communicate with others; he can engage in expressive language. This verbal behavior, like the receptive, is of two types: auditory and visual. Expression presupposes reception, as indicated by the discussion above. Therefore, the ways in which the child expresses himself reveals the integrity of his receptive language. If he cannot remember words, sequences, syntactical structures, and spellings, or if he cannot discriminate words that sound or look alike, his expressive language will be deficient. This pattern of relationship between reception and expression cannot be overlooked in diagnosis or remediation. On the other hand, reception can be basically intact with expression alone being deficient. The input and output systems of the brain are only semi-autonomously interdependent.

It is rare for a child to manifest a pure condition, one not complicated by other deficits, but apraxias occur without other serious impairments. Both expressive aphasia and dysgraphia can be found when other involvements are minimal; they are analogous, aphasia impeding the utterance of words and dysgraphia representing the detriment to writing. Both are apraxias, which as a condition does not include paralysis. Historically, expressive aphasia was the first language disorder to be identified. One of the leaders in clarifying this condition was Broca, after whom the area in the brain was named (Nielsen, 1946). He maintained that when a lesion occurred in the "third left frontal convolution" the patient would not be able to utter words normally. These first observations pertained to adults; an otherwise normal person became ill, having a type of "stroke," after which he was unable to speak.

Detriments to output are more easily observed than to input; thus expressive aphasia was recognized prior to receptive. Input disorders continue to be difficult to identify in both children and adults. Of great significance perhaps is the fact that the early workers made no distinction between language and speech; some dictionaries still do not do so. As a result, expressive aphasia was described as a *loss of speech*, when in actuality it is a disorder of language. Because of this confusion, taking the phrase "loss of speech" literally, some persons continue to be reluctant to accept the concept of aphasia in children. This concept, now verified in a number of ways, assumes that it is *language*, not speech, that is incapacitated. This being the case, as a condition it may be present prenatally or occur preverbally, but it cannot be identified until after the age at which spoken language is acquired. Because it is a language disorder, having an expressive aphasia does not necessarily mean one has acquired speech and then lost it. From the point of view of age at onset, aphasia is like deafness and various other conditions in that it can occur prenatally, congenitally, or at any time after birth throughout the life span. The analogous disturbance affecting the written word, dysgraphia, also common in children, seems not to be controversial. The same situation, however, prevails because usually dysgraphia is congenital but cannot be properly diagnosed until after the child has attained the age required for acquisition of the written word.

Apraxias can affect both verbal and nonverbal functions, but it is the verbal about which more is known. In Chapter I, we indicated that as a disorder apraxia is not fully understood but, in contrast with agnosia, it is an impairment of output. Also, unlike dysarthria and ataxia, the motor system per se is not deficient. Moreover, unlike amnestic aphasia in which words cannot be recalled, the problem is not one of being unable to bring to mind what one wishes to say. Memory for what one wishes to say or write and the motor system for saying or writing it are intact. Therefore, the defect is in the association, the interaction between these systems.

Some authorities view apraxia in terms of memory and describe it as a deficiency in which the motor patterns, as they relate to speaking, cannot be learned and remembered. This concept is useful, but it is advantageous to think also in terms of interneurosensory processes. We have stressed the significance of these processes in brain function; apraxia is an illustration. To speak, as well as to write, assumes not only ability to recall and to hold words in mind but also ability to relate these signals to the appropriate motor system, to activate the motor system for the appropriate expressive movements. In speaking, the associations which must be made are auditory and motor. In writing, the associations are more complex, involving auditory, visual, and motor equivalents. Tactile-kinesthetic sensory signals too can be impaired in both speaking and writing. Therefore, each of the neurosensory equivalents may be intact as separate entities and function normally under various circumstances, but be deficient specifically in relation to language, per se. The result is expressive aphasia and/or dysgraphia, highly consequential types of learning disabilities in children. They first must be recognized diagnostically and then planned for in terms of remedial education.

These apraxias must be differentiated from other conditions affecting learning and behavior. Two such involvements of expressive language that entail motor capacities are *dysarthria* and *ataxia*. Dysarthria, a paralytic condition that affects speech production and articulation, may be due to disorders of either the central or peripheral nervous system. Ataxia, caused only by deficits in the central nervous system, is a condition in which there is no paralysis and the relevant muscles are innervated, but the motor activity cannot be coordinated normally (Cobb, 1948). The resultant incoordination takes the form of impulsive, jerky movements and tremors, and disrupts balance. Ataxia may affect either speech or writing, or both, besides gait and general use of the hands (Myklebust, 1965). Dysarthria and ataxia often are seen in association with learning disabilities such as aphasia and dyslexia.

Conceptualization

We have considered three types of learning disabilities—those affecting perception, imagery, and symbolization. Another disturbance which has been recognized for many years and of much consequence is a deficiency in *conceptualization*. This deficit was first recognized in adults. One of the great pioneers in psychoneurology, Hughlings Jackson (Taylor, 1958), emphasized the importance of loss of abstraction when lesions occurred in the brain. More recently, Goldstein (1948), Goldstein and Scheerer (1941), and Myklebust (1965) have shown the significance of reduced abstract-concrete behavior in relation to brain dysfunctions. Werner and Kaplan (1963) have made noteworthy contributions through their studies of abstract behavior and symbol formation. Cassirer (1953) and Langer (1957) evolved arguments in philosophy to show the significance of conceptualization in Man's evolution and how this type of behavior is unique to human beings. When psychoneurological impairment disrupts this process, one of Man's most unusual attributes is inhibited. Ability to conceptualize is a salient facet of that which makes man Man, but even so there are many gaps in our knowledge concerning this aspect of behavior (Anderson, 1959).

In order to consider deficits in conceptualization in terms of psychoneurological learning disabilities, it is necessary to describe more precisely this type of behavior. Conceptualization does not refer only to the ability to abstract; abstraction and conception are not synonymous. There are many types and degrees of abstraction, from the rat distinguishing between reward and punishment to a high degree of creativity. Likewise, there are many levels of concept formation. This behavior, however, assumes not only ability to abstract but ability to categorize—categorical reasoning. Whereas one cannot conceptualize without engaging in abstraction, one can engage in abstraction without conceptualizing.

Although the processes of abstracting and of forming concepts overlap and are interwoven, it is desirable to distinguish between them. The continuum from a high degree of abstraction to a high degree of concreteness can be viewed in terms of the individual being stimulus-bound; the more stimulus-bound, the more the behavior is dominated by present, observable circumstances. In contrast, the more abstract the behavior, the more total experience plays a significant role in the mental processes.

When conceptualizing, abstraction must be included, but the critical factor is the manner in which experience is classified and categorized. To illustrate, in early life the child's experience *chair* refers only to a specific chair, perhaps his own which is present and observable. Later he generalizes *chair* to include other chairs, whether or not they are observable. Still later he learns to classify and categorize his experience *chair* relative to the concept *furniture;* he conceptualizes it in terms of a group or groups of experiences. Another distinction to be noted is that experiences that are abstracted (such as the experience *chair*) can be observed, whereas *the class or category that forms a concept is not in itself observable.* Rather, it represents a group of experiences with a common denominator, usually obscure and abstract, but having some association one with another. It is this common denominator—the process of recognizing the relationships among experiences—that sometimes constitutes the deficit in learning in children with neurogenic disturbances. Jackson (Taylor, 1958) called attention to this with his emphasis on propositionalizing, as did Goldstein (1948) by stressing the significance of the abstract-concrete attitude. Ostensibly, it is the thought process that is disordered, so the psychology of thinking is relevant when analyzing these deficiencies in conceptualization.

In any event, the student of psychoneurology and learning disabilities cannot avoid consideration of interrelationships among the processes of perception, imagery, symbolization, and conceptualization. A deficit at any one of these levels of experience interferes with ability to form concepts, and inasmuch as brain dysfunctions commonly interfere with these processes, it is not surprising that both children and adults with these problems often have been referred to as being concrete.

If verbal facility is affected, as in receptive aphasia, when the basic symbol system for thought (the auditory) is impeded, concept formation becomes more difficult. Most concepts necessitate word usage; thus, though it is possible to form the concept *furniture* without use of the word *furniture,* it can be formed more readily when the relevant word is available for its identification and crystallization. Research evidence concerning the precise manner in which language disorders and concept formation are related is not yet available. In terms of remedial education, experience indicates that the teacher must be aware that some children form concepts spontaneously when they acquire the necessary verbal facility. On the other hand, many must be assisted in learning to generalize and categorize. These children often have difficulty with multiple word meanings, with proverbs, and with metaphors.

In general, the psychology of concept formation is somewhat better understood than its neurology. Many workers, nevertheless, have been concerned with brain function, not only as it relates to learning, per se, but to imagination and creativity; gradually this significant area of knowledge is expanding. To some extent the neurology of inner language is relevant, including studies of the frontal lobes which indicate that this area of the brain carries a unique responsibility for this aspect of behavior (Milner, 1954; Penfield and Roberts, 1959). Given areas of the brain may have more responsibility than others, but it appears that any brain dysfunction altering learning may obstruct ability to conceptualize. Inasmuch as this is Man's highest achievement, encompassing all facets of his learning and experience, it is particularly vulnerable to both psychic and organic disturbances.

NONVERBAL DISABILITIES

In the discussion of semi-autonomous systems and brain function (Chapter I), we stated that there are both verbal and nonverbal neurogenic learning disabilities. Theoretically, and from clinical evidence, it appears that the brain receives, organizes, and categorizes experience both verbally and nonverbally (Myklebust, 1967). All experience cannot be defined as verbal; Guilford (1959) concludes that most interpersonal behavior is nonverbal. Much of what one learns and much of one's everyday functioning are determined by situations, circumstances, and feelings that are not and perhaps cannot be wholly verbalized. Experience with children who have deficits in learning clearly reveals that in many instances their greatest, if not their only, problem is in nonverbal learning.

On the basis of the concept of semi-autonomous organization, we must predicate that the brain is comprised of systems that specialize in verbal and systems that specialize in nonverbal functions. Research evidence increasingly supports the hypothesis that those serving verbal behavior are largely in the left hemisphere and those serving nonverbal behavior in the right (Hécaen and Ajuriaguerra, 1964; Penfield and

Roberts, 1959). Because it has been demonstrated that when damage occurs in one of the hemispheres the function might be transferred to the other hemisphere, we cannot presume that a specific process can be accomplished only by a given system on a given hemisphere. Nevertheless, one of the hemispheres serves mainly verbal learning whereas the other seems to serve mainly nonverbal learning. We are led to the conclusion, therefore, that there is a *neurology of learning which relates to verbal functions and a neurology of learning which relates to nonverbal functions.*

Again, the concept of semi-autonomous functions is useful as a background and frame of reference for both diagnosis and education. On the other hand, the concept as presented oversimplifies the complex operations which occur in the brain. The presumption is too much a matter of "all or none." It infers, for example, that certain processes are operative or non-operative, and if non-operative, that nature proceeds to transfer the entire function to the analogous system in the opposite hemisphere. While research evidence is inconclusive, it can be observed clinically that nature operates more efficiently. In children who have acquired a mild motor involvement in the fingers on the dominant hand, often seen in the presence of a moderate ataxia, careful evaluation by motor tests reveals *bilateral* cerebral dominance for certain motor functions. Fine motor movements, such as required for buttoning and writing, are transferred to the opposite, nondominant hand, whereas gross motor movements, because they are unaffected, are not transferred; they remain where they were, on the dominant side. Since nature works so wisely and effectively, we do not recommend interfering with handedness. To do so seems naive in view of present indications of the manner in which the nervous system modifies itself for optimum functioning, both in self-preservation and in learning.

The extent to which the nervous system adjusts itself to the need for or lack of need for transfer so far as verbal learning is concerned is not known. Nonetheless, through the use of sodium amytal injections a temporary inactivation can be induced in one hemisphere at a time. It appears that language too can be bilaterally represented—certain language functions, those not significantly impeded, remain on the dominant side while the ones vitally disturbed are transferred. This possibility is consistent with other observations, like that occurring in motor functions as well as with our concept of brain function. It follows that hand and verbal dominance are not necessarily related; dominance for language should not be inferred from hand dominance. The dominant hemisphere for verbal behavior, partial or otherwise, is not easy to establish and often requires specialized techniques.

In this discussion of nonverbal learning disabilities, there is the assumption that neurological systems, predominant in the right hemisphere, have been developmentally disrupted by endogenous or exogenous involvement in the same manner as detriments occur for verbal learning. It is incumbent upon special education to provide methods and techniques *also* for the child who has this type of deficit. His verbal abilities may exceed those of the normal child and yet he cannot learn to perform simple nonverbal routines like judging the distance between himself and an approaching vehicle or the spatial orientation involved in hanging his coat on an ordinary hanger. Compared with those who have verbal academic deficiencies, less is known about these children, diagnostically and remedially, but it is necessary to include them when planning a program of special education: see Chapter VIII.

Interpersonal Relationships

Perhaps most interpersonal, attitudinal relationships are nonverbal in nature. Attitudes have been emphasized psychodynamically, but not psychoneurologically. When a child lacked feelings of relationship with others, as seen in autistic children, his problem was viewed only in terms of emotional disturbance. Though the works of Creak and Ini (1960), Goldfarb (1961), and Rimland (1964), among others, the neurological status of these children has been questioned.

Although the nature of the association between brain dysfunctions and obliviousness or poor interpersonal relationships is largely unknown, many workers now make a point of securing intensive neurological and electroencephalographic studies when they encounter "autistic-like" children. Moreover, as shown by the findings of Goldfarb, the results often are positive. These results do not prove that other factors are unimportant, but they provide a different frame of reference for the medical and educational management of children who are severely withdrawn and unable to maintain interpersonal relationships with others.

Nevertheless, the question of self-perception, person perception, and social perception is more inclusive. Some children with nonverbal neurogenic learning disabilities who are *not* withdrawn and oblivious have only slight ability to recognize and identify the attitudes and feelings of others, even when permitted to view their facial expressions. They cannot distinguish between the manifestations of sadness and happiness, anger and gentleness, seduction and helpfulness, politeness and impoliteness, etc. This can be revealed, sometimes dramatically, by showing them pictures of persons who are obviously angry, happy, etc., and asking them to identify accordingly. Their lack of facility is sometimes strikingly apparent.

Both self-perception and person perception can be studied through use of the Drawing of the Human Figure Test (Myklebust, 1964). In one of our studies children with learning disabilities scored three-fourths of average on this test even though they fell within the normal range on the Wechsler Intelligence Scale for Children. Likewise, Cohn (1960) showed that scores on the Draw a Person Test varied according to the status of the brain's functioning at a given time; differences appeared prior to and following seizures. That such distortions follow certain types of dysfunctions in the brain has been recognized for a number of years. Badal (1888) emphasized the problem of *finger agnosia* and Babinski (1918) stressed the importance of *anosognosia,* an inability to perceive and recognize body parts. Some time ago we called attention to the problem of *speechreading aphasia,* which is the inability to associate meaning with movement of the lips (Myklebust, 1964). In view of these observations, there is little question but that ability to perceive parts of one's own body and thus perhaps the body parts of others may be disrupted neurogenically.

There are many challenging and intriguing implications for differential diagnosis, as well as for remedial education. We have used the Human Figure Drawing Test as an indicator of total psychoneurological status and of progress under a regimen of remediation. The results have been highly rewarding. Our emphasis here, however, is that a nonverbal learning disability may include inter-personal relationships and self-perception as well as perception of others. Keeping in mind the definition of a learning disability (Chapter I) and the ways in which brain dysfunctions disturb learning, we next consider the role of special education and basic principles for remediation.

CHAPTER III

Special Education and Learning Disabilities

Firmly entrenched in our philosophy of education is the idea that every child should have an opportunity to learn to the best of his ability. As a group, children with learning disabilities have not had this opportunity. Usually a curriculum as established by the school system has been provided, but the children have been unable to cope with it. Consequently, they have failed and have been classified as mentally retarded, emotionally disturbed, or simply as underachievers. Some have been deprived of all educational services because their problems precluded a place for them in school. To illustrate, the parents of a six-year-old nontalking, hyperactive child with superior nonverbal intelligence were told that their son was not ready for school and that they should wait until he could communicate and exercise better control of himself. It is our belief that with proper facilities, professional personnel, and curriculum most of these children can be educated through the local school system.

Until recently society placed children with learning disabilities in programs already existing rather than considering them as a homogeneous group with its own special needs. Fortunately, criteria for diagnosis and classification now have been developed so that this group can be defined and special education provided. The learning disability population is not totally new; childhood dyslexia was recognized by Hinshelwood as early as 1898 (1917). As a population, however, it has grown and become more widely recognized. With advances in science fewer children expire at birth or in infancy, but some who survive have disorders of learning. Also, due to refinement of diagnostic procedures in medicine, psychology, language pathology, and education it is possible to isolate new conditions. Finally, as a result of our changing society, we have become aware of children with deficits in learning. The emphasis on academic achievement and higher education has made demands on children that are beyond the ability of some to learn under typical educational programs.

Recognition of children with learning disabilities has far-reaching implications. Establishing a legal definition educationally makes it necessary for school administrators to provide special education programs, for communities to consider financial resources, for universities to develop training programs, and for state offices of public instruction to initiate teacher certification standards. This greater awareness also requires that various professional persons combine efforts to further expand diagnostic and remedial services.

First, and foremost, proper programs have a marked effect on the child himself. Often the child with a learning disability is labeled slow or lazy when in reality he is neither. These labels have an adverse effect on future learning, on self-perception, and on feelings of personal worth. On the other hand, when the problem is recognized and the child and family realize that remediation is possible, the child's attitudes change as do the attitudes of those around him. Sometimes it seems that improvement is initiated with the diagnosis; parents report that the child is better even before the educational program begins. Merely knowing that he has ability, that there are reasons for his failure and that something can be done is of great benefit. Being confused by the discrepancies in their abilities, most of these children desire help. In view of their average or above ability, they feel they can compete with their peers; yet at times they fail miserably. This frustration was expressed by an eleven-year-old boy who came to his remedial teacher saying, "If I don't finish my arithmetic workbook by the end of the week, I won't pass into sixth grade. I can't do it . . . but I know I *can* . . . but I have to have help." When schools provide adequate diagnostic and educational assistance, many children show marked improvement and the emotional tensions resulting from repeated failure are reduced.

Proper programming is of benefit to society as well as to the individual. If these children remain in regular classes without special education, they often become school dropouts. They cannot be readily employed because of their educational limitations and hence may remain dependent throughout their adult years with a long-term drain on the economy. If special programs are established and appropriate remediation provided, the majority become independent and self-supporting citizens. Even if special education is necessary throughout the elementary and secondary school years, or even beyond, the cost is nominal.

It must be emphasized that existing special education programs are inadequate. Although it sometimes is recommended that these children be placed in rooms already available for the handicapped, they should not be with the deaf, the retarded, the crippled, or other health impaired. In contrast to the programs for the deaf where the educational procedures are geared to the sensory deprivation, it is necessary to utilize all sensory capacities to effectively benefit the child with a learning disability. Likewise, a plan that purports to solve the problem by merely reducing goals is seriously inadequate since placement in a class for slow learners or lessening homework and other demands is *not* a program for this type of child. None of these measures considers his specialized needs.

Counseling services designed only to assist these children in learning to live with their problems also are inadequate. Although certain children require assistance in dealing with the frustrations which follow repeated failure, they urgently need a positive educational program aimed at overcoming the learning disability. Similarly, it is a mistake to assume that typical tutorial programs alone will solve the problem. Although an intuitive teacher may be able to understand and help the child, the remedial program must be more encompassing. In order to learn to the best of his ability, a child with a learning disability must have an inclusive special education program. Society needs the unique resources of his mind, and for maximum benefits to be realized, the effort must be made at as early an age as possible.

EDUCATIONAL PLANNING

The overall educational objective for children with learning disabilities differs only slightly from that for all children; the objective is to assist them with learning so that they can actualize their potentials and become an effective, integral part of society. Our concern is not solely with academic achievement and improvement of isolated functions, but with attainment of social maturity—ability to communicate, to care for oneself, to be successfully employed, to become independent and self-supporting. The plan is one that looks at individual requisites for purposeful living. As Whitehead (1929, p. 18) states, "There is only one subject matter for education, and that is Life in all of its manifestations."

Planning involves applying broad objectives to the development of a practical solution. Every educational program has both abstract and concrete goals. Many school systems express interest in the child with a learning disability but do not know how to proceed. One superintendent stated, "We would like to help these children; they are of concern to every teacher who has them, but we do not know what to do." It becomes the responsibility of the professionals, the persons trained in this field, to establish the necessary criteria and guidelines. Perhaps no area of special education requires more interdisciplinary cooperation. The skills, knowledge, and techniques of psychologists, neurologists, ophthalmologists, pediatricians, psychiatrists, otolaryngologists, and electroencephalographers, plus all members of the educational staff may be required to provide an adequate program.

The single most important factor in planning for a child with a learning disability is an intensive diagnostic study. Without a comprehensive evaluation of his deficits and assets, the educational program may be too general, or even inappropriate. The diagnostic study should include an evaluation of sensory acuity, intelligence, language (spoken, read, written), motor function, educational achievement, emotional status, and social maturity (Myklebust, 1954). In addition, an evaluation should be made by the pediatrician, the neurologist, the ophthalmologist, and by others as indicated by the nature of the child's deficiencies. These combined skills make it possible to consider aspects of the problem that require remedial effort from various points of view. Many children benefit from proper medical attention. The primary concern here, however, is with the educational program which derives essentially from the psycho-educational evaluation.

This evaluation should yield a multi-dimensional definition of the disability because only then can the teacher proceed with development of the remedial program. The implication is that it is necessary to have immediate access to all diagnostic findings because it is from these that the educational approach must be evolved. Sometimes teachers are required to begin remediation without adequate knowledge of the deficits and integrities. Although information can be obtained from personal contact with the child, precise planning is possible only when these observations are supplemented by detailed diagnostic information.

Multi-dimensional Considerations

There are various ways of defining problems of learning: according to subject matter, according to the sensory modality through which learning is impaired, according to the level of the involvement (i.e., perceptual, symbolic, etc.), and on the basis of verbal versus nonverbal deficits. The first dimension is concerned with *intrasensory and intersensory disabilities*. Thus we need to know whether the disability falls within a single modality, whether it extends to more than one modality, and whether it includes intersensory functions. This dimension assists the teacher in knowing which input channels are intact and the types of learning processes to be enhanced by training. However, she should not only know which modalities are involved and whether intersensory functions are impaired, but the *level of the involvement* according to the hierarchy of experience. Rarely does the deficiency encompass all learning through a given modality. As shown in the discussion in Chapter II, the detriment usually can be described as being primarily perceptual, at the level of imagery or of symbolization, or mainly in concept formation. This is the second dimension.

A third dimension comprises yet another facet consequential to educational planning. The brain seems to function on the basis of whether sensations are *meaningful or nonmeaningful* and whether they are *verbal or nonverbal:* see Chapter I. Hence, the teacher must consider the deficiency in terms of being nonverbal-nonsocial, social-nonverbal, or verbal. To illustrate, some children can be described as having a deficiency in auditory perception, in visual imagery, in comprehending the spoken word (receptive aphasia), or in understanding what they read; this type of reading disorder suggests that the problem is one of gaining meanings (abstracting-conceptualizing).

The fourth dimension relates the *effect of the disability to types of educational achievement,* such as reading, written language, and arithmetic. It is essential to know if a disturbance of visual perception is interfering with arithmetic, with reading, or if it impedes nonverbal behavior and prevents average performance in physical education or in art. In the upper grades the effect on specific subject matter—e.g., geometry, graphic arts, geography, or foreign languages—must be considered. A student with visual-spatial distortions may do satisfactory work in some areas of mathematics but fail in geometry. This dimension is especially important for purposes of guidance and for determining the amount and type of special assistance that a student may need.

A fifth and still broader dimension is the *effect of the learning disability on total social maturity,* on overall functioning in society. Because our goal is for the individual to become an independent, self-supporting citizen—an integral part of society—we are concerned with those aspects that prevent him from attaining this objective. Our interest is not solely in academic success. Therefore, in developing the educational plan, we must ascertain which aspects of self-help, locomotion, communication, or other areas of function are impaired and in need of remediation.

The multi-dimensional approach to the learning disability is essential in order that the educational plan be sufficiently broad in scope. A uni-dimensional approach leads to a restricted educational plan; if the emphasis is on a specific disturbance without consideration for broader areas of function, the instruction concerns only the development of skills. On the other hand, an approach that considers only generalized deficits in reading or arithmetic is not sufficient to meet the child's needs. A remedial plan which includes both specific and generalized objectives permits the teacher to work on the deficits and to relate her efforts to all of the areas involved.

Although the educational plan should encompass all dimensions of the learning disability, there must be a balance between the specific and the general, operating in such a manner that the end result is an integrated program. Often the child is taken from one specialist (or one special teacher) to another without a coordinated central plan. Liason work is stressed in the discussion of school planning in Chapter IX.

States of Readiness

Another significant factor in educational planning is the concept of *multiple states of readiness.* In educational circles readiness is sometimes viewed unitarily, yet broadly, as readiness for school or readiness for subject matter, such as reading. Because of the nature of brain dysfunctions and the numerous types of learning disabilities that occur, it is highly advantageous to adopt a diversified concept of readiness, not only readiness for school subjects but for a level of self-control and responsibility. A hyperactive child might be ready to learn to read so far as auditory, visual, and integrative functions are concerned but be unable to cope with a group setting, with social stimulation from others his own age. Similarly, a child with adequate self-control might be ready to read so far as visual functions are concerned, but be unready auditorially. Therefore, *readiness is an encompassing concept* to be viewed from many standpoints. It is not satisfactory to wait until the child attains what is considered to be a normal state of readiness. Rather, the remediation must provide opportunities for growth according to the readiness levels that are present.

This is in contrast to saying, "meet the child at his level." In the field of learning disabilities it is imperative to meet him at many levels. A ten-year-old may be functioning at his age level in comprehension of the spoken word but at the six-year-old level in reading. Without an understanding of these discrepancies, it is impossible to plan an adequate educational program. The teacher must determine the stages of readiness and maintain a critical level of stimulation in each area of learning. If the child is understimulated, he fails to learn, and if the demands are above his level, he becomes frustrated and discouraged.

This concept of readiness includes recognition of other environments and subcultures in which the child finds himself. The various activities at school, at home, and in the community must be evaluated in relation to his learning disability to ascertain those which he cannot manage. The teacher through training prepares him for those with which he cannot cope. For example, if a child cannot find his way from one class to another, she determines whether he has problems in spatial or time orientation. Similarly, if he is unsuccessful on the playground, she explores his ability to follow instructions and the rules of the game. Motor skills and self-control also must be considered since many facets of a learning disability can interfere with out of class activities. A high school boy, who had serious orientation and spatial relationship problems, could play in the band when seated but he could not march with the band on the football field until he was instructed in right-left orientation, in following directions, and in walking to a specific rhythm. Other situations with which the teacher must be concerned include art and music classes, and home and community activites—the dinner party, shopping trips, unsupervised play in the neighborhood.

It is clear that remedial teaching cannot be a perfunctory presentation of a certain set of materials in a standardized sequence. Rather, it requires a thorough knowledge of the child, his various levels of function, and a comprehensive understanding of the material which is to be taught. It requires a *clinical teaching* approach.

THE PEDAGOGICAL RATIONALE

With greater cognizance of the nature and magnitude of the problem of learning disabilities, there is a growing awareness that specialized methods for educational remediation must be developed if these children are to have maximum opportunity for self-actualization. Though additional research and experience is necessary before conclusions can be reached as to the most effective educational procedures, it is practicable to suggest pedagogical principles and procedures that have proved highly successful.

There are many types of learning disabilities (see Chapter II) but a basic underlying homogeneity serves to unite and characterize this population. This homogeneity is derived from the fact that it is the neurology of learning that has been disrupted, thereby altering and determining the psychology by which these children learn. Unlike the mentally retarded, they have normal potential for learning; hence, the educational objectives differ; unlike those with deafness or blindness, they receive information through all sensory modalities. However, the brain dysfunction precludes organization and use of these sensations in the normal manner; they cannot learn in the usual way. Further comparisons with other types of handicapped children assists in clarifying why special education is necessary for those who have learning disabilities.

The Sensorially Impaired

The neurology of learning is not disturbed in the deaf or the blind child. His problem is one of under-stimulation; he is deprived of a type of information vital to total awareness, learning and development—there is a deprivation of input. Because he is lacking in audition or in vision, the processes whereby he learns are altered. To the extent possible he must learn, adjust, and understand the world in which he lives through compensatory use of his residual senses; it is apparent that many do so successfully (Myklebust, 1964). But learning without a given type of experience is not comparable to learning when all types of information are received normally. Therefore, we do not assume that the same psychology of learning, that the same pedagogical principles, can be applied to the sensorially deprived as to those with learning disabilities.

The Mentally Retarded

There may be an overlap between the psychologies by which the mentally retarded and the learning disability child learn. However, to emphasize the similarities tends to obscure, if not distort, important differences. One cannot deny that the neurology of learning has been disturbed in the mentally retarded, but the fundamental effect has been to reduce potential for learning in general. Though some retarded children have isolated *high* levels of function, the pattern is one of generalized inferiority; normal potential for learning is *not* assumed. In comparison, children with learning disabilities have isolated *low* levels of function. The pattern is one of generalized integrity of mental capacity; normal potential for learning *is* assumed. Therefore, the processes differ whereby these groups of children learn in that with the retarded there is no overall intellectual competence through which to gain awareness and insights for development of the deficient areas. In other words, the learning disability child differs both quantitatively and qualitatively from the retarded. He has more with which to learn and the patterns and processes by which he learns are different. Pertinent data are forthcoming (Behrens, 1963; Boshes and Myklebust, 1964; Luria, 1961; Zigmond, 1966).

The Emotionally Disturbed

In comparing learning disability and emotionally disturbed children, numerous variations can be noted. With the emotionally disturbed, remediation is planned along the lines of lessening the demands, then ultimately reintroducing demands as their affective tolerance warrants. The process is one of bringing about greater acceptance of reality, development of insight, and strengthening of ego functions. It is the *normal* learning processes that have been impeded; consequently, diverse pedagogical methods and procedures are not a primary consideration. When the emotional disturbance is alleviated, these children learn like the normal child. The neurology of learning has not been disrupted.

Those with Learning Disabilities

The learning disability child requires material (auditory, visual, tactile) to be presented in modified manners. Birch (1964) and Zigmond (1966), among others, have shown that perceptual organization and integration differ in children in whom the neurology of learning has been altered. Various assumptions can be made as to how normal children integrate auditory, visual, and tactile experience and these assumptions hold *because* the normal child is capable of such integrations. To make these same assumptions for children who have learning disabilities is naive. We cannot infer that because they understand the spoken word they can convert this auditory form into the read or written form—that what they see can be integrated with what they hear or feel. They have need for a special type of teaching because they achieve by idiosyncratic processes. How these children are taught makes the difference between learning and not learning. They have normal potential so they learn successfully when taught according to their peculiarities.

Other Approaches

Monroe (1932), in her excellent and provocative work, emphasized the need for developing a profile of deficiencies by type of error as well as a profile of deficits by school subject. We have found profiling to be of utmost significance in planning programs of remediation for individual children. Nevertheless, Monroe did not proceed on the basis of the child's specific profile of deficits and integrities. She began with auditory discrimination (of speech sounds) and gradually taught the child to associate (transduce) these sounds with their visual equivalents, often asking him to both trace and view the written word while doing so. She observed that certain children could not blend syllables to form whole words (a common type of auditory learning disability). We assume that her methods were highly beneficial to many children, perhaps mainly to those with deficits in auditory learning. However, questions arise: Should an auditory approach be used with all children? Does tracing assist in learning visually? Monroe's hypothesis seems to have been that the fundamental involvement in a reading disability is a deficiency in the integration of auditory sensations. Many children do have such deficits, affecting not only ability to read but also the acquisition of spoken and written language. But a considerable number do not have deficiencies in auditory learning and for these children her postulation appears inappropriate.

Another noted authority (Fernald, 1943) made quite a different presumption. She viewed the child's problem as a deficit in visual learning with the further hypothesis that the "look and say" method complicates the process of learning to read. Because of this hypothesis, she did not stress auditory functions, per se. Rather, she developed a method whereby she taught children visually, but it consisted of finger tracing in the first stage. The tactile (finger tracing) modality was considered primary although other inputs were emphasized. In stage two, after tracing, the child was required to look at the words and then to write them without looking at copy, *saying them to himself while doing so.* Auditorization of the word while writing it was considered important because, "It is necessary to establish the connection between the sound of the word and its form, so that the individual will eventually recognize the word from the visual stimulus alone" (Fernald, 1943, p. 40).

Fernald assumed complex interrelationships in intersensory perception and learning, the route being from tactile to auditory to visual. Based on her hypothesis, the approach was to establish more effective visual learning through the tactile-auditory modalities. Again the question arises: Do all children learn most effectively through this sequence, through this patterning of incoming sensations? Those with deficits in tactile learning might have difficulty with stage one, finger tracing. Moreover, unless the child can auditorize, he will not be able to say the words while writing them, and those with deficits in visual learning might achieve more successfully by other methods. We postulate that some do.

Several workers have stressed perceptual processes as a basis for teaching children with neurological disturbances, including the slow learners. Perhaps this emphasis can be traced to the noteworthy contribution of Strauss and Lehtinen (1947). Cruikshank (1961) has asserted that because these children have perceptual disturbances, structuring and intensification of the stimulus are critical to improvement in learning. Inherent is the inference that all learning disability children have perceptual disturbances and that this involvement is essentially visual. A similar frame of reference characterizes the work of Kephart (1964), but he emphasizes "ocular" features, spatial orientation, and motor patterns for developing visual perceptual abilities. Frostig (1964) also stresses visual perception and has prepared materials for training children with learning disabilities.

Despite the significance of these contributions, the learning disability child cannot be viewed only in terms of perceptual disturbances. Not all, perhaps not even the majority, of them have such disturbances and hence are not principally in need of structuring of the environment, of incoming stimuli. Moreover, when perceptual disturbances are present, they might include auditory or tactile processes as well as, or instead of, visual processes; auditory perceptual dysfunctions are common.

The most successful pedagogical principles are those based on both psychological and neurological considerations—those that have a psychoneurological foundation. As implied throughout this volume, the principles that we have found most valuable have their origin in the frame of reference that there is a psychology of learning which characterizes children with learning disabilities. This does not preclude the fact that they may overlap with, or in some respects be similar to, those postulated for other types of handicapped children, or even for the normal.

A final statement of principles, a final method or approach, is not anticipated for the learning disability child any more than for the normal. On the other hand, through experience as well as from research, a level of knowledge has been gained so that we can avoid gross exaggeration of methods and of claims for success. Likewise, we can avoid a conglomeration of approaches and an illogical, ill-conceived emphasis on any one behavioral aspect or function. Though there are limitations to all approaches, certain principles are evolving and a rationale for special education can be stated. It is in these terms that we discuss the approach that we have found most effective in promoting learning in this group of children. This approach, as much as possible, incorporates contributions from education, psychology and neurology.

PRINCIPLES FOR REMEDIATION

Individualizing the Problem

Teaching of children with learning disabilities must be strikingly individualized. The teacher should have the child's characteristics clearly in mind. In addition to common information—intelligence level, home background, emotional status—she should know the nature of his problem in learning, the deficits, the integrities, the levels of function in spoken, read, and written language, the nonverbal and medical aspects. She must have the total "syndrome" in mind in order that the educational procedures can be applied with precision and accuracy.

Teaching to the Level of Involvement

In the preceding chapter we stressed the importance of interpreting the learning disability in terms of the level of experience—perception, imagery, symbolization, or conception—which is predominantly involved. To prevent overgeneralization and oversimplification, it is necessary to ascertain this level and to structure the educational remediation accordingly. For example, a disturbance of revisualization or of reauditorization processes might impede verbal learning, but in this case it is pedagogically unsound to proceed as though these are simple aphasias, dyslexias, or dysgraphias when, in fact, they are not; the approach is to begin with the visualization or auditorization defects, not with their verbal manifestations. This means teaching to the level of the involvement as closely as possible.

Teaching to the Type of Involvement

The type of disability that characterizes a child's deficit in learning is a significant variable, so teaching according to the type of involvement constitutes a critical principle. We have emphasized the meaningfulness of *type* by our classification of nonsocial-nonverbal, social-nonverbal, and verbal. These distinctions highlight the fact that the problem may comprise meaning versus non-meaning, or verbal versus nonverbal factors in learning. That meaning is a psychological and neurological factor in learning is being reiterated. As a pedagogical variable, it is of great consequence, and the same is true of differentiating between verbal and nonverbal. We indicated previously that the neurology of verbal behavior differs from that of nonverbal behavior; the left hemisphere of the brain is mainly responsible for verbal functions, with the possibility that the right is predominantly responsible for the nonverbal. There are a number of pedagogical implications and it is on this basis that concepts of *transfer* are postulated.

The principle of teaching to the type of the involvement also means that the approach corresponds to the determination of whether the deficit entails *intra* or *inter* sensory learning and whether there are deficiencies of integration. The methodology, as discussed in the following chapters, assumes that the teacher recognizes that the deficit falls within a given type of function and that she proceeds with remediation with this fact in mind.

Teaching According to Readiness

The significance of multiple readiness levels has been presented. Here we emphasize as a principle that the teacher should be aware of the various readiness levels and that the remediation should provide for a balanced program, with the program's emphasis shifting in order to bring about greater equilibrium and stability in all of the areas of function.

Input Precedes Output

Learning assumes both input and output; the child comprehends before he speaks and reads before he writes. These variables, so vital to the concept of learning disabilities, might also be viewed as types of involvement. However, in terms of principles for remedial instruction, they warrant separate consideration.

In training it is helpful to note that the agnosias are input (receptive) disorders and that the apraxias are output (expressive) disorders. Deficits in input are the more debilitating, especially when the disorder is auditory in nature. That is, input problems tend to modify and reduce learning severely and inclusively. The child who cannot comprehend the spoken or read word, or perceive time and space, is reduced in total experience. He is emotionally immature, showing concomitant effects in ego development. He lacks the usual tools for thought, understanding, and adjustment. In contrast, the child who cannot speak or write at least has tools for purposes of inner language; thinking processes, emotional growth, and adjustment are less debilitated. These factors, the input-output variables, often become the basis for school classification and grouping, which in itself suggests their importance in terms of principles and methods. Those with receptive disturbances present a generalized problem because their learning disorder is the more severe and requires maximum *special* education programming.

Teaching to the Tolerance Levels

Teaching to the tolerance level is a fundamental principle that has evolved from our experience with children (and adults) who have learning disabilities due to dysfunctions in the brain. This principle has grown in significance since we have done electroencephalograms on children while they are in the act of learning (Myklebust, 1967). That both psychological and neurological tolerance levels are often altered in these children has been acknowledged; it remains for special education to teach the child accordingly. Overloading, in particular, must be avoided. The teacher should be aware that a given type of stimulation may grossly impede learning or interfere with learning through other sensory modalities. Unless the principle of teaching to the tolerance level is meticulously followed, the child not only may not profit from instruction but his total well-being might be further disrupted.

Multisensory Stimulation

The multisensory approach in remediation can be described as an attempt to stimulate in every way possible, with the hope that somehow something will be beneficial. When indiscriminately used with children who have learning disabilities, this approach must be described as unfortunate. The number of sensory modalities to be activated for input can be determined solely on the basis of the child's total capacities and tolerance levels. If both auditory and visual stimulations are given, because of the nature of the brain dysfunction one may obliterate incoming signals from the other. Moreover, some children can tolerate incoming information from just one modality at a time, or from only certain modality combinations such as auditory-tactile. The multisensory approach must be analyzed by the criteria of overloading and tolerance levels. Though rare, it is apparent that undue stimulation will bring about catastrophic reactions or even seizures in some children. As discussed previously, the special educator should recognize that a given approach applied indiscriminately does not foster learning and may be detrimental. The method used should be by choice, not by chance.

It is of vital importance to stress that indiscriminate application of the multisensory approach may be no more unwise or detrimental than indiscriminate application of a unisensory approach. As discussed below, teaching only to the deficits or only to the integrities, only on the basis of perceptual involvement or only in terms of motor processes, is to apply a unisensory approach in an indiscriminate manner. Such procedures ignore the significant individual differences which especially characterize children with learning disabilities. Tolerance levels and other relevant factors also are overlooked. Special education has always emphasized the meeting of every child's needs according to the nature of his total capacities and handicaps. It must continue to do so.

Teaching to the Deficits

Teaching only to the deficits is a unitary, hence limited, concept of remediation. Although an objective of the educational plan is to raise the deficits, to assume that this can be done only, or even most effectively, by approaching the remediation largely through the deficient avenue is misleading. Children in whom the disability is mainly visual sometimes are unable to tolerate more than minimal stimulation through this modality. The same is true for some in whom the principle involvement is auditory, and for still others in whom the greatest deficit is in tactile learning. The approach of choice is to raise the deficits without undue stimulation or demand on the disability itself.

There are other limitations to teaching only to the deficits. This approach fails to consider the importance of interneurosensory learning. The special education plan concerns much more than raising the level of function in a deficient area. The remedial instruction is gauged in such a manner that the deficit is raised but also so that the information gained through one modality, whether or not it is deficient, is integrated with all of the other information being received. We cannot assume, as we can in the normal child, that if we raise an auditory ability, e.g., memory, that the child with a learning disability is capable of generalizing this facility to other areas of function. Boshes and Myklebust (1964) and Zigmond (1966) have shown that the learning disability child's inability to integrate various types of information differentiates him from the normal child. Such conversion of learning must also be remedied. This is one of the most troublesome and limited aspects of educational programs that revolve around stress on deficits, motor-patterning, visual-spatial-patterning, structuring, associating, or perceptual training. No restricted, unitary approach is sufficiently encompassing to allow adequate control of the various factors which warrant analysis, consideration, and emphasis.

Teaching to the Integrities

Those who advocate teaching to the integrities, to the areas of least deficiency, purport to reach the deficit areas through the unaffected modalities. This may be simply another approach with the same weaknesses mentioned above. Moreover, it assumes interneurosensory learning which as an assumption might be seriously in error. Often it is these *inter* learning processes that are not intact, so the integrity area (through which the stimulation is being given) develops unitarily and becomes functional out of proportion, even to a greater extent than existed prior to remediation. All experienced persons have seen the child who has become "completely visual" or "completely auditory." Because integrity areas have become unduly functional, the child is no longer capable of integrating certain classes of information—i.e., auditory, visual, verbal, or nonverbal. Certain inter-neurosensory learning processes are now permanently deficient.

Training in Perception

To provide training only in terms of perceptual disturbances is to assume that this involvement is a universal consequence of dysfunctions in the brain. We have pointed out that this is far from the true circumstance because many types of deficiencies in learning result from neurological disturbance. Stressing perception when it is unnecessary or unwarranted does not benefit the child and can be detrimental since it imposes restrictions on other learning processes of consequence to total development.

Controlling Important Variables

As this principle implies, for effective learning the teaching must be in terms of the variables that typify a given child or group of children. Some require emphasis on control of *attention*, on prevention of distractibility. For others it is essential to control proximity; simple structuring (having the child closer to the teacher, a greater distance from another child, etc.) can mean the difference between learning readily and not learning. *Rate* also is a significant variable, as illustrated frequently throughout the remaining chapters. Most children with learning disabilities, at least at the time of beginning the special education training, are benefitted by skillful manipulation of rate, whether the remediation is mainly for verbal or for nonverbal deficiencies. In some children *size* is critical to effective learning. The teacher should explore the influence of varying the size of objects, pictures, and print.

Both Verbal and Nonverbal

The principle of both verbal and nonverbal means that the child must be taught so that he shows gains in all areas of experience. If the greater deficit is in verbal learning (aphasia, dyslexia, dysgraphia), language training is mandatory. However, development of verbal facility includes relating words to nonverbal experience. When nonverbal functions are disturbed, usually the educational remediation process is even more subtle and complex because then the problem necessitates enhancement of meaning, of inner language broadly conceived.

Deficiencies in nonverbal learning often entail time concepts (hours, days, weeks, seasons), direction, and relational concepts (fastest, half-full, half-way, not quite so full, taller, closer, later, after a while, too short, too high, etc.). The principle of both verbal and nonverbal implies a flexible approach to teaching, with constant awareness that words and nonverbal experience must be stressed in an "in and out" manner; first one is stressed and then the other, as indicated by the child's deficits and idiosyncratic disruptions in learning.

Psychoneurological Considerations

Psychoneurological Considerations summarizes the point of view expressed in this volume. It emphasizes that the educational approach takes cognizance of the fact that it is a brain dysfunction that has altered the ways in which the child learns, and that highly consequential medical problems may be involved. Moreover, the findings of the neurologist, electroencephalographer, and ophthalmologist are of considerable value to the educator. With the assistance of these specialists, we have acquired detailed statistical evidence which reveals that classifications on the basis of these findings are directly related to the ways in which the child learns most successfully (Behrens, 1963; Boshes and Myklebust, 1964; Hughes, 1967; Lawson, 1967; Zigmond, 1966). Therefore, the educational approach is guided, not alone by behavioral criteria but also by physical findings which disclose the status of the nervous system. Only when both are incorporated can the educational remediation be most beneficial.

CLINICAL TEACHING

Traditional approaches for the education of children with learning disabilities seemed limited, if not unsuitable, so we found it necessary to originate pedagogic principles and procedures. Because neither scientific evidence nor experience are yet extensive, we anticipate various revisions and adaptations. Nevertheless, the principles, methods, and techniques discussed and illustrated throughout the remainder of this volume have developed from research and actual remediation experience with a large number of children ranging in age from preschool through high school years. We designate this approach as the method of *Clinical Teaching*.

The critical connotation for the special educator is the term *clinical*. In Webster's Dictionary (1963, p. 423) we find "clinical" defined as "depending on or involving direct observation of the patient" and "applying objective methods to the description, evaluation, and modification of human behavior." Both statements, each in a different way, serve admirably to emphasize the basic attributes of this concept of remediation. It is dependent on direct observation of the child and these observations are based on objective, diagnostic information (including medical), and the intent and purpose of the remediation is to modify behavior. Hence, in our training of educators, psychologists, and other specialists, in our work with parents and with the children themselves, we refer to this approach as *Clinical Teaching.*

Clinical Teaching implies that the teacher is fully aware of the child's disability, of his strengths and deficits, and that her efforts are to bring about a balance between his tolerance levels and the stimulation provided. She considers his problem in multi-dimensional, not in unitary terms, and recognizes the need for controlling certain behavioral variables while activating or manipulating others. The procedures are not viewed in terms of dichotomies, such as deficits versus integrities or multisensory versus unisensory. Any one of these may be the method of choice under specified circumstances. Included is the inference that to prevent the integrities from becoming developed out of proportion to the deficits, it is necessary to *hold* the high points of ability while properly developing the low points. This is accomplished through emphasis on *balance.* If the teaching is done through intact areas of function, it is done in a manner that fosters integration with the deficit areas, always with the awareness that if the integrity areas are raised, the deficit areas must be raised in the same proportion, or preferably to a greater extent, so that more uniformity of abilities is achieved.

Clinical Teaching does not assume that the same methodologies are applied to every child. Rather, it stipulates that each child presents a problem with its own idiosyncratic characteristics. The teacher is equipped to adjust her approach to the dynamic pattern of the relationships between the strengths and weaknesses peculiar to each individual; she adjusts her approach, the child is not expected to adjust to her methods. She expects him to perform according to his potential but she is aware that chronological age (not mental age alone) and opportunity for learning are influential and must be considered when planning a remedial program.

To be a clinical teacher requires a degree of sophistication in that she must be informed in both the psychology and the neurology of learning. There is regard for the importance of concepts, such as meaningfulness, verbal versus nonverbal, input before output, semi-autonomous systems, seizure-prone, overloading, balance, monitoring systems, simultaneity, hierarchies of experience, and neurosensory processes. Sophistication and knowledge likewise are assumed relative to the significance of developmental factors. Moreover, the child is viewed not only in terms of his learning disability but through other facets of behavior—i.e., his social maturity, his emotional adjustment, his acceptance of and by other children, his neighborhood, his friendships. Clinical Teaching does not stress academic success alone; the pervasiveness of the problem, even in those whose potential for learning remains above average, is kept clearly in mind. Hence, this approach is broad, inclusive, and dynamic. Only an approach of this type can be expected to meet the urgent challenge presented by this group of handicapped children.

This approach is summarized in the Schema below. The fundamental principles which must be considered involve: the integrities, deficits, tolerance levels, number and types of sensory modalities to be activated, type of involvement, level of involvement, relationships between reception and expression, nature of verbal and nonverbal disturbances, states of readiness, and the need for assistance with total integration.

Schema illustrating the Clinical Teaching approach to remediation of psychoneurological learning disabilities.

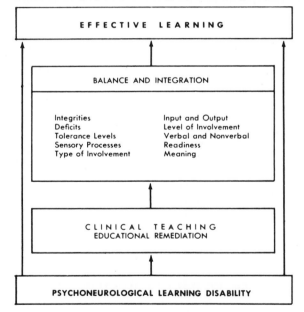

Underlying these considerations is the principle that the teacher must develop the greatest possible degree of balance among the behavioral functions by individualizing the program for each child or each group of children. She recognizes that her approach depends on and involves *direct observation of the patient* (child) and that success can be achieved *by applying objective methods to the description, evaluation, and modification of human behavior.*

CHAPTER IV

Disorders of Auditory Language

Children with learning disabilities present many types of deficiencies in auditory behavior, both verbal and nonverbal. Because these are so fundamental to psychological processes, we first investigated the ways in which different conditions (deafness, emotional disturbance, mental retardation, receptive aphasia) distorted auditory functioning (Myklebust, 1954). Relationships were found between a given condition and the manner in which the child behaved. Children with mental illness sometimes ignore sound, even when presented at the pain level of intensity. The hearing impaired respond consistently when their reduced threshold is considered. For the mentally retarded the problem is one of level of comprehension; their ability to respond varies on the basis of the procedures and stimuli used.

A dysfunction in the brain can inhibit auditory learning and at times impede all aspects of auditory functioning, verbal and nonverbal. This severe type of involvement, as a result of damage to the central nervous system, was one of the first auditory receptive disorders to be recognized (Nielsen, 1946). Following a brain disease, the individual was unable to comprehend sound. Traditionally, this condition is referred to as generalized *auditory agnosia*. Freud (1953) first used the term agnosia as a diagnostic classification; Jackson (Taylor 1958) preferred the term *auditory imperception*. This degree of debilitation of auditory processes is seen also in children. Hardy (1956) and Taylor (1964), among others, emphasized the need to differentiate this marked deficit in auditory capacity from profound deafness in early life. Both psychogalvanic and electroencephalographic audiometry are revealing when making such a diagnosis. For everyday clinical purposes, we use the informal techniques described previously (Myklebust, 1954).

GENERALIZED DEFICITS IN AUDITORY LEARNING

Generalized deficits in sensory processes comprise one of the most complex problems encountered by the teacher of the child with learning disabilities. We have stressed that neurogenic disturbances of auditory capacities are especially debilitating to the child's behavior. Audition is the organism's primary distance scanning sense. It is the basic avenue through which the individual maintains contact with his environment, day and night. Moreover, it is the primary channel for language acquisition and interpersonal communication. Gesell and Amatruda (1947) commented that audition is the "social sense."

Because generalized deficits in auditory learning are grossly disturbing to the child, we shall consider this problem in some detail. The number of children having this deficiency is not known. School systems have not had programs for these children so they have been erroneously or knowingly classified either with the deaf or with the mentally deficient. Those for whom the techniques discussed here have been most rewarding are neither deaf nor mentally deficient. They are severely disturbed in auditory perception and, in addition, cannot interpret any sound, whether of the social-nonverbal type or of the spoken word. At times, they have deficits in auditory memory.

The child with a generalized deficit in auditory learning hears, but he does not interpret what he hears. He understands neither spoken words nor environmental sounds. He is unable to structure his auditory world, to sort out and associate sounds with particular objects or experiences. Because he fails to make these associations, he responds inconsistently to sounds and sometimes he is thought to be deaf or hard of hearing. Auditory involvements of this type are considerably more debilitating than those where only verbal comprehension is affected.

In some ways these children are similar in behavior to the deaf. Since they do not interpret sounds, they become more visually and tactually oriented. They prefer colorful and mobile toys rather than those which produce sound. Most of them appear quiet and use few vocalizations. However, the vocalizations used vary in pitch and inflection, indicating a more normal vocal quality than found in the deaf. The following summary was written by a psychologist after seeing a child who had a severe auditory receptive disability. Note particularly the description of the responses to sound.

Psychologist's Report   Billy: C. A. 6 years, 7 months

Billy is a dark-haired, very tractable, sweet dispositioned boy. He was interpersonally responsive to play activity. He did not respond to verbal directions, but quickly followed gestured commands.

He at times reacted to faint footsteps in the hall, and, at times, to clapping behind his back, but he never responded to his name said in varying degrees of loudness. He used very appropriate gestures. For instance, when he squeezed a dog that made a noise, it gave him great pleasure, but when he pressed a similar dog and no noise was emitted, he shrugged his shoulders, shook his head, and slightly extended his arms with hands in an upward position. When he squeezed the dog that made a noise, he smiled and became very alert looking; when he pressed the non-noise dog, he lost the smile and a look of bewilderment came over his face.

He was well-motivated on nonverbal tasks and was decidedly pleased with himself when he successfully completed a task.

There was considerable vocalization with gross variations in tone—not at all like the peripherally deaf child. These vocalizations at times appeared to be a real attempt at communication.

It is obvious that the child heard sounds and was aware of them, but because he did not relate sounds to experience his responses were inconsistent and inappropriate. He could not understand the spoken word so he could not acquire language. His primary means of communication was gesture and pantomime. He used his voice to gain the attention of others and demonstrated good vocal inflection, but he did not associate sounds with concrete objects nor understand the simplest words, even at the level of naming or labeling.

Educational Procedures

In teaching a child with a generalized deficiency in auditory learning, the primary objective is to help him utilize all of his capacities. If he is permitted to rely solely on vision and taction, he will gradually behave more and more as though he were deaf. Although it is possible that the severity of the disability will preclude acquisition of the spoken word, every attempt should be made to help him develop all of his potentials. If he cannot acquire spoken language, it is important for his protection that he learn to understand the meaning of the social sounds in his environment. He should be able to sort out a particular sound from the conglomerate auditory world, know when to ignore it and when to respond; he should be able to relate the sound of a train with the object and react appropriately. Even if he can use sounds only for signalling or warning purposes, he will become more socially competent. The ultimate goal, however, is to teach him to understand the meaning of both social sounds and the spoken word.

The primary task of the teacher is to help the child relate sounds to the proper units of experience, and in so doing perhaps the fundamental instructional principle is *simultaneity. It is essential that the auditory stimulus be carefully timed with the experience.* A few seconds' delay can be a deterrent in learning. For example, when teaching the meaning of the sound of an airplane, it is not sufficient to take the child to the window and see the plane after the sound has diminished, while there are traffic noises, or when children are playing in the vicinity. Under these conditions it is too difficult for him to differentiate one sound from others and to relate it to the appropriate object.

Meaningful Auditory Environment. In the initial stages of training, the auditory environment should be structured as much as possible. The classroom should be some distance away from traffic and continuous playground noise. Since these children do not understand sounds, they often do not know which ones to ignore and thus overreact to extraneous noise.

As they learn to associate sounds with experience, their responses become more suitable. But until they are capable of coping with environmental sounds, they should not be placed in an overwhelming auditory world. It causes distraction and interferes with learning.

Most children have adequate auditory stimulation in their home and school environments for the development of spoken language. However, if they do not respond when spoken to, the tendency is to rely on gesture. Visual cues are necessary but they should not be used exclusively since words and sounds must be heard in order to be learned. It is essential to talk to the child but not to use excessive verbalizations. The speaker should face him when talking because he gains meaning from watching facial expressions.

The daily classroom routine should be planned so that auditory and nonauditory activities are alternated. Because children with severe auditory receptive disabilities have considerable difficulty in listening, they fatigue easily. They need periods of quiet after working on auditory tasks. At times they become so frustrated and fatigued that they withdraw from the situation by covering their ears. It is necessary to watch for such signs of fatigue and to provide quiet periods during which they can regain their equilibrium.

Awareness. When a child gives no consistent responses, it is important to begin training by making him aware of *sound* and *no sound*. Without emphasizing meaning, the teacher merely tries to help him to respond consistently to sounds. Toys such as bells, drums, toy pianos, or telephones are used to produce sounds and these are presented in a relatively quiet environment. The teacher shows the child each toy object and encourages him to manipulate it so that he has an active part in starting and stopping the sound. For example, the child is asked to push the piano keys or to ring the bell. Meanwhile the teacher, with facial animation and gestures, indicates that the child should listen. She might cup her ear and look quizically each time she hears the sound.

Toys should be selected which are attractive both visually and tactually, but it must be made certain that it is not only the tactual or visual experience that the child enjoys. One boy with auditory agnosia enjoyed squeaky rubber animals, not for the sounds they produced, but for the pleasurable sensation of flattening the toy and feeling the air being emitted from the tiny hole. He was intrigued by the tactual sensation of the air and the change in the size of the animal, and as a result he did not attend to the sound.

In addition to working with toys, the child with a generalized auditory disability should be encouraged to explore objects in his daily environment in order to become more aware of the presence and absence of sound. He might be asked to turn the radio on and off; as he turns the switch the teacher tries to make him conscious of the sound by using gestures and facial animation. He can be encouraged to perform tasks such as sharpening pencils; as he turns the crank he should listen for the sound. At home, under the supervision of an adult, he might turn on mixers, vacuum cleaners, or other appliances which are not dangerous. The environment should be as quiet as possible when new sounds are introduced so that the child hears only the sound produced by the object selected. As he manipulates them and turns them on and off, he not only becomes more aware of sounds but he also begins to relate them to objects and experiences.

When awareness has been established, the child should be encouraged to respond *consistently*. It is not sufficient that he merely be aware of sounds; he must learn to understand them and to react appropriately. Eventually, after meaning has been developed, he should learn which to ignore and which to listen for, but initially, he needs help to respond consistently.

(1) Select a toy piano or a bell with which the child is familiar and have him close his eyes or put his head down on the table; ask him to sit up or uncover his eyes each time he hears the sound. If he cannot comprehend the task, help him by holding his hand and simultaneously tapping the table each time the bell rings. Continue this procedure until he responds to the sound without assistance. In some instances the child is not asked to close his eyes but instead is told to raise his hand or tap the table each time he hears the sound. The exact procedure depends upon the degree of distractibility and integrative capacity. Although certain children can respond with their eyes open, others respond more consistently if their eyes are closed because they are unable to cope with both visual and auditory stimuli at the same time. As the sounds take on meaning, the children have less difficulty. Highly stimulating visual activities are not presented when they are expected to listen. They should be seated at a table, told to wait and to respond as soon as they hear the sound.

(2) Have the child respond to the cessation of sound; ring a bell behind him and ask him to raise his hand or tap the table each time the sound stops.

(3) Select identical toys, e.g., two bells or two drums. Stand behind the child and ring the bell; he is to ring his bell when he hears the one behind him. To make certain that he understands the task, it may be necessary to pantomime the "game" and to help him with the first few trials.

(4) Reduce the amount of structure and teach him to respond to meaningful sounds. Ring a bell in the same way each day to indicate lunch time. Initially, ring the bell so that he can both see and hear it; later conceal it to see whether he responds to just the sound.

Select other sounds to represent various activities during the school day, such as a drum for recess time or a whistle for dismissal. If buzzer or bell systems are utilized, help the child to respond to them appropriately. Usually these are more difficult to learn because there is no concomitant visual experience to associate with the social sound. When actual objects are used, the child receives simultaneous visual and auditory experience.

As the child shows improvement, other meaningful sounds are introduced. Sounds which are important for self-protection should be taught as early as possible. The sounds of cars, trains, airplanes, and fire trucks should be included, as well as those of the telephone, doorbell, and a knock on the door. Each one should be introduced in a structured manner to avoid the task of selecting a certain sound from the conglomerate field. For example, when teaching the sound of a knock at the door, the classroom should be quiet and the child's attention guided in the proper direction.

Later, after considerable work has been done with actual objects, recorded sounds are applicable. The sound of a train is presented with a toy train or with a picture of a train. All recordings should be clear and of sufficient duration to permit the child to distinguish each sound; a short sound effects recording is inadequate for teaching purposes. Each sound should be played several times since he needs to hear it repeatedly before he can make the correct association with the object.

Localization. In addition to understanding sounds, the child must be able to localize them; only when the general source of a sound is known can one react appropriately. When a car approaches from the left, we must determine whether to move, and if so, in what direction. "Hide and seek" games of the type suggested by Myklebust (1955) are useful in improving localization and listening behavior. The teacher gives the child a toy, such as a cricket or a bell, and shows him how to play with it. Then she plays the game of "find the sound." She hides behind the door, rings the bell, and encourages him to find the sound. If he fails she may set an alarm clock and hide it. While it is ringing, she and the child "search" for the sound. Other techniques include the following:

(1) Seat the child at a table and ask him to close his eyes; then ring a bell on his right and have him turn toward the sound. If he is not successful, ask him to open his eyes and simultaneously follow the sound by both looking and listening. As he learns to direct his attention, ask him to close his eyes and repeat the initial procedure. Later, make the task more complex by moving to different positions in the room and presenting sounds from various directions.

(2) Teach him to "follow the sound." Blow a whistle while walking around the room and have the child follow. After he understands the

task, have him close his eyes and follow just by sound; make certain that there are no obstructions.

Discrimination. Children with auditory receptive disabilities often need special training in discrimination. They can distinguish gross but not fine differences. They might be able to differentiate between a knock on the door and the ring of the telephone, but not between a telephone and a doorbell. For training to overcome these difficulties, the following procedures are suggested:

(1) Select two noisemakers having very different sounds, e.g., a drum and a bell. Have the child gain experience with the toys so that he knows the sound which accompanies each object. Then stand behind him with an identical set of toys and ring the bell to see if he can point to the correct object. As he progresses, select sounds more nearly alike and continue the exercises with variations to assure the necessary motivation and enjoyment.

(2) When success has been gained with two sounds, introduce a third one, making the task more complex. For example, use a drum, a bell, and a clapper, gradually working toward finer discriminations.

(3) Record a series of common, everyday sounds, such as those made by trains, airplanes, animals, and household appliances, and select pictures to go with each of them. Then place three or four pictures in front of the child and play one of the sounds. He is to identify the picture associated with it.

Memory. Auditory memory is critical for language development. Retaining a sequence of sounds within words and a sequence of words within sentences is essential for comprehension and for expressive use of the spoken word. Those with severe auditory receptive disabilities frequently are deficient in auditory memory and require specialized training accordingly. The exercises outlined below have been found beneficial.

(1) Face the child and clap your hands once. Ask him to imitate you. Next, clap twice and have him do the same. Then see if he can imitate a pattern of three. When he understands and can follow the sequence while facing you, stand behind him and have him imitate from audition alone. Initially, the task should be presented both auditorially and visually because he may need to both see and hear. With practice and emphasis on listening, he should be able to remember and imitate the number of sounds he hears.

(2) Draw a circle on the blackboard, then clap once to indicate that one figure represents one sound. Next draw two circles and clap twice. Follow with three and then with four. Ask the child to look at each series of figures and clap the correct number of times for each set. Then stand behind him and clap a certain number of times; ask him to point to the

set of figures corresponding with the number of sounds that he hears. If the child has number concepts, the teacher can write the numerals 1, 2, 3, or 4 on the blackboard, then clap and have him point to the number representing the number of claps. These exercises can be performed with drums or sticks, but the tactual and kinesthetic experience of clapping seems more advantageous.

Amplification. The question has been raised as to whether amplification is desirable in working with children who have severe auditory receptive disabilities. It is rarely beneficial to increase the intensity of sound because the primary problem is an inability to associate sound with the proper unit of experience. Increasing intensity is merely confusing. Moreover, since such children do not respond more consistently to loud sounds than to soft ones, amplification is of little value. Individual hearing aids are particularly confusing because extraneous background sounds are amplified and auditory perception is disturbed. On the other hand, amplification during carefully supervised periods of instruction can be of benefit, so portable binaural amplification units sometimes are applicable when new sounds are being introduced. The earphone with a slight increase of intensity structures the auditory world so that the child can listen more effectively. If amplification is used, comparative quiet is essential since intensification of background sound interferes with learning.

Children who have deficits in both auditory acuity and comprehension usually benefit from amplification. Under these circumstances the decision should be made by those trained in audiology as well as by the teacher. Children with this type of multiple involvement are in need of educational procedures which consider both the sensory deprivation and the disturbance in the central nervous system.

Auditory Inflection and Rhythm Patterns. A child with severe auditory receptive difficulties may respond appropriately by detecting the inflectional and rhythmic patterns of language. He, like the young normal child, does not fully comprehend the individual words of a question, such as, "Do you want to go bye-bye?" but he associates the entire verbal pattern with the experience of going away. After hearing the sentence said with the same inflectional pattern, the child grasps the general meaning and later the individual words. In teaching children with auditory agnosia we often capitalize on this ability before attempting to teach word meanings. Two or three sentences are selected and repeated in the same way at the same time each day. For example, the teacher might say, "Time . . . to . . . go," with a distinctive melody, and immediately after saying it indicate that it is time for the children to leave. After several repetitions the children associate the experience of going home with the inflectional pattern. Other phrases, such as, "lights . . . out" or "lunch . . .

time," are repeated with different inflectional and rhythmic patterns. Later the teacher alters the cadence of the sentence to determine whether the child understands the words. As he improves in his ability to comprehend, social sounds, words, and meaningful verbal symbols are introduced according to the principles outlined in the following section.

DISORDERS OF AUDITORY RECEPTIVE LANGUAGE

Children who have auditory verbal comprehension disabilities resulting from central nervous system dysfunction hear but do not understand what is said. Unlike those with generalized deficiencies, they comprehend nonverbal-social sounds but they are unable to relate the spoken word to the appropriate unit of experience. Language disabilities of this type have been described in both children and adults and have been designated as receptive aphasia, sensory aphasia, auditory verbal agnosia, or word deafness (Goldstein, 1948; McGinnis, 1963; Myklebust, 1954; Orton, 1937; Schuell, (1964), Wepman, 1951). Even though writers have used varied terminology, they agree that these disabilities should be differentiated from the language deficits resulting from deafness or mental retardation. Frequently such a distinction is not easy to make in those who have serious impairments, but it is essential in planning an adequate educational program. The receptive aphasic, as discussed here, is neither deaf nor mentally retarded; consequently his educational needs are different. Usually he demonstrates average or above average ability on nonverbal measures of intelligence but is deficient in verbal functions.

Typically, those with receptive aphasia have normal auditory acuity but sometimes it is difficult to assess their hearing by means of pure tone audiometry. Their responses are inconsistent and vary from one time to another. Listening in itself is demanding and they fatigue easily. Therefore, audiometric testing may need to be done in several short sessions by experienced audiometricians. Periods of diagnostic teaching and careful observation of responses to environmental sounds sometimes are necessary to obtain information regarding their level of auditory acuity. This determination should be made as early as possible since the educational procedures for the receptive aphasic with *no* hearing loss vary from those for children who have both a hearing impairment and a language disorder.

Occasionally parents and teachers are bewildered by the child's lack of consistent response to sound, finding it hard to discipline him because they are uncertain about whether or not he can hear and understand. Other parents are less concerned about hearing and comment, "I know he can hear—he just doesn't understand what we say." Teachers indicate that these children look dazed and at times do not even respond to their names. Some, though they can hear, cannot listen and become frustrated in conversational situations. During story time in school, it is not unusual for them to cover their ears or to withdraw from the situation.

Children with receptive aphasia often are highly creative in diverse ways. Because of their limitations in auditory learning, they tend to enjoy painting, drawing, or similar activities. One boy constructed beautiful models of boats from scraps of wood and a twelve-year-old girl sewed doll clothes without either patterns or instructions. Their verbal deficits, however, interfere even in art classes because they do not know the names of the utensils they are to use. An art teacher commented that a seven-year-old boy could not complete assignments if she used only verbal instructions, but when she provided a finished sample of the work to help him understand, he did the best work in the class. Without demonstrations he could not grasp the assignments.

An eight-year-old boy with a severe auditory comprehension problem drew the picture shown in Illustration 1. Because he had some ability to read, he was given sentences and asked to draw a picture to go with each one. (His performance intelligence quotient was 96 but his verbal quotient was only 65.) He could understand simple instructions given auditorially but became completely confused in a classroom discussion or during casual conversation. This same boy drew highly complex three-dimensional figures and animals. One day in class while learning the names of birds he indicated that he wanted to draw one. First he sketched the body, but before starting on the wings, he got up, moved about the room waving his arms like a bird, sat down, drew the wings of the bird, cut them out and inserted them into the body. Such actions illustrate how he was over-compensating for his auditory deficit by using vision, taction, and kinesthesis. It also suggests that the visual and auditory systems can operate semi-independently.

The primary characteristic of receptive aphasics is their inability to comprehend the spoken word; however, the degree of involvement varies. When it is severe, they may not comprehend any words nor even recognize that words are words. Consequently they fail to recognize their names and cannot respond to simple commands like "Open the door". When the condition is less severe, they have trouble only with more abstract language or certain parts of speech. Some can grasp simple words such as nouns but not words that represent actions, qualities, feelings, or ideas. That is, they can understand the nouns *milk* or *daddy* but not the verbs *drink* or *walk*. Several attempts were made, with little success, to teach an aphasic to *point* to various objects. Each time the teacher tried to help him internalize the meaning of *point*, he thought she was naming the finger or pencil being used in the act. He could not perceive that the word *point* represented an action, not an object.

I ride a horse.

I ride a bus to school.

I ride my wagon very fast.

ILLUSTRATION 1. Drawings by an eight-year-old whose auditory comprehension level was three to four years.

Similar problems are evidenced with other parts of speech or meaning units. Even teen-age receptive aphasics might fail to grasp the multiple meanings of prepositions like *under* or *around*. A fourteen-year-old girl who was told, "Draw a line around the picture of a milk bottle," responded, "But I can't get around it—I can't get in back of it." She had not conceptualized the multiple meanings of the word *around* and could not complete the exercise.

Adjectives and related descriptive words are difficult for the receptive aphasic. He must know that these words represent qualities, not objects or actions but characteristics related to objects, feelings, and experiences. He must realize that objects can be described as well as named. This is illustrated by an eight-year-old who could not understand concepts or words such as *hard*, *soft*, and *sharp*. The teacher, in an attempt to establish the meanings, selected several objects for him to examine. She tried to explain the sharpness of a knife by having him feel the point and by comparing it with a needle. The child became very frustrated and said, "No, No, that not sharp—that knife." He could not yet realize that the word *sharp* referred to a particular quality and not to the object itself.

Seen somewhat less frequently is the inability to comprehend the *names* of objects. Normally, simple nouns are learned easily but occasionally can be the most troublesome. It seems that the sound unit representing the name of the object is so short that some individuals are unable to grasp it during the normal flow of language. Initially, they appear dysnomic (unable to recall) since they use so few nouns expressively. Yet when asked to identify objects by name, they cannot do so because they do not comprehend them. In several instances children could follow commands such as, "Point to the one we use to lock the door," but not, "Point to the key." Because of these discrepancies in ability, the comprehension of both single words and longer verbal units must be evaluated and planned for.

In reality the child must learn "what means what" (Simon, 1957). He must learn *what* verbal symbol represents *what* experience. Language would be simple if it were nothing more than associations and if one verbal symbol represented a single experience. This, however, is not the case. The same auditory symbol can represent a number of unlike objects or experiences and the meaning depends largely upon the context. A word such as *cover* represents an object in one situation but an action in another. Not only does the same symbol represent dissimilar experiences but also a single object often has more than one name. The complexity of language is never more evident than when the symbolic process is disrupted.

In the normal acquisition of language, children hear a steady flow of words, but to understand them, meaning units must be differentiated. This is not an easy task for the receptive aphasic. On occasion he will mis-cue and associate the wrong symbol with the experience, as did a five-year-old boy in class when he was learning the nursery song, "Open, shut them." While singing he was to hold his hands with palms up and then alternately open and close his fists. He performed the proper action and repeated the words correctly, but while opening his fists, he said the word *shut* and while closing them, he said *open*.

Even older children may improperly differentiate words. Their problems may not be apparent in the spoken form but appear only in the written. A twelve-year-old who was asked to write a definition of the word *opponent* wrote *opsitem* for *opposite team*. He had heard this particular meaning unit and thought of it as one word. In another instance, he wrote *whichs* for *which is*, and wrote the word *weightlessness* as three words, *weight less ness*. In reading, words are clearly delineated by spaces. This is not true of the spoken word so the process of differentiating meaning units is highly complex.

An inability to understand words must be differentiated from disorders related to distractibility, listening, or auditory memory. Inasmuch as any one of these problems can affect the child's comprehension, the specific deficit should be determined. If a child can comprehend but not remember what he hears, he is in need of remediation for a memory disturbance. Similarly, if he comprehends in a structured auditory environment, his need is not for work on comprehension and word meaning; his deficit is more one of auditory perception than of receptive aphasia.

Auditory Comprehension and Related Learning Disabilities

A disorder of comprehension inevitably affects verbal expression. Myklebust (1954) emphasized that input precedes output and that children who fail to understand do not use meaningful spoken language. Those who have a severe receptive aphasia may be unable to use any words, in which case gesture, pantomime, and occasionally drawings assist in indicating their needs. Others use words or sentence fragments in keeping with their level of comprehension. The child who does not understand the names of objects will use few nouns. The one who does not understand words representing qualities or feelings may use no adjectives. Those who do not understand the use of past or future tense will use sentences with verbs only of the present tense.

Some children are echolalic and merely repeat what they hear without understanding. Even though words are used, they do not constitute expressive language. As a rule, echolalia occurs only when the verbalizations they hear are above their level of comprehension. The following transcription of a five-year-old shows that he understands simple commands and questions, but not complex language.

Teacher: (Shows picture to child) Where's Mommy?
Child: Mommy. (points correctly)
Teacher: Where is the shoe?
Child: Shoe. (points correctly)
Teacher: What is the boy doing?
Child: What is the boy doing? (echolalic)
Teacher: What is the Mommy holding?
Child: Mommy holding? (echolalic)
Teacher: Show me the kitten.
Child: Kitty. (points correctly)

Facility with expressive language usually is below the receptive language level. For example, if the auditory comprehension age is at an eighteen-month level, the average expressive language age is about six months lower. If additional expressive deficits exist, the discrepancy between comprehension and expression may be greater. Children having mixed receptive, memory, and expressive deficits require educational remediation in all areas.

Reading. Receptive disabilities of the auditory type generally affect reading, writing, and arithmetic as well as spoken language. Reading is a visual symbol system superimposed on previously acquired auditory language (Myklebust and Johnson, 1962). Therefore, it is apparent that an inability to learn spoken language interferes with learning to read. Occasionally these children learn to read simple words but they rarely progress beyond this level and tend to have many problems of reading comprehension. Those who are echolalic in spoken language sometimes are *word-callers* in reading. They transduce visual symbols to auditory symbols (or the printed letter to its sound), but they cannot translate either form into meaning.

The letters below illustrate the problems of receptive aphasia, its effect on oral expressive language, and the child's attempts to compensate for his auditory difficulties by trying to read. His limited comprehension is evident in both the auditory and visual forms.

Paragraphs from a Mother's letter:

Bill is now seven years old. He spoke no intelligible words at all until he was past two, and didn't use meaningful sentences to any extent until he was five. He has, however, used a lot of nonsense phrases from nursery rhymes, television commercials, etc. He also uses repetitive speech patterns; for instance, he used to end every sentence with "isn't it," and now he ends them all with "okay."

He has within the last year and a half learned to answer questions, more or less, and respond to a greeting. He has for some time been able to follow directions as long as he is not required to use much judgment.

According to his tests, Bill can read much better than he can talk. We are told that he can read at a first grade level, although we don't know how much of it he comprehends. We have given him very little help with this, other than answering his questions when he wants to know what a word is. We think he picked up his letters, and many words, off the television.

He does not seem much interested in having us read him stories, play games with him, etc., at least for more than a few minutes.

Paragraphs from a Teacher's letter:

Bill has used very little speech in his school experiences. His conversational speech consists of one or two word answers which are difficult to understand. When he reads he seems to pronounce words more clearly.

I was not able to communicate at all with him at first. I tried informal conversation with him. At no time did I get a response. Yet when I showed him the first pre-primer he appeared thrilled. Immediately he read the title. He read the entire book but at no time was I able to elicit a comment or an answer to an informal question about the story.

Most receptive aphasics are deficient in auditory skills, including discrimination, rhyming, and blending sounds into words. As they improve they acquire facility in phonics and in syllabication but initially, they need a global language approach to reading similar to that outlined for auditory dyslexia in Chapter V.

Written Language. The written language of the child with receptive aphasia also is affected to varying degrees, depending upon the extent of the deficit and other complicating learning disabilities. Myklebust (1965) states that *when a receptive aphasia is present, there is a marked effect on written language if the aphasia is present from early life.* As a rule, written language is concrete and in keeping with the levels of spoken and read language. Although they may be able to copy, these children cannot spontaneously formulate good sentences.

The following illustrations reveal the contrast between the language and non-language ability of a thirteen-year-old receptive aphasic. Although she had excellent visual integrities for nonverbal learning as shown in Illustration 2, her auditory receptive capacities were more nearly that of a six-year-old. The effect of her deficits is evident in the written language in Illustration 3.

The concreteness of the written language of a twelve-year-old receptive aphasic is shown in Illustration 4. She had not learned the words *period, comma,* or *question mark,* yet she remembered how they looked and where they should be placed. She had marked difficulty in understanding nouns

ILLUSTRATION 2. Visual nonverbal abilities of a 13-year-old receptive aphasic.

the boy   plays the toys
in school . the Dolls
pretent something to eat
Dinner and Play house
keeper that was playing
at school. his mother
with her child going to
the store bruy some milk,
coffee, candy, and cereals.
the boys and girls is hun-
gry something to eat and
Drink.

ILLUSTRATION 3. Written language of a 13-year-old receptive aphasic.

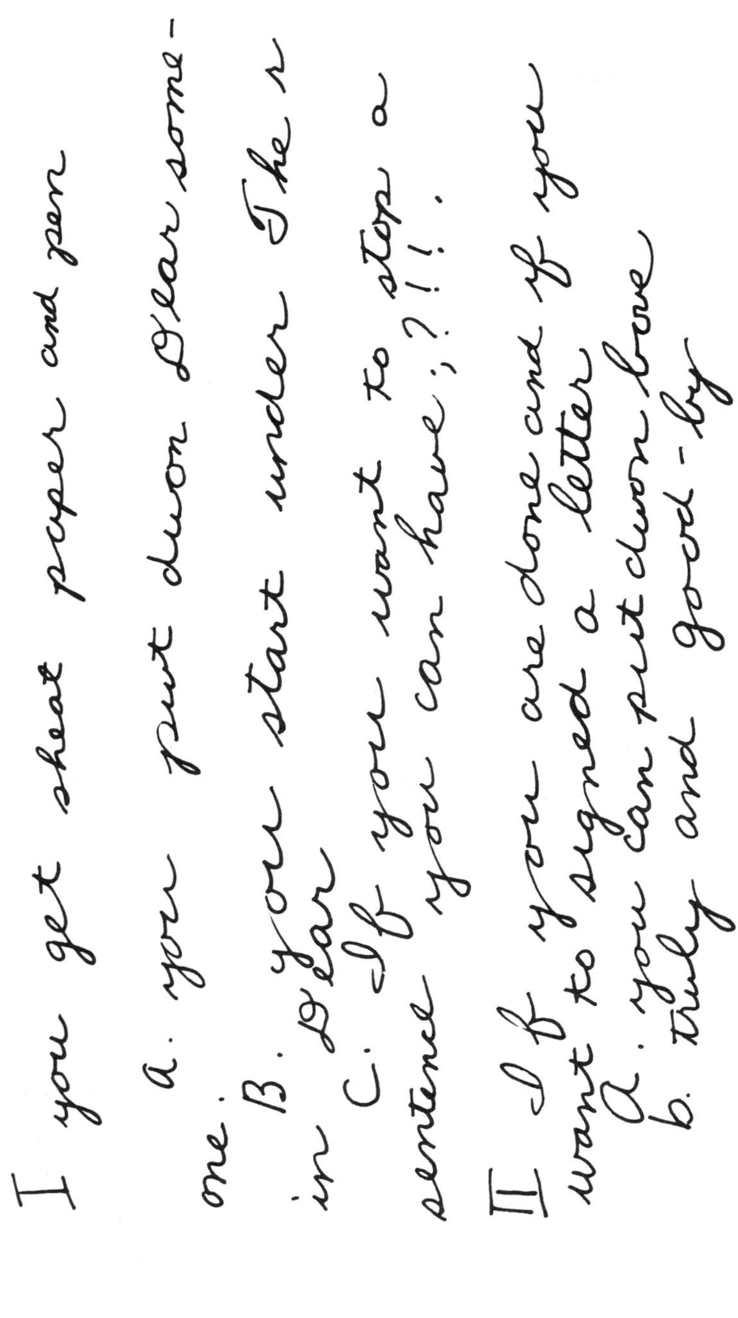

I you get sheat paper and pen

a. you put dwon Dear someone.

B. you start under The r
in Dear

C. If you want to stop a
sentence you can have.;?!!.

II If you are done and if you
want to signed a letter if you

a. you can put dwon love

b. truly and good-by

ILLUSTRATION 4. Concrete written language of a 12-year-old receptive aphasic.

and multiple meanings of words, as well as in auditory discrimination, which caused misperception and misarticulation of many words. She confused words like *steak* and *skate*, resulting in errors of word usage, and often said, "We had *skate* for supper last night," or "Children should *mine* their parents."

Mathematics. Some children with auditory receptive language disorders learn to calculate but do poorly in arithmetical reasoning because they do not comprehend the words. A ten-year-old boy with a wide discrepancy between verbal and performance ability was at the top of his class in computation but at the bottom in reading and written language. Although he could not grasp the meaning of story problems, he was rapid and accurate if the numbers were set up for him.

A fourth-grade girl received a "B" on one part of an arithmetic test and a "D" on the other. In analyzing this discrepancy, it was observed that in the first part she was merely required to calculate problems already arranged for her, but in the second half of the test she was to match words, such as *set* and *numeral*, with the definitions. This she could not do. Her problem was not a true dyscalculia (an inability to learn arithmetic because of a neurogenic deficiency), but one of verbal comprehension affecting arithmetic. It seems that number symbols are more stable than words, not varying in meaning to the same extent.

Case Illustration

A case summary of a seven-year-old girl with severe auditory receptive disabilities was written by the school social worker. Note the description of behavior in school, particularly failure to respond to her name and to verbal instructions. Like many children with psychoneurological learning disabilities, she also had minor motor disturbances, reflected in her inability to button clothes and in her gait. The test results demonstrate the discrepancy between visual and auditory functioning. Though she was average in most nonverbal functions, she did not achieve above a three-year level on auditory verbal tasks.

> I have observed Mary in the classroom, in the halls, and on the playground for 22 days only, but already I feel that this child needs special help of some kind. Her difficulties are not those of self-control so far as the classroom discipline is concerned. She is a very good little girl, and she tries to be very cooperative when helped. I believe that she has very good average intelligence.
>
> Her difficulties, though, are numerous. She has many speech difficulties, and has problems expressing what she wants to say. Her bodily coordination often is poor. She walks in an odd way, and bumps into people and things. However, this is not always true, for then, again she will move about just as an average first grade child does.

She very often has an extremely short attention span. Then, again, she seems interested, and the span is longer.

Most of the time, she seems completely confused about doing anything, even following the simplest directions. With kindly guidance by the teacher in a one to one relationship, she will try to think things through and carry out directions. With such guidance, she can often achieve reasonable results in academic subject matter. Once in a great while she seems to be able to do things all by herself, but this is seldom.

Retention is rather poor. Things that seem to have been learned in the morning or the day before are not remembered in the afternoon or on the next day; or, if remembered, it is only a small portion of the total concept.

Small muscle coordination is not good. First grade manuscript writing is very hard for her to do unless teacher guidance is given at each step. She has difficulty in putting on any clothing; she gets things on inside out. Even large buttons bother her. She seems either unaware of her mistakes, and has to have help or else she turns to me to do everything for her.

She often seems in a complete daze in the classroom. At other times this is not so evident. Often, she does not seem to hear anyone, even saying her name, and remarks have to be repeated many times to gain her attention. At such times, she seems to be in another world, and finds it difficult to come back to ours.

She tires very easily. She also seems extremely unsure of herself, but she responds, and seems so grateful for praise, encouragement, guidance, and affection. She is well-liked by everyone.

Educational Procedures

The primary educational goal for the receptive aphasic child is development of auditory language. Since he is able to hear, every effort should be made to help him understand what he hears. The child who cannot comprehend will remain at a low level of adjustment. Rather than permitting him to compensate only visually, emphasis is given to understanding the spoken word. Remedial procedures are suggested below.

Begin Training Early. There is a tendency to adopt a *wait and see* policy with children who are not talking. Often the advice given to families is, "Wait six months or a year and he probably will start talking in sentences." In rare instances this might occur; however, experience indicates that prognosis for language development is better when proper training is begun early. Children referred between the ages of three and four years make more rapid progress than those not referred until five years or older. Those deprived of early training become more like the deaf since they tend to overcompensate for their disability and are more visually and tactually oriented to their environment. In addition, they develop more emotional problems, perhaps as a result of their inability to communicate. Training should begin as soon as the problem is identified.

The auditory environment should be structured. The child must have an opportunity to hear and acquire words in a meaningful setting. Even though he may not respond when spoken to, it is fundamental that teachers and parents talk to him but not use excessive verbalizations or language above his ability to understand.

Input before Output. In communication systems a message must be received before it can be transmitted. Therefore, training in comprehension precedes work on expression. In most instances spontaneous verbal expression occurs with improved comprehension. Although children can be taught to merely say words, these repetitions are only auditory-motor patterns when meaning is not included. This does not mean that verbal responses are discouraged. Furthermore, using newly learned words strengthens comprehension. The basic premise of input before output is that a child should not be expected to use words until he first understands them.

Meaning Units. Children with auditory receptive deficits have trouble sorting out "what means what." They cannot differentiate sounds (words) and relate them to the proper unit of experience. Hence, the teacher periodically must reduce the amount of language she uses and explain the new word to be introduced. Instead of saying, "Give me the cup" or "Mark the ball," isolate the key word *cup* and other words to be taught. Reducing the carrier phrase, i.e., the length of the statement, often aids comprehension. A five-year-old, on a reading readiness test, could not perform on the word meaning subtests when instructions were given normally, "Mark the ____." However, when the isolated words *bottle* or *carrot* were said, he understood and answered correctly.

In many instances comprehension is established only when the meaning units are structured, isolated, and timed with the presentation of the symbol. As soon as a word is understood in isolation, it is reintroduced into context or short sentences. Language is not composed of single words or sentence fragments, and we do not mean to imply that all words should be taught in isolation. Nevertheless, the child who has receptive aphasia is unable to associate meaning with words as they normally are spoken in sentences. Thus, the task of the teacher is to help him differentiate meaning units and to associate these with the appropriate verbal symbols.

Simultaneity. The principle of simultaneity is critical. The spoken word and the experience must be carefully timed to make the exact association. The normal child can perform these sorting and abstracting processes with ease, but in remediation of learning disabilities the teacher must help in differentiating the words and in relating them to the appropriate referents.

Repetition. Repetition is required for all learning but more so for children with language disorders. Many have serious memory problems in addition to deficits in comprehension, so in order for them to learn and retain, the words and concepts must be gone over again and again. Only then do they become meaningful to them.

Selection of Vocabulary. *Experience.* Words are meaningful when the individual has the experience with which they are to be associated. A multitide of sensory impressions must be received and integrated before comprehension can occur. The vocabulary for language training is selected on this basis, according to the individual's experiences. An arbitrary list of words is totally unsuitable. Moreover, words common in one part of the country may be inadequate for children in another geographic area. Also, each child's daily routine varies, making it essential to individualize the vocabularly in accordance with his needs.

Whole Words. Only meaningful words and sentences are taught. Work is not done on isolated sounds or nonsense syllables since these elements do not constitute language. Teaching begins with concrete words which represent common experiences. Generally these are nouns, verbs, and a few simple adjectives (hot, cold) or adverbs (up, down) easily associated with daily happenings.

Auditory Configurations. Words that sound different should be taught during the initial stages of remedial training. The use of similar sounding words requires a high degree of auditory discrimination that some children with receptive deficiencies do not have. For example, even though *cap, cup,* and *cat* are familiar objects, these words should not be taught at the same time. One aphasic girl still finds it difficult to distinguish between the words *cup, key,* and *cap,* but when these are contrasted with *pencil* or *mitten,* she can do so successfully.

Concepts. Words are not simple auditory-motor associations. When a child learns the word *cup,* he must know that this auditory unit refers to more than a single object, that it represents objects of varying sizes and is used for containing milk, coffee, tea, or other liquids. Later he must learn that another object from which he drinks milk is not a cup but a *glass.* Still later he must learn that the word *glass* or *glasses* represents an object worn over the eyes or that it is a material used for making bottles, jars, and windowpanes. Meanings of words change radically, even from a noun to a verb, as in the words *fly* and *point;* in these instances the idea to be conveyed is derived from context and from repeated experiences. The task of the teacher is to help the child understand auditory symbols as they occur in various contexts and then to use them appropriately. (Other suggestions are given below.)

The richness of the meaning of words comes only with numerous and varied experiences. According to Vygotsky (1962), *words are saturated with sense.* The word *apple,* for instance, is the name of a specific object but it may evoke innumerable memories of trips to apple orchards in the fall, bobbing for apples at parties, the smell of freshly baked apple pie, or the drudgery of picking and peeling bushels of apples. In good language training, the teacher does not stop with the teaching of a simple association; instead, she extends the child's experiences and enriches word meanings for him.

Parts of Speech. In the language remediation program there should be regard for the various parts of speech. As indicated previously, words are not always taught in isolation. However, the teacher should be keenly aware of the nature of the experiences to be provided in order to make a symbol meaningful. Word meanings cannot be taught in drill sessions. Experiences must be arranged to promote an understanding of both words and sentences. Each verbal unit must be carefully analyzed so that the situations can be structured in such a way that the words become meaningful.

Children first master concrete verbalizations, words or sentences directly related to their experiences: simple nouns, e.g., *milk* and *spoon*, are taught first. These are followed by simple verbs, prepositions, adjectives, adverbs, and pronouns. This does not mean that the adverb *more* is not understood by the young child, or that he comprehends all nouns before all other words. It suggests only that some parts of speech are more difficult because the experiences they represent are more abstract.

The following discussion regarding the parts of speech discloses the complexity of the problem; illustrative procedures are given for each.

Nouns. The primary objective in teaching simple, concrete nouns is to establish the principle of *naming*. The teacher helps the aphasic learn that the word *shoe* represents the name of the object. The principles outlined in the preceding section and those given below are useful.

(1) Select two or three familiar objects, for instance, a *shoe* and a *mitten*, and place them before the child. Hold one of the objects and say its name three or four times, making certain that he is both listening to the word and attending to the object. Reduce all carrier phrases; do not present entire sentences, such as "See the pretty mitten" or "This is a shoe." Merely say the single word *shoe* a number of times. Follow this with the second object, repeating its name several times. Then place both objects in front of the child, saying one of the words—he is to point to the right object. If he cannot correctly identify the object named, repeat the procedure and occasionally use negative practice. If he picked up the shoe when the word *mitten* was said, hold up the shoe and in a questioning way say, "mitten? . . . no . . . shoe . . . shoe," emphasizing the correct word. With gestures and facial animation, indicate that the auditory word *shoe* does not represent the mitten but only the shoe. Encourage him to say the

word only after he understands it. However, after he comprehends, arrange experiences so he will have to use the word. Also use the word in context so that he hears it in relation to other words.

(2) Remember to teach words as concepts, not just as labels, since most verbal symbols represent more than a single object. *Shoe*, for example stands for the child's shoe as well as mother's high-heeled shoe or father's tennis shoe. Training should include work in both general and specific meanings, for while some words represent many things, others, such as names of persons, denote a single individual. Although a child needs a broad concept of the word *Mommy*, he uses it specifically to refer to his own mother.

(3) Begin work with real objects, progressing to toys and then to pictures. Some children with learning disabilities do not understand that an object can be represented in pictorial form. Unless they realize that the picture of a shoe represents the real object, the word meaning will not be fully established. If problems are evidenced in this area, it may be necessary to match objects to miniature objects or toys, and then to pictures (see Chapter VIII).

(4) It is assumed that parts of the body are among the first words children learn. Very early in life they are asked, "Show me your nose" and "Where is your eye?" Even though lessons on body image are included early in language programs, these are not necessarily the first words to be taught. Children with learning disabilities may have disturbances of body image and hence be confused when words representing body parts are introduced.

When names of body parts are taught, use dolls and simple pictures since occasionally children can identify an arm on a doll or a picture when they cannot do so on themselves. Problems of body image in adult aphasics have been discussed by Critchley (1953) and in children by Kastein (1964), Kephart (1960), and others. Each individual must be studied to determine whether more success is attained by relating the word to the child's own body or to other types of figures.

(5) As the child progresses it is necessary to teach the more abstract nouns and words less easily pictured. Nouns denoting categories can be taught by having him sort groups of pictures and then supplying the word for him. Give him pictures of toys and foods, such as those in Illustration 5. Ask him to cut out the pictures and place all of the things we eat on one page and those we play with on another. After he finishes, follow with the statement, "We eat these, they are *foods*," emphasizing the name of the category.

More advanced exercises can be designed to foster understanding of higher level concepts, e.g., *furniture, appliances, occupations.* Often the

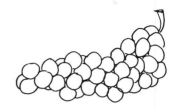

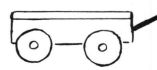

ILLUSTRATION 5. An exercise for teaching abstract nouns.

child can give a functional definition of an object but not of the symbols representing categories. For example, some upper elementary school children have trouble naming specific occupations of individuals in their communities. When they see a picture of a dentist, they may say, "He fixes our teeth," being unable to designate him by the word *dentist*.

It is impossible to predict all of the words a child does not understand, particularly if he has begun to acquire language. Therefore, the teacher must be alert to his errors and correct them, listening carefully to his language and noting his problems. One teacher showed a picture in which several cars were stopped on a busy highway because of a stalled auto. The driver was looking under the hood, obviously trying to remedy the situation. The children were asked to tell what was happening. A nine-year-old in the class said, "Oh, oh, there's a traffic." Another in the group said immediately, "You're silly, that's not a traffic, that's a *traffic jam*." The job of the teacher was to indicate as clearly as possible the differences in the meanings of *traffic* and *traffic jam*. By discussing experiences and pictures, she illustrated that in one context the word *traffic* represented a general condition: in another it described a type of condition. In addition, the auditory unit *jam* had to be differentiated from the same unit when used to represent a sweet substance we put on bread.

It is the responsibility of the teacher to observe the child in his various classes and to discuss his problems with the other teachers. She should note whether he knows the names of the utensils or equipment used in art classes, in physical education, and in the regular classroom. She must know that when he is given directions he cannot grasp, she must adapt her teaching to his needs so that he is helped to function more adequately in the group. The text books for each of his courses should be examined to note the nature of the vocabularies and the concepts which he might not understand.

Verbs. The basic goal in teaching verbs is for the child to learn that the word now represents an action, not the name of an object. If the word *eat* is used in association with an apple, he must understand that it denotes an action and not the object. When the word *walking* is introduced, he must know that it is not the name of a person but that it represents something the person is doing. Comprehension of verbs is often difficult for aphasic children. They tend to grasp the naming principle quickly but prefer to label objects rather than ascribe qualities or denote action. The teacher must assist these children to internalize actions and associate them with the proper words. Useful procedures include:

(1) Engage the child in simple activities, e.g., walking or running. Simultaneously say the single word *walk* or *run* several times. Reduction of language and simultaneity again are very important. After two or three

presentations, ask the child to run or to walk. These procedures are repeated until he comprehends the words. In some instances it is necessary to physically lift the child or, in the most realistic way possible, to have him experience a given sensation. In the case of a five-year-old who did not understand the word *jump,* the teacher lifted him a few times and simultaneously said the word. After several repetitions, he followed correctly when given commands involving this word.

(2) Although direct experiences are most valuable, pictures can be used to teach verbs. Negative practice occasionally is instructive. The pictures in Illustration 6 show two animals and a man running and then standing still. The child must understand that the word *run* refers to a particular type of movement, that the man or animals are not named *running* but that this word represents the action in which they are engaged.

(3) Verbs not easily pantomimed or pictured are difficult to teach. Thus the meaning of words such as *grow* must be mastered over a period of time and through actual experiences. Rarely is it possible to see something grow within a short period of time but children periodically can observe plants or keep height charts of themselves to gain the meaning of this word. After the concept is established, they might be given exercises of the type in Illustration 7 and asked to circle the things that grow.

(4) Receptive language ability is related to understanding correct usage of verb tense. There is a tendency to think of the development of syntax primarily in terms of expressive language, but it also comprises a high degree of receptive and integrative ability. The child must be aware that he uses one verb form when he talks about things in the past and another when he talks about things to happen in the future. Even though he is not conscious of formal rules of grammar, he must associate certain experiences with a given linguistic form. The teacher should help the aphasic make these associations. The person who speaks only in the present tense—"Go to the movies," "Have dinner out"—does not tell us whether he has already gone or whether he will go in the near future.

Until the aphasic internalizes the experience with the correct linguistic form, he cannot use proper syntax. This awareness can be taught by using concrete experiences or pictures, and associating them with an appropriate sentence. For example, select pictures which illustrate activities that have been completed, are in process, and that will occur. Place two or three pictures in front of the child, say a sentence and ask him to point to the one that corresponds with what was said.

Picture presented	Teacher says
A cat eating	The cat is eating his dinner
A cat by an empty bowl	The cat ate his dinner
A family riding in a car	They are riding in the car
A family walking toward a car	They will go for a ride in the car

Running   Not Running

ILLUSTRATION 6. Exercise for teaching the word *run*.

ILLUSTRATION 7. An exercise for teaching the concept *growth*.

Before a child can use proper syntax, he must understand the correct and incorrect forms. The *syntactical aphasic* may know that he omits or substitutes words but he does not know which words to select or how to put them in order. Those with receptive disabilities, however, need help only at the level of comprehension. Direct experiences in the classroom should be applied whenever possible. Before starting an exercise or assignment, in anticipation of the next activity the teacher shows the material and uses a simple sentence, such as, "We are going to paint," or "We will paint." She repeats the sentence two or three times and gives the impression of an event which will occur. Then while the children are painting she may repeat other appropriate sentences: "The children are painting," or "Johnny is painting." Often it is helpful to have the children say the sentences while they are engaged in the activity. Such verbalizations must not merely be repetitions, but should be coordinated with the experience. Generally, presentations of this type aid both comprehension and expression.

Adjectives. Adjectives represent qualities; they stand for concepts. The child must understand that the words *pretty, old, hot,* and *tiny* stand for qualities. They are not names of objects nor do they denote actions, and they can be used to describe more than one object or experience. The words *hot* and *big* are not the names of things but tell something about an object or experience. An adjective cannot be taught in isolation. Watson and Nolte (1956, p. 33) explain that "Beautiful is an adjective, but in isolation it doesn't make sense because it has no noun or pronoun. The sentence must name a beautiful something."

In order to fully comprehend the adjective, frequently it is necessary to work simultaneously on verbal and nonverbal aspects. Training begins with the meanings of adjectives directly related to sensory experience since concrete words are more readily understood. The teacher arranges *sets* of experiences because adjectives are learned more easily when comparison is made between two or more objects. Adjectives usually represent relative qualities, such as size, space, or feelings, and can only be meaningful in relation to other experiences. A child comprehends the word *big* when it is compared with something not big, and the word *cold* when it is compared with something less cold. Selected procedures are given below.

(1) Take the child to a sink and permit him to turn on both the cold and the hot water. Make certain he knows the noun *water*. Place his hand under the stream of hot water and simultaneously say the words *hot water*; do the same with the cold water. The point of this technique is not to improve his tactual discrimination nor to feel the difference in the temperature, but rather to relate the words *hot* and *cold* with the proper experiences. Then permit him to touch other things that are hot and cold

(a radiator, a cool windowpane). The purpose is to teach him that the same auditory unit *hot* may be applied to various objects, not only to water. Furthermore, the presentation should provide him with a word to represent previously acquired experiences.

(2) Select pictures like those in Illustration 8 to represent *big* and *little*. Note that the same object is used in each set of pictures so only the contrast in size is presented. Do not draw a big boy and a little girl, or a small maple tree and a little evergreen, but control all variables except size. From these the child learns that the word represents a particular quality. When work is done with comparative adjectives, such as *long, longer, longest*, draw identical objects varying only in size. As he improves, other variables can be introduced, the concepts are broadened, but in the initial stages of training it is essential to control all factors except the specific one being emphasized.

(3) Teach the adjectives related to auditory experience. Select two bells, one producing a loud sound and one a soft sound. Permit the child to ring them and give him the words to describe each sound. As he progresses, teach the words *tinkling, clanging, gonging*, and other adjectives descriptive of sound.

(4) Words relating to smell and taste are taught by bringing foods for the children to sample. An eight-year-old boy, limited in verbal comprehension, was asked to find the foods that tasted sweet. He said, "Me can't do . . . What sweet means?" He had not been deprived of the experience, nor was he unable to differentiate the taste of foods, but he had not related the experience of sweetness with the symbol.

(5) Teach words that denote feelings. Aphasics have only a few words to express anger, surprise, or happiness. Although most of them have experienced these feelings, they have not understood the words used to describe them. Teaching begins with direct experience whenever possible, but it is also helpful to use pictures showing happy and sad faces; see Illustration 9. The teacher first asks the children to tell whether they think the faces look the same. After they see the differences in the configuration of the mouth, etc., she supplies the words *happy boy* or *sad boy*.

Some children fail to comprehend because they are deficient at the level of experience. For them the problems and training procedures are different, as described in Chapter VIII. If they have deficits in visual-spatial ability, they are unable to differentiate size and distance and therefore do not perceive the meaning of words such as *long, short, wide, narrow*; however, they understand adjectives related to auditory experiences. Likewise, those having tactual perceptual disturbances cannot be expected to grasp the meanings of the words *smooth* and *rough*, inasmuch as these experiences would not have been established.

ILLUSTRATION 8. An exercise for teaching the concepts *big* and *little*.

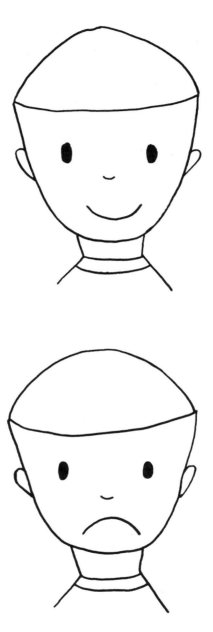

ILLUSTRATION 9. Pictures for teaching *happy* and *sad.*

Often the receptive aphasic child is hyperactive and distractible so he has a limited attention span. He darts quickly from one thing to another without touching, looking, or listening long enough to gain depth of meaning. Every effort should be made to increase his ability to attend. The training should be sufficiently structured so he has ample opportunity for looking and listening. School age children might be given exercises like those shown below to review concepts that have been introduced and to encourage the use of descriptive words.

Exercise for Teaching Descriptive Words

If a pile of dishes fell, what kind of sound would you hear?	crashing squeaking scraping shuffling whistling
If you felt some fine velvet cloth, it would feel	rough soft sticky scratchy hard
If you heard two children whistling, you might think they were	angry happy sad sick tired
If you touched the seat of a car which had been standing in the sun for a long time, it would feel	damp cold hot moist wet
If you heard that something was made of gold, you would think it was	red, white, and blue yellow and shiny black and rough green and white soft and white
If you saw a person frown, you would think he was	happy cross satisfied hungry sorry

Prepositions. Mastering prepositions, especially when used in a command, is one of the most difficult learning problems we have observed. Many children fail assignments, not because they are unable to do the work, but because they cannot follow when directions include prepositions.

Occasionally, a child may fail because of an inability to recognize the nouns and verbs used in the command. A child cannot be expected to put the ball *in* the box unless he knows the words *ball* and *box*. A disturbance in body image can interfere with his performance. If he does not know the names of body parts, he cannot follow commands, such as, "Put your hands *under* the table," or "Put your hands *behind* you." Moreover, an auditory memory problem can prevent him from retaining a series of words, thus making it impossible for him to follow the directions.

Prepositions often denote location; therefore, to comprehend the words *on*, *in*, and *under*, the child must have ability to deal with the concepts of space and time. The following procedures are suggested:

(1) Ask the child to alternately place his hands on the table and under the table; simultaneously repeat the phrases *on the table* and *under the table* until he comprehends. Then give him specific commands: "Put your hands on the table," or "Put the ball under the table."

(2) Use similar procedures to teach the words *in* and *on*. Give the child a ball and ask him to put it in the box or on the box. Then follow with a series of commands or with pictures. First give him the pictures of empty boxes and ask him to draw a ball *in* the box, *under* the box, etc. When he understands these words, have him tell where each ball is.

(3) While learning the meanings of the words *on*, *under*, and *behind*, the emphasis is on the *concept* of location. The child must know that these words refer to a position in relation to another object. Pictures such as those in Illustration 10 can be used in teaching this concept. Note that the objects, chair and ball, remain constant and only the position of the ball is altered. The purpose is to help the child concentrate on the one factor that will help him comprehend the word.

(4) As he progresses, he must learn that these words are used in many settings, as shown by the pictures in Illustration 11. In this exercise both the objects and the locations are varied to assist him in generalizing the concepts.

(5) Prepare pages of pictures for the exercises listed below. The first set is highly structured so it is not necessary for the child to think about many facets of the instructions; he concentrates on a change of the preposition only. Later, he is required to listen and attend to more complex commands, including changes in the various parts of speech.

a. Give the child a picture of a house and say:

Draw a line under the house.
Draw a line over the house.
Draw a line around the house.

(Change only the preposition; hold verb and object of the preposition constant.)

on

under

in front

behind

ILLUSTRATION 10. Pictures for teaching prepositions.

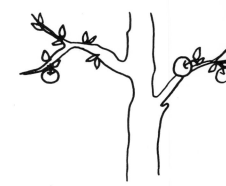

on

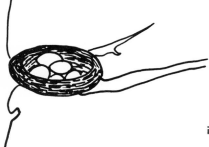

in

under

ILLUSTRATION 11. Exercise for teaching the prepositions *on, in* and *under.*

Draw a line under the dress.
Draw an egg in the nest.
Make an X above the plane.
Draw a circle around the fish.
Draw a line from the fish to the nest.

ILLUSTRATION 12. Exercise for reviewing prepositions with school-age children.

b. Give the child a series of pictures
and say:
Draw a line under the barn.
Draw a line under the cat.
Draw a line under the house.

(Change only the object of the preposition; hold verb and preposition constant.)

c. Give the child a series of pictures
and say:
Draw a line under the barn.
Draw a line over the cat.
Draw a line around the house.

(Change the object of the preposition and preposition; keep verb constant.)

d. Give the child a series of pictures
and say:
Draw a line around the house.
Put an X on the barn.
Make an X under the cat.

(Change all variables.)

Similar exercises can be prepared for school-age children who are able to read but who need practice in following instructions. See Illustration 12: pictures are drawn at the top of the page and instructions are written below.

General Significance

It should not be inferred that language is composed of single words and short phrases, or that training is limited in emphasis. We are concerned with a child's total understanding, with his ability to grasp general significance, with his reaction to ideas, with his capacity to evaluate and make judgments about the language he hears. Thus, even though deficits must be isolated, as a foundation the approach is one of language development broadly conceived. It includes consideration of the dimensions outlined previously: the development of receptive before expressive language, the development of auditory before visual, progression from concrete to abstract language, and finally, development from simple to more complex verbalizations.

Increasing the complexity of language places many demands on integrative capacity. When a story is read, the child must be able to listen for longer periods of time, to store more information, to know individual words, and to grasp general meanings by relating ideas. The teacher works gradually but steadily toward this type of comprehension. In doing so, many exercises are designed; see Illustration 13. The child is given a series of pictures, listens to the teacher read the sentences, and follows the instructions. He cannot listen only to one or two words, but must continuously relate and associate ideas.

ILLUSTRATION 13. Pictures for teaching sentence meaning and comprehension of stories.

Both the length and complexity of the story are modified according to individual needs:

When Daddy comes home from work, he puts the car in the garage.
Mark the place where Daddy puts the car.

Last week was my baby brother's birthday. He was one-year-old. Mother baked a cake for him and we all sang "Happy Birthday."
Mark what Mother baked.

In school we do many things. Sometimes we read books, sometimes we paint, and sometimes we make things with clay.
Show me one of the things we use in school.

My mother knits pretty sweaters for my sister and me. She buys yarn at the store and sometimes we help her roll it into a ball. At night when she sits in her rocking chair and knits, our cat, Snowball, gets the ball of yarn and plays with it. The yarn gets all tangled and we have to roll it into a ball again.
Mark what Mother uses for knitting.

In geography we have been learning about Eskimos. They live in the north where it is very cold and where it is sometimes hard to find food. In the winter they go ice fishing. They make small holes in the ice, drop the line into the hole, and wait for the fish to nibble the bait.
Mark what the Eskimos eat during the winter time.

Training should be provided so the child learns to react to ideas and to judge the validity of what he hears. True-false questions and verbal absurdities are beneficial. The child cannot accept everything he hears verbatim, but should become aware of the necessity for evaluation. An eight-year-old, prone to listening to individual words without grasping general meanings, was given the sentence, "It was raining so I took my boots off when I went outside." When asked whether he thought it was a good idea, his comment was, "Well, it's a complete thought." Although he could understand and remember details, he could not comprehend general meanings. Therefore, he was given exercises such as those below and asked to find words or phrases which did not make sense in the story.

True-False Statements

Dogs have two legs.
Both cars and bicycles have four wheels.
Most balls are square.

Find the Absurdity

Mother mixed the flour, eggs, sugar, butter, and other things to make cookies. Then she put them in the refrigerator to bake.

Last Sunday we went for a ride in the country. We drove past many farms and saw all of the animals. On the way home we got a flat tire and Daddy had to fix it. He was happy because there was not a spare tire in the trunk and he had to walk to a nearby house and call a service station.

Throughout the training the teacher should lead the child's thinking so that whenever possible he sees the relationships for himself. All statements should be worded in a manner that permits him to gain new insights. This can be done only by reducing the level of complexity to the point where he can understand the meaning, then gradually raising the level. Active learning is superior to passive and the excitement of individual discovery stimulates motivation for further learning. An example of this principle is given in the transcription below.

Our ultimate goal in receptive language training is that the child comprehends so he can participate in his school and home environment. We hope to provide him with a foundation on which other forms of symbolic behavior can be superimposed, enabling him to express himself effectively and become a dynamic participant in society.

Procedures for Teaching the Concept of "Fly"

The following is an example of how a teacher helped a child understand a new concept and respond appropriately to a question:

Teacher: (Showing the series of pictures in Illustration 14) Billy, tell me which ones have wings.

Child: Wings . . . no wings . . . no, no wings. (He obviously did not understand the word)

Teacher: Do you have wings?

Child: (Still not comprehending, he becomes quite frustrated) No . . . no wings.

Teacher: (Attempting to see whether the child understands the concept of flying) Which ones can fly?

Child: No fly, no, no, no.
(It is apparent that the child did not need help in saying the words *fly* or *wings*, but he did need to associate experience with the words. He also needed to see relationships and to have guidance in forming concepts. The next lesson was devoted to the comprehension of the word *wings* and to the concept of *flying*. Note the pictures and the progressions which were used (Illustrations 14 and 15). First the teacher went back to the level of picture identification to make certain that the child recognized each of the pictures. He responded correctly to all simple commands, such as "Show me the bird". The teacher then began to increase the level of language.)

Teacher: (Takes either a toy bird or a picture of a bird and lifts it up in the air) Look, Billy, the bird goes up, up, up. (Note she does not yet use the word *fly*.)

Child: Yah, bird up high. (Takes the picture and does the same)

Teacher: (Takes the picture of the airplane and does the same) Does the airplane go up?

Child: (Nodding) Up, up, airplane big . . . up.

Teacher: (Takes the picture of the chair) Does the chair go up? (Absurdities sometimes help to establish meanings)

Child: (Laughing) No, no, no, chair not go up.

Teacher: (Takes the picture of the house) Can the house go up?

Child: No, house down.

Teacher: (Takes a picture of a bird which is flying) See, Billy, the bird has *wings*. (Points to the wings and says the word again) Wings. Do you have wings? (Then the teacher answers the question herself) *No*, Billy has arms, not wings. You have arms, but see, the bird has no arms. (Points to the picture again)

Child: (Shows understanding) Bird, no arms.

Teacher: (Takes the picture of the bird again) The bird has wings.

Child: (Child now responds with the phrase) Bird has wings.

Teacher: (Uses picture absurdities again—a bird with no wings and a boy with wings) See, this bird has no *wings*, he cannot *fly*. (The child laughed at these pictures because he knew they were incorrect. The teacher then takes the picture of the chair) Does the chair have *wings*? No, the chair has no *wings* . . . it cannot go up . . . it cannot *fly*. The bird has *wings* . . . it can *fly*, it can go up . . . see the bird *fly*. (Use the out-of-doors and real experience whenever possible. Takes the picture of the dog) Can the dog fly?

Child: No, dog cannot fly.

Teacher: (Teacher takes a few single pictures of animals and inanimate objects and continues to ask the child whether these objects have wings or whether they can fly. The child seemed to comprehend the words and concepts so she went back to the original question, using a series of pictures.) Billy, which ones can fly?

Child: (The child now responds to the questions in this form) Bird can fly . . . plane can fly.

(The child now shows some grasp of the words and of the concepts. It is true that he does not recognize their subtleties. Later he should realize that some creatures that have wings do not go up in the air, and that the word *fly* is also the name of a particular insect. New meanings are added with additional experience and training.)

ILLUSTRATION 14. Pictures for teaching the concept _fly_.

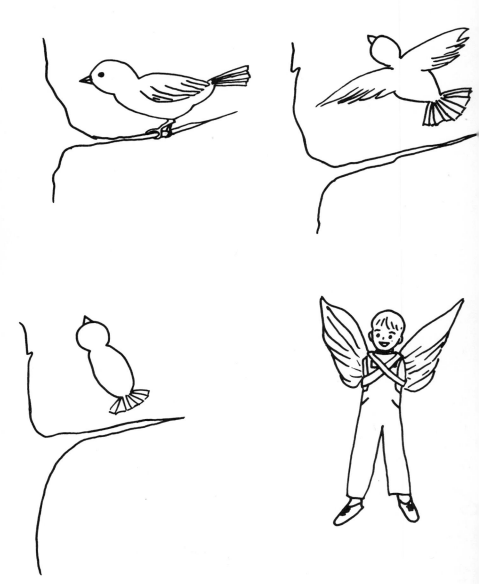

ILLUSTRATION 15. Pictures for teaching the concept *fly*.

Auditory Memory Span and Comprehension

Auditory memory span refers to the amount of information an individual can retain in proper sequence, particularly for purposes of immediate action or recall. Many children with neurogenic learning disorders are limited in the amount of information they can remember; consequently they have difficulty taking a series of commands or in comprehending complex verbal instructions. These problems should be differentiated from those in which comprehension of words is affected since remedial procedures vary with the nature of the deficit.

The receptive aphasic fails to execute commands because he does not comprehend, whereas the child with a limited memory span follows single commands but cannot retain a series. The latter child is constantly being reprimanded and thought to be naughty or stupid; in school he fails his assignments, not because of an inability to do the work but because he cannot remember the sequence of instructions. This means that much effort is required for the older students to take class notes since they cannot remember what they hear while writing. Unless alleviated or remedied, many vocational problems result; they are unable to take instructions from employers and are thought to be inattentive or incompetent. The following procedures are recommended for the improvement of memory span.

Meaningful Material. Various studies indicate that rote learning of nonsense material is more difficult to remember than that which is meaningful. Therefore, no work is done with nonsense materials and rote drills. Emphasis is placed on meaningful associations, organization, and retention in a practical manner so as to be useful in everyday activities.

Attention. Although problems of attention and memory should be differentiated, they frequently occur together. Therefore, the teacher must be certain that a child is listening and attending before presenting him with a task. He must be "ready." Some cannot prepare themselves or voluntarily establish a mental set. Words such as *wait, listen,* or *ready* are used before giving an assignment. In addition, wait a few seconds after saying the attention-getting word since a brief moment of quiet before the presentation facilitates listening and recall. The attention-getting device need not be auditory; a visual cue, e.g., a flashlight or tactile stimulation (a tap on the shoulder), may be more helpful to some children.

Organizational Skills. With maturity most persons develop organizational skills for performing routine activities, in studying or in working. Rather than attempt to recall random lists or bits of information, efforts are directed toward organization and systematic planning. The housewife who when going to market thinks, "I must get two things from the dairy counter and four things from the frozen foods section," has used organizational skills to aid recall. Similar skills must be developed in children with memory span disorders if they are to achieve. They should be taught to organize, to revisualize or reauditorize a task before starting it. If a child cannot remember a series of instructions, the teacher might utilize visual cues (diagrams or maps) to remind the child where he is to go and what he is to do beforehand, or he might be shown the first letters of the names of the objects he is to remember. Others, who benefit from reauditorization, are encouraged to say a word list or repeat the instructions before they begin the task.

Examples of Techniques:

(1) Nonverbal memory span training is done with those who have severe disabilities. The suggestions in the section on memory for generalized auditory disorders are beneficial.

(2) Words in series: Select pictures or a series of objects that are used together and place them before the child (stove, sink, refrigerator; pencil, pen, paper; hat, coat, gloves). Say the words for him and ask him to repeat the names while simultaneously looking at the pictures. Then remove the pictures and ask him to say the series.

Play situations of a practical nature are arranged for children of various ages. Preschoolers enjoy playing store, giving and taking orders. One child in the group buys three or four items on the shelf and the "storekeeper" must remember and select those ordered. Older children enjoy playing restaurant and giving each other orders. Each one is encouraged to use clues which stimulate recall. Some write the first letter of each word; others only need to indicate the number of things they are to remember. Still others repeat each word several times in order to memorize it.

Exercises are prepared for tape recorders which can be used for independent work. Sheets of pictures are given each child and he listens to directions, such as, "Listen, I will say the names of some things on your paper. You are to listen and mark the ones I say. Ready? Mark the apple, the orange, and the grapes . . . . Next. Ready? Mark the table, the chair, and the lamp." After he has completed the exercise, he can listen to the tape a second time and evaluate his responses or correct his errors.

(3) A series of instructions are more difficult to remember than a series of words because the physical act of executing the command often interferes with recall. Nevertheless, practice should be given. It is wise to begin with a series of instructions using pencil and paper tasks rather than

those involving excessive movements. For example, give the child a sheet of paper with pictures and ask him to:

Draw a line around the house and a circle around the dog.
Put a green mark under the cow and a red mark over the cat.

In all instances it is critical to make certain that the child understands individual words and phrases before giving him a series of instructions.

Use a series of instructions necessitating moderate physical movements:

Touch your nose and clap your hands.
Put your hand on your head and cross your legs.

Gradually work toward a more complex series of commands, such as those normally given by parents at home or by teachers in school:

Go to the cupboard and get a ball and the blocks.
Put the ball on the table and the blocks in the box.
Get three scissors; put one on the white table and two on the green table.
Open the top drawer and get two red pencils and one blue pencil.

(4) Auditory memory span with a verbal response: In each of the preceding exercises the responses were of a nonverbal nature; the child was asked to perform, not to speak or write. The following techniques can be used with children who have the ability to speak but who are limited in auditory memory span.

a. Sentence repetition: Give the child sentences to repeat, beginning with two or three words and gradually adding more. To facilitate recall, keep the ideas related, as shown below:

I see.
I see a dog.
I see a dog and a cat.
I see a black dog and a cat.
I see a black dog and a white cat.
I see a black dog and a white cat fighting.
I see a black dog and a white cat fighting in the street.

b. Read sentences as those listed below and ask questions about each.

I went to the store and bought lettuce, bread and milk.
Question: What did I buy?
        Where did I go?

Mr. and Mrs. Jones live at 318 Elm Street.
Question: Where do Mr. and Mrs. Jones live?
        Who lives at 318 Elm Street?

Flight Number 415 leaves Tuesday at 3:45 P.M.
Question: Which flight leaves Tuesday at 3:45 P.M.?
        When does flight Number 415 leave?

DISORDERS OF AUDITORY EXPRESSIVE LANGUAGE

Many children with language disorders have no problem in understanding the spoken word but are deficient in using it to express themselves. They perform well in nonverbal activities and on verbal tasks not demanding an oral response. They demonstrate good ability on measures of picture identification and reading readiness tests which require only pointing or marking, but if asked to name the pictures or to describe an event, they cannot do so. In school they follow instructions and perform successfully except when asked to speak.

Within this group there are various types of problems and each should be delineated before initiating a remedial program. Although all of the disorders described below are sometimes considered to be forms of the broad category, *expressive aphasia*, it is essential to differentiate among the types of disabilities. Many combinations of deficits occur but three are more prevalent than others. Each is discussed with regard to the nature of the disability and the educational procedures found to be beneficial.

(1) The first group has a deficit primarily in *reauditorization* and word selection. These children understand and recognize words but they cannot remember (or retrieve) them for spontaneous usage.

(2) The second group has difficulty learning to say words; they comprehend and reauditorize but cannot execute the motor patterns necessary for speaking. There is no paralysis but they cannot voluntarily initiate the movements of the tongue and lips because of an *apraxia*.

(3) The third group has *defective syntax*. They are able to use single words and short phrases but are unable to plan and organize words for the expression of ideas in complete sentences. They omit or distort the order of words, use incorrect verb tenses, and make other grammatical, syntactical errors long after such skills have been acquired by normal children.

Reauditorization

The inability to recall words has been observed in both children and adults who have language disorders. This problem has been called a word-finding difficulty or *anomia*. Although some authorities limit the disorder to an inability in the recall of nouns, usually the problem is more generalized and affects the recall of other parts of speech. Eisenson (1957) refers to this disorder as an amnestic type of aphasia. The person's primary difficulty is in the evocation of certain types of words (names, qualities, relationships). In some instances it appears that the words of greatest consequence to meaning are the hardest to remember. For example they can recall ejaculations (*okay* or *all right*) but cannot remember the words essential for transmitting an idea.

We recorded the spoken language of a young woman who told the entire story of a traffic accident which she had witnessed. She could understand words but could not spontaneously recall them.

> Well, there was this big . . . (demonstrated a crash by doubling her fists and hitting them together; she also covered her ears to indicate noise). O, my gosh, it was awful . . . just awful. You know . . . running, running . . . stop . . . look . . . oh, isn't this terrible? (Here she suggested that everyone came out of their houses to see what had happened and commented on the accident.) Then at last, two . . . (held up two fingers and then demonstrated the word *cars* by pantomiming the act of driving) Ooh . . . ooh (indicating sirens) . . . one white . . . one blue (ambulance and police car) . . . took out one big . . . one little (showed that one was a tall person and one a child) . . . go away fast, oh, it was just terrible . . . it was just awful.

Observations of individuals with reauditorization disorders confirm the hypothesis of Russell (1961) who suggests that recognition of the familiar and remembering appear as two separate processes, yet the latter might well be an elaboration of the first mechanism. Learning disabilities can occur either at the level of recognition or at the level of recall. A child who fails to recognize words visually cannot read. On the other hand, he might be able to recognize but not revisualize them, in which case he can read but not write. Similarly, a child might comprehend a word when it is spoken but not be able to recall it. Children with reauditorization deficits experience great frustration in communicating. They try to relate happenings but give up in desperation because they cannot remember how to say what they have in mind. In school they raise their hands to respond but by the time the teacher calls on them, they have forgotten what they intended to say.

Below is a transcription of a nine-year-old boy. He tried to tell us how to make a model but could not remember the names of the materials. It took him approximately thirty seconds to recall the word *plastic*. Note his use of nonspecific words, such as *junk*, *stuff*, *what-cha-ma-call-it*, which he usually substituted for nouns. If the materials had been present, he could have easily constructed the model. However, he could not recall the verbal symbols for giving an explanation of the process, so he concluded by saying, "I can't explain it . . . I can't remember."

> John, tell me something you like to make or do.
> Uh, w . . . well . . . well . . . models.
> What sort of models do you make?
> Oh, airplanes and ships.
> How do you make them? Tell me about it.
> Well, out of . . . um . . . out of . . . oh . . . what-you-ma-call-em . . . out of . . . what-you-ma-call-ems . . . I can't uh . . . let's see . . . out of . . . plastic.

Good! What do you do? How do you do it?
>W . . . W . . . well, I paste . . . I paste junk and stuff like that on it . . . the wings . . . and stuff like that.

And what else do you do?
>W . . . w . . . w . . . well, I . . . um . . . oh . . . hm . . . can't explain it; uh . . . uh . . . uh . . . out of wood, and I have all sorts of nails and stuff like that I use.

How do you do it?
>W . . . w . . . well, I uh . . . oh, I sort of do it like . . . um . . . oh, I forget (laughs) . . . um . . . (long pause—perhaps 20 seconds). Let me see . . . hm, I can't remember.

Preschool children who have limited language due to disturbances in auditorization processes communicate largely by gesture and pantomime or by using simple vocalizations. Generally, they can repeat the words after the teacher says them. This ability distinguishes them from apraxic children who cannot utter words even in imitation. Those with auditorization deficits can say the words after they are said for them. Those with expressive aphasia cannot; they must be taught to produce speech sounds. The child with reauditorization deficits must be assisted in learning how to retrieve the words he wants to use. In contrast, the apraxic child remembers what he wants to say but cannot relate the word to the motor system. Sometimes those with auditory memory problems must be taught words of two or three syllables because they cannot remember the sequence of the sounds; however, they do not need help on motor patterning for words.

At times these children can recall words only when an object or picture is present. They might try to ask for *milk* but cannot do so until they see the glass or perhaps until it is placed in their hands. The visual-tactual experience facilitates auditory recall. Older children often develop highly skilled ways of compensating for such deficits in memory. A teen-age girl with severe dysnomia said that whenever she went into a restaurant she always ordered something in sight and commented, "One of those, please," or she pointed to an item on the menu and said, "I think I'll try this." In a clothing store she either waited on herself or pointed to something in order to avoid asking for it by name.

An analysis of the ways in which the individual tries to convey his ideas is helpful in teaching. If we observe that a person can say it if he sees it, visualization techniques might be used to teach him to reauditorize. The following are typical of the adaptations made by children and adults who are unable to remember words.

Nonverbal Sounds. Young children frequently try to convey an idea by using sound effects or nonverbal sounds. It may be a barking sound for the word *dog* or the sound of a horn if they cannot remember *car*. A five-year-old boy trying to tell about helping his father cut the grass could not remember the words so he used the sounds of the mower, the clippers, the water sprinkler, and other objects. This same child often hummed a song to represent an object he could not name. Even though he was able to repeat the word *boat* immediately after the teacher, he could not say it spontaneously when he saw one; therefore, he hummed the song "Sailing, Sailing." Similarly, when he could not recall the word *cake*, he hummed "Happy Birthday."

Gesture or Pantomime. Some children are unable to produce any sounds so they resort to pantomiming or drawing pictures. A five-year-old tried to tell what the barber used to cut his hair, but rather than using the sound of the clippers, he pantomimed their use. On other occasions he drew pictures to indicate his needs.

Delayed Response. Given sufficient time many children eventually can evoke the word they want, but it may take several seconds. Often they comment, "Don't tell me . . . it's coming . . . I want to try to think of it myself." Others are grateful if the listener provides a cue through a multiple choice, such as "Do you mean ____ or ____?" However, some say that the feeding in of multiple selections actually interferes with recall. In these instances a few seconds of quiet are provided, rather than a series of words from which to select those they have in mind but cannot retrieve.

Circumlocutions or Functional Definitions. Children whose greatest problem is with recall of nouns may describe the object by use or by definition rather than by name. Instead of saying the word *fork*, they might say, "eat" or "it's that long, shiny thing that has points on it and you use it for eating." A nine-year-old girl tried to say, "needle and thread," but could only say, "it's sharp and it has a little hole in one end and you put some kind of string through the hole, but I know it isn't string." When asked if they were *pin* and *yarn*, she knew these words were incorrect but could not say needle and thread until they were said for her. Characteristically, she quickly identified them as correct when she heard them.

Word Associations. When the child is unable to recall a word, he may substitute one from within the same general category or one similar in meaning. He says *cake* instead of *pie*, or *dog* instead of *cat*, even though he knows that the alternative he selected is incorrect. The substitution usually is closely related so the proper meaning is conveyed; however, meaning sometimes is vague or distorted.

The child who says, "I need a *paper holder*," instead of paper clip may communicate a general idea to the listener, but the man who took his granddaughter to the ticket window of a football stadium and said, "I want a paper for my wife," did not convey accurate meaning and was very embarrassed because he substituted the word *paper* for *ticket* and *wife* for *granddaughter*. He selected words from within the appropriate category but they were seriously inappropriate in meaning. Such errors can place the individual in harmful, dangerous circumstances.

Written Response. Older children may use the written word as a means of communication. Some cannot evoke the auditory symbol even after writing it, but others can say it if they see it, using a visual symbol as a cue to auditory recall. Others need only to see or trace the first letter of a word, after which they can say it.

Pertinent information on various modality functions can be gathered from such observations. In terms of semi-autonomous systems it is apparent that auditorization can be distorted even though visualization is intact. Furthermore, interneurosensory processes are evident when an individual utilizes the stored information from one modality to supplement that which is deficient in another.

Oral Reading. A disturbance in word recall generally is revealed through spoken language but it also can affect oral reading. Both children and adults with this problem may be able to read silently but less well orally. They associate meaning with the visual symbol but cannot call up the correct auditory symbol. As a result, their oral reading is filled with substitutions or is significantly below their silent reading ability. An eight-year-old girl, asked to read the sentence, "The bird flew back to its nest," could not recall the exact words so she read it as, "The chicken went back to his home."

Older children often look at a word and say, "I know the word and I can give you a definition, but I cannot say it." They can read silently but cannot transduce from the visual to the auditory. For instance, a twelve-year-old was given a group of words and was asked which of three meant the same as the one that was underlined: *inspection*, termination, examination, protection. His comment was, "I know it is the second one and I know it means you have to sort of look into things and make sure they're all right, but I can't say the word."

The child who has severe reauditorization difficulties may show non-fluencies or hesitations in his connected speech. His parents become concerned because they feel he is beginning to stutter. They should be advised to reduce demands for spoken language and to call no attention to the hesitations. As memory skills improve, the nonfluency diminishes and remediation for stuttering is unnecessary.

Educational Procedures

The major objective in teaching a person with reauditorization deficits is to facilitate the spontaneous recall of words. We attempt to help him recall the appropriate word at the appropriate time. Auditory memory disabilities are some of the most difficult to alleviate, but improvement can be expected. The following procedures have been found useful in working with children and adults.

Meaningful Auditory Stimulation. The emphasis should be on the recall of a useful vocabulary for each individual. No time is spent on memorizing a series of digits or nonsense syllables. Extensive auditory stimulation is provided since the child must have words repeated many times in a meaningful setting before he can recall them.

Organization of Input. Ideas which fit together are easier to remember; hence, material should be organized so as to make the most efficient use of memory abilities. Children must be made aware of ways to organize their ideas and materials so they have an area or category to scan when trying to find the most suitable word. As a means of organizing the input, words are presented in context, in pairs, in association, and by category. The human brain, like a giant computer, scans the stored information while looking for the desired response. When the information is stored in an organized manner and when the child is aware of this organization, his memory tends to be more effective.

Facilitation of Recall. When a child cannot readily recall words, he must have a means of finding them. But not all individuals respond to the same type of cue. Each person must be studied to ascertain the most effective techniques for his idiosyncratic needs. Some perform best with visual cues, others when given a partial sentence, an associated word, or the first sound of a word. Suggested remedial techniques include the following:

(1) *Usage in context:* One of the most successful means for developing facility in reauditorization is to teach the words as used in a sentence. When unable to say a word spontaneously, a child often can do so if the teacher says a partial sentence as, "I write with a ___" or "I sit on a ___." Sentence completion exercises are beneficial for evoking the necessary words. The following exercises can be prepared for dual channel tape recorders, as well as for other types of electronic equipment, or for direct work with the child.

Paste pictures of objects on cards. Record sentences on magnetic tape to accompany each picture, i.e., "I sleep in a ___," "I eat soup with a ___." The child is directed to look at the picture, listen to the incomplete sentence, and provide the missing word. After practicing with the sentences as cues, he is asked to name the picture without hearing the sentences. If he cannot remember the word, encourage him to reauditorize the sentence to himself until he can look at the object and say the word spontaneously. These same procedures can be used for work on other parts of speech. Examples of sentences with omitted adjectives are:

The stove feels hot but ice feels ____.
Snow is cold but an iron is ____.
Some men are fat, others are ____.

(2) *Word associations.* In our language many words are associated because of common usage in everyday living and often are said together. Units like *bread and butter, salt and pepper, table and chair* are familiar to all of us. The normal individual may think of these words in pairs but can say them either singly or together. Certain children with language disorders cannot. They look at a picture of butter but can say it only when someone says "bread and ____." The first word of the pair is a cue for the second. Making children more aware of these associations is one way for improving recall.

Present pictures on cards, e.g., *shoes and socks, needles and pins, bread and butter, salt and pepper.* Ask the child to look at the pictures and repeat the words. If he profits from visual cues, write the words beneath each picture. After he can repeat the word pairs, present the pictures again but say only the first word in each pair and ask him to say the second. If he cannot do so, give him the first sound of the word as an additional cue. When he can say each pair, point randomly to single pictures and ask him to name them. If he cannot, encourage him to silently reauditorize the set but to say aloud only the one to which the teacher points.

The use of word opposites is an effective means of teaching word associations. Many children learn to recall words after working with pairs, e.g., *young-old, fat-thin, hard-soft, fast-slow, big-little.* Pictures or objects should be used to reinforce the words. Various parts of speech which are presented in meaningful groups are beneficial in facilitating recall. Words related to the sense of taste or touch are taught, e.g., *sweet, sour, bitter, salty* or *hard, soft, smooth, rough.*

(3) *Words in series or categories.* Many children are able to learn a series, such as the days of the week, but are unable to isolate and name a particular day out of sequence. Even though they have difficulty with immediate selection, it is helpful to capitalize on their ability to serialize as a means of improving word recall. Assume that a child cannot remember names of articles of clothing. Teach a series of five or six items and present them in a logical sequence from top to bottom, e.g., *hat, shirt, pants, socks, shoes.* Repeat the series and simultaneously point to each item. Continue until he can name the articles with his eyes open or closed. Then randomly point to various items and have him name only one. Encourage him to reauditorize, to think of the series until he can bring out the correct words. After considerable practice most children can "find" the appropriate word without going through the entire series. Other series to be taught include eating utensils, in order from left to right, *napkin, fork, plate, knife, spoon.*

(4) *Visual cues*. Those who can read and who profit from revisualizing words should be given cuing techniques accordingly. Gradually reduce the visual cues until the auditory symbol can be spontaneously evoked. Paste pictures on cards and print the name of the object below it. Ask the child to look at the picture and say the word. Practice until he can say each one quickly. Then erase letters from the end of the word until only the initial letter remains. The objective is to have him name the object by seeing only one letter and then without any visual cue.

Exercises can be prepared for children to read aloud. This sequence illustrates progressive reduction of cues. During the first lesson the child can be given two complete words from which to select his response. Later he is given only the first letter and eventually, he is given no cue.

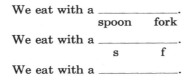

$$
\begin{array}{l}
\text{We eat with a \underline{\hspace{3cm}}.}\\
\qquad\qquad\qquad\text{spoon}\quad\text{fork}\\[4pt]
\text{We eat with a \underline{\hspace{2.5cm}}.}\\
\qquad\qquad\qquad\text{s}\qquad\text{f}\\[4pt]
\text{We eat with a \underline{\hspace{2.5cm}}.}
\end{array}
$$

(5) *Kinesthetic and tactual cues*. Encourage the child to feel an orange or a pencil as a means of aiding recall. Initially, use real objects but later ask him to rekinesthetize or remember the feel when trying to think of a word.

Rapid Naming. Rapid naming drills are particularly profitable for those who are slow to respond. Put six or eight pictures in front of the child and have him name them as quickly as possible. Time him and repeat the procedure until he can give words at approximately one per second. Children enjoy timing themselves and keeping records from week to week. An eleven-year-old girl was pleased that she could name 15 articles of clothing in one minute whereas two weeks earlier she required three minutes.

"Warm-up" sessions at the beginning can be used by having the child name objects in the room as quickly as he can. If he finds this arduous, the task can be reduced by first asking him to point to the objects as they are named for him. Even though he has no difficulties in comprehending, it helps him to hear the words before he is asked to recall them spontaneously.

Self-monitoring. Most children with severe disturbances in reauditorization are aware of their errors. Some will not even attempt an answer if they feel it is incorrect. Others, especially those who tend to perseverate, should be encouraged to inhibit an answer which they think is wrong. For example, a child tried to recall the word *orange* but continued to say *banana* even when he knew it was not right. His repetition of the incorrect word caused further frustration. Therefore, his attempts were inhibited by telling him to wait and remain silent for a few seconds. At times it is necessary to shift to nonverbal activities and resume verbal instruction later. However, the child often improves if given a few moments of quiet and encouraged to internally "hear" the words before saying them.

Continued Usage. It is important to keep the child using words, since recall improves with rehearsal. Many situations can be arranged in the classroom that provide an opportunity to respond verbally in a meaningful setting. The teacher should consider each individual's disability and state questions in a way that he must answer by using words that are difficult to recall. If a child indicates that he wants a paintbrush, the teacher should not merely say, "Do you want the brush?" but rather should word the question so that he responds by using the word. If he needs a multiple choice selection, she might say, "Do you want the pen or the brush?" He hears the complete word but has to respond by saying it. The teacher may also give a partial sentence, "We paint with a____," or she may give the initial sound *b*. Active learning in a meaningful setting is superior to drills on word lists.

Auditory-Motor Integration

A second group, composed of children who have an expressive language deficit, is unable to *say* words; the children comprehend and can recall but cannot associate words with the motor patterns for speaking. It is the inability to *imitate* words which often differentiates this population from others with disorders of spoken language. (Children with reauditorization problems can repeat but not remember words; those with syntactical deficits can use single words expressively, but cannot formulate sentences.) This disturbance is a form of expressive aphasia and has been variously designated as motor aphasia, apraxia, verbal apraxia (Agranowitz and McKeown, 1959; Eisenson, 1957; Nielsen, 1946; Wepman, 1961).

Most writers agree that apraxia refers to an inability to act or to move various parts of the body in a purposeful manner, although the power of the movement is intact. Head (1926) stressed that apraxia must be differentiated from paralysis and disorders of comprehension which affect the individual's ability to execute a motor act. Nielsen used the term *apractic aphasia* to differentiate it from other disabilities. He states that the adult aphasic knows what he wishes to say, i.e., he has clear thoughts; he can hear the sounds silently in his head, but he has forgotten how to make the movements necessary to produce speech sounds. He can move the muscles for chewing, clearing his throat, etc.—it is only the movements required to utter speech that he has forgotten.

More recently, Wepman (1961, p. 81) defined apraxia as, " a disruption in the ability to transmit or express a motor response along a specific modality; difficulty in the articulation of speech, in the formation of letters in writing, or in the movements of gesture and pantomime." In discussing verbal apraxias, Wepman states that they "are relatively independent of the symbolic process. It can be shown in an apraxic patient, for example, that he understands what is said to him, formulates symbols, has available the syntax of language, but cannot recall or control the motor act of articulation." Our observations of children are similar. Although the congenital aphasic is different from the adult in that he never acquired the motor patterns for the spoken word, there are similarities both diagnostically and educationally. Many of the procedures outlined in this chapter for remediation of expressive aphasia can be used with either children or adults.

Apraxic involvements may be manifested in general motor performance and in visual-motor skills as well as in the use of spoken language. Thus a child might be unable to learn the nonverbal motor patterns required for riding a bicycle. Others cannot write (see Chapter VI). Those who are unable to learn the auditory-motor patterns for speaking do not necessarily have problems in writing; however, both systems can be affected. One six-year-old compensated for his oral deficit by writing, but another boy the same age could neither speak nor write.

The expressive aphasic child is unable to coordinate the auditory-motor patterns for speaking. He has not learned that he can produce a particular sound by placing his tongue and lips in a certain position—that he can say *m* by closing his lips and humming. It is hypothesized that rudiments of this auditory-motor integration emerge as a child babbles. While making noises in his crib, he realizes that he produces a specific sound by moving his tongue and lips in a certain way. He also discovers that if he wants to duplicate the sound, he must repeat the movement. A similar development occurs when a child establishes visual-motor coordination and learns to draw. He becomes aware of visual patterns when he moves his crayon in one direction and learns to change the picture by altering the movement. Children with expressive aphasia do not make this discovery. Consequently, they cannot talk until they learn to coordinate a sequence of sounds with a sequence of movements. Information from case histories indicates that they are silent babies. They do not babble as much as the other children in the family and their vocalizations during early periods of training consist of vowel sounds with varying inflections. The findings suggest that even sound effects which the children used contained no consonants, e.g., *ooo-ooo* for train, *ee-ow* for meow, *ow-ow* for bow-wow.

Children with severe impairment have no spoken language and therefore communicate largely by gesture and pantomime. Some who are particularly bright teach themselves to read and write a few words so they can express their needs. The following letter written by the mother of a four-year-old boy illustrates the problem. Fred was accepted for training shortly after the evaluation, remained in our program for two and a half years and when dismissed had good spoken language. At the time of dismissal he scored 128 on performance intelligence and 120 on verbal. All academic achievement was above his grade level.

Mother's description of her son who had severe expressive aphasia

Fred was a quiet baby and babbled very little. He makes more babbling noises now (4½ yr.). He has never used words or jargon, but has developed a great deal of gesture for use in communication. He understands everything we say to him and enjoys stories and other verbal activities. He has begun to print words but only a few of these are used for purposeful communication.

When Fred was 3 yr. and 9 mo. old he began to imitate animal noises. Most of these were produced with vowel sounds and an occasional *b* or *k*.

I remember a few weeks before his third birthday he repeated "bah, bah, bah" all one day. Thinking it might mean "bye-bye," I took him out in an attempt to satisfy his wish and encourage him to continue, but he never repeated the sound after that day, so I may have been mistaken. At about the same time on three separate but identical occasions he made the sounds "wah dow." I interpreted it to mean "want down" and helped him down. Then he learned to get down for himself and the sounds to my knowledge have never been repeated. Whether these were simply coincidences or not, I don't know.

He communicates very well non-verbally by facial expression, hand and body movements, etc. He will frequently "act out" verbs like fall, jump, etc. and nouns like escalator, revolving door, airplane, etc.

When he was three years and 10 months old, I suddenly realized that Fred was reading words: dog, cat, etc. because he'd make the sound for the animal when he saw only the word. At three years and eleven months he started making words all by himself with his alphabet blocks. Later he started printing the words; he was unable to make lower case letters well, but could translate lower case letters on toy blocks into capital letters.

Pronunciation may be distorted until the motor pattern is fully established. Head (1926) reported that a mild disability causes mutilation of letters and syllables resulting in slowness and difficulty of articulation, which at first resembles a slight dysarthria. Yet apraxia is different from dysarthria. The child with paralysis knows where he wants to place his tongue or lips but he cannot do so because of restricted movement. In contrast, the apraxic has adequate movement but does not know how or where to place his tongue. When observing an aphasic child trying to imitate a movement, it appears as though his tongue is lost in his mouth.

Occasionally a child can imitate the movements of the oral mechanism but cannot repeat sounds. For instance, he can imitate a movement such as opening and closing the lips without sound but cannot repeat *ma-ma*. He can tranduce the visual-motor pattern (watching the speaker's mouth) to his own speech mechanism but cannot coordinate auditory-visual-motor patterns. Others can produce isolated phonemes but cannot blend them into words because they cannot follow a sequence of movements. Those who are unable to retain a motor pattern may distort words by saying *puc* for *cup*. Transpositions of sounds can be due to a disturbance in either auditory or motor sequentialization. The teacher should explore the child's ability to hear the differences in words. Generally, the apraxic can correctly think the sound of the word but not the motor plan, so he usually knows when he says it incorrectly. Those with auditory sequentialization problems are less aware of their errors because they do not have a clear auditory pattern of the word. While the expressive aphasic's ability to monitor his errors auditorially is of value in learning to speak, it disturbs him because he knows how the word should sound and also knows that he cannot say it correctly; he often refuses to try to say a word unless he is sure he can produce it.

At times children forget how to produce sounds they have learned. A six-year-old, feeling very unhappy, came to class one day and said, "I lost my 'uh'." He pointed to his throat indicating that he had forgotten how to make the *k*. Only after two or three sessions of diligent practice could he again say the sound. Others, for whom the motor pattern is nearly established but not totally automatic, sometimes forget how to start a word. However, when given a preparatory set, such as, "lift your tongue" or "close your lips," they proceed and say the word correctly. In the previous section we described the child with reauditorization problems and his need for preparatory auditory cues—e.g., the first sound of a word. The apraxic, however, does not find an auditory cue beneficial; he must watch the speaker or be told where to place his tongue and lips. He must have cues for the motor plan, not for the words themselves.

Educational Procedures

The primary objective in teaching the child with deficits in oral expressive language is that he learn the auditory-motor patterns for speaking. Every effort is made to teach him control of the oral musculature so that he can produce sounds and blend them into meaningful words.

Inventory of Movements, Phonemes, and Words. Before teaching new sounds, the teacher takes an inventory of the movements, phonemes, or words that the child can produce and capitalizes on them. Rather than presenting new and difficult sounds, she utilizes the ones made on a vegetative level and tries to raise them to a voluntary level. Occasionally a few consonants or words such as *okay* can be uttered, but not repeated or used consistently. The teacher listens carefully to the spontaneous vocalizations or jargon, noting the sounds emitted and then attempts to *make the child aware of these sounds and the movements used in producing them.* Finally, she tries to *develop voluntary repetition for purposeful communication.*

These objectives can be achieved by engaging the child in meaningful parallel play, where he is most apt to make sounds involuntarily. Play with toys that require gross motor activities usually causes the child to vocalize. After a sound is uttered, repeat it and note whether he can follow with other repetitions. For example, if during his play he utters *uh oh* when an object falls off the table, repeat the sounds exactly as given and encourage him to say them again. If he succeeds, have him hold the *oh* and call his attention to the position of his lips. At times it is beneficial just to comment, "That's nice, do it again. Do you feel where your tongue is?" On other occasions have him watch in a mirror or trace around his lips with his index finger.

Symbolic Vocalizations. As soon as the child is conscious of the sounds he can produce, the teacher helps him make the vocalizations symbolic and meaningful. Even though his first attempts may not be articulated perfectly, he should be encouraged to use them for communication. When he says *ee* consistently to represent the word *eat*, he has the rudiments of expressive oral language. If he says *o* for *open* or *uh* for *up*, he not only reinforces the necessary motor patterns but finds that people now respond to his vocalizations.

While we do not encourage or reinforce incorrect motor patterns, it should be remembered that young children do not articulate words perfectly when they begin to use the spoken word. Therefore, we should not assume that the first attempts of the aphasic must be perfect. He becomes discouraged with excessive corrections. However, when he produces sounds meaningfully, he feels more a part of his environment; he is motivated to use words and thus reinforces the motor patterns. When oral expression begins, the teacher pronounces words correctly. She does not repeat inaccurate attempts since the child must hear the proper pattern to imitate it. In the early periods of training when trying to make him aware of his vocalizations, she imitates his sounds but words are said correctly.

Language training is done in a meaningful setting. Young children do not respond well to drill type of activities. Not only does a meaningful setting stimulate vocalizations but it provides a climate in which the child can reinforce the motor patterns by using newly learned words.

The Motor Plan. Nearly all training of preschool children can be done in relatively informal settings, but brief periods of structured activities are necessary for learning new and more difficult expressions. The procedures for teaching new words depend both upon the deficit in auditory-motor function and on the intact systems. Some learn best from watching the speaker, others need to watch themselves in a mirror, still others may be confused by visual input and profit more from instructions given auditorially. Various *teaching routes* must be explored and the techniques modified according to the individual's combination of deficits and integrities.

Although typically there is overlap and modification of techniques, three fundamental approaches should be followed. The goal is to achieve spoken language, but because of the nature of the learning disability, not all learn in the same way. The first approach utilizes extensive visual cues, the second verbal directions, and in the third motor-kinesthetic cues are emphasized. Examples of each are given below:

(1) *Visual*. Some expressive aphasics learn to produce sounds if they observe the speaker's lips. They watch, not to comprehend (as would a deaf person), but to learn how to *say* words. They cannot *listen and do* but they can *look, listen, and do*. Others can only *look and do* because they cannot coordinate the visual-auditory-motor patterns.

Before teaching words it is critical to ascertain whether the child understands imitation as a basic process. If he cannot follow, he cannot be expected to imitate the refined movements for speech. Have him *follow the leader* and imitate various movements, such as putting his hands over his head, under his chin, and behind his back. If it seems beneficial, have him watch himself in the mirror to make him aware of body positions; most children also enjoy imitating hand puppets. As he learns, progress toward imitation of finer movements, e.g., blowing, smiling, licking the lips. Move the tongue from side to side and up and down rapidly, open and close the jaw, purse and retract the lips—all without sound. Emphasis is on the nonverbal visual-motor sequence. After he is able to imitate these movements, gradually introduce sound. Have him open and close his mouth a number of times, then while continuing this movement tell him to start making a sound. This should result in *ma–ma–ma*. Encourage repetition to strengthen the motor pattern, then immediately try to convert the sounds into a meaningful symbol, which in this instance would be *mama*. Have him repeat the word and use it purposefully.

Select other words that are visible on the lips and follow the same procedures, establishing the motor pattern, introducing sound, reinforcing it, and converting it into a word. Generally words composed of vowels, bilabial or linguadental consonants are easiest, e.g., *up, eat, no, daddy, night, meat, pie, boy.*

There are various reasons for beginning with the nonverbal motor pattern. First, some individuals cannot tolerate stimulation from all sensory modalities. Second, those who monitor their errors best auditorily do not like to hear their own incorrect productions, so they feel more success this way. Finally, those who perseverate do not have the problem of shifting from incorrect productions if the motor pattern is first well established. Techniques for blending and reinforcing sounds are outlined below.

(2) *Verbal instructions.* Some children with deficits in oral expressive language cannot learn from listening or from watching the speaker but must have detailed instructions for proper tongue and lip placement. They cannot look at a person elevating his tongue and duplicate the pattern. However, when given either auditory or written instructions, e.g., "Lift your tongue" or "Make your lips go into a circle," they perform successfully. Many people experience a similar problem when trying to learn the new motor patterns required for playing golf. They watch the instructor but cannot achieve the proper patterning until the instructor says, "Don't bend your elbow" or "Bring the club all the way back to your shoulder." They do not relate a visual-motor pattern to their own body schema.

The teacher will find it helpful to analyze the sounds of our language so she can state quite specifically what the child should do with his tongue and lips. For example, when presenting *m*, she might say, "Close your lips and hum," or for *f*, "Bite your lower lip and blow but do not use your voice." Suggestions for tongue and lip positions are outlined by Agranowitz and McKeown (1959) and Nemoy and Davis (1945).

Most children reinforce the motor patterns through use. However, some of our young adults keep a list of sounds and how to produce them as a reminder if they forget how it should be done. A teen-age girl, severely apraxic after an embolism, learned to speak only after she was given written instructions. Detailed instructions for every sound were written to correspond with the printed symbol:

ee	Spread your lips and make a sound
ah	Drop your jaw and use your voice
th	Place your tongue between your teeth and blow—do not use your voice
n	Press the tip of your tongue behind your teeth—use your voice and feel the sound come out of your nose
f	Bite your lip and blow—do not use your voice

In this young lady's case, the only route to auditory expressive language was through the visual symbol system. Before she could learn to say words she had to see them written phonetically. She converted these printed symbols into an auditory pattern and then could speak. She relied so heavily on the visual phonetic symbol that she could not say *enough* until it was first written *enuf*. The letters represented auditory-motor movements which she blended to form words. Later she revisualized the spelling and finally could say the words spontaneously. Phonetic spelling was her only satisfactory cue to motor patterning.

(3) *Motor-kinesthetic*. The third procedure emphasizes the motor-kinesthetic approach. The teacher guides the child's tongue and lips or jaw into position, makes him conscious of the kinesthetic sensation, and reinforces the pattern through repetition. Devices such as tongue depressors or lollipops are used to guide the tongue and lips. For example, hold the front of the child's tongue down with a tongue depressor and encourage him to say *k*. Release the tongue depressor and see if he can duplicate the position and the sound. Touch the alveolar ridge with a lollipop to illustrate where he should place his tongue for the *t*, *d*, or *n*. A sticky substance, peanut butter or a caramel, can be placed at various points in the roof of the mouth to indicate the point at which the tongue should make contact.

Work from gross to fine imitation with emphasis on taction and kinesthesis. Ask the child to bring his thumb and index finger together several times. Have him continue the movement and place his fingers near the corners of his mouth. Encourage him to open and close the lips while simultaneously moving his fingers. Add the sound and say *ma-ma*. Have him make a circle with his thumb and index finger. Then place the fingers over his mouth and have him form the lips in a circular position to say *oh*. Another technique is to have him place the thumb by one corner of the mouth and the index finger by the other. Ask him to move the fingers apart, spreading the lips into a smiling position. Add voice and say *ee*.

Often it is essential to teach the expressive aphasic how to blend sounds into words. Although some learn whole words from the procedures suggested in the preceding section, others cannot remember a sequence of movements. Blending can best be accomplished by starting with combinations of vowel and nasal sounds. The blending of a plosive consonant with a vowel is much more difficult because the child does not have the feeling of one sound moving easily to the next. Therefore, combinations such as *m–e*, *n–o*, *m–y*, *ea–t* should be taught first. In all instances the blending should be of sound combinations which constitute meaningful words. Goldstein (1948) stressed that the learning of senseless combinations of syllables does not help the person learn language and that all attempts should be made to provide the individual with words for purposeful communication. The first words to be taught are selected on the basis of ease of production and frequency of usage so that the child has ample opportunity to practice what he has learned.

When the child is learning new words of more than one syllable, over-articulate and repeat the words slowly to give him an opporutnity to watch each movement. Like a slow-motion film the teacher says, "but–ter–fly," first very slowly encouraging the child to follow, them gradually increasing the speed until the rhythm and inflection are normal. This technique is particularly important for the child who transposes syllables or distorts the sequence of sounds within words.

As indicated earlier, children with deficits in oral expressive language need a preparatory set or a motor cue before saying a word. This tendency is prevalent when words are nearly established but not fully automatic. The type of cue depends upon the most effective route for learning. It may be visual, e.g., having the child watch your lips, or a verbal instruction, e.g., "round your lips." After the initial cue, the remainder of the word comes easily.

Throughout the training period the teacher arranges many situations where the child has an opportunity to use newly learned words. If he has just learned to say *home*, the teacher formulates questions so he can respond by using this word, thereby reinforcing it. At no time should he be forced to speak or be deprived of something he needs because he cannot imitate the spoken word. He should be encouraged three or four times but then his attempts are accepted whether or not they are perfect.

Formulation and Syntax

The third group of children with deficiencies in oral expressive language has a disability in the formulation of sentences. The children understand what they hear and can use single words and phrases but they cannot formulate and organize words according to correct language structure. They tend to omit words, distort the order of words, use incorrect verb tenses, and make other grammatical errors long after such skills are normally acquired. This language disorder has been designated as *form-ulation aphasia* or *syntactical aphasia*.

In studying agrammatisms it is helpful to consider normal language development. Although much remains to be learned about the acquisition of syntax, the findings of Brown and Bellugi (1964), Chomsky (1957), Ervin (1964), and Lenneberg (1964) are useful in studying normal as well as abnormal verbal behavior. While it appears that a child merely listens, learns, remembers, and repeats sentences, the development of syntax is far more than simple repetition. Ability to formulate sentences is a complex skill requiring many integrities, including ability to understand, to remember word sequences, to manipulate symbols, and to generalize principles for sentence structure.

A child cannot remember every sentence he hears, but he holds certain structural patterns in mind, makes abstractions about the relationship of words, and then generates sentences of his own. Initially, these are very simple word groupings, such as noun-verb combinations (not like the sentences he hears his parents use), but he follows an orderly sequence developmentally and with maturation learns to plan more complex sentences. He selects and arranges words to correspond with experience. He learns, for example, that when he sees one child performing an activity, he says, "The boy is skating," but when he sees a group he must add an *s* to the word *boy* and change *is* to *are* in order to form the correct sentence, "The boys are skating."

Normal children and certain types of aphasic children are able to recognize sentences as being correct or incorrect long before they can express them correctly. To illustrate, pairs of pictures and sentences were given to children with syntactical disorders. Two pictures were selected, one showing *a* boy running and another showing a *group* of boys running. They were asked to point to the picture that corresponded with the sentence, "The boys are running" or "The boy is running." In nearly all instances those whose language deficit was primarily syntactical could select the correct picture even though they could not use proper sentence structure expressively. Similarly, when asked to tell whether a sentence sounded right, e.g., "The boys *is* running," they could distinguish errors but not correct them. These observations are similar to those of Goodglass (1963, p. 38) who found that "often the typical motor agrammatic understands very well the distinctions which he does not express in his own speech."

Syntax and Memory. Even though syntax involves more than simple repetition, the role of memory in learning a language should be emphasized. A child must retain certain linguistic patterns in mind and store them to make the abstractions necessary for correctly generating sentences of his own. Often aphasics with syntax disturbances have a limited auditory memory span. Goodglass found that agrammatic adult aphasics were able to repeat only three or four unrelated words at a time. A similar tendency can be observed in children with language disorders; they fall below the norm on tests involving auditory memory span, including those not requiring verbal responses. Initially, it was our impression that they could retain a sequence of words if they were not required to repeat them. Test results, however, do not support this conclusion. When asked to point to a series of objects, or to execute a series of commands, they omit items or distort the sequence. Their performance on auditory memory span tests requiring a verbal response is also deficient, sentence repetition often being most seriously disturbed.

As a whole, this group tends to be low both on Auditory Attention Span for Unrelated Words and on Auditory Attention Span for Syllables (Baker and Leland, 1935). The latter test measures the child's ability to repeat sentences of increasing length. Recently we observed an interesting trend in the performance of dyslexic and aphasic children on these two tests of auditory memory span. Although both groups of children fell substantially below the norm on these tests, some with formulation difficulties performed better on memory for unrelated words than on memory for sentences. It seems that those who have syntactical deficits can more successfully remember a list of unrelated words than sentences where both meaning and structure must be held in mind.

Of prime significance in acquiring syntax is the ability to manipulate language structures. A child hears certain sentence patterns, perceives the plan of words, and then begins to construct sentences of his own. Chomsky (1957) and Lenneberg (1964) discuss the ways in which young children practice with their newly learned sentence plans. They grasp certain automatic grammatisms, select words to insert into the structure and in so doing, combine the semantics and syntax of the language. A professor described this phenomenon in his two-year-old son. After several meaningful experiences, the child began to say the sentence, "Put the car away." After using this sentence two or three evenings, the boy seemed to realize that this structural pattern could be used in other settings. For several days following he was heard practicing with the sentence plan, sometimes in the presence of others and sometimes by himself. Typical sentences he used were, "Put the toys away," "Put the socks away," and finally, although somewhat erroneously, "Put the baby away."

Taylor (1963) states that children demonstrate their skill in manipulating structures when they produce a sentence and substitute a nonsense word for a vocabulary item they do not know. This tendency is noted especially in children who have severe auditory retrieval disturbances. They seem to understand the relationships of words within a sentence but cannot evoke the words they need and therefore substitute a syllable or sound. A five-year-old, for instance, substituted the nonsense word *tia* each time he could not recall the word he wanted. Children with syntactical disturbances do not acquire these automatic grammatical structures. They develop vocabulary but do not learn how to correctly put words together. Some cannot formulate any sentences; others may use sentence fragments or grammatically incorrect sentences.

An analysis of case history information reveals that children with syntactical disturbance are referred for study later than those with other language problems. Since most have acquired some vocabulary, the parents are hopeful that sentences will emerge spontaneously. This is not true. A study of their language development discloses a wider discrepancy between the emergence of the first word and the first two-word combinations than for the normal child. Generally, a child uses his first word at about twelve months of age and combines words by eighteen or twenty months. In the syntactical aphasia population there was an interval of as much as three to four years between the emergence of the first word and the first sentence. For twelve such children the mean age for the first word was sixteen months whereas the mean age for the first two-word combination was forty-two months. This is contrasted with one of our studies of receptive aphasics in whom the first word was expressed at two years and the first sentence at three years. Once they acquire meanings, they do not have difficulty with syntax.

The mother of a boy with syntactical aphasia kept a meticulous record of her son's early life, including his language development. She noted that he had a vocabulary of approximately one hundred words before he began putting words together. When he first combined words, they were in list rather than in sentence form. At breakfast time he merely said, "Juice, toast, milk." At no time did he use noun-verb combinations (want milk) or adverb-noun combinations (more toast). Although direct parallels cannot be drawn between the development of oral and written language, a similar phenomenon was observed in acquisition of the written form. Myklebust (1965) found that children write lists of words before they construct sentences.

On occasion parents try to remedy the language problem but with little success. The mother of a four-year-old wrote, "He uses some words but just does not seem to know how they should go together or even that they should go together. I worked with him for a month recently on 'I am a boy.' He can say each word but not together as a sentence. In desperation, I finally threatened to withold his favorite blanket at nap time if he didn't repeat the sentence. He just said, 'No,' and climbed into his bed without tears or protest and settled down for his nap."

Similar observations were reported by the father of a four-year-old, as shown in the letter below:

Right now Billy's speech is limited to a few monosyllables: Maw (for Grandma), Paw (for Grandpa), Ma, Da, mine, and bye. He also attempts some other words, but the enunciation is so garbled that it is hard to understand him even when you know what he is trying to say.

. . . on occasion he has tried to put two words together, but usually gets them in reverse order. For example, if he is telling you the light is on he'll say 'on light,' although, of course, it is not clearly enunciated.

He never attempts to put more than two words together, although he manages to work out a mixture of signs and mangled key words that get across to a listener (who is tuned in on his wave length) his thoughts or desires.

He has a younger brother, who at 15 months speaks a good deal more clearly than he does.

We do not think there is any impairment of his mental processes, for he apparently comprehends everything that is said. He can follow simple orders and carry out simple tasks without difficulty.

Fortunately, he also possesses a sweet disposition, and he doesn't seem to mind repeating as often as necessary something that he is trying to tell you. Recently, however, he has become somewhat reluctant to repeat words that we have asked him to say. He may try once, possibly twice, but won't try the third time.

He plays well with other children. He is aggressive enough that they don't push him around and agreeable to sharing toys and playthings. His muscular coordination is probably less than normal, although he likes to ride a tricycle, climb, and play on a swing or slide. He manages to keep up with the other kids.

The most severely deficient use only single words and pantomime because they cannot formulate sentences. Others manifest serious deficits in word order. Syntax and formulation often is markedly disturbed in those who acquire language and then lose it as a result of a disease. Often they retain a vocabulary and fragments of automatic structure but they cannot use complex sentences. Note the responses of an eleven-year-old who became aphasic after a severe illness:

Question: Why is it nice to live in a big city?
Child: Shopping to at the stores.

Question: What kind of transportation is called Public Transportation?
Child: Public transportation is the people what the bus and busways.

Question: Why should the driver not look at the scenery when he is driving in the country?
Child: The driver not looking at the scenery—you have to stay on the road as you travelling.

The language of some formulation aphasics is described as being *telegraphic* because they speak in the style normally used in a telegram. Key words are retained so meaning is preserved, but many words, e.g., articles, prepositions, connectives, and other parts of speech, are omitted. Typical telegraphic speech appears as: "Mom—dad—me—go—store."

Although young children omit words when they first acquire sentences expressively, they make rapid progress so that, according to Brown and Bellugi (1964), by three years some children produce all of the major varieties of simple sentences up to a length of ten or eleven words. Typical omissions in the early learning of language are possessive inflections, the modal auxiliary *will*, other forms of auxiliary verbs, *is* and *have* and the inflected endings of words, *ing* and *ed*. Similar omissions are observed in aphasics but their errors persist for a much longer time.

The errors of the aphasic are present both in spontaneous language and in imitation. When given the sentence, "Mommy and Daddy went to the store," they might say, "Mommy, Daddy go store." A basic problem is the inability to organize and program the correct sequence of words. A young man verbalized this difficulty very well. When asked to repeat, "We went to the store for some bread and butter," his response was, "I know . . . I know meaning . . . bread and butter . . . the store . . . just can't put it together." He was suggesting that he had the general meaning but could not organize the words into the proper structure.

It has been suggested that young children omit words but preserve the word order (Brown and Bellugi, 1964). While this tendency is observed in many with language disorders, it is not a universal characteristic. Some cannot remember the sequence and fail to give the words in correct order even in direct repetition. The following are examples:

Four-year-old
Teacher: Turn the page.
Child: Page turn.

Six-year-old
Teacher: The wheels fell off the truck.
Child: Wheels off truck fell.

The following are errors in spontaneous sentence formation:

Five-year-old
Cut I.
Milk got me none.
Me out eat.

The expressive language level is in keeping with the types of sentences that the child is able to formulate. Some use only noun-verb combinations because they cannot manipulate other structures. The errors that persist are those involving word order, verb tense, word endings, pronouns, possessives, prepositions, connectives, articles and wording of questions. Formulation disabilities usually are reflected in the written as well as in the oral language form. If a child cannot express ideas orally, it is doubtful that he can write them (Myklebust, 1965). Note the language forms of a nine-year-old boy while viewing a picture:

Oral

Little boy like play house. Mom, Dad, kids, eat dog go 'way.

Written

One upon a little boy love to play house toy people. And here are some of the thing he play where a man mother to boy a baby and chair glass and a table.

Observe the lack of sentence structure and the overuse of listing. This boy could read third grade material aloud without making errors. If the stories above were written correctly, he would not have omitted words in reading them. Also, if his sentences were read back to him, he would recognize them as being incorrect but be unable to correct them.

Educational Procedures

The primary educational goal for children with formulation disorders is to *develop a correct, natural, spontaneous flow of language*. The teacher acts as a guide, giving the child the vocabulary and syntax necessary for meaningful expression of thoughts and feelings. One of the dangers in presenting procedures for educational remediation is that they appear rigid and stereotyped. Language training goals are precisely the opposite.

Automatic Grammatical Structures. This approach is similar to current *audio-lingual* methods used in teaching foreign languages, but with structure and repetition. By structure we mean a planned presentation of experience, coordinated with sentence patterns in keeping with the child's mental and language levels. In essence we utilize planned presentations to help the child *learn the structure of language*. Structure in this latter context has been discussed by Bruner (1963, p. 7) who states that "grasping the structure of a subject is understanding it in a way that permits many other things to be related to it meaningfully. To learn structure, in short, is to learn how things are related." Bruner cites a number of examples of structure but states that "the often unconscious nature of learning structures is perhaps best illustrated in learning one's native language. Having grasped the subtle structure of a sentence, the child very rapidly learns to generate many other sentences based on this model though different in content from the original sentence learned." The young normal child seems to learn these structures with little effort; the aphasic does not. He has difficulty retaining the pattern and in planning and organizing the words he hears. Therefore, one of the major objectives is to help him grasp the principles whereby words are organized into sentences. This is done, not by using formal rules, but by an approach which facilitates his learning. Every attempt is made to foster the building of automatic grammatical structures into which he can insert appropriate and meaningful words.

There is no clearly prescribed age for initiating work on syntax. As in normal language development, many of the early utterances of the aphasic child are one-word sentences, an integral part of syntactical development. As soon as a rudimentary vocabulary emerges, work should begin. Most teachers are concerned about the types of language structures to stress during the early stages of training. The best guides are the observations of normal children. Generally, the first two-word utterances are noun-verb combinations (daddy go), adjective-noun phrases (big boy), and adverb-noun phrases (more cooky). As stated previously, the first sentences of both the normal and aphasic child rarely are correct syntactically, so we cannot expect perfect sentences at the outset.

The teacher should *provide a series of sentences auditorially, sufficiently structured with experience so the child will retain and internalize various sentence plans.* It might appear that these principles are similar to those for language learning in any child. While it is true that in general the goals are the same, the experiences and the sentences must be much more closely planned and coordinated. Simultaneity, auditory stimulation, structure, and repetition are critical. The normal child abstracts grammatical principles by making spontaneous associations, but those with learning disabilities must have many more concrete presentations.

Experience and Sentence Plans. *Arrange meaningful experiences either through play activities or pictures.* Then provide phrases or sentences which coincide with the experience and encourage the best response possible from the child. Begin with nouns and verbs understood by the child, e.g., eating, sleeping, daddy, baby. Engage him in an activity and use controlled sentences, "Daddy is eating, Mommy is eating, Baby is eating." Each sentence should be said while presenting the appropriate object, and the wording of each sentence should remain the same except for the noun. The length of the sentences should not be varied, since it is necessary to control as many variables as possible. In this particular sequence the verb remains constant but the nouns are altered; in a later sequence the noun remains constant and the verbs are altered. Repeat each series of sentences for the child and encourage responses from him. In some instances ask him to repeat the entire sentence or permit him to complete them—e.g., "Daddy is ____," "Mommy ____."

After working with one set of objects and a single verb, the teacher may shift the verb to the word *sleeping*; she uses the same figures but now says, "Daddy is sleeping," "Mommy is sleeping," "Baby is sleeping." From these presentations the child begins to form the grammatical automatisms necessary for formulation of syntactically correct sentences.

In addition to structured presentations, other cues are helpful. Use *visual cues* to indicate the number of words in phrases or sentences. Because many children are limited in auditory memory span, it is beneficial to provide them with various types of visual support. Young children respond well to the simple technique of raising a finger for each word in the sentence. Although cues of this type do not help them remember specific words, they serve as reminders for those who tend to omit auxiliary verbs and prepositions. A five-year-old trying to say, "The man is eating," could only remember, "The man eating," but said, "Me know . . . one more . . . me know no." Making them aware of the number of words within a sentence seems to help them in acquiring syntax.

Auditory-kinesthetic cues can be used as a means for remembering both the number of words in a sentence and the auditory rhythmic pattern. It is well known that cadence, rhythm, and inflectional patterns are important for the development of syntax; therefore, in some instances we tap out the sentence pattern on a table while saying the sentence.

Amplify the unstressed words or word endings in a sentence. It has been suggested by some writers that the reason children omit auxiliary verbs and word endings is that they do not hear them clearly. In sentences, such as, "The boy is running" or "The boy walked," stress is placed on the noun and the verb. When encouraging sentence repetition, the teacher says the unstressed words somewhat louder and emphasizes them. Word endings, such as *ed* and the *s* of possessive, should be stressed auditorially, and perhaps visually, by asking the child to watch the speaker's lips.

Sample Techniques. Simple sentence construction of the noun-verb-object type are developed in the same way as described previously. After the child uses noun-verb combinations, "Mommy—eat" or "Mommy is eating," pictures are selected to illustrate various people eating a specific food. The teacher then gives a group of simple sentences, "Mommy is eating soup," "Daddy is eating soup," etc. First the whole sentence is repeated so the child hears the total pattern, then words are omitted for the child to insert, and gradually he learns to say the entire sentence.

Present, past, and future tense verbs are difficult for many children because they must determine how to select and shift words in a sentence. Good results are often achieved through group activities. The teacher has one child walk around the room while she, together with the rest of the group, says, "Johnny is walking." After Johnny sits down, she says, "What did Johnny do? Johnny *walked*." Each time she encourages a response from the group. A similar technique is suggested for developing the correct use of verbs, such as *see* and *saw*. The teacher flashes a picture on the screen, and while the picture is present, she says, "What do you see?" and encourages a response, such as, "I *see* a dog"; she then turns off the light and asks, "What did you see?" and encourages the sentence, "I *saw* a dog." In this way a modification of experience promotes modification of the language structure.

Pictures are used in addition to direct experiences. For example a series of three pictures might be drawn to illustrate past, present, and future tense verbs. In picture Number 1, the child sees a cat walking toward a bowl of food; he is encouraged to say, "The cat is going to eat" or "The cat will eat his dinner." In picture Number 2, the cat is eating and the child is encouraged to use a sentence in the present tense, such as, "The cat is eating dinner." Finally, in picture Number 3, the cat obviously has finished eating and he is asked to say, "The cat ate his dinner" or another sentence using the past tense.

Similar pictures might be selected for work with prepositional phrases. After a child acquires sentences, such as, "Mommy is walking," he is encouraged to express more complex ideas (or use more complex constructions). Pictures are drawn to show that mother can walk to various places (the store, the beach, the school); with each one an appropriate sentence is given for the child to say or to complete. Gradually, more variables are introduced so that he can say, "The boy is riding to the park" or "The cat is climbing up the tree."

A comparable approach is used to teach adjective-noun combinations. Pictures are selected and phrases provided to help the child understand that a descriptive word generally precedes the name of the object. For example, several pictures are shown of things that are funny. The purpose is not to develop the concept of funny or sad, as outlined in the section on disorders of comprehension, but for him to learn the position of the adjective in relation to the noun. Practice phrases are: a *funny boy*, a *funny hat*, a *funny clown*. With repetition, most children acquire these phrases and formulate sentences accordingly. Gradually sentences with varied structures are emphasized. To avoid stereotyped language the child is taught to express ideas in different ways. When he has success with simple sentences, i.e., "I see a cat" and "The cat is black," he is shown how to combine them into a single, more interesting sentence, i.e., "I see a black cat."

Sentence building is one of the most challenging and difficult exercises we have used with both children and adults who have language disorders. The person is simply given a word and is told to use it in a sentence. This is not easy because words must be arranged around a single word with no cue provided for sentence structure. Differences are observed in performance when both the children and adults are given a noun or verb as compared with a preposition or a conjunction. Those with moderate deficiencies in formulation may be able to construct sentences around nouns or verbs but not around prepositions or adverbs.

A twelve-year-old boy with formulation difficulties constructed the following sentences using the words *boy*, *throw*, and *big*. Most of his simple sentences in normal conversation were syntactically correct but when he had to plan sentences with prepositions, conjunctions, adjectives, or adverbs he had problems organizing the words. Note his sentences:

> This is a good day for a *boy* to be out.
> The boy can *throw* the ball.
> The amount of . . . the *big* . . . the light . . . the amount of *big* light . . . the *big* light in the living room went out.

Children who are unable to construct a sentence from one word without assistance may only need a starter or a cue for success. At times this could consist of giving them the first few words of a sentence and at other times two or three additional words. For example, if they cannot use the word *to* in a sentence, they are asked to try to think of a sentence with the words *mother—to—store,* or if they cannot think of a sentence using the word *quickly,* they are given the words *dog—quickly—road.*

When the child reaches the point of formulating whole stories, various motivating devices are utilized, e.g., film strips, movies, slides. Picture sequences from reading readiness books are also useful. They are cut apart and mounted on single cards for the child to arrange in the proper sequence. First, he looks at each picture in the sequence and tells what is happening. Second, with the help of the teacher, he is encouraged to use appropriate transition phrases or words, e.g., "Next, they . . ." or "After it rained they . . . ." This type of instruction continues throughout the language program. The teacher leads the child from simple to more complex constructions, always accepting his responses but noting his errors and helping him correct them.

Some children have disturbances of both motor-patterning and syntax. They cannot be expected to express themselves in good speech because they cannot work on producing the motor pattern and good syntax at the same time. While trying to formulate sentences, the child should not be required to articulate perfectly. Nevertheless, each lesson is planned so that he receives help on both the production of words and proper syntax. Young children are given training only in the improvement of auditory language. School age children, however, simultaneously are given work with the written form. The exercises below are beneficial:

(1) *Scrambled sentences.* Give the child three or four flash cards containing single words and ask him to arrange them into sentences. Those with the greatest problem may need to be told what the sentence should say, but eventually they should be able to look at the words and arrange them without auditory cues. Written exercises as in Illustration 16 are also helpful.

(2) *Specific sentences.* Depending upon the type of errors made by each individual, specific exercises are designed (Illustrations 17, and 18, 19).

SCRAMBLED SENTENCES

Write each sentence correctly.

1. run   can   I

   I   can   run

2. ball   play   the   boys

   The   boys   play   ball

3. cold   today   is   it

   It   cold   is   today

4. work   to   father   went

   Father   to   work   went

ILLUSTRATION 16. Exercise for improving word order.

Write a word in each blank.
Make a good sentence.

1. I came ___in___ the car.

2. Come ___with___ me to the party.

3. Sunday we went ___at___ the zoo.

4. Put the dishes ___On___ the table.

5. I write ___with___ a pencil.

ILLUSTRATION 17. Exercise for improving errors of omission.

Use of Adjectives

1. The bark of the tree feels __rough__.

2. I had a __big__, __jucy__ orange for lunch.

3. The baby chicks were __soft__ and __furry__.

4. Did you see the __fluffy__, __white__ clouds in the sky today?

ILLUSTRATION 18. Exercise for improving use of adjectives.

Use the words <u>is</u> or <u>are</u> and finish each of the sentences.

1. The boy *is doing homework* .

2. The leaves *are many colors* .

3. They *are going.* .

4. The wagon *is   old* .

5. Some girls *are very good* .

ILLUSTRATION 19. Exercise for teaching subject-verb agreement.

Finish the story.

Have you ever been to *the* circus?
When I went *and* visit my *gramother* in
hicago last summer, they took *Billy*
and me to the big circus that came
to the city for three weeks. First,
we watched the parade of all the
animalls and tried to see how many
of them we could name. Next, we saw
some funny *clouns* riding on *horses*.
They did *tricks* that made everyone
laugh. While we watched the circus
we ate *peenuts* and *candy*. We were
all sorry when it was *over*. I hope that
I can go again sometime.

ILLUSTRATION 20. Exercise for teaching story formulation.

The first is for children who tend to omit *prepositions and conjunctions,* the second for those who use relatively few *adjectives,* and the third is primarily for children who have difficulty with *subject-verb agreement.* (Note the exercises for the use of the words *is* and *are* in Illustration 19.)

(3) *Sentences for stories.* The exercise in Illustration 20 is designed for children who need help in formulating *sentences for stories.* The child must insert a word which makes the story meaningful.

In summary, it is the task of the teacher to provide as many language learning situations as possible. She has in mind the type of error she wishes to correct and the type of new sentence construction she wishes to teach. She controls many variables so that the child can learn the principles by which words are organized into sentences. The goal is to develop facility in the expression of ideas and feelings.

CHAPTER V

Disorders of Reading

The impact of a reading disability perhaps never can be fully understood by the person who can read and write. When in a foreign county we experience frustrations because we are unable to read the language, but this situation is not comparable to being unable to read in any language. Initially parents of children with reading disabilities are concerned with academic achievement or the vocational limitations which result from school failure. Such concerns are justified but the effects are more debilitating. An inability to read not only creates problems in school learning but limits social maturity, social relationships, and the assumption of responsibility. It leads to dependency on others to an extent not expected of children with normal intelligence. It is from questions such as the following that we realize how a reading disability restricts one's everyday activities and total adjustment.

What happens when one cannot read signs of danger?

How can one use public transportation when he cannot read the names on trains and stations?

How can one look up a telephone number in case of emergency?

What are one's feelings when one goes to a restaurant with friends and cannot read the menu?

How can one complete application forms for employment, for a driver's license, and for the armed services?

There are many reasons for reading failure in children, including mental retardation, sensory impairment, emotional problems, neurological disturbance, and inadequate teaching (Eames, 1960; Gates, 1947; Monroe, 1932). Our concern is with the group who cannot read because of dysfunctions in the brain. This disorder has been designated *word blindness* (Orton, 1937), *developmental dyslexia* (Critchley, 1964), and *dyslexia* (Myklebust and Johnson, 1962). In all instances these designations concerned children with normal intelligence and no significant emotional disturbance, but who could not read. Although widespread interest in this problem has developed only during the past few decades, it was recognized at the end of the nineteenth century by Hinshelwood (1900) and Morgan (1896). Hinshelwood described a thirteen-year-old boy who could not store visual images but could learn auditorially. Orton (1937) made a notable contribution through the concept of *strephosymbolia,* and

147

Gillingham and Stillman (1940) developed procedures for teaching children with this type of disturbance. In recent years various professions both in the United States and abroad have become interested in dyslexia (Bender, 1958; Bryant, 1963; Money, 1962; Rabinovitch, 1954). Outstanding work has been done in Scandinavia by Hallgren (1950) and Hermann (1959), in South America by de Quiros (1962) and in England by Critchley (1964). Although opinions differ regarding etiology and other aspects of the problem, there is agreement that these children have been overlooked and are in need of much attention from educators.

LEARNING TO READ

The child of average intelligence is expected to learn to read even if he has only reasonably good teaching. Learning to read, for many children, seems not to require much effort. They appear to attain this ability almost incidentally. They quickly make associations between the printed symbol, the auditory symbol, and meaning.

Several years ago the incidental method was introduced. Basically, the procedure emphasized acquisition of a reading vocabulary from meaningful activities without formal teaching. Some learned from this method but there were criticisms from educators who felt there should be a more systematic approach, especially since children taught in this manner sometimes had difficulty in attacking unfamiliar words.

While controversy over methods continues, some children learn by any method and others in spite of them. Currently, there is agreement regarding the interrelationships of auditory and visual language and also that neither whole words nor phonics should be stressed exclusively. New procedures, such as the International Teaching Alphabet, the colored alphabet, and programmed instruction are being investigated for normal as well as for handicapped children.

Children who do not learn to read are usually categorized as being either mentally slow or emotionally disturbed. The dyslexic child is neither. Typically, he is of normal intelligence and wants desperately to read. To understand why he cannot, it is essential to be familiar with the ways in which the normal child acquires this skill. It has been suggested that reading is a visual symbol system superimposed on auditory language (Myklebust and Johnson, 1962). Johnson (1960) stated that reading is a symbol system twice removed from the realities which they represent. This statement implies a developmental progression as described by Myklebust (1954). That is, the child first integrates nonverbal experiences directly. Next he acquires auditory, then later a visual verbal system which represents both the experience and the auditory symbol.

The acquisition of each symbol system requires a number of integrities. It assumes ability to integrate nonverbal experience, that the individual will be able to differentiate one symbol from another, attach meaning to it, and retain it. For example, in acquiring auditory language the child must differentiate the symbol *cat* from the other symbols that he hears; he must associate this particular auditory unit with the animal; next he must store the symbol for future use and be able to recall and say it when communicating with others. Likewise, in learning to read he must be able to discriminate *cat* from other visual symbols, associate it with experience, with the auditory symbol, and remember it.

If a child has difficulty integrating meaningful experience, or learning through either the visual or auditory modality, a disturbance of reading can be expected. If he does not associate meaning with symbols, he may develop word-calling ability but not comprehension. In this instance he can *transduce* from the visual to the auditory but not *translate* symbols into meaning. Deficiencies in discrimination, interpretation, or retention of either auditory or visual symbols can cause problems in reading, as discussed below. Because of the variety of involvements, a unitary approach cannot be used in remediation. *The procedures of choice depend upon the nature of the dyslexia.*

In remediation a major objective for the dyslexic is to develop integration of experience, the spoken word, and the printed word. Throughout the training, emphasis is given to such integration as well as to reciprocity of functions, as illustrated by the Schema below:

Schema illustrating the processes required for learning to read

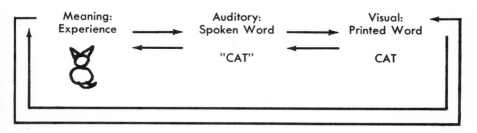

Attainment of this objective requires intensive study of each individual so that the remedial plan matches the pattern of deficits. It is insufficient to raise the areas of deficiency to a state of "normal reading readiness." If the teacher waits for an overall state of readiness, some children will never learn to read. An auditory dyslexic, for example, could not "hear"

the rhyming parts of words until he first *saw* them in printed symbols. Similarly, a visual dyslexic could not quickly match three-letter words until he was reading at a second grade level.

The approach to remediation often circumvents the major disability but simultaneously includes work on the deficits. Visual dyslexics rarely learn from a global word approach because they cannot retain an entire sequence of letters, but they can learn individual sounds and blend them into words. Auditory dyslexics, on the other hand, *can* learn words as wholes, but in the early stages of training, they do not learn through phonics. With proper training both types of dyslexics can acquire a sight vocabulary and phonetic skills. It is the initial training which varies.

As we have stated elsewhere, dyslexia is rarely found in isolation. Other disabilities are manifested as a part of the total syndrome (Johnson and Myklebust, 1965; Myklebust and Johnson, 1962). Although all of the characteristics are not expected to be found in a single child, the following often occur with the reading disorder.

Memory Impairments

Many types of memory disturbances result from central nervous system dysfunction, including deficits in span as well as immediate and delayed recall. Frequently the disorder affects learning through one sensory modality more than another; thus a person might function well visually but not auditorially. Since reading requires both auditory and visual memory, an impairment in ability to retain information in either modality can cause difficulty. The child with auditory memory problems may be unable to remember letter sounds or to put sounds together to make words. Those with visual memory impairment may be unable to revisualize letters and words.

Memory for Sequence

The inability to sequentialize has been observed in many children with learning disabilities. In reading they fail to remember the sequence of letters or sounds within words so they misread or misspell words. Dyslexics also might have difficulty learning a series, such as the days of the week, the months of the year, or the alphabet. Some know that there are twelve months in a year and can give the names of the months but not in the correct order. In a study of sixty dyslexics, only sixteen were able to give the months of the year correctly (Johnson and Myklebust, 1965).

Left-Right Orientation

A number of investigators have noted left-right disorientation in both children and adults with neurogenic involvements (Bender, 1958; Benton, 1959; Critchley, 1953; Rabinovitch, 1954). Typically they cannot identify left and right on themselves, on others, or on inanimate objects. Because of this disability they do not understand directions involving the use of the words *right* and *left* and are thought to be disobedient when they fail to follow instructions. They are confused when asked, "Put your name in the upper right-hand corner" or "Get the books on the left side of the bottom shelf." In physical education classes they cannot follow the rules of the game.

Time Orientation

The inability to tell time or even to acquire a sense of time has been stressed by many diagnosticians and by parents of dyslexic children. The mother of two boys said, "I have noticed that Tom, our seven-year-old, really has a better sense of time than Jim, our thirteen-year-old who has learning problems. Jim has never seemed to catch on to the happenings around him that would help him know what time it is. I don't think he even notices when the sun is going down and that this could be a cue that it is time to come home for dinner. He had a terrible struggle learning to tell time and still does not always know what day of the week or month of the year it is." The frustrations which result from time disorientation are expressed by a nine-year-old who said, "Mrs. Smith, I am glad you taught me how to tell time and told my parents to buy a watch so that I would know the time, but why is it that the other kids just *know* when to come in from recess?"

Body Image

Considerable emphasis has been given to the study of body image in children with learning problems (Bender, 1958; Critchley, 1964; Kephart, 1960). In the dyslexic population we have found only little difficulty in identifying parts of the body on command; however, their drawings of the human figure were lacking in good organization and detail. In one of our studies (Johnson and Myklebust, 1965) the mean Intelligence Quotient on the Goodenough Draw-a-Man was 84, whereas the mean on the Wechsler Intelligence Scale was 103.

Writing and Spelling

As indicated previously, writing is possible only after ability to read has been achieved. Therefore, the dyslexic child usually is unable to write or is unable to write more than he can read. Except for those who are dysgraphic, the limitation in writing is a result of the inability to read. The majority can copy. Until a child can interpret and remember words, he cannot use them for spontaneous written expression.

Dyslexic children are seriously deficient in spelling because the written form requires simultaneous ability to revisualize and to reauditorize letters. Hence, if either of these is deficient, it will result in reading and spelling disorders.

Topographic Disorder

An inability to read graphs, maps, globes, or floor plans is manifested by a large number of dyslexics. They cannot associate meaning with these representational materials or spatialize symbolically. Some are unable to understand the keys used with maps and therefore have little ability to make determinations regarding distance. Topographic disorders of this type interfere with school subjects (geography and mathematics) but also with many practical everyday activities.

Deviate Motor Pattern

Although dyslexic children do not have gross motor involvements, many have minor disturbances including inferior locomotor coordination, balance, and manual dexterity. Parents report that they fall more easily and that they are more awkward than others in the family. Some cannot ride bicycles because of balance problems; others cannot construct simple models because they cannot manipulate small pieces of material. When motor tests are administered, they fall below average, particularly on tests of locomotor coordination. In addition, they have a greater degree of laterality disturbance as compared to the normal (Orton, 1937).

VISUAL DYSLEXIA

A disturbance in learning through the visual modality often interferes with ability to read. It is known that defects of sight and of the visual fields may impede learning to read, but the chief concern in this discussion is with children who can see but who cannot differentiate, interpret, or remember words because of a central nervous system dysfunction.

Not all visual learning disabilities, however, affect reading. Some affect nonverbal functions more than reading; others interfere with several forms of symbolic behavior including arithmetic and music. Still others are limited almost entirely to reading. In this chapter the emphasis is on disabilities related to reading and pre-reading functions, but the teacher should be alert for other disturbances which may be present. The degree to which reading is affected depends upon the severity of the disorder. Some are so severe that the children are totally unable to read; others with less involvement have difficulty only with syllabication of multi-syllable words or with development of a sight vocabulary.

Analysis of diagnostic findings and observations indicate that the following characteristics prevail among visual dyslexics:

(1) They have visual discrimination difficulties and confuse letters or words which appear similar. Some fail to note internal detail and confuse words such as *beg* and *bog;* others cannot see the general configurations of words such as *ship* and *snip.* In learning to read it is necessary to assimilate both the details and the general configuration, as well as the relation of the parts to the whole.

(2) *Rate* of perception is slow. Although accurate in discriminations, some scrutinize words slowly and cannot rapidly recognize them as being the same or different. The letter matching exercise in Illustration 21 was given to a group of dyslexics. Those with auditory involvements could complete it in less than a minute. In contrast, an eight-year-old visual dyslexic required five minutes of concentrated effort. Not only was he slow in scanning letters but he had to look at the model several times while completing a single row.

Those whose rate of visual perception is limited have difficulty recognizing both pictures and words presented tachistoscopically at a rapid rate. The response of one child was, "I saw something on the screen and I saw some straight lines but I do not know what it was."

(3) Many show reversal tendencies both in reading and writing, tending to read *dig* for *big.*

(4) Some have inversion tendencies and misread *u* for *n* or *m* for *w.* The effect of such a disturbance is shown in the writing of a six-year-old who tried to copy the letters in Illustration 22.

(5) Visual dyslexics have difficulty following and retaining visual sequences. When given a series of block letters to arrange in order, they cannot duplicate the pattern. If they see the word *pan* and are given letters to arrange in the same way, they distort the order and spell the word *pna* or *nap* or *apn.* Some follow the sequence when a model is present but cannot revisualize the sequence from memory; they know all of the letters in the word but cannot remember their order.

(6) They have many visual memory disorders. Some cannot remember either nonverbal or verbal experiences. A fourteen-year-old nonreader could neither describe his home nor remember whether his very blond brother had light or dark hair. This revisualization deficit may affect other forms of behavior so that numbers, musical notes, or other types of figures cannot be remembered. In most instances, however, the greatest problem is in memory for the printed word.

(7) Drawings by visual dyslexics tend to be inferior and lacking in detail. Relevant details are omitted, even in drawing simple objects from their everyday environment.

(8) Many have problems with visual analysis and synthesis. When given two-piece puzzles of letters or words they are unable to arrange the

VISUAL DISCRIMINATION

1. <u>a</u> c d a e o u i a
2. <u>b</u> t d p d b k q b
3. <u>c</u> o c e c c o e u
4. <u>d</u> l d h p t d b q
5. <u>e</u> e o a u c c e e
6. <u>f</u> l f h t f h f l
7. <u>g</u> y g p g q p b d
8. <u>h</u> l h h f l f t k
9. <u>i</u> i l i t h j i l
10. <u>j</u> i l t j i t j t

ILLUSTRATION 21. Exercise for developing rapid visual discrimination of letters.

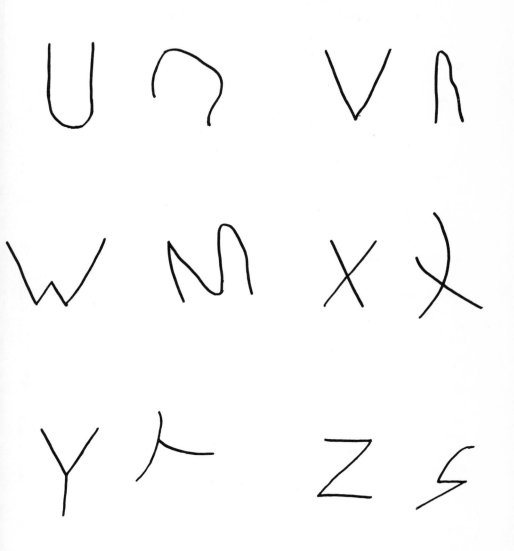

ILLUSTRATION 22. Copying of a six-year-old dyslexic.

parts properly. Some also have difficulty doing jigsaw puzzles indicating that they cannot relate the parts to the whole.

(9) On reading readiness and reading diagnostic tests visual dyslexics show a marked breakdown on visual skills as compared with auditory skills. They are especially deficient on subtests involving visual memory and coding. Hence, it is important to do an item analysis of the test findings since a child can demonstrate average reading readiness by his composite score, because of falling above average on auditory functions.

(10) They prefer auditory activities. On occasion a child is so good auditorially that he memorizes stories he hears at home or at school and it is only when he is asked to read a word in isolation that the teacher realizes that he cannot read, that he merely remembers what he hears other children say.

(11) Certain types of games or sports are troublesome. A nine-year-old boy enjoyed playing catch with his father but could neither participate nor even watch a baseball game because he could not visually grasp what was happening. Many do not enjoy activities such as building models; however, others perform well until they are given the printed instructions.

Educational Procedures

The visual dyslexic rarely is able to learn by an ideo-visual approach since he cannot associate words with their meanings. He cannot retain the visual image of a whole word and consequently needs a more phonetic or elemental approach to reading. A fifteen-year-old said that he could recognize only three words immediately; they were *stop, no,* and *yes.* He was of average intelligence, spoke fluently, was excellent in shop and woodworking, but could not read. One might ask why a boy with these integrities had not acquired more words on his own or from regular classroom instruction. This is the critical issue; he was unable to make spontaneous associations between the printed word and its meaning. Certain methodologies stress teaching fifty to one hundred sight vocabulary words before beginning work on phonics or analytical skills. The dyslexic boy mentioned above had spent eight years in school but had learned only three words. It was virtually impossible for him to learn fifty words or even ten words as unique wholes.

For this type of disability reading instruction begins with the presentation of short visual units (generally single letters) which can be blended into words. Simultaneously he receives training in other deficit areas, e.g., visual memory and sequentialization. The purpose of the instruction is to give him a systematic means of attacking words, but also to aid him in learning a sight vocabulary. Because of his specific visual deficits, instant recognition of whole words may occur only after months or even years of training. We cannot wait until a child builds up all visual skills before teaching him to read. After ten months of training a severe visual dyslexic remarked that he could finally see words in his mind.

The purpose of all reading instruction is to give the child a means of identifying the words he sees. The normal child uses many clues including word form, context, structural and phonetic analysis. Because of specific learning deficits the dyslexic has only a few clues available. He is much more limited in the means whereby he can identify words. It should be emphasized that his problem is not one of verbal comprehension, but is an inability to release or unlock meanings. If he were able to transduce the visual symbol to its auditory equivalent he would have no difficulty understanding the material.

The approach to remediation which has been most successful with this type of dyslexic is similar to that described by Gillingham and Stillman (1940), referred to as an alphabetic or phonovisual approach. Basically, it involves teaching isolated sounds or phonograms and blending them into meaningful words. Since this approach requires a high degree of auditory integrity, the teacher must evaluate the child's ability to blend sounds. If he is unable to combine two or three sounds, this approach is not the most satisfactory; a whole word approach with some emphasis on taction and kinesthesis would be used.

Teach letter sounds. Select two or three consonants which are different both in appearance and sound (m, t, s). Make certain that the child can differentiate one letter from another. Each letter is written on a flash card in lower case with heavy, black ink. It is unnecessary to use large print since some children with visual disabilities cannot grasp the whole if letters are too big. Letters varying from two to three inches in height have been most successful. The important factors are the clarity of the stimulus and the consistency of form. (If letters are not well formed or if lines are irregular, the child cannot recognize them quickly.) The type of print should be kept constant. The letter a, for example, should not be written as it is in text books at one time and in lower case manuscript at another. Similarly, capitals should not be introduced until the child has a degree of ability to read words in lower case print.

While holding one of the flash cards *say the sound of the letter*. The letter name (*es* for *s*) is not introduced at this time. Many dyslexics are confused if given both the sound and name of the letter. The letter is pronounced as it is heard in a word so he can relate the auditory and visual components of words. After it is said for him *ask the child to say the sound*.

When using this approach to reading it is important that neither the teacher nor child say consonants followed by a vowel sound. The *p* should be said lightly and not pronounced "puh." If the vowel sound is accentuated it is nearly impossible for children to blend sounds into words. An eight-year-old tried to sound out the word *pat* but said, "puh—a—tuh—puh–a–tuh? What does that mean?" Gillingham (1956) also stressed the importance of an easy production of consonant sounds to avoid distortions in pronunciation.

Teach words that begin with each sound. Next, ask the child to think of words that begin with each sound. Generally the visual dyslexics are able to think of several words; those with auditory involvement need help with this type of task.

Teach identification of letter to its sound. After presenting three or four consonants, show the child the flash cards and ask him to identify the letter that goes with the sound you say. ("Give me the *m*.") The purpose is to build a strong association between the visual and auditory symbols and to help him transduce from one form to the other. When he hears a sound, he must know how it looks, and when he sees a letter, he should be able to recall the sound.

In some instances it is necessary to utilize taction and kinesthesis. If, after several trials, the child is unable to make the visual-auditory associations, he should be encouraged to trace over the letters while simultaneously saying the letter sound. This step is not always necessary and should be used only when indicated. *Some are confused by the multisensory stimulation and do less well when bombarded from all modalities.*

Word-sound associations. These are rarely taught. Whereas some methods stress the teaching of a sound in association with a key word (*a* for *apple*), we have found this technique confusing to many dyslexics. A boy who had been taught by this method was unable to dissociate the key word from the sound and therefore could not read words correctly. When trying to sound out the word *pet* he said, "p—elephant e—t." He had been taught to think of the word *elephant* in connection with the short *e* and could not eliminate it when attacking new words. Those who are good auditorially sometimes memorize sounds and key words for the entire alphabet while listening to the teacher say them, but still are unable to read because they have not associated the sound with the letter.

Occasionally the auditory dyslexic profits from sound-word associations since he needs to hear a sound in relation to a word. In rare instances the visual dyslexic uses a word cue but of a different type. He profits from a visual nonverbal cue used in association with a letter. A fourteen-year-old could not remember the sound of *w* so he carried a small card in his pocket with the letter written next to the picture of a window. The picture helped him think of the sound.

After the dyslexic has learned three or four consonants, *present one or two vowel sounds.* Generally the short *a* and the short *i* or the long vowel

combination *ee* are the easiest to learn. Those who have both auditory
and visual problems may need to have the long vowels presented first
inasmuch as they are easier to differentiate auditorially. If, however, the
dyslexic is good auditorially and can discriminate short vowels, these are
presented first since he has only a single visual unit to remember, whereas
he must remember two-letter combinations when learning long vowel
sounds (*ai, ay, ea, oa*). The stress is on the simplest auditory-visual
correspondence possible, that is, on letter-sound representations.

Only one sound is taught with each letter or letter combination; exceptions will be presented later. Some reading specialists do not recommend
teaching isolated sounds on the basis that children will have to unlearn
some things they learned previously. If, for example, they learn the short
sound of *e*, they must learn that it sounds different in the words *me* and
men. Nevertheless, slow readers need a systematic approach to reading in
the early periods of training and they need not be told all of the exceptions
until they have established some ability to read. The teacher of children
with learning disabilities who presents all of the possible sounds of the
single vowel *e* in the first few lessons will only confuse the children.
Therefore, one sound is given for each letter.

Blend sounds into meaningful words. As soon as the child knows a few
consonants and vowels, teach him to blend these sounds into meaningful
words. He is not taught to blend sounds into nonsense syllables but to
read the words in his spoken vocabulary. The blending must be done
smoothly to prevent jerkiness, distortions, and faulty pronunciation of
the word. To avoid breakdowns in blending it is helpful to begin with
words composed of nasal consonants and vowels so there are no pauses
between letters (*man, am, nap*). Occasionally a line is drawn under the
words to illustrate the need for smooth, even blending of the sounds.
Immediately after the sounds have been blended into a word, *ask the child
to tell what it means and use it in a sentence.* In the past, critics of a strong
phonics approach felt that comprehension might suffer; however, if
meaning is included there is little need for concern.

The visual dyslexic has no difficulty comprehending what he reads; his
problem is *reaching* the meaning. He cannot go from the visual symbol to
meaning; therefore, our emphasis is on auditory-visual associations. One
of the major reasons for teaching only meaningful words is that this provides the child with a means of monitoring what he reads. When sounding
out words, he can use meaning as a checking device. Thus, when sounding
out the word *man*, he does not accept his own inaccurate attempts (*m–u–n*
or *m–i–n*) because he realizes that these do not constitute words. When
he is asked to practice on nonsense syllables he has no idea whether he
has produced them correctly. Only when he knows that all of the words

in a given list are meaningful can he become more adept at checking his own errors.

Present word families. When success has been gained on a few simple words, present word families. From the word *man* show him how he can change the initial consonant to form other words (*pan, fan, ran*). Final consonants also should be varied to form other words (*pat, fat, rag, rat*). An important factor to remember in teaching the dyslexic is that he cannot manipulate the letters to form word families "in his mind." The letters must be observable so that he can see how the words are alike, then he must go through the physical operation of changing the initial or final consonants. Hence, anagrams or cutout letters are used frequently.

Introduce two-letter consonant blends. The child is now required to remember longer visual units, but, if necessary, he can still read individual sounds. He repeats the blend several times and is encouraged to think of both the sequence of the sounds and the letters. He must relate a temporal sequence with a visual sequence and note the change in sounds when letters are arranged in a different order (*ts, st; sk, ks*).

Many new words can be added to the reading vocabulary after consonant blends are learned since they can be placed in either the final or the initial position (*plan, stand, grab, step, rust, stop, rest, bets, best*). The child is encouraged to think of the blend as a single unit but he may need to sound them out individually until they are well established.

Introduce long vowel combinations and consonant groupings that are represented by a single sound. The child is now told that he will see two or more letters but he will hear only one sound (*ay, ee, oa, th, wh, ch, sh*). This is frequently a difficult step for the visual dyslexic whose memory span is short. However, if he has achieved success in reading words which have a consistent sound for letter correspondence he usually can master it. Very few rules are taught. Some advocate teaching principles, such as, "When two vowels are seen together the first one says its own name"; however, rules assume ability to remember, to generalize, and to apply principles. Children with learning disabilities are inferior in this type of application so they do not respond well to use of rules. Some can memorize the rules but not apply them; others, whose memories are deficient, are frustrated because they cannot remember the rules. Therefore, the vowel or letter combinations are presented with a simple statement—e.g., "When you see these two letters together, they usually say ____." Likewise, the terminology "short vowels" or "long vowels" is confusing because some think of a letter which should *look* short or long. Moreover, it requires that they go through a translation process to determine the meaning of a short vowel or a long vowel.

The reading vocabulary taught in the early stages of training is highly phonetic. Words are selected on the basis of the consistency of sound to letter or auditory-visual correspondence so that the child has a systematic means of attacking them. The words should include sounds or combinations of sounds that have been taught and should be part of the spoken language vocabulary.

A considerable amount of writing and spelling is used in this approach to teaching reading. No child is asked to write that which he cannot read, but as soon as he has learned to sound out a few words, he is asked to write them. Writing reinforces reading and assists development of transducing processes. When he sees the letter, he should know how it sounds, and when he hears it, he should know how it looks. Throughout the training there is emphasis on helping the visual dyslexic look for pronunciation units within words. When he looks at a word, he should see letters or letter groupings which represent auditory patterns.

Simple sentences, paragraphs and stories. As soon as the child can read several words, write simple sentences, paragraphs, and stories for him to read. A few sight vocabulary words (I, the, you, they, and others) which are essentially nonphonetic are introduced through context, but the majority should be easy to sound out. Although the sentences and vocabulary are slightly stereotyped at first because of the phonetic vocabulary, children are pleased when they can finally read more than single words. If they can attack most of the words in a paragraph systematically, they can begin to grasp the sight vocabulary from context. The teacher can write stories about the child's experiences and, using a sense of humor, she can write clever stories which contain his reading vocabulary. Students in training have written delightful short stories entitled "Slim Jim," "The Fat Cat," etc.

In writing the stories the sentence structure should be similar to the child's spoken language so he has a means of anticipating the next word in the sentence. Some children's books contain phonetic vocabularies but have rather distorted sentence structure. Although appealing to the average youngster, they are difficult for the dyslexic who must rely on the "feel" of the next word in context. He senses this only when the sentence structure is similar to his spoken language.

The child should have a large enough reading vocabulary so that he does not experience failure when reading books are introduced. Before trying to read a page he is asked to scan it to see if there are words he does not know. The teacher then helps him with the difficult words before he begins. This is to prevent a break in the flow of his reading and thinking.

Improving Visual Deficits

As indicated previously, an elemental phonic approach is used with the visual dyslexic in the initial stages of training. However, every effort is made to build deficient visual functions so that eventually he can learn to read without going through auditory analytical processes. Not all visual dyslexics need every procedure outlined here; some may require assistance only in noting sequence or directional detail. Nevertheless, the teacher should be aware of the several types of disturbances and be prepared to deal with them.

Prepare materials carefully. Because the problem is one of visual interpretation, it is especially important that materials be selected and prepared with care. Figures should be neat, boundaries should be well defined, and printed materials should be clear and well spaced. Some children do not grasp the whole if materials are unusually large, but those to be traced must be large enough so the child can feel the variations in line and form.

Improve scanning and develop orderly inspection of materials. When teaching visual discrimination and memory skills, it is necessary to develop improved habits of "looking." Frequently children with learning disabilities are not consistent or orderly in their inspection of materials. Those who are distractible skip back and forth from the beginning to the end of a word and, rather than making a careful inspection, fixate on details and do not notice the important features.

Although the ultimate goal is to help these children recognize words immediately, it may be necessary to "lead their looking." For example, encourage systematic scrutiny of words such as *walk* and *wall* by covering all of the letters except the two *w*'s. Gradually expose the second, third, and fourth letters and encourage the child to compare words letter by letter in this systematic fashion.

In work concerned with skill in matching or discrimination, make certain that the children understand the concepts of *same* and *different*. Many times they fail tasks, not because of a visual discrimination problem, but because they do not know what they are expected to do; they do not understand the language used in the instructions. When comprehension problems are noted, the teacher should reduce the language to the lowest possible level.

Balance input stimulation. It cannot be assumed that children with visual learning disturbances profit from doing exercises designed to improve the visual skills of normal children. They do not make generalizations from casual visual inspection; they must have supplemental cues to help them see similarities and differences in letters and words. The task of the teacher is to determine whether the child improves most by providing stimulation from all modalities, from combining audition and vision, from combining kinesthesis and vision, or from periodic reduction of vision and emphasis on kinesthesis. Although the diagnostic test results are useful, the teacher may need a trial learning session to determine the most effective means of achieving this vital balance for learning.

General Form and Configuration

The child who tends to identify letters or words on the basis of detail should have training to assist him in scrutinizing the general outline of a figure. Strauss and Lehtinen (1947) stress relating the whole to the part in order to recognize a figure immediately and uniquely. The child must learn that a *j* and an *i* are not the same even though they have dots over them; he must note the general shape of the letters. Likewise, he must learn that an *e* and a *c* are not the same even though their general configuration is similar. The following techniques assist children in noting the outlines and form. It is beneficial to begin below the child's level of functioning to give him a feeling of success. Therefore, initially, work with pictures and pre-letter forms is recommended:

(1) **Match pictures to outline drawings.** Select a picture of a cup and draw a heavy black line around the edge. Prepare an outline of the cup on another card and have the child match the outline to the picture.

(2) **Match objects to outlines.** Select several flat objects (penny, paper clip, key). Draw outlines of the objects on paper and have the child place the object within the proper form. If he has difficulty, ask him to trace around the object with his finger and feel its shape and form. Next ask him to select other objects and draw around them; then ask him to remove the object and observe the shape that he has drawn.

(3) **Draw designs or pre-letter forms** on flash cards with heavy black ink. Draw a second set on onionskin paper. Have the child superimpose figures and determine whether they are the same.

(4) **Prepare figures** (squares, rectangles, triangles, circles, and other geometric figures) from posterboard, cardboard, or wood. Leave the designs unmounted so the child has ample opportunity to feel the entire figure and superimpose one figure on another. If the figures are mounted, he is unable to readily compare the forms. Give him two of the cutout figures and ask him to tell whether they look alike. If he cannot, have him close his eyes and feel if they are the same. Although even preschool children are expected to be able to distinguish between similarities and differences in geometric figures, it is not unusual for older children with learning disabilities to find this difficult.

(5) **Prepare exercises** as in Illustration 23 for those who cannot perceive the general configuration of words. First have the child draw around the word *where*, observing that the *h* is taller than the other letters. Next have him write each letter in the boxes provided. At the bottom of the page he must relate the general outline of the word to its shape and write it in the proper box.

where

home

mitten

and   that   kitten

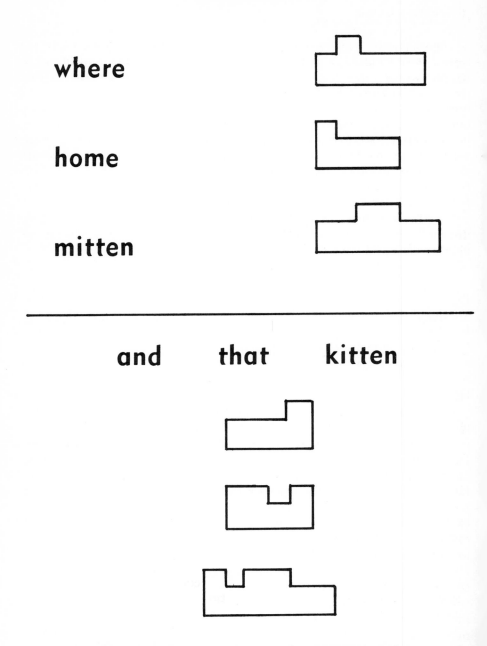

ILLUSTRATION 23. Exercise for teaching general configuration.

Perceiving Detail

In contrast with the problem discussed above, some children identify words on the basis of general configuration without perceiving detail. They misread words such as *come* and *came* because they do not see differences in the second letter, or they misread words with *e* and *o* because they fail to note the horizontal line in the *e*. Without discouraging their use of general configuration, exercises should be given to assist them in becoming aware of internal and external details in figures, letters, and words.

(1) **Prepare drawings** as in Illustration 24. Draw the internal designs (the door of the house or the horizontal line of the circle) in a different color so the child will observe it more closely.

(2) **Prepare figures** for use on the flannelgraph. Cut two large outlines of figures (houses, faces, etc.). Place parts of the figures within the outline (doors, window, eyes, nose, different shaped mouth, etc.) and have the child tell whether they are the same, or have him arrange parts in the same way as the teacher's model. Cutout figures are preferable since the pieces can be manipulated to illustrate similarities and differences. Often the child with a learning disability is unable to work with mental images so he must be shown how things look by moving a part from one place to another.

(3) **Use anagrams and cutout letters** for those whose greatest problem is in reading. Arrange sequences of letters, i.e., *come* and *came*, and ask the child whether they are the same. Show him the differences by removing the *o* from one word and superimposing it on the *a* in the second word. Then ask him to select a letter that would make the two words exactly the same.

Orientation of Letters

Analysis of visual reading skills should give consideration to problems associated with orientation of letters on the page. In English there are many symbols which are similar in general configuration but which differ in their position when printed. For example, the *u* and the *n* are merely inverted versions of the same general configuration. Similarly, the *b, d, p* and *q* are the same shape but vary in rotation and orientation on the page. Some dyslexics are able to make differentiations of general shape but have great difficulty with rotated figures. A disability of this type affects both reading and writing.

Money (1962) states that children are confronted with two different spatial problems, position and orientation. In the child's early development he learns that a dog is a dog whether it is standing up or lying down but when he begins to read, he learns there is only one acceptable position for each letter. He cannot write the letter *u* upside down because then he

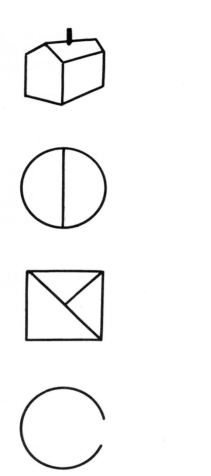

ILLUSTRATION 24. Exercise for teaching perception of details.

has written a symbol which sounds different and which changes the meaning of a word.

As with other discrimination skills the concept of *position* must be clear to the child. He must be fully cognizant of what is expected; if he does not know that he is to give attention to the position of letters, he will not be successful. The teacher can establish the importance of position by having him perform various activities, i.e., turning objects in various positions to demonstrate differences in appearance.

When working on pre-letter forms or letters it is suggested that unmounted figures be used so they can be rotated and manipulated. Often the child cannot visualize or manipulate figures in his mind. Cutout figures which can be rotated or superimposed on others are useful in helping him perceive similarities and differences.

(1) *Select two or three toy* cars and place them in various positions on a table. Ask the child to tell whether they are all going the same way or ask him to select the car that is going in a different direction. Similar exercises can be done with pictures like those found in reading readiness books, but real objects are recommended first.

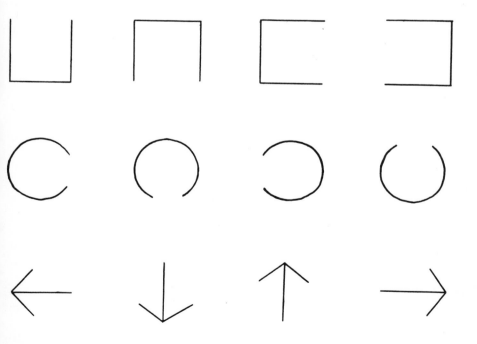

ILLUSTRATION 25. Exercise for teaching position of figures.

(2) *Prepare exercises* as seen in Illustration 25. Ask the child to look closely at the first figure in each row and find another that is the same. If he has difficulty, prepare figures, i.e., arrows or three-sided figures, from posterboard. Turn them in different directions and have the child match those that are the same or tell which one in a group is different. If he fails to *see* the differences, taction should be used to help him *feel* the patterns. A seven-year-old who could not match the figures finally learned to make the discrimination after tracing over them. The teacher guided his finger over each figure and simultaneously said, "left-down-right" or "down-right-up," etc. She continued with each of the designs and after about four repetitions the boy said, "I got it . . . I can *see* it. They're all going a different way." This realization came only after combining tactual-kinesthetic stimulation with auditory directions.

Visual Sequentialization

Among the learning disabilities seen in dyslexics is a disturbance in sequentialization. They are unable to follow specific patterns or remember the order of letters in words. Reading involves not only the differentiation of letters but the patterning of letters within a word. The letters of the word *dog* cannot be written in any other order. Disturbances of sequence are common and often persist longer than others. Long after a child has fluency in reading, his problems in sequentialization may be evident in spelling as illustrated below:

> Model Sentence: This is a girl.
> Child's Writing: Htis si a gril.

The teacher must first establish the concept of sequence, helping the child understand that it is a particular *order* which he should try to visualize. If the deficits are serious and the child is in the early grades of school, use nonsymbolic activities rather than letters.

(1) *Arrange colored beads* on a string according to a specific pattern, e.g., red, blue, red, blue, and have him continue the pattern, or have a pattern completed and ask him to make one like the model. Increase the complexity of the pattern as he improves (red, blue, blue, red, blue, blue).

(2) *Have the children* in class line up according to specific orders—boy, girl, boy, girl. Let them observe themselves in a large mirror so they can see the order, or rhythmically chant the order in which they are to stand. Sometimes they learn to revisualize a sequence by auditorizing.

(3) *Prepare patterns* of pictures or designs to be placed on bulletin boards or walls of room. Start the pattern and ask the children to complete the sequence.

(4) *Make paper chains* of colored strips, encouraging the children to develop their own patterns.

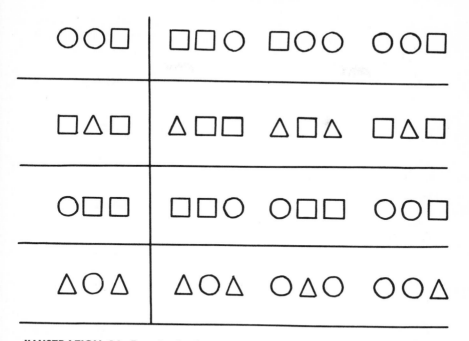

ILLUSTRATION 26. Exercise for improving visual nonverbal sequentialization.

(5) *Older children* are given printed exercises as shown in Illustrations 26, 27, and 28. These materials can be prepared for duplication or converted for use in various types of teaching machines. The Autoscore* has been especially useful for children with visual learning disabilities. The purpose of the first exercise is to help the child perceive a nonsymbolic sequence. He is to find the pattern of circles, squares, and triangles that is like the first in each row (Illustration 26). The second exercise (Illustration 27) is to be used with those who have begun to read but who persist in making errors of sequence. A picture cue is provided to make them think of the sound of the word; then the auditory sequence (temporal sequence) must be related to a visual-spatial sequence. The last worksheet (Illustration 28) also is for children who distort sequence in reading or spelling. They are to select a word from one of the five on the right which shows how the letters should be arranged.

Rate of Discrimination

Many dyslexics can match and discriminate words if given enough time, but speed of perception is seriously deficient. As a result they fail to

* Autoscore: Astra Corporation, New London, Connecticut.

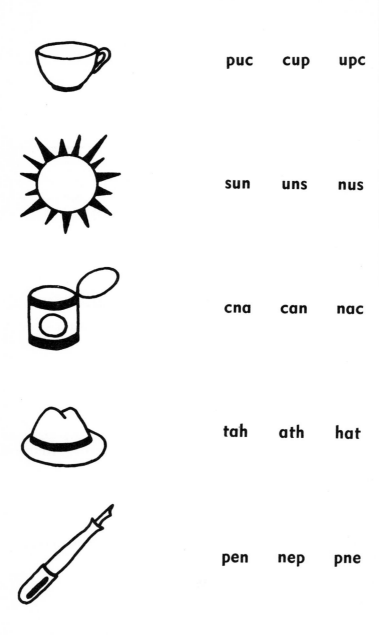

ILLUSTRATION 27. Exercise for teaching sequentialization of letters in words.

	swing
	sting
string	spring
	string
	sling
	trail
	lariat
train	train
	tain
	rain
	fast
	safe
fast	tars
	hats
	staff
	shoe
	show
show	wash
	wish
	sash
	pets
	step
stop	stop
	bets
	spit

ILLUSTRATION 28. Exercise for teaching letter sequence.

develop a sight vocabulary and cannot instantly recognize words. Although our chief concern is with accuracy in reading, time also should be spent on improving rate.

(1) *Prepare exercises* like those in Illustration 29. The child is not required to read the words but must find a word in each row that is the same as the first. Time records are kept to demonstrate progress. A fourteen-year-old nonreader, working steadily, completed the exercise in seven minutes and twenty seconds. Two weeks later his speed was two minutes and thirty seconds.

(2) *Utilize tachistoscopic presentations.* Present various stimuli including pictures, letters, digits, and words at varying speeds. Initially the child is presented with a set of figures and is asked to find the one that corresponds to the one seen on the screen. Later he is given no visual cue and is asked to tell what he saw. Encourage rapid recognition of the

VISUAL DISCRIMINATION

Draw a ring around the words that are the same in each row:

no	in	on	no	an	me	no	ma	no
bed	dab	bid	bed	bad	dub	bud	bed	bed
lap	tap	lap	pal	lip	lap	lab	lap	pal
top	tap	pot	tip	top	pot	tpo	pit	top
now	new	nor	now	won	win	won	now	now
rat	rat	tar	rag	tar	rat	tan	rot	tar
was	sew	war	saw	was	saw	was	saw	was
spot	tops	spot	step	pots	spot	tops	step	
meat	neat	team	meal	meat	meet	meat	team	neat
star	star	rats	stir	tars	star	rats	star	stir
keep	peek	keep	peel	seep	peek	leap	weep	keep
ten	tan	tin	net	ten	ton	net	not	ten
from	from	term	from	from	them	form	from	from

ILLUSTRATION 29. Exercise for developing rapid visual discrimination of words.

figure by preparing sets of pictures or words which are grossly different in configuration (a bat, a ball, a house). As he improves increase the difficulty by requiring closer discrimination of pictures (apple, orange, egg).

Similarly, when using words, show the child a card containing three words of varying lengths (hat, mitten, something). Flash one of the words on the screen and ask him to mark the one on the card that is the same as the one seen on the screen. Tell him not to be concerned about reading the words but to concentrate on the length and general configuration.

When visual dyslexia is present, learning does not occur in the usual manner. Although the goals and materials may be similar to those for normal children, specific techniques to improve the deficit in learning must be applied. Each procedure is designed with a particular goal in mind but the ways in which it is used depend upon the combination of deficits and integrities found. Our concern is not only with achievement in reading but with processing. Through these procedures the child develops strategies which are useful to him in learning to read and which are transferable to other learning situations.

AUDITORY DYSLEXIA

Although reading is primarily a visual symbol system, many auditory integrities are essential for its acquisition. These integrities include ability to distinguish similarities and differences in sounds, to perceive a sound within a word, to synthesize sounds into words, and to divide them into syllables. If a child cannot perform these intrasensory auditory functions, he will have difficulty learning to read. Although some who cannot normally learn to read have a history of speech or language disorders, these are not universal characteristics. The auditory capacities necessary for reading, especially those involved in relating a temporal sequence to a visual-spatial sequence, differ from those required for speaking. The latter concerns the relationship of a temporal to a motor sequence. Thus, there is not always a direct correlation between speech and reading problems.

The *ways* in which reading is affected in the auditory dyslexic vary from those of the visual dyslexic. The visual dyslexic cannot learn whole words; but this may be the principle means whereby the auditory dyslexic learns them. He cannot synthesize sounds into words or analyze words into parts; consequently, he does not learn with an alphabetic or phonic approach. The auditory dyslexic, unlike the child with visual disabilities, may be able to associate the word *milk* with the liquid inside the carton after seeing it several times; however, he does not relate visual components of words to their auditory equivalents. That is, he sees the similarities in word parts but does not relate them to their auditory counterparts so he does not make the generalizations required in learning to read.

Moreover, unlike the normal child he does not relate a part of a word to the whole and therefore must learn each new word as a unique entity. The average first-grader is taught the word *look* and retains both the auditory and visual image. Later when he sees the word *book*, he mentally compares it with the word *look*, sees the similarities in word endings, relates it to the sound, and changes the initial consonant so he can read the new word *book*. The auditory dyslexic does not have this facility. As a result he does not learn to read words unless he can make a direct association between the symbol and the experience, or unless each new word is said for him.

Characteristic problems of the auditory dyslexic are:

(1) They have numerous auditory discrimination and perceptual disorders which impede use of phonetic analysis. One of the most common is the inability to "hear" the similarities in initial or final sounds of words. The child does not perceive the similarities in the words *boy* and *big* or the final sounds in the words *mat* and *cat*. Others are unable to hear the double sounds of consonant blends in *rust*, *bent*, or *sift* and thereby read or spell them as if they had only one final consonant (rut, bet, sit).

Discrimination of short vowel sounds is one of the greatest problems of the auditory dyslexic. Although he understands words such as *pin*, *pan* and *pen* in context, he is unable to perceive differences among them when they are heard in isolation. Neither can he recognize a rhyme or think of words that rhyme. In contrast with the normal six- or seven-year-old who enjoys making nonsense words that sound alike (silly, willy, nilly, dilly), many auditory dyslexics, even at high school age, are unable to think of two words that rhyme. They cannot listen for a part of a word and think of another whole word with the same ending. A thirteen-year-old boy said, "I just can't hear that part in the word." Because of one or more of these auditory disturbances, rarely is the dyslexic able to make generalizations about new words that he encounters.

(2) These dyslexics have difficulty with auditory analysis and synthesis. Although their spoken language generally is good, those with a disturbance of analysis cannot break a word into syllables or into individual sounds. When given the word, *table*, they cannot separate the syllables, or when given a one-syllable word, *cat*, they cannot dissect it into its individual sounds. Generally they find it easier to analyze words into syllables than into individual sounds, but many can do neither. A disturbance in auditory analysis affects both reading and spelling. It interferes with the development of syllabication skills for reading, and because of an inability to break a word into its various components, entire syllables may be omitted when writing.

Those with problems of synthesis cannot combine parts of words to form a whole. Consequently, when trying to sound out a new word, they cannot retain each of the syllables and put them together. We have observed children with this disability who knew all of the letter sounds but, because of an inability to blend, were unable to learn to read by a phonic or elemental approach.

(3) Many in this group cannot reauditorize sounds or words. When they look at a letter they cannot remember its sound, or when they look at a word they are unable to say it even though they know its meaning. The auditory dyslexic, therefore, may be able to read silently better than orally. He associates words with meaning but cannot transduce the visual symbol to the auditory. Like many adult brain damaged individuals, he substitutes words when reading aloud. An eight-year-old could match sentences to pictures, but when asked to read the sentence, "The dog is eating his dinner," she read, "The puppy is eating the food." In speaking, we have freedom to select a word from several with similar meanings, but in reading the auditory symbol must correspond precisely with the visual symbol. Because of these various types of disturbances, it is critical that more than one measure of reading be used. A sixth-grade boy scored at grade 4.2 in silent reading vocabulary, grade 3.8 in silent reading comprehension, but only at grade 2.9 in oral reading because of numerous substitutions when reading aloud.

(4) Some have a disturbance in auditory sequentialization. If their non-verbal skills are impaired, these children cannot follow a rhythm pattern and may not enjoy music. If auditory verbal symbolic functions are affected, they may distort the pronunciation of multisyllable words (*emeny* for *enemy*), or when writing, they may transpose letters because they cannot retain a sequence of sounds.

(5) Behaviorally, auditory dyslexics tend to prefer visual activities. Many are good in shop, woodworking, and athletics. They are inferior on tasks which involve auditory memory, sequence, and discrimination. On reading readiness and reading diagnostic tests they are below average in memory for sentences, in blending, syllabication, and rhyming.

Educational Procedures

Children with auditory involvements respond best to a whole word or ideo-visual approach during the initial stages of reading instruction. Because of their problems in auditory perception, memory, and integration, they are unable to handle the skills required for phonetic analysis; in fact, some may be able to develop auditory skills only after having learned a sight vocabulary. As with the visual dyslexic, however, debilitated functions cannot be ignored. Even though able to learn by a global method, he cannot possibly retain visual images for every word; therefore, he must acquire a systematic means of attacking unfamiliar words.

The visual dyslexic begins by learning the sounds of letters and integrating them into wholes; the auditory dyslexic, in contrast, works from the whole to the part.

Develop auditory-visual correspondence. Often it is necessary for the teacher to begin instruction by explaining to the children that things have names we can *hear* or *see* and that what we *say* also can be written. Some auditory dyslexics, in particular, are unaware of the relationship between the spoken word and the printed symbol. In attempting to achieve auditory-visual integration, it is essential that the child know what constitutes a word. Many do not know that a unit of letters divided by spaces represents a word; some think, for example, that each letter represents a word. Therefore, the teacher should illustrate that the spaces are the dividing lines between words we can see or say. She might select a child's favorite book, "The Three Bears," and say the title for him. For example, "Listen, I will say the name of your book and I want you to tell me how many words you hear." While reading the title, speak the words slowly and hold up a finger for each word. Show him the cover of the book and ask him to tell how many words he sees. Finally, ask him to point to each word as you say it. Ability to relate an auditory symbol to a visual symbol is critical for both reading and spelling. If it is not clear, children tend to add, omit, or substitute words when they read, or they combine two words into a single word when they write. A ninth-grader wrote *plejalegeance* for *pledge allegiance.* Auditory-visual correspondence should be emphasized in order to learn the sounds of individual letters as well as of individual words.

Select a meaningful reading vocabulary. We begin with words that are in the child's spoken vocabulary and which are different in both auditory and visual configuration. Words are selected which look and sound different so that he can identify them more easily. First, nouns are presented and the child learns to match the printed symbol with an object. Make certain that he auditorily knows the name of each object before teaching him to read it. Ask him to say the name of each one and then show him the printed symbol. Words are written in manuscript form, not in cursive writing.

Relate printed symbol with experience. Label various objects in the room (door, window, toys, crayons) to help him relate the printed symbol with experience. Also point out words on cartons, boxes, or cans (milk, paste, paper). Reading is not limited, however, to object-word associations. The child should *see, hear,* and *say* the word. Since our concern is with the development of reading and auditory skills, a certain amount of oral reading is emphasized. The sequence of presentations is critical. Some cannot make the association between the printed symbol and meaning if they are asked to simultaneously say the word aloud. We first make sure that the child knows the auditory name of the object, then concentrate on matching the printed word with the object, and finally ask him to say the printed word. For reinforcement and review, exercises such as the one in Illustration 30 are provided. The child draws a line between the picture and the word. Verbs are presented in a similar fashion. First the child is told to *run, jump, or walk* and then he is shown the printed words that represent the spoken words.

Teaching machines have been useful in developing a basic sight vocabulary.

(1) The Language Master* is an electronic device into which the child inserts a card containing a picture, a printed word, and a strip of magnetic tape. When the card goes through, the child hears the word spoken twice and simultaneously sees the picture and the printed word—he sees the picture of a ball, the printed word *ball*, and hears it said twice. The child can repeat the word because dual channel tape is used and recording is provided. With equipment of this type it is critical that the child's attention be directed to the words both auditorially and visually. If he only listens and repeats the word, he will not learn to read. Similarly, the child who is deficient in meaning must relate the picture to the word; otherwise he is only transducing from the auditory to the visual without integrating meaning.

Teaching machines are not essential for good remediation but they increase effectiveness. They should not merely keep the child occupied; the materials must be designed for teaching new words or for review of those presented earlier.

(2) The Autoscore is effective in teaching a sight vocabulary but has no provisions for auditory instruction. It is used to supplement and review rather than for presenting new words. A picture is drawn on the left side of the card and two to five words are printed on the right. The child places a stylus in a hole to indicate his response. If it is correct, a light flashes to signal that he should proceed to the next item. If his response is incorrect, a buzzer sounds; the unit does not progress until he answers correctly. Although the same type of exercises can be prepared for seatwork by having the child draw a line from the picture to the correct answer, he receives no immediate reinforcement.

Introduce simple phrases and sentences. Following a developmental progression similar to that suggested for teaching children with auditory verbal comprehension disorders, we next present other parts of speech

* Language Master, Bell and Howell Co., Chicago, Illinois.

shoe

airplane

clock

key

ILLUSTRATION 30. Picture word matching exercise for dyslexics.

such as adjectives or prepositions, and develop short phrases and sentences (a red ball, a red hat, a red dress; a blue ball, a big ball, a little ball; in the house, in the barn, in the box). Sentences and action pictures can be prepared for the Language Master or for a dual channel tape recorder. A picture is pasted on the card and a sentence is recorded which is in keeping with the child's reading level. (The girl is eating. The girls are eating. The boy is running. The boys are running). The child listens to each sentence and watches each word as it is said.

Many children enjoy reading sentences which are written in the form of commands or instructions. Sentences, such as, "Turn on the light" or "Put the chair by the table," are written on cards and the child is asked to "read and do." This procedure is an effective means of evaluating reading comprehension and also provides a variation from the usual school routine. Other reading instructions can be prepared for seatwork. A series of pictures are drawn at the top of the page and instructions with a vocabulary in keeping with the child's reading level are printed below (Draw a line under the house; color the dress yellow; put an x by the tree).

Use experience stories. Many remedial teachers have found that experience stories help children learn to read. The child tells about something he has done and the teacher prints what he says. He is then encouraged to read his own story. Or, the reading lesson may begin with a direct experience, e.g., a trip to the post office, or a walk around the school grounds to see buds on flowers and trees. When the class returns, they talk about the things they have seen and write a story. Klausmeier et al. (1956) state that one of the problems in using experience charts is the number and difficulty of the words that must be included to make an interesting story. Not all of the words in an oral discussion can be taught for a sight vocabulary in one lesson, but the teacher guides the vocabulary so that it is within the reading range.

Frequently the experience stories are written with pictures drawn below some of the printed words. Thus, if the story begins, "Today our class went to the post office," a picture of boys and girls might be drawn under the word *class* and a picture of the post office under the word *post office*. These picture-word associations improve retention of a sight vocabulary. Children who are good visually (as are many of the dyslexics with auditory impairments) like to draw the pictures themselves. One of our severe auditory dyslexics learned a sight vocabulary of 300 words in ten weeks by drawing a picture to accompany each new word.

Another activity from which the children derive pleasure is writing a daily newspaper. They tell about the things they have done; the teacher types the material on stencils and duplicates it so each child has a copy to take home to read, thus receiving further enjoyment and reinforcement.

An important factor for the teacher to remember in using these techniques is that the child should not memorize the story auditorially, but that he establish an auditory-visual correspondence. He is not to rely solely on memory but to relate the words he says to the words he sees. To ascertain whether he is reading, the teacher says a word within the story and asks the child to point to it, or she points to words in random order and asks him to tell what they are.

Improving Auditory Deficits

While an ideo-visual approach is used to develop a basic reading vocabulary, simultaneous emphasis is given to debilitated auditory functions. Without this two-pronged plan the auditory dyslexic may not be able to read unfamiliar words. His visual memory, although good, is inadequate for remembering all words he encounters and he cannot always rely on context to identify words. Therefore, some structural and phonetic analysis is necessary. If auditory skills remain undeveloped the affect on spelling is even greater than on reading.

Auditory Discrimination

Considerable emphasis has been given to disorders of visual perception in children with neurological dysfunction, but comparatively less attention has been given to auditory processes. A few writers (Monroe, 1932; Myklebust, 1954; Robinson, 1952; Schuell, 1964; Wepman, 1960) have stressed the importance of auditory functions in both spoken language and reading. Robinson found that a functional auditory disturbance, such as inadequate auditory discrimination or insufficient auditory memory span for sounds, was present in about forty-six percent of her sample with reading disability. More recently, Wepman reported a positive relationship between poor discrimination and poor reading. He also found that poor discrimination may be at the root of both speech and reading difficulties but often the imposition affects only reading or spelling.

The exact degree of auditory efficiency that is necessary for learning to read normally is unknown, but current research should yield more information about the balance of functions required. Gates (1947, p. 231) observed that "other things being equal–the more familiar the child is with the sound characteristics of words and the more skillful he is in identifying and blending the sound units of words, the better he is equipped to utilize the phonetic techniques." Berg (1958) used the term "listening skills" in relation to reading and concluded that:

When listening ability is low, reading ability tends to be low.

When listening ability is high, reading ability is not predictable.

When reading ability is low, listening ability is not predictable.

When reading ability is high, listening ability is to a small extent predictable, likely to be high.

Tests of auditory discrimination, like those developed by Templin (1957) and Wepman (1958), are useful in determining whether a child can distinguish similarities between syllables or words and whether remediation is indicated. However, these tests do not identify children whose primary disability is between perceiving sounds within words. Many dyslexics can tell whether two words are the same, but they cannot tell whether parts within words are similar. Because of this disability they cannot think of words that rhyme or that begin with the same sound and they cannot relate a part of one word to another. Durrell's findings (1956) are similar. He noted that the ability to tell whether words pronounced by the teacher are the same or different has little or no relationship to auditory perception of word elements—high ability in this does not indicate that the child has the background of noticing the separate sounds in words that is required by reading. The latter skill involves more auditory analysis and synthesis. Generally, the dyslexic who fails gross discrimination tasks will be poor in analysis and synthesis but the reverse is not necessarily true.

Since various types of auditory disturbances interfere with reading, the teacher must explore a child's ability to hear similarities and differences in words, to distinguish similar parts of words, to follow an auditory sequence, to blend sounds into words, and dissect word wholes into syllables or individual sounds. Not every dyslexic is deficient in all of these skills, but appropriate remediation should be provided as indicated.

Match sounds. Because many children have both discrimination and memory problems, they should not be required to remember a sound until they can compare two sounds presented simultaneously. Ask the child to say a consonant sound which can be sustained (m, s, sh, v). Tell him to continue emitting one of the sounds while you say others (r, m, l) and ask him to stop as soon as you say the one he is producing.

Encourage reauditorization. After the child can distinguish similarities and words by matching them, make the task more complex by having him reauditorize the sound (say it to himself). Tell him, "This time I want you to listen for the *m* but try to remember it without saying it aloud. I will say some other sounds and when I say *m* (the one you are thinking of) raise your hand." The latter procedure is similar to that described by Van Riper (1947) but should be preceded by sound matching so the child has an opportunity to listen and compare sounds.

Utilize visual and kinesthetic cues. While the child is producing a sound, have him concentrate on the position of the tongue and lips or watch himself in the mirror. Orton (1937) notes that differentiation of short vowel sounds is apt to be defective and that children with this difficulty learn by themselves to cultivate a visual aid, e.g., watching the lips of the speaker. Those who do not learn these strategies spontaneously need to be instructed to utilize cues from other sensory modalities. If visual cues are effective, show the child pictures of persons saying various sounds such as *oh* or *m* and have him relate the sound to the picture.

Sequentialization

Many dimensions of sequentialization are critical for learning. When learning to use spoken language, a child must hold a pattern of sounds within a word, a series of words within a sentence, and series of ideas within a story. Reading methodologists stress the importance of visual patterning inasmuch as the child must understand that letters in words remain in a particular order. Auditory sequentialization in reading is equally important and is frequently found to be deficient in dyslexics. They tend to omit or distort syllables in talking, reading, and spelling. The objective in remedial training is to instill consciousness of both the number and the order of sounds within words.

Develop awareness and recognition of nonverbal auditory patterns. Present two sets of sounds and ask the child to tell whether they are the same.

(a) *drum—jingle—drum*   vs.   *drum—jingle—drum*
(b) *drum—drum—jingle*   vs.   *jingle—drum—drum*

Present a series of rhythmic taps or code-like patterns and ask him to listen to the pairs of sounds and tell whether they are the same.

(a) . . -   vs.   . . . -
(b) - . -   vs.   - . -

Imitate sound and rhythm patterns. Place several noisemakers in front of the child. Present patterns, as described above, and ask him to imitate them. Also start a rhythmic pattern (using drums), interrupt it, and see if the child can continue it. Many dyslexics can imitate the pattern once or twice but cannot hold the sequence and continue it repetitively.

Coordinate auditory and visual patterns. Sometimes it is easier for a child to work with auditory and visual sequences simultaneously than with intrasensory auditory information. He cannot retain an auditory sequence without seeing the visual pattern. Use the code-like patterns suggested above, explaining that a short sound will be represented by a dot and a long sound by a dash. Then show him a visual sequence (. - .) and ask him to listen for the auditory pattern and determine whether it goes with the one he sees. If drum beats are used, present the visual sequence with spaces of varying lengths between dots.

(a) .. ..
(b) . ...

Develop awareness of the number of syllables within words. Repeat words of varying lengths and ask the child to tap the number of syllables in each. Modify the speed with which you say words since the rate of auditory perception is critical; some dyslexics can differentiate the number of syllables only when the sounds are heard at the rate of one per second. Gradually increase the rate until he can differentiate the number of syllables when the words are spoken at a normal rate.

Emphasize the rhythmic sequence of words. Ask the child to listen to multisyllable words and relate the rhythm of the word to visual nonverbal patterns. For example, say the word *tomato*, with a slight stress on the medial syllable and show him a nonverbal visual pattern that corresponds with the accent and rhythm of the word (. - .). Later ask him to listen to words and then draw the rhythmic sequence he hears. He need not be concerned with the sounds the letters make or with spelling, but merely concentrate on the number and pattern of syllables within a word. Note the progress of a nine-year-old dyslexic, as shown in Illustration 31.

October		
Teacher Said	*Child Drew*	
Northwestern	— —	
applesauce	— .	
typewriter	— .	
February		
Teacher Said	*Child Drew*	
potato	. — .	
Illinois	. . —	
Massachusetts	.. — .	
university	.. — ..	

ILLUSTRATION 31. Improvement in auditory sequentialization.

Blending and Integration

Ingram (1960), Gates (1947), and Myklebust and Johnson (1962) studied children who, because of synthesizing difficulties, could not construct words from their sound components. Dyslexics with this problem may know all of the letter sounds but not be able to read because they cannot combine them into words.

Blend syllables into words. After the child can differentiate the number of syllables within words, have him combine parts into wholes. Say the words *ta—ble* or *bas—ket—ball* by syllable and have him put them together. Initially, repeat the words with only a slight pause between syllables but gradually increase the length of the pause to foster reauditorization. Exercises of this type can be prepared for independent work on dual channel tape recorders. The teacher says the whole word so the child knows what he is to say; then she repeats individual syllables and asks the child to put them together.

Combine individual sounds into words. Normally it is easier for children to blend syllables than individual sounds, but emphasis should be given to both skills. Children who cannot distinguish the double consonants in *stop, lift,* or *crust* misread and misspell them. First make the child aware of the number of sounds by saying the words very slowly and making a mark on paper for each sound. After he can tell the number of sounds, repeat the word slowly, sound by sound (*s—t—o—p*), and have him blend them together.

Analysis and Synthesis

Gates (1947) observed that young children hear words as total sound units and do not realize that the same sounds occur in many different words. Typically, however, by the age of six or seven they recognize similar features in words and find pleasure in rhyming or thinking of words that start with the same sounds. In contrast, the auditory dyslexic does not make these differentiations and may not be able to do so until after he has learned a few sight vocabulary words. Although most ear training in kindergarten and first grade is oral, the dyslexic with auditory deficits needs the simultaneous presentation of visual symbols in order to learn to hear the similarities.

Utilize visual symbols to improve auditory discrimination and analysis. Write two or three words the child has learned to read and that begin or end with the same sound.

sit	ma*n*
sand	pi*n*
supper	ru*n*

First ask him if he can *see* anything that is the same in the groups of words. Ask him to underline the parts of the word that are the same. Next ask him to listen carefully when you say the words and see if he *hears* the similarities. Amplify and sustain the initial or final sounds to make certain he detects them. If he is unable to distinguish the similarities, structure the sound by using a small portable amplifier. Increase the volume slightly and repeat each word, amplifying the sounds he is to listen for. Finally, ask him to say each word, uttering the underlined sound more loudly than the others. The feedback he receives from saying *sun* or *supper* is beneficial. Training should include discrimination of sounds in the initial, final, and medial positions of words.

Use concrete, manipulative materials. Before children can execute the complex mental operation of analysis and synthesis, they must work directly with materials they can manipulate. They need to see the physical change in the appearance of a word when it is dissected and relate it to the auditory pattern. Perhaps the single most important factor in working with dyslexics is to help them perform simultaneous auditory-visual analytical operations. Use cutout letters or anagrams and ask the child to spell a word he knows, such as *man*. Ask him to say the word, then remove the initial letter and replace it with a different letter (f). Explain that the word now says *fan* but that only the first sound changed; the remainder of the word still looks and sounds the same.

Demonstrate the ways by which words can be analyzed. They can be separated by syllables and by individual sounds in many different groupings. Select words from the child's reading vocabulary in which there is close auditory-visual correspondence (letter-sound relationship). Begin with words containing consonants which can be sustained rather than with plosives. Show the child the whole word *sun* and say it. Then while he is observing, separate the letters, placing them about an inch apart. Take the first letter, say it and simultaneously move it toward the second letter; then move both toward the third letter, continuing to say the sounds while moving them together. Encourage the child to both look and listen; then ask him to perform the operation. Separate the sounds of the words in other ways so that he can see and hear various groupings (s—un, or su—n).

Encourage reauditorization and mental manipulation of sounds. The normal child works with the spoken words and pictures before the printed symbol, but the auditory dyslexic may not be able to hear sounds within words or select pictures beginning with the same sound until he first learns the printed word. Hence, the sequence of presentations in remediation is of importance.

(1) Prepare written exercises which provide visual clues to aid auditory discrimination. Write groups of rhyming words and have the child underline the ones that look the same at the end; then instruct him to say the words so he can hear as well as see the similarities.

(2) Prepare other exercises like those shown in Illustration 32, and ask the child to write a word in the blank space that rhymes with the underlined word. Provide a multiple choice so he can see the difference in the word endings. Gradually eliminate the printed symbol as he improves and

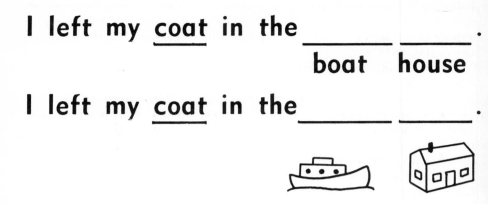

I left my <u>coat</u> in the _____ _____.

boat   house

I left my <u>coat</u> in the _____ _____.

ILLUSTRATION 32. Exercise for teaching auditory dyslexics to perceive rhyme.

replace it with a picture to encourage reauditorization without seeing the visual equivalent. Initially, it may be necessary to say the words, emphasizing the rhyming part, but gradually he should complete the exercise by thinking the words to himself.

(3) Attempt to improve and reinforce short vowel discrimination by utilizing pictures and visual letters. Present the child with a series of pictures and ask him to draw a line between the picture and the vowel sound he hears in the word.

Pictures	*Printed Letters*
pan	i
pen	a
pin	e

(4) Reduce the visual symbol (the printed word) but provide auditory stimulation until the child can internally hear the components of words. For example, give him the words in Illustration 33 and ask him to underline the one you say.

UNDERLINE THE WORD THAT YOU HEAR

1. top	tap	tip	
2. ten	tin	tan	
3. fun	fin	fan	
4. hot	hit	hat	hut
5. hum	him	ham	hem
6. pit	pat	pet	pot
7. bad	bed	bid	bud
8. big	beg	bag	bug

ILLUSTRATION 33. Exercise to improve auditory discrimination of short vowels.

ILLUSTRATION 34. Exercise for development of rhyming ability.

(5) Continue to reduce the printed symbol but provide the spoken word to assist the child in making the proper discriminations. Prepare pictures like those in Illustration 34 and ask him to mark the one that rhymes with *me* or *sock*. Later, when he can reauditorize rhyming words, use the same pictures but have him cut them apart and match those that rhyme (block and clock; bee and key).

As a parallel exercise, show the child a series of pictures and say the words (table, top, tree, boat) and ask him to mark the one that does not start with *t*. Next, provide no auditory clue (do not say the words for him), and ask him to mark the one that starts with a different sound than the others. Similar procedures are used with rhyming words. Show him pictures and say the words *ring, king, bat* and instruct him to mark the one that does not belong. Eventually reduce the auditory stimulation completely and ask him to look at the pictures, think the words, and mark those that do not start or end in the same way.

Develop higher level syllabication skills and encourage analysis of words by syllables. Select multisyllable, phonetic words from the child's sight vocabulary and write them on flash cards (corner, candy, finish). Give him a card that constitutes the first syllable of a word (cor) and then give him two or three cards and ask him to select one that completes the word. Encourage him to say them aloud while he tries to find the correct one (cor—dy; cor—ish; cor—ner). It is important that dyslexics not only learn to sound out syllables but that they be aware of meaningful and nonmeaningful units.

When he gains some facility with the manipulation of concrete materials, provide exercises as in Illustration 35. In this instance, he cannot physically manipulate the syllables but must look at them, relate the sounds to each other, and determine which groupings make a word.

Another effective exercise for teaching syllabication and spelling to dyslexics is shown in Illustration 36. Word lists are prepared in printed form and on dual channel magnetic tape. The child looks at the words in the first column, listens to the teacher and repeats them. Secondly, the teacher says each syllable, leaving a space on the tape for the child to repeat each one and then integrate them into a whole word. He is permitted to review the tapes as many times as necessary and listens to his own production to monitor his errors. The purpose of the exercise is to help the child visually identify pronunciation units in words. By separating the syllables both auditorially and visually he learns to recognize similar units in many different words. Gradually the size of the space between syllables is reduced until he can revisualize the smaller units within the whole. This technique of dividing syllables has been more effective than others, such as color cues or drawing lines between syllables. Both colors and additional lines tend to distort the image of the word as a unit, whereas the division by spaces reinforces the auditory and visual analysis.

Marked progress was noted with many dyslexics using these procedures. A class of three fourteen-year-olds received two one-hour sessions per week and improved two grades in reading over a six-month period. All three students had difficulty with auditory sequentialization and synthesis. Progress was made not only in achievement scores but in basic auditory memory processes. One of the girls in the group scored at an eight-year-level in auditory memory for sentences at the beginning of the training and at the twelve-year-level after six months of remediation.

WHICH ONE DOES NOT MAKE A WORD?

par	ty
	lor
	king
	fect
	cel

	end
ex	act
	pect
	cite
	cuse

	tain
	ment
mo	tion
	bile
	tel

ILLUSTRATION 35. Exercise for developing synthesis and syllabication.

1.	re	mem	ber	remember
2.	un	der	stood	understood
3.	de	vel	op	develop
4.	en	er	gy	energy
5.	dis	as	ter	disaster
6.	re	main	der	remainder
7.	im	prove	ment	improvement
8.	pro	tec	tion	protection

ILLUSTRATION 36. Exercise for developing analysis and synthesis.

Stress on Tactual Learning

Dyslexics who have both auditory and visual disabilities often profit from being taught through the tactual modality; procedures similar to those recommended by Fernald (1943) are used. Essentially, this is a tracing-sounding-writing method. The child selects a word he wishes to learn and the teacher writes it on a card in large script or print. He traces over the word with his forefinger, saying each part of the word as he traces it. Fernald stresses the necessity of tracing with the finger rather than with a pencil or crayon since the child learns through both tactual and kinesthetic stimulation. We modify the method according to the child's pattern of deficits and integrities. First, we use a more controlled vocabulary rather than having the child select any word he wants to learn. These first words are meaningful nouns or verbs and are relatively phonetic. The second modification pertains to the balance of stimulation. Earlier we indicated that overloading may occur when stimulation is given through modalities. Therefore, while some children need and profit from looking, saying, and tracing, others learn better by only looking and tracing; some trace over sandpaper letters with their eyes closed.

Before using these methods, a determination should be made as to whether the child perceives similarities and differences in objects or forms through touch. If he does not, there is little point in having him trace. Often we begin by having the child close his eyes, feel certain objects (a brush, a comb, a pin) and tell what they are. Later we ask him to trace over a form (circle or square) and tell what it is, or to select one of a group of visual figures that corresponds with the one he felt.

READING COMPREHENSION

The purpose of reading is to acquire meaning from the printed word. In this chapter the emphasis has been on factors which interfere with the child's ability to *reach* meaning. We do not minimize comprehension, but our clinical teaching experience and certain research studies suggest that the major problem of the dyslexic is not in *understanding* what he reads but in *transducing*, in visual-audio processing. In other words, dyslexics fail to comprehend because they cannot convert the visual symbol into the previously acquired auditory symbol.

We explored the extent to which dyslexics have difficulty with meaning by giving them comparable forms of a reading vocabulary and reading comprehension test. The first was given orally; the children listen to five words and tell which one means the same as the first, or they listen to a paragraph and answer questions. The second form was given visually (the children read). The discrepancy of performance in children who were purely dyslexic was marked. Most scored at age level or above when the test was given orally, but as much as six years below age level when they were required to read. In contrast, receptive aphasics do not show this discrepancy; their oral vocabulary is comparable to their reading level. Some with severe auditory memory span disorders do slightly better when they read because they can listen, remember, and assimilate all of the words. This rather simple, clinical procedure is helpful to the teacher in determining how much time should be spent on comprehension and how much on syllabication or word perception skills.

Many children with mixed problems need training both in word attack and in meaning. Smith and Dechant (1961) include the following as basic to understanding:

1. Ability to associate meaning with the graphic symbol

2. Ability to understand words in context and to select the meaning that fits the context

3. Ability to read in thought units

4. Ability to understand units of increasing size: the phrase, clause, sentence, paragraph, and whole selection

5. Ability to acquire word meanings

6. Ability to select and understand the main ideas

7. Ability to follow directions

8. Ability to draw inferences

9. Ability to understand the writer's organization

10. Ability to evaluate what is read: to recognize literary devices and to identify the tone, mood, and intent of the writer

11. Ability to retain ideas

12. Ability to apply ideas and to integrate them with one's past experience

These authors add that a child's comprehension can be improved by using techniques such as surveying main headings, reading for the principal ideas, reading in thought units, and forming the habit of grouping supporting details about main ideas in a thought-outline form. Passages can be written which encourage the child to note details, to follow precise directions, and to abstract general meanings. With proper selection of stories and by carefully phrasing questions, the children will comprehend.

ORAL READING

One of the major reasons for having a child read aloud is so that we can analyze the types of errors he makes (substitutions, omissions, etc.), and also to further differentiate between problems of word attack and meaning. Previously we have discussed learning problems which prevent certain children from reading orally and others from reading silently. Those with severe reauditorization disabilities cannot convert the visual symbol into its auditory counterpart; they can read silently but not orally. Similarly, those with expressive aphasia can read silently but cannot form the motor pattern for saying the words. Some children must read aloud in order to comprehend, and still others do not comprehend when they read aloud. Those with inferior comprehension (word-callers) read correctly, but because the words are meaningless they do not attend to phrasing, to thought groups, or to punctuation.

Each child must be evaluated to determine his idiosyncratic needs and the most effective means for teaching him to read. Those who cannot reauditorize or say words should not be held back in reading because of their disability. They learn to read by associating pictures with words and often make good progress. Simultaneously, work is done on the deficits so that they will learn to read either silently or orally. If they can comprehend words only when they say them aloud, they should be permitted to work by themselves so as not to disturb others; gradually they are encouraged to sub-vocalize or whisper the words. Oral reading often is emphasized for the word-callers, those who read without attending to thought groups. The phrases are spaced on the page according to units of meaning, e.g., *Mother and Dad   went to the movies   last night.* Periods and question marks may be drawn in different colors to insure attention to them.

CHAPTER VI

Disorders of Written Language

"Man has not always written, nor is writing the earliest phase of language development. When children write they are responding to an innate urge which has moved mankind in dynamic ways through the ages—it was the primeval urge to *record* human experience and preserve the story of man's adventures that gave impetus to the development of writing" (Zirbes, 1955, p. 2). Relatively little research has been done on written language, but the role of this form of verbal behavior in a world of mass communication is alerting educators of their responsibility to shift emphasis from skills to a dynamic language process. Recently, a new standardized scale, the Picture Story Language Test, was devised for study of the development and disorders of written language (Myklebust, 1965). This scale makes it possible to objectively appraise facility with the written word. It is of value to psychologists and educators in assessing language disorders in children and adults, as well as in determining directions for remediation.

Writing is a highly complex process and, according to Myklebust, is one of the highest forms of language, hence, the last to be learned. It is a form of expressive language, a visual symbol system for conveying thoughts, feelings, and ideas. Normally, the child first learns to comprehend and use the spoken word and later to read and express ideas through the written word. Although oral and written expression are not identical, it can be assumed that the visual symbol systems (reading and writing) are learned by superimposing them on auditory language.

Any language—auditory, visual, tactual—involves a code, an arbitrary symbol system which represents experience. For the code to serve as a means for communication, two or more people must be able to use it for transmitting and receiving messages. The speaker or writer encodes his thoughts with the proper symbols and the listener or reader decodes the messages. When a child writes a story, he demonstrates the ability to interpret and use a visual code; he transmits his ideas by writing symbols which are interpreted by the reader. This same story may be read aloud (converted to auditory symbols) since the written symbols represent an auditory code.

Ability to use written language requires many integrities, including adequate auditory language and experience on which to base the written form. In addition, according to Hughes (1955, p. 11), ". . . writing requires keeping the idea one has in mind . . . the ordering of ideas in some sequence and relationship . . . some planning and design for the correct placement of the word or idea on the paper at one's disposal. Then it requires the selection and utilization of acceptable forms for each letter in proper combination for the word. The fine discriminations, integrations, memory and coordination of hand, mind, and eye required for the act of writing are infinitely complex."

In the normal child these processes develop in an orderly pattern so that by the time a child is approximately six years of age, he is ready to begin to write. He has developed the visual and auditory discriminations required for reading and the visual-motor integration necessary for forming letters; he has, at least to a point, acquired the cognitive and language functions necessary for selecting and organizing words into simple sentences. As he matures and receives proper instruction, the thoughts which he is able to express become increasingly abstract and sentence usage becomes more complex.

Facility with written language does not, however, develop solely on the basis of maturation. The child must be taught. Olson (1949) states that the child will make the responses of which the organism is capable, providing the environmental situation stimulates and elicits the response which the organism is capable of making. Hughes (1955, p. 7), apropos of this concept, adds that "in a pre-literate society the child would not write even though the organism was capable of discrimination between letters or characters and possessed the neuromuscular coordination that permitted the brain to dictate fine coordinating movements of hand and eye required in writing."

With maturation and proper instruction, the average child acquires the written word. However, children with learning disabilities often fail to acquire written language despite normal mental ability and above average school opportunities. The specific basis for the failure depends upon the nature of the disorder and may require intensive diagnostic evaluation. Although there are differences in the growth patterns of normal children, those with learning disabilities often have a much greater degree of variability in performance. A twelve-year-old might function at age level in ideation but be at a ten-year level in oral spelling and only at a seven-year level in visual-motor coordination. Even though able to convey ideas, he cannot do so in writing because of deficits in the visual-motor system. In contrast, another twelve-year-old might have superior visual-motor coordination but because his visual memory ability is that of a seven-year-old, he is prevented from writing; he cannot remember how words look.

Often it is through pathology and the disruption of language processes that we come to realize the complexity of verbal behavior and the critical need for intensive study of all aspects of learning. Throughout this volume we emphasize that disorders cannot be defined only according to broad areas of achievement but that specific reasons for reading, writing, or arithmetic failure must be identified if appropriate remediation is to be provided. In Chapter III, the concept of multiple states of readiness is stressed; it is reemphasized here because of the complexity of the writing process and the numerous possibilities for failure. In analyzing a disorder of written language, the teacher must consider many levels of function, including visual-motor coordination, visual memory, reading, spelling, syntax, and formulation ability. From studies of these aspects of behavior, specific problems are isolated and selected for remediation.

Since the written is the last form of language learned by the child, it is apparent that disabilities in other areas of verbal behavior can interfere with its acquisition. Nevertheless, some learning disabilities are unique to the written form and these are of chief concern in this chapter. Illustrations are presented to show the interrelationships of all types of language functions, but the emphasis is on specific problems of the written form and their remediation.

WRITTEN LANGUAGE AND DEFICITS IN AUDITORY COMPREHENSION

As indicated in Chapter IV, most children with a disturbance of auditory verbal comprehension have problems in written language. Because of limitations in word meaning, their written language tends to be concrete and rarely above the level of the spoken. Most can copy and some can memorize visual configurations in order to spell simple words correctly, but content and syntax are usually deficient.

A number of learning disabilities occur in conjunction with a receptive impairment and thus compound the effect on written language. For example, severe auditory discrimination problems can be reflected in writing as well as in reading or speaking. If a child is unable to distinguish the differences in *wish* and *witch*, he may misunderstand the meaning, misarticulate, or misspell the words. Those who have the additional difficulty in visual learning have an even greater problem in gaining facility with the written word.

The remedial program is planned according to the deficit or combination of deficits present. The critical factor is accurate identification of the disability so that remediation can begin precisely at the point of breakdown. Remediation for the receptive aphasic does not begin with writing but rather with auditory verbal comprehension.

WRITTEN LANGUAGE AND DEFICITS IN
ORAL EXPRESSIVE LANGUAGE

Children with problems in oral expressive language usually have disturbances in writing, but the exact nature of the deficits varies with the auditory involvement. Those with oral syntax disorders tend to write the way they speak because they have not acquired the correct grammatical structure for either form. They cannot properly select and organize words into sentences inasmuch as they do not have an adequate auditory verbal system on which to superimpose the written. Typically, they omit words or word endings, use improper verb tenses and pronouns, or distort the order of words within the sentence; see Illustration 37 for the writing of an eleven-year-old.

Children who have reauditorization deficits or dysnomia are less consistent in their written errors than are those with difficulties in formulation. Some are unable to recall words for either oral or written expression; others can recall the visual image of a word that they cannot recall auditorially, so their written work might be slightly superior. Usually there is not a wide discrepancy between these two forms.

In a few instances, those with severe auditory memory problems are able to write sentences better than they can say them because they are able to use visual monitoring. Due to auditory memory deficits, they cannot remember the words they have said nor relate them to the remainder of the sentence; they cannot recapitulate or anticipate. They reveal knowledge of proper sentence structure by their ability to monitor errors in the visual form. Many say, "It's better when I see it."

One of the most striking examples of this phenomena was seen in a young adult aphasic who was told to give a sentence about a picture showing a man eating cake and ice cream. His auditory verbal response was, "man . . . eating . . . cake . . . ice cream." When asked to write a sentence, he used the same words in the identical sequence but left space on the paper to insert the missing words as he knew his response was incorrect. As he went back over his written sentence, he first wrote the word *the* in front of the word *man*, then wrote *and* between the words *cake* and *ice*

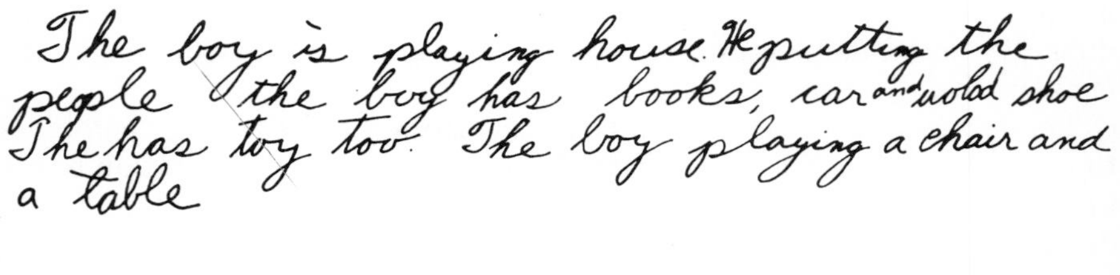

The boy is playing house. He putting the people the boy has books, car and old shoe The has toy too. The boy playing a chair and a table

ILLUSTRATION 37. Written language of an 11-year-old with syntactical aphasia.

cream, then *is* before the word *eating,* and finally *some* before *cake.* He was able to monitor his errors visually so the sentence was perfect when completed; however, he could not correct his oral syntax since it required auditory capacities beyond his ability.

First attempt:	man	eating	cake	ice cream
Insertions:	The	is	some	and
	1	3	4	2

Final attempt: The man is eating some cake and ice cream.

Children who have only an expressive aphasia sometimes demonstrate good facility in written language to compensate for their oral expressive limitations. If they have no difficulty with receptive language, reauditorization or formulation, and only an inability to relate words to the motor system, they might use the written form for communication. This would not be true unless the child had been taught to read.

WRITTEN LANGUAGE AND DISORDERS OF READING

The child who cannot read cannot write. He may be able to copy but he cannot use written symbols for purposeful communication. Output cannot precede input. Until he learns to interpret the written form, he cannot use it expressively. All types of dyslexia impede acquisition of written language and spelling but the effect varies with the nature and degree of the involvement.

Visual dyslexics make errors unlike those in whom the disability is primarily auditory. Generally, the errors of the visual dyslexic are related to visual discrimination, sequence, or memory, as discussed in Chapter V and as shown in Illustration 38. Children with visual memory impairments can have disturbances in both reading and writing, or only in writing. If the ability to retain a visual image for purposes of reading is impaired, it is evident that writing will be limited. Further on in this chapter it will be shown that certain visual memory problems affect only writing because those with this involvement retain the visual image of a word for purposes of recognition but not for full recall.

The auditory dyslexic omits syllables within words because he does not distinguish all of the parts within the whole. Others misperceive and thus miswrite the words; see Illustration 39. The thirteen-year-old girl who wrote this story did not hear the differences in *them* and *then* or in *much* and *mush,* so she wrote as she heard them. Her auditory problems can be noted in her use of *work* instead of *worked* in the second line. While this appears to be a syntax error, she could not detect the word endings and consequently omitted them when writing. To assist dyslexics with

ILLUSTRATION 38. Writing of an eight-year-old with visual dyslexia.

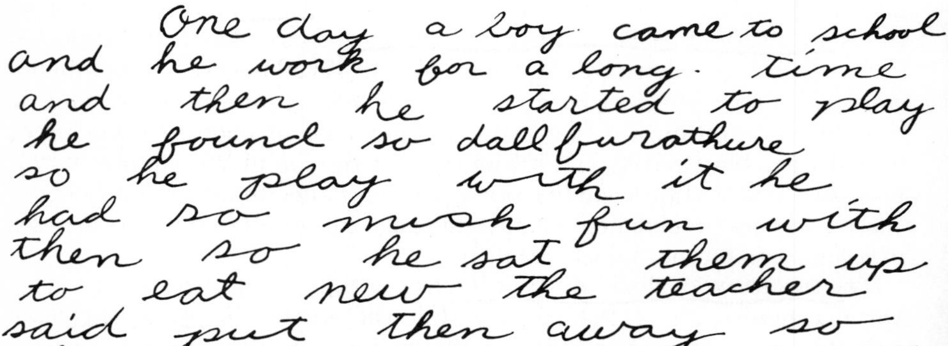

One day a boy came to school
and he work for a long. time
and then he started to play
he found so dall furathure
so he play with it he
had so mush fun with
then so he sat them up
to eat new the teacher
said put then away so
he put then away and
he though he whoud play.
with them the next day.

ILLUSTRATION 39. Written language of an auditory dyslexic.

writing and spelling, we first work on the input process of reading and the respective deficits. Often, writing improves with reading and proper instruction in spelling, grammer, and English.

DISORDERS OF WRITTEN LANGUAGE

Certain learning disabilities occur only in the written form; other forms of verbal behavior are intact. The disturbances observed most frequently are of three main types: (1) *A disorder in visual-motor integration*; the person can speak and read but cannot execute the motor patterns for writing letters, numbers, or words. He may be able to spell orally but cannot express ideas by means of visual symbols because he cannot write. This condition is designated *dysgraphia*. (2) *A deficit in revisualization*; this individual recognizes words when he sees them and hence can read. However, he cannot revisualize letters or words, so he cannot write spontaneously nor from dictation. He cannot evoke the visual image from hearing the spoken form. (3) *A deficiency in formulation and syntax*; in this instance the person can communicate orally, can copy, can revisualize and spell words correctly, but he cannot organize his thoughts into their proper form for written communication. He does not write the way he speaks; he makes errors in written formulation that he does not make in speaking.

DYSGRAPHIA

Dysgraphia is a disorder resulting from a disturbance in visual-motor integration. The child with this type of involvement has neither a visual nor a motor defect, but he cannot transduce visual information to the motor system. He sees what he wants to write but cannot ideate the motor plan. As a result, he is unable to write or copy letters, words, and numbers. *It is the ability to copy which differentiates dysgraphia from other disorders of writing.* The dyslexic, for example, cannot write because he cannot read; yet he can copy. Similarly, a child with a visual memory disturbance can copy but he cannot write spontaneously because he cannot remember how the letters look.

Dysgraphia is a type of apraxia affecting the visual-motor system. Apraxia also may occur in the auditory-motor system, in which case spoken language is affected. Although it is possible to have a disturbance in both areas, it is more common for only one system to be affected. In terms of the semi-autonomous systems concept, this is an important factor to consider. A child who is apraxic for speech is not necessarily apraxic for writing. Similarly, the dysgraphic does not necessarily have difficulty in talking. Many dysgraphics overcompensate for their visual-motor deficit by developing superior auditory skills, good spoken language and reading ability.

Very early in life the normal child learns to make visual motor associations. As he scribbles on a paper, he finds that he can produce a particular visual pattern by moving his arm in a certain way; he discovers that he can make a different picture by changing the direction of his movement (Lowenfield, 1952). He likes what he sees and tries to remember what he did in order to reproduce it. He retains both visual and kinesthetic images so that he can copy many kinds of figures. As he matures, he perceives how complex lines and figures fit together and learns to draw and write. In learning to make these associations, the child also learns to transduce information from one system to another. When he sees a figure, he knows what movements to make in order to copy it, and he knows that if he makes a series of movements in a certain sequence, he can produce a specific visual pattern. Dysgraphic children cannot make these associations or profit from similar experiences; therefore, they cannot write.

Apraxia may exist with or without a symbolic disturbance. Although dysgraphia impedes the ability to convey ideas, it is different from a language problem which affects the ability to organize and express ideas clearly. Orton (1937, p. 99) observed that ". . . a developmental agraphia may coexist with a reading and spelling disability but a writing disability is encountered not infrequently as an isolated disorder."

The allied learning problems which occur with dysgraphia are most frequently in arithmetic, in visual-spatial relationships, and in nonverbal visual-motor functions. The arithmetic disturbance common to children with dysgraphia is three-fold: they have difficulty writing numbers, aligning numbers properly on the page, and understanding concepts related to space, distance, and time. On the other hand, many learn arithmetic facts quickly and can answer questions orally.

Nonverbal visual-motor functions also are often disturbed in the dysgraphic child. He cannot transduce visual information to the motor system or imitate what he sees; therefore, he may be unable to tie his shoes, open a bottle, or follow a sequence of movements in a game. Copying letters or other visual symbols is difficult because the symbol provides no clue to the movement patterns he should use. A child can watch and possibly imitate when his father uses a hammer because he has an opportunity to observe a sequence of movements, but when he looks at a written figure on a page, he has no idea how to make it. Even if he watches someone write, he rarely has the advantage of seeing the entire sequence and direction of movements inasmuch as the letter may be partially covered by the writer's fingers or the movements are too rapid for him to follow.

There are many degrees of dysgraphia. Those with the greatest involvements are unable to hold a pencil properly or to draw a straight line. An eight-year-old girl, trying to copy a vertical line, finally gave up in desperation and said, "How do I do it? Where do I go?" Even when she was told how to hold a pencil and how to proceed, she could not copy unless the teacher guided her hand. Some children can draw simple designs but cannot copy figures that require a series of complex, reciprocal movements. The boy who tried to write the numbers shown in Illustration 40 could draw circles and lines but could not copy numbers or letters. He had excellent spoken language and could read above his grade level but could do no written work.

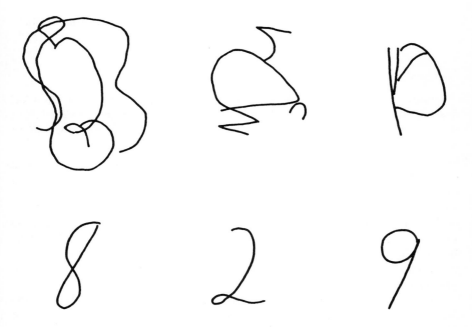

ILLUSTRATION 40. Copying of an eight-year-old dysgraphic.

Older dysgraphic children sometimes reproduce a legible word but distort the sequence of movements when they write. The eleven-year-old who wrote the word *goat* in Illustration 41 knew how the word should look but did not know the sequence of movements to use in order to write it. Therefore, he drew small sections of each letter. It is essential to watch the dysgraphic child write because this performance gives an indication of the deficiences to be corrected.

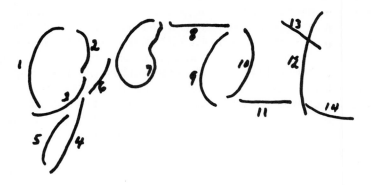

ILLUSTRATION 41. Writing of an 11-year-old with disturbance of visual-motor sequencing. (The numbers show order of writing.)

Delineation of the Problem

Program planning for children with dysgraphia requires a detailed description of the problem. Before inaugurating a program of remediation it is necessary to know precisely what a child can or cannot do, and to know *how* he learns. Teachers need more than a statement of diagnosis and a summary of objective test information; they must know how a child performs and how he attempts an assignment. The teacher who observes that a child reauditorizes while he writes, or that he never watches his hand while he writes, gains valuable insight into the nature of his problem. Clinical observations of the child engaged in a learning task can substantiate a diagnosis and also determine how he should be taught. Through observation we determine the systems that are or are not intact and gain information about the sensory channels to be used for presenting new material.

The study of writing ability should include a specific tabulation of the figures, letters, and numbers a child can copy as well as a description of his performance while he writes. Noting his grasp of a pencil, his posture, and the sequence of movements used in copying a figure are relevant in outlining the educational procedures to be applied in remediation.

It is emphasized that in this section we are concerned only with a child's ability to copy. This skill should be differentiated from those which involve knowledge of letter names, letter sounds, spelling, language, and other verbal functions. The objective is to gather information on visual-motor integration and ability to transduce from one modality to another as it pertains to writing.

Pre-Writing Skills

Grasp of writing utensils. Many dysgraphic children do not know how to hold a pencil. They see what they are to do and try to manipulate their fingers properly, but cannot imitate what they see. Some hold the pencil in both hands and try to write; others refuse to touch writing utensils because they have experienced repeated failures. Those with less severe problems hold the pencil too close to the point or the eraser; others grip the pencil too tightly or too loosely. If there are problems in manipulation of crayons or pencils, measures should be taken to teach correct grasp. Suggestions are given below.

(1) Young children should be given primary-size pencils and large crayons. Even though they do not have a muscular involvement, preventing them from gripping a narrow pencil, they can manipulate larger pencils better. Hexagonal crayons are helpful because the flat sides are easier to grip. Felt-tip pens are also useful.

(2) Short pencils should not be used. They force the children to grip too tightly and their writing becomes jerky or small. Short pencils also cause them to use undue pressure, which in turn brings about fatigue and frustration.

(3) The pencil should be held above the sharpened part between the thumb and the middle finger with the index finger riding the pencil. If children have difficulty remembering the correct position, a piece of adhesive can be placed on the pencil, a small notch cut in the wood, or paint applied on the specific area where the fingers should be.

(4) If children have good verbal facility and seem to learn by using the auditory channel, detailed instructions of what they should do can be given, e.g., put the pencil in your right hand, put your index finger on top of the pencil, put your thumb on the left side of the pencil, put your middle finger on the right side of the pencil, curl your other fingers slightly and let them rest on the table. These directions provide a pattern which is reauditorized so the act can be performed automatically; the child should verbalize each position and movement. Cobb (1948) suggests that no movement becomes automatic without a plan. This plan must be auditorized for some dysgraphic children.

(5) If children lack good auditory skills and if kinesthesis seems to be the best modality for learning, they are asked to close their eyes and while their fingers are molded into place, their hands are guided. A firm grip can be used, but relaxation is encouraged and large sweeping movements are used initially.

Position of paper. Observe the way in which the child places the paper on his desk. An incorrect slant will cause him to write in an awkward manner. Nearly everyone has noticed a backhand awkward left-hander who has not learned to slant his paper to the right rather than to the left. There are also inferior writers who place the paper with lines running perpendicular to the body so they write with their hands moving vertically rather than horizontally.

Paper for manuscript writing should be placed parallel with the lower edge of the desk. Teach the children how to move their paper up and away from the body as they work toward the bottom of the page. Paper for cursive writing is tilted at about a sixty degree angle to the left for right-handers and to the right for left-handers.

Posture. Children with learning disabilities often have poor writing posture. Some keep their heads too close to the paper; others move constantly and as a result slide their paper or cover their work with their arms so they cannot see what they are doing. Encourage a good, upright sitting posture. Select appropriate chairs, tables, and desks for each child and make certain that both feet are kept firmly on the floor and that he can see all of the work on his desk. Papers should be stabilized or anchored to the desks for hyperactive children. Masking tape is effective for this because it can be removed easily from both the desk and the paper. Blackboards should be large and in a position so that the child need not reach above his head or stoop when he writes.

If a child has unusual posture, such as a marked tilt of the head, it is wise to suggest a visual examination. Visual field defects and other disturbances might be present.

Study of Processes

Visual Discrimination. Although ability to discriminate visually should have been evaluated before a diagnosis of dysgraphia was made, it is important to make certain that a child can differentiate one letter from another. If he cannot distinguish similarities and differences in words, he will not write them correctly since a disorder of input affects output. Visual discrimination can be estimated by giving the child exercises of the type found in Chapter V. If difficulties are seen, the remedial procedures discussed there should be applied previous to work on writing.

Nonverbal Visual-Motor Patterning. It is helpful to note whether the child can imitate various nonverbal motor patterns and also to observe how he learns them. By exploring his ability to learn motor patterns, we ascertain the most effective means for teaching him. The purpose of the following sequence of activities is to determine his specific needs. We know that it is hard for him to take in a visual pattern and transduce the information to the motor system, but we must find a route which will help him achieve this goal.

First, ask the child to imitate pretend movements, such as eating, blowing, or turning a key in a lock. *Do not* give a verbal command; reduce

the auditory stimulation and merely perform the act and ask him to imitate what he saw. Do the same with non-meaningful activities—touch the
thumb and index finger. Second, ask him to perform similar activities but
give verbal instructions simultaneously. Say to him, "Show me how you
eat—lift your arm, move it toward your face," etc. Perform the act and
ask him to do the same.

A third technique is to ask the child to close his eyes and then guide
his hand in a particular movement pattern until he can do it by himself.
Have him open his eyes and watch what he does. From his performance,
we can gain insights concerning which system and procedure is most
helpful in teaching him. Knowing that a child has a disturbance in visual-
motor integration is only stating the problem; our job is to find the
expeditious routes for learning.

If a child can imitate an activity when he is given verbal directions, he
can be taught through the auditory modality. On the other hand, if his
performance is better when he closes his eyes, the implication is that he
cannot tolerate multisensory stimulation, so a unisensory, tactile-kinesthetic stimulation should be stressed. Typical "teaching circuits" or
routes we have used with a dysgraphic child are:

(1) Visual to auditory to visual-motor.
    Present a clear visual pattern; follow with a detailed auditory verbal
    description of the movement plan; have him watch and imitate.

(2) Kinesthetic to visual-motor.
    Have him close his eyes; guide his fingers and hands in the desired
    movement pattern; have him open his eyes and watch what he does.

(3) Kinesthetic to auditory to visual-motor.
    Follow the procedures outlined in (2) but while the child has his eyes
    closed, verbalize the movement pattern with him, e.g., down—turn
    right; go across—go up. Have him open his eyes and continue the
    pattern.

The routes to be used depend upon the presence of other learning disabilities, upon the amount of stimulation a child can handle from one or
more modalities, and various other factors. The child who has a receptive
aphasia in addition to dysgraphia does not profit from extensive verbal
directions, and the dyslexic might need more emphasis on saying letter
sounds while tracing. The purpose is to find the route which most clearly
compensates for all of the variables so that the child can learn to write.

Ability to copy figures. Children of school age are asked to copy geometric designs and pre-letter forms which are the components of manuscript letters. They include horizontal, vertical, and angular lines and
circles, squares, triangles, half circles (rotated in different directions),
intersecting lines, and hooks. Children seven years and older are able to
copy these figures. Maximum performance can be gained from distractible

children by covering all of the figures except the one to be copied, or by presenting the designs on separate cards.

It is unnecessary to be concerned with ability to name the figures; stress only ability to duplicate the visual pattern. Occasionally, children who have good auditory capacities perform better when the figure is named. For example, some cannot draw the designs until they are referred to as a ball, a box, a Christmas tree, or a fish hook.

While the child draws, observe the hand movements, hand preference, and the sequence of movements, noting whether the lines are drawn from top to bottom, from left to right, or whether the pattern is inconsistent; attention also should be given to whether the figures are unusually small or large, whether they fall within a given space and whether the drawing is done too quickly and is inaccurate or whether it is done slowly and laboriously. Observe which figures are copied successfully and categorize the errors by type of figure, line, and angle. After analyzing the deficiencies, proceed with remedial procedures as outlined below.

Educational Procedures

Writing involves integration of information from the visual modality, from taction, and from proprioception. Certain dysgraphic children are unable to assimilate these sensations and experiences simultaneously. Therefore, in training it is necessary to begin by presenting visual and kinesthetic patterns separately, gradually working toward integration of the two.

Visual Learning. Draw a vertical line or a circle on the blackboard. Use chalk that leaves a strong visual impression. Explain to the child that you want him to learn how to draw the picture and that he must watch very closely. Leave the model on the board and draw another identical to it. Draw slowly so that there is sufficient opportunity to observe the movement patterns. While drawing keep the figure exposed, not covering it with your hands. Repeat the pattern two or three times, always moving in the same direction. A pocket flashlight can be used to illustrate the movements. Hold it several inches away from the blackboard and trace around the figure with a beam of light, being sure that the child watches closely. An opaque projector also is invaluable in teaching. It has a control which projects a small, white arrow on the screen and which is used as a pointer. The teacher directs the movement of the arrow around each design projected on the blackboard until the child is familiar with the visual-movement pattern. If the child has good verbal facility, the plan is repeated while simultaneously tracing over the figure and saying, "left—down—right"; make certain that the words are understood. No attempt is made to have the child duplicate the drawing, model, picture, etc. at this time; he only watches the movement patterns.

Kinesthetic Learning. Have the child close his eyes and guide his hand over the figure which was presented visually. Draw the design in the air or on the blackboard with the index finger. Use large movements at the beginning to emphasize kinesthetic feedback. Continue to guide his hand until he can follow the pattern without assistance.

Present all figures in the same spatial plane. If the figures were shown in the vertical plane, do not shift the kinesthetic pattern to a horizontal plane. The kinesthetic image obtained from drawing in the air is different from one on a table or desk. When the child draws a vertical line on the blackboard, he feels his hand moving downward from head to toe, whereas when he draws at his desk, he feels his hand moving toward his body. It should be remembered that the words used to indicate directional patterns vary according to the position of the child and his work surface (Kephart, 1960). The word *down*, for example, does not represent the same directional pattern when a child is standing at a blackboard as when he is sitting at a table.

Coordinating the patterns. After the child has followed each pattern visually and kinesthetically, we help him to coordinate them. If he cannot tolerate the visual-tactile-kinesthetic stimulation, he is asked to close his eyes and his hand is guided as suggested in the preceding exercise. As soon as he can follow the kinesthetic pattern by himself, give him a piece of chalk and have him draw the figure on the blackboard with his eyes closed. Then have him open his eyes and see what he drew. Next, with his eyes open ask him to draw another figure that looks the same. Note any differences in his ability to draw with his eyes open or closed. Critchley (1953) observed that some brain damaged adults can draw figures with their eyes closed but not with their eyes open. We have had experience with children whose performance deteriorates when they are forced to watch what they are doing. One boy developed tic-like movements of his head if he was told to draw and to continually watch his hand. Until he had established the movement plan, he could not copy figures with his eyes open.

Introduce each new exercise by presenting the pattern visually, then kinesthetically, and then in combination. In addition, the following principles are recommended:

(1) *Work from gross to fine movement patterns.* Draw large figures before working with small designs on narrow-lined paper.

(2) *Encourage development of orderly movements.* Teach drawing of lines and figures by using a consistent sequence of movements in the proper direction. If children do not learn correct sequence, their writing often is slow, labored, and inaccurate. Insert directional cues, such as arrows, to illustrate the movement plan.

(3) *Reinforce the visual-motor patterns by repetition.* Motor patterns for writing should become so automatic that it is unnecessary to concentrate on the formation of individual letters while expressing ideas. The person who drives a car cannot think about each movement of his hand or foot; his attention must be directed to watching traffic and road signs. Similarly, with the dysgraphic child the goal is that his act of writing become automatic, freeing him to concentrate on the ideas he wishes to convey.

(4) *Use materials from which good visual feedback can be obtained.* The objective of the training is to develop visual-motor integration; therefore, the child must have an opportunity to *see* what he does. Although tracing in the air or tracing over sandpaper is recommended to develop kinesthetic imagery, it is not used to coordinate visual-motor patterns. Materials such as finger paint, wet sand, and stencils in addition to crayons and pencils are recommended. Finger paint and wet sand are particularly useful for children who refuse to work with writing utensils, and they also provide tactile stimulation. Finger painting can be done either on an easel or a table, but writing in sand or clay must be done at a desk or on a horizontal plane. When using finger paint, have the child close his eyes, guide his hand in the proper direction, and have him paint the figure with his index finger.

(5) *Teach the movement plan through verbal directions.* While tracing over a figure, repeat rhythmic chants, such as "down—across—up." The auditory rhythm patterns help many children establish visual-motor integration and develop a smooth flow of writing. The use of this procedure depends upon the child's verbal facility and his ability to comprehend the spoken word. It is not used with children who become frustrated with auditory stimulation. The auditorily distractible child tends to listen to the auditory patterns instead of concentrating on the visual-motor plan. If children are unable to tolerate verbal directions, reduce the auditory stimulation and emphasize kinesthetic-tactile methods.

Reinforcement Techniques. The following techniques can be used to reinforce newly learned patterns:

(1) *Stencils and templates.* Make simple stencils from cardboard, posterboard, or plastics. Cut designs from the center of each as shown in Illustration 42. The material should be sturdy so that the child can feel the edge of the cutout. Clip the stencil over the paper to prevent it from moving while he is tracing. First, have him trace around the inside edge of the design with his index finger and then have him repeat the movement with a pencil or crayon. Remove the stencil and show him the figure he drew. This technique is effective because even though a child overshoots the boundary of the stencil when he is drawing, he sees a good picture when he removes the template. He gets an accurate visual perception of the figure as well as a feeling of success.

Starting points and directional cues should be marked on each stencil to indicate the plan of movement and to develop consistent sequences. The teacher might color or paste small red and green dots on the template to show the starting and stopping points. The red "stop sign" is an important cue for the perseverative child who continues to trace around the inside of the figure without purpose. Arrows can be drawn on the stencil to show direction.

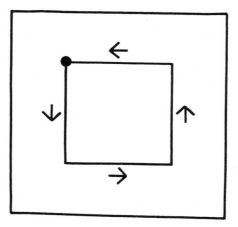

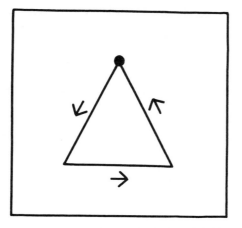

ILLUSTRATION 42. Stencils for teaching dysgraphics.

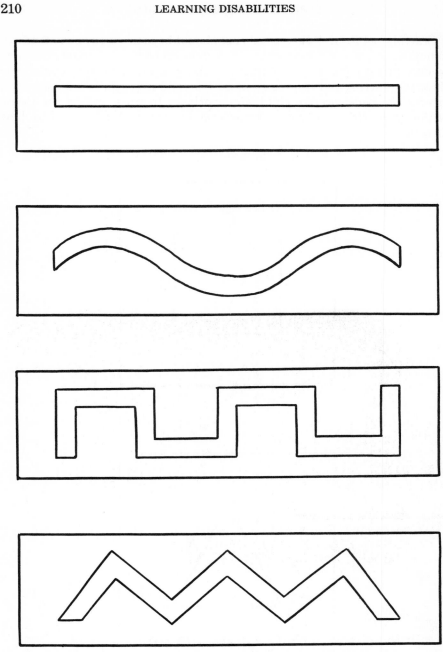

ILLUSTRATION 43. Stencils for improving visual-motor patterns.

(2) *Drawing roads.* Most children enjoy tracing over the patterns shown in Illustration 43 and they refer to them as roads that are straight, hilly, or mountainous. The linear patterns, in a developmental sequence, are cut from stencils or are drawn on paper to be copied. Initially, the road may be one-half inch wide but it is gradually reduced in width as the children improve. Eventually they should be able to trace directly on another pencil line. After they can trace complete patterns, prepare incomplete designs to be finished.

(3) *Tracing folds.* Fold pieces of paper into squares, rectangles, and triangles. Open the paper and ask the child to trace the folds with the tip of his index finger and then with a pencil. The tactile impression from tracing the fold is beneficial.

(4) *Tracing with copy paper.* Draw figures on white paper using heavy black ink. Fasten onionskin or copy paper over the model figures so that the child can see the lines. Make certain there is enough light. Glass-top drawing boards with a light attached underneath the drawing surface also can be used for tracing.

(5) *Dot-to-dot figures.* Draw one complete figure and an outline of the same figure by using dots. Ask the child to connect the dots and make a picture like the one that is finished. If he can recognize numbers and knows them in sequence, write numbers by each dot to show the direction of the movements.

Letters and Numbers. When the children are able to copy the designs and pre-letter forms, they are taught to blend movements and to form letters. Make an inventory to determine which ones are easily copied. Analyze each letter by breaking it into its simplest components and demonstrate how the parts fit together. For example, assume you are teaching a child to write a lower case, manuscript *b*. Cover the semicircle of the letter and ask him to tell you what he sees; he might respond, "I see a line." Then cover the line and expose only the half circle and ask him to tell what he sees. Explain that is all he has to do—draw a line and a half circle. Emphasize the spatial relationships and initially place dots or markers to indicate where the parts should be joined. With this type of breakdown, writing letters becomes less of an obstacle since most children have little difficulty if they can draw the individual components.

Use directional cues on letters until they are written automatically. The exercise in Illustration 44 shows how this is accomplished. Letters are written with dotted lines and arrows are superimposed on the lines to indicate the direction of the next movement. Charts of this type are available for all letters in primary teachers' manuals.

Dysgraphic children must be taught to blend movements easily and smoothly. Each segment of a letter should be joined with another to avoid jerkiness. For example, if a letter is composed of four different segments, teach the child to blend two parts together until the pattern is automatic, then add a third, and finally a fourth.

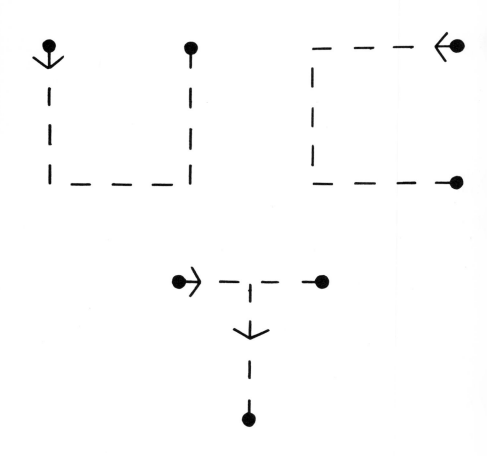

ILLUSTRATION 44. Directional cues for writing letters.

Manuscript versus Cursive. Some controversy exists regarding the initial type of writing that should be taught initially to children with learning disabilities. Normal children are taught manuscript writing because the movements are simpler to make. However, some authorities (McGinnis, 1963; Strauss and Lehtinen, 1947) suggest that cursive should be taught first so the children need not transfer from one form to another. Advocates of cursive writing feel that it is necessary for children to learn to read all forms, including lower and upper case, and cursive, and assume that if they have been taught to write the cursive form, it will help them learn to read it. Furthermore, they feel that the problem of spacing letters and words is minimized if cursive rather than printing is taught. Since cursive words are written as units, it is not necessary to teach children to leave a small space between letters and a larger space between words.

Despite these arguments, our experience is that manuscript writing is the easier for the dysgraphic child. The movements are less complex and there are fewer reciprocal movements and changes of letter forms. In connected cursive writing, the visual-motor pattern for a letter changes, depending upon its position within a word. For example, the *n* in the word *no* is not the same as the *n* in the word *on*. Modifications of letter forms do not occur in manuscript writing and therefore it is recommended. The complexities of cursive can be taught after the visual-motor patterns for printing are well established. The problems of spacing and letter alignment are a greater obstacle in manuscript writing, but they can be overcome by techniques such as those suggested below.

Timing the shift from manuscript to cursive writing depends not only upon ability to copy but upon the number and nature of the learning disabilities present. Normally, children print for one to two years and are then taught cursive writing. Severe dyslexics, however, may be unable to read more than one form of a word and become confused if they are taught cursive writing too early. A third-grade boy could read words only in lower case manuscript form; he could read the word *from* if it occurred in the middle of a sentence but not if it was the first word of the sentence with a capital letter. Reading different forms of the printed word requires facility in translating one symbol into another and many children with language disorders do not have this ability. *Therefore, they are taught one form for both reading and writing until they can read it successfully.* Eventually, they should be able to read all forms of the printed word, but at first, *it is important to learn one type thoroughly.* The dyslexic boy mentioned above had no difficulty copying either manuscript or cursive writing, so we knew that as soon as he could read and revisualize words, he would be able to write them.

Cursive writing is taught in much the same way as manuscript writing. Letters are broken down into the simplest components and blended together. An example of how a twelve-year-old boy learned to write an *h* is given in Illustration 45. He first learned to print and then to write.

Spacing. As they begin to write sentences, dysgraphic children (particularly those with visual perceptual problems) often have trouble learning to leave the proper amount of space between letters and words; see Illustration 46. Some do not leave spaces between words and others leave

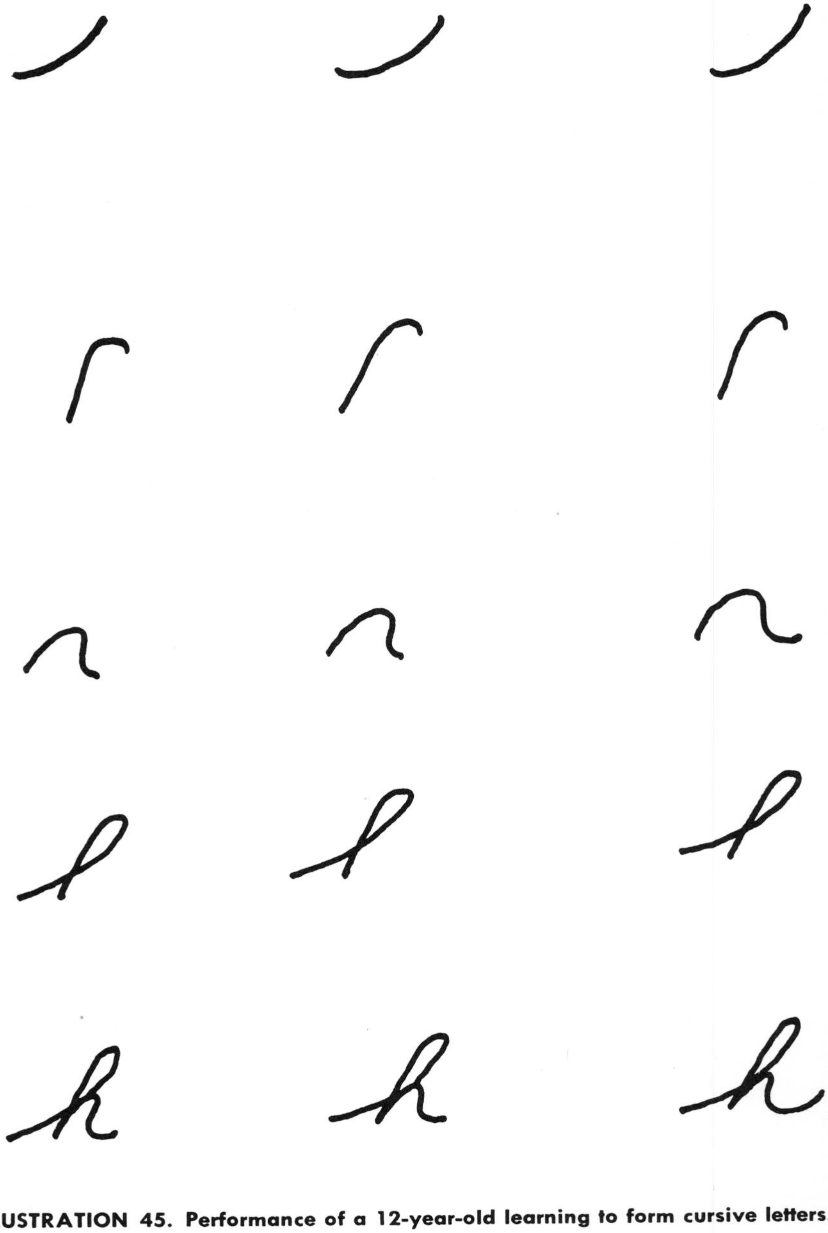

ILLUSTRATION 45. Performance of a 12-year-old learning to form cursive letters.

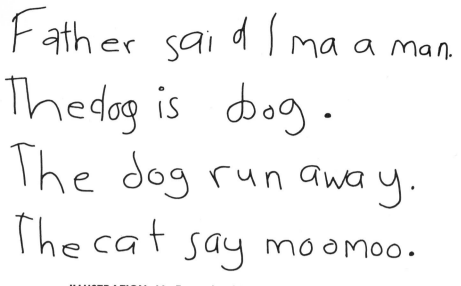

ILLUSTRATION 46. Example of inability in spacing words.

irregular spaces with little regard for word units. They may write sentences in this way:

Iseethedog.   or   I se e t he do g.

In order to improve spacing, they must be able to identify errors. Exercises such as the following are suggested:

(1) Place anagrams or cutout letters on a flannelboard or desk. Arrange the letters to make a sentence but do not leave spaces between the words. Tell the child what the sentence should say and ask him to separate the words by moving the letters. As you say the sentence, pause after each word to indicate the place where one word ends and another begins. Later, arrange sentences on the board but do not tell him what it says; see if he can determine how the letters should be separated.

(2) Prepare exercises such as the one in Illustration 47. Tell the child what the sentence says, then give him a colored pencil and ask him to mark where spacing should appear. As children perform exercises of this type, they learn to appreciate the difficulties facing the reader who tries to read improperly spaced writing and become more conscious of their own errors.

(3) After children can identify errors and arrange words correctly, ask them to *write* sentences. Structure the task by drawing a series of rectangles

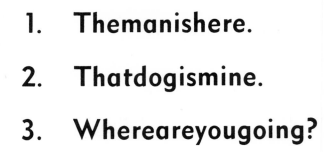

1. **Themanishere.**

2. **Thatdogismine.**

3. **Whereareyougoing?**

ILLUSTRATION 47. An exercise for improvement of spacing.

Numbers from Copy

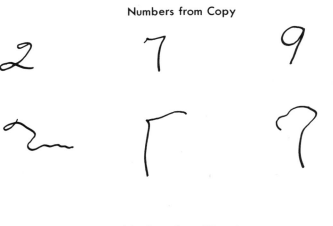

Numbers from Dictation

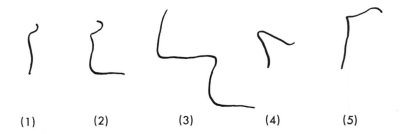

(1)   (2)   (3)   (4)   (5)

ILLUSTRATION 48. Writing of a seven-year-old dysgraphic prior to remediation.

in which each word is to be written. Make the rectangles of varied sizes to correspond with the length of the word and leave a space between each figure. Give him a sentence and ask him to write a word in each space.

Erasures and Corrections. Erasures and corrections are small but significant problems to be considered in teaching dysgraphic children. When they write, they often make mistakes but do not take time to correct them. Instead, they write over the error or they do not fully erase it. As a result, the words they write are not clear. These children must see an accurate visual pattern of the letter if they are to improve. Therefore, they should be taught and encouraged to completely erase incorrect figures.

ILLUSTRATION 49. Writing and drawing by the same child after 18 months of training.

Progress

Most dysgraphic children show good progress if they are taught to make the appropriate visual-motor associations. Those who do not learn to write properly or who write very slowly can be taught to use a typewriter. They need special techniques to establish the motor patterns for typing but these are less complex than the visual-motor patterns required for writing.

The preceding work samples (Illustrations 48 and 49) illustrate the progress of a seven-year-old boy. At the beginning of remedial training, he refused to pick up a pencil, tore the paper, and broke crayons; he was severely frustrated because of his constant failure. He learned to print all of the letters of the alphabet within a period of four months and learned cursive writing in 18 months. Shortly before his dismissal he not only could complete written assignments but asked to draw pictures and write stories as a reward if he finished other work ahead of time.

DEFICITS IN REVISUALIZATION

Writing disabilities frequently result from deficits in visual memory. With this type of involvement the person can speak, read, and copy but he cannot revisualize words or letters. His disability is similar to the dysnomic who can comprehend but not reauditorize words. However, the disturbance is in the visual processes rather than in the auditory.

Revisualization problems occasionally are seen in conjunction with a visual dyslexia but both can appear as isolated disorders. When the two are found together, the child might have a mild dyslexia, with reading only one grade below level but with spelling three or four grades below. This discrepancy cannot be attributed to dyslexia alone. When the revisualization deficit occurs in isolation, all areas of achievement may be at grade level with the exception of spelling and writing. For example, a ten-year-old scored at grade 5.0 in reading, grade 4.9 in oral spelling, but only grade 3.5 on written spelling because of his limitation in ability to revisualize letters and words. Often there are differences between the scores on multiple choice spelling tests and dictated spelling tests because the first requires only recognition, not full recall.

Revisualization deficits can also affect numbers, but writing is interfered with more because of the complexity of words and the sequence of letters to be remembered. Recall of nonverbal visual stimuli may be impaired, in which case problems are evidenced in revisualizing objects or people. Drawings of the human figure are lacking in detail, such as the one in Illustration 50 drawn by a twelve-year-old boy.

These children are not dysgraphic; they can copy, as shown by the writing of an eight-year-old in Illustration 51. In contrast, note his lack of ability to write letters from dictation; see Illustration 52. He could give letter names and sounds when he saw them (he could transduce from the visual to the auditory system), but be could not revisualize the letters from the auditory presentation. He knew the attempts, as seen in Illustration 52, were incorrect, but he could not revisualize the ones he wanted.

ILLUSTRATION 50. Drawing of a man by a 12-year-old with poor revisualization ability.

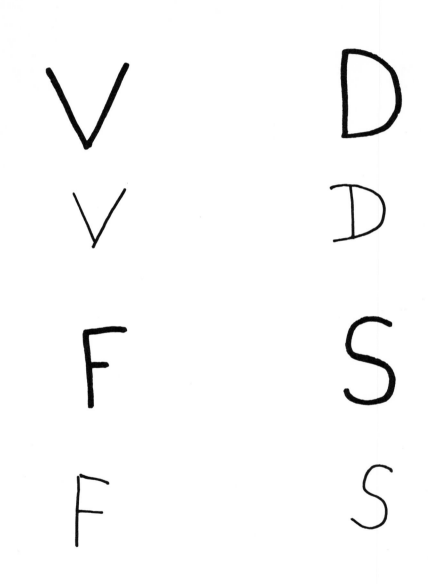

ILLUSTRATION 51. Copying of an eight-year-old with a visual memory disorder.

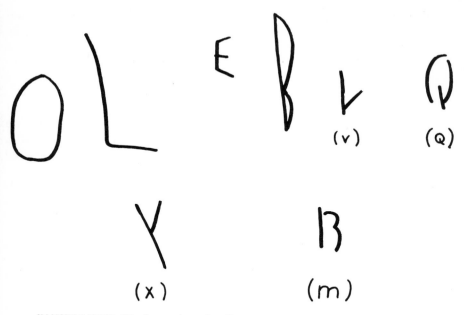

ILLUSTRATION 52. Examples of a disturbance in revisualization by the same eight-year-old.

Educational Procedures

Selection of Materials. Materials for training in visual memory should be carefully selected. All pictures, letters, and words should be clear with well defined lines so the child has ample opportunity to see and to remember them. Printed, typed, or dittoed exercises are examined to see that all letters are complete. Material projected from a tachistoscope or other visual aids is focused so the image is sharp and clear. Small type is avoided.

Charts of letters or numbers that are used in the classroom are written with heavy ink or crayon and with adequate space between. The charts are placed so that the child with visualization problems is not required to view them from an angle or from a distance. As indicated later in this discussion, children often refer to these charts when they cannot remember how letters or numbers look.

Because of memory disabilities, it is necessary to prepare materials that are unlike those used in the normal educational setting. Print of a larger size or of a different color can be used to intensify certain letters or figures. For example, words that are especially difficult to revisualize are typed in a contrasting color to strengthen the visual impression. Materials for tactual presentation are constructed from sturdy posterboard, plastic, or wood so the boundaries and differences are easily perceived.

Attention. Memory is dependent upon good attention. The individual who wants to remember what he hears or sees must remain attentive while engaged in an activity. Certain children with learning disabilities are distracted by sights and sounds around them and they find it hard to concentrate for a long period of time. Those in whom the problem is severe should have a structured environment, as outlined in Chapter VIII. Others, only mildly distractible, do not need a modified environment but profit from procedures designed to improve attention. They miss an assignment or the first part of an instruction because they are not ready. They are neither disobedient nor provocative; they are slow in preparing themselves to listen or to look.

When problems of attention occur together with a memory deficit, attention-getting signals must be used in training. Verbal instructions, such as "Ready" or "Next," are helpful but visual cues are stressed. The teacher gains the child's attention with a pocket flashlight. While working with flash cards or word charts, she holds the light near each picture or letter (somewhat like a pointer) to make sure that he looks at all of the figures. Orderly and thorough inspection of material is encouraged. If necessary, the entire letter or word is outlined with the beam of light. When tachistoscopic devices or other visual aids are used, a light is flashed on the screen in the position where the stimulus will appear so that the child knows where to look, the purpose being to prepare him for learning. Since children with learning disabilities tend to have difficulty readying themselves, we begin with attention-getting devices and gradually reduce them as internal controls and proper habits of attention are established.

Facilitating Recall. The objective of the remedial teaching is to assist the child in revisualizing letters and words, hence making it possible for him to write and spell properly. To attain this goal, the image must be adequately stored and a means for cuing should be provided. As stated previously, the children in this group can hold an image for purposes of recognition (reading) but not for total recall. Therefore, we have found it beneficial to work from *recognition to partial recall* to *total recall*. In using this progression our assumption is that the child first requires sufficient opportunity to see and work with the entire stimulus, then with only partial cues, and finally to revisualize them without external assistance.

The primary means for evoking responses from children with revisualization deficits (until memory improves) is through the auditory or kinesthetic-tactile modalities. Often these children are heard spelling words aloud while writing them, indicating the need for audition to serve as a mediating process. Some, however, have not learned that they can use this type of strategy to improve their written work. A post-encephalitic teen-ager learned to compensate for his severe revisualization deficit by relying on kinesthesis. He learned new spelling words by tracing them several times. Later, if he could not remember them, he wrote each one two or three times and commented, "That didn't feel right when I wrote it."

Recognition. Even though children with revisualization deficits can read and recognize figures, work is done to improve visual storage of letters and words so that they are more readily available for spontaneous writing. By using the term "recognition," we mean that the child does not have to *write* a response. He will be required to complete letters or words from memory after he has acquired facility with tasks such as those below.

(1) Expose a picture for approximately four or five seconds. Remove it and present a second one and ask the child to tell whether it was the same as the first. Initially, the time of exposure should be long enough for the child to inspect it thoroughly but the time delay between the two presentations should be relatively short. As he improves, the time of presentation should be decreased and the time delay between presentations increased. We have observed teen-age children who could not retain an image for more than four seconds. Gradually, however, as they learned to use cues from other modalities, they made marked improvement.

(2) Present a picture, letter, or word, as suggested above, but give the child a sheet of paper with three, four, or five figures and ask him to circle the one he saw. Increase the complexity of the task by presenting two or more figures and asking the child to mark *all* of the ones he saw. Those who benefit from auditorizing should be encouraged to say the letters or numbers as they see them and while waiting for the second presentation. A twelve-year-old visual dyslexic with severe spelling deficits could retain only two digits until he learned that visual memory could be improved if he said the numbers over and over to himself.

(3) Revisualization can be improved by making the child aware of the "feel" of the letters. On occasion visual recognition has been improved by using skin writing, especially in those who have deficits visually *and* auditorially. Place a number or letter in front of the child and ask him to look closely at the figure. Then the letter is traced on his back or on the back of his hand while he follows the pattern visually. After several presentations a letter is traced on his back and he is asked to tell whether it is the same as the one in front of him, or to select the one from two or three that corresponds with the one he felt.

(4) Exercises such as the one in Illustration 53 are given to children to improve spelling, especially the spelling of non-phonetic words. Two or more spellings of a word are written and the child is asked to select the correct one. This type of exercise generally precedes writing from dictation since the latter requires complete revisualization.

(5) The Autoscore has been useful for training in visual memory. Exercises (see Illustration 53) are prepared for all age levels, with recognition of the spelling vocabulary of each child. Although it is not essential that the exercises be prepared for teaching machines, immediate reinforcement permits the child to work independently until he has all of the answers correct. Other materials are prepared for lower elementary age groups by drawing a picture and writing two or three spellings of the word next to it. Older students are given sentences with a word omitted and from several spellings are asked to select the correct one.

(6) Verbal descriptions of letters and objects facilitate recall. Ask the child to look at objects or letters and have him describe them in detail. Later, give him riddles, such as, "I am thinking of something to eat that is round, red, and has a stem on top," or give him letters, "I am thinking of a letter that is a straight line with a dot over it." The objective is for him to transduce from the auditory descriptions to the visual image.

Partial Recall. At this level we are concerned with ability to revisualize a whole figure from seeing only a part. The child is given a partial design or letter and is asked to complete it. Children with the severest disabilities usually cannot complete the partial figures unless they are told what the object is supposed to be. They cannot look at the part and revisualize the whole. Therefore, in the beginning periods of remediation, it is necessary to say, "Make this into a *sun*" (or an *apple*, or into an *h* or an *m*). Thereafter they should be encouraged to complete the figures without further suggestions.

(1) Prepare sets of picture completion exercises as shown in Illustration 54. The first picture in each row is complete but each successive picture has a part omitted. Ask the child to look carefully at the first figure and to complete each of the others without looking at the model; however, permit him to use it as necessary. As facility develops, give him incomplete pictures with no model to work from.

(2) Prepare simple designs, i.e., circles or squares, and ask the children to make them into as many pictures as they can. For example, by using the circle they might make a sun, a face, a clock, or a ball. By using the perpendicular lines, they could make a box, a suitcase, a door, or a house.

(3) Similar exercises can be given with letter completion. (Illustration 55 shows ways in which a page is prepared.) The child is asked to look at each part and to add lines to make a letter. As suggested before, some must be told what letter to make, but with progress in learning, they should complete them without verbal cues.

(4) Partial recall must lead to total recall. The techniques mentioned by Skinner (1961) in his work on visual memory using programmed instruction and teaching machines have been helpful. Words are first written completely to provide an opportunity to study the total con-

CIRCLE THE CORRECT SPELLING

please   thuoght
plaese   thought

would   becuase
wuold   because

littel   pencil
little   pensil

ILLUSTRATION 53. Spelling exercise for improving visual recognition and recall.

figuration and the sequence of letters. Gradually letters are omitted from various positions and the child is asked to write in the missing letter(s). At the end of the exercise only blank spaces remain and he must write the entire word from memory. Skinner feels that memory is improved by these procedures without the child being fully conscious that he is memorizing. An example is given below. This technique has proved to be one of the most effective for teaching a non-phonetic sight vocabulary to children with dyslexia and spelling difficulties. Many learn phonetic words when procedures for coordinating auditory and visual sequence are used (Chapter V), but this specific technique is for English words which have no consistent phonetic pattern (laugh, does, enough, etc.).

c a t
c _ t
c a _
_ a t
_ _ t
c _ _
_ a _
_ _ _

ILLUSTRATION 54. Exercise to improve revisualization.

*

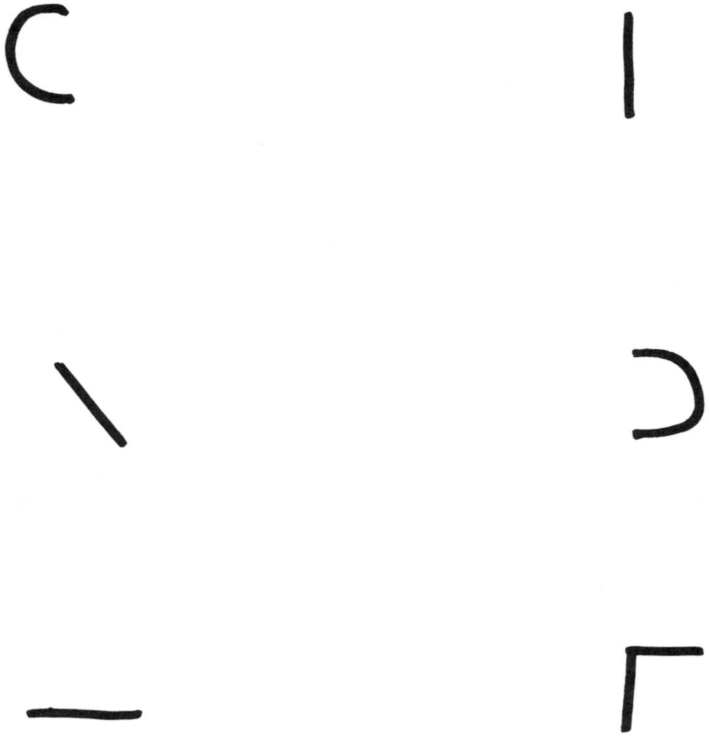

C

I

\

⊃

—

Γ

ILLUSTRATION 55. Letter completion exercise.

If revisualization deficits interfere with a student's completion of daily assignments, it is suggested that he be provided with charts containing the letters of the alphabet and numbers to which he can refer while doing his work. These letter and number charts serve as a kind of crutch until visual memory improves. Often it means the difference between success and failure in classroom activities. The child who knows how to spell a word orally should not be penalized because he cannot revisualize a letter, nor should the student who can do oral arithmetic problems be forced to revisualize numbers while doing written calculation. Although certain periods of the day should be devoted to the improvement of visual memory, he requires a guide while engaged in story writing or other written work. Even though many classrooms have letter and number charts on bulletin boards, it is helpful if individual cards are prepared to eliminate the difficulty of looking back and forth from the paper to the blackboard.

DISORDERS OF FORMULATION AND SYNTAX

Problems of written formulation are not manifested until the child has acquired a rudimentary level of reading and spelling. In the first and second grades he is expected to write only words or simple sentences. As soon as he can read more fluently and has been taught to spell, he is expected to write stories, letters, and answers to examinations. It is at this point that those with written formulation difficulties begin to fail in school. This group of children, by nature of their problem, is referred for diagnostic study and remediation later than others. Those with auditory comprehension deficits generally are identified during the preschool years, and many dyslexics during the first and second grade; however, those with written language disorders may not be identified until they are in the third grade, or even until they are in high school. Since written language is the last verbal system learned, the reasons for later identification are apparent.

Children with disorders of written formulation can have superior auditory language, good reading comprehension, and ability to copy the printed word, but they cannot express ideas in writing. According to Vygotsky (1962), pure thoughts cannot be expressed because of what is lost in the translation from thought to symbol. Observations of children with learning disabilities indicate that some can convert thoughts into one symbol system better than into others. Those with a disturbance of written formulation have greater difficulty encoding to visual symbols than to auditory. Although oral and written language are not identical, it is expected that there be reasonable integration between these forms in order that ideas can be expressed whether by speaking or writing.

Disorders of formulation and syntax vary both in nature and severity. In some instances the greatest problem is in ideation and productivity, while in others it is primarily syntactical. In the majority, however, both are present. Children with a disturbance in ideation and productivity are limited in output and use more concrete language. They may spend several minutes before initiating a simple sentence and finally give up with the comment, "I just can't put ideas on paper." They can *tell* stories or relate incidents but they cannot translate thoughts into written symbols. To determine the discrepancy between oral and written language, several children were given the Picture Story Language Test (1965), once according to the standard procedure and once orally. Although there is no standardization for the oral Picture Story Language Test, clinically it is useful to compare the transcriptions of the oral and written stories. Total word count on the written story often is less than half that of the oral story, and the Abstract-Concrete scores tend to be lower.

A disturbance of written syntax can occur in conjunction with a disorder in ideation or isolation. In contrast with children who have both oral and written formulation problems, children who have only written syntax difficulties have fluent use of the spoken word. They make errors in the written form that are not made in the spoken. The most frequent errors are word omissions, distorted word order, incorrect verb and pronoun usage, incorrect word endings, and lack of punctuation. This population does not have delayed or distorted spoken language, but it is of interest that many of their errors are the same type as found in children with deficiencies in oral syntax. The primary reason for referral is their limited ability to express themselves in written language.

The stories in Illustrations 56 and 57 reveal the written language problems of a high school student with average intelligence, good auditory language and reading ability. The first illustration is a transcription of the story he gave orally and the second is a short story about Fall. When his written story was read to him, he was appalled at the errors but rarely could he identify his mistakes when he read his own material.

Many students with written formulation disorders do well in school until they are required to write essay questions or themes. They participate in class discussions and perform on objective tests but fail much of the written work. A high school English teacher wrote as follows about a girl in her class: "I do not see how it is possible for any person to be so successful on one type of examination and completely fail on another. I am sending Jane's two final English examinations for you to see. On the objective part she received an *A*, one of the highest grades in the class. On the essay section, however, I could not give her more than a *D*. She seems completely unable to pull ideas together, to put them in sequence, or really demonstrate what she knows."

Spelling disabilities should be differentiated from those of written language. Many bright students avoid words they do not know how to spell and consequently reduce the level of their written work. When told not to worry about spelling, to concentrate on ideas, it is possible to determine more about the level of their ideation and formulation ability.

The picture in front of me tells the story of Billy who is trying to improve his speech by doing various exercises. In the one shown he is trying to show family life through the use of toys. He's now trying to re-enact a situation . . . uh . . . in his family when it's time to eat dinner. Each time he does this he tries to improve himself, trying to have normal speech. He's progressing fine, but he just needs a little more help . . . a little more time.

ILLUSTRATION 56. Oral language by a 19-year-old boy.

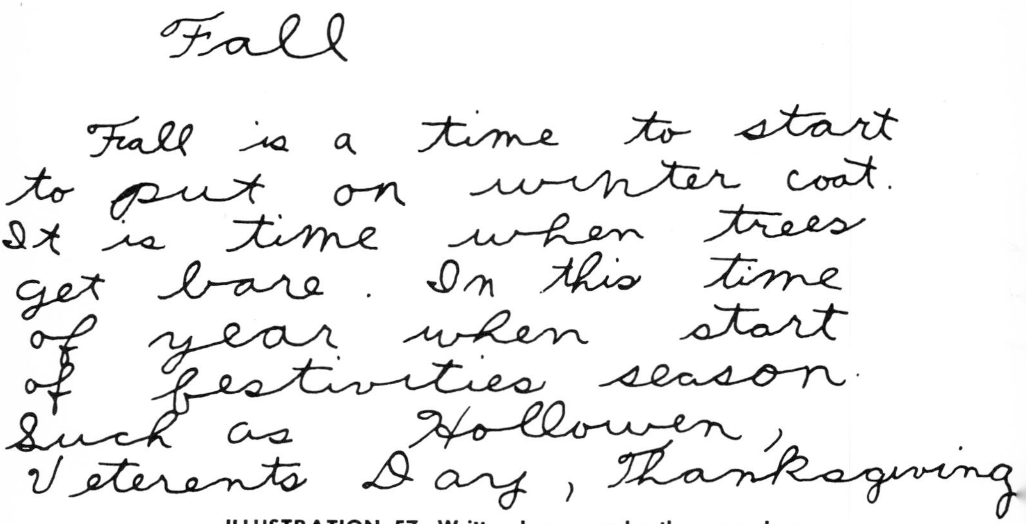

Fall

Fall is a time to start to put on winter coat. It is time when trees get bare. In this time of year when start of festivities season. Such as Hollowen, Veterents Day, Thanksgiving

ILLUSTRATION 57. Written language by the same boy.

Disorders of written formulation are very frustrating. Often the child feels he is able to compete with his peers in school activities until he is expected to convey information by writing. In the early grades there is less demand for written expression but by mid-elementary or by junior high school, the student feels his inadequacy because the discrepancy between the knowledge he has acquired and the knowledge he can convey continues to grow. Despite the frustrations and the complexity of the problem, progress can be made if proper remediation is provided. The high school student who wrote the story entitled *Fall* (Illustration 57) is now in a small liberal arts college doing average work. His progress in writing after eighteen months of training can be seen in Illustration 58. Residuals of the disability are evident but he continued to improve so that the level of his written language was more nearly in keeping with his other verbal behavior.

Educational Procedures

Awareness of Errors. Training begins by having the child write sentences and listening to the teacher read them aloud. When he identifies an error auditorially, the corrections are made on paper; in this way he can see the exact position of the omitted word or the transposition of words within a sentence. Next he is taught to monitor his own material by reading it aloud very slowly, checking word by word that he says exactly what is written. Later he is taught to say the sentence to himself (reauditorize) while scrutinizing the printed form.

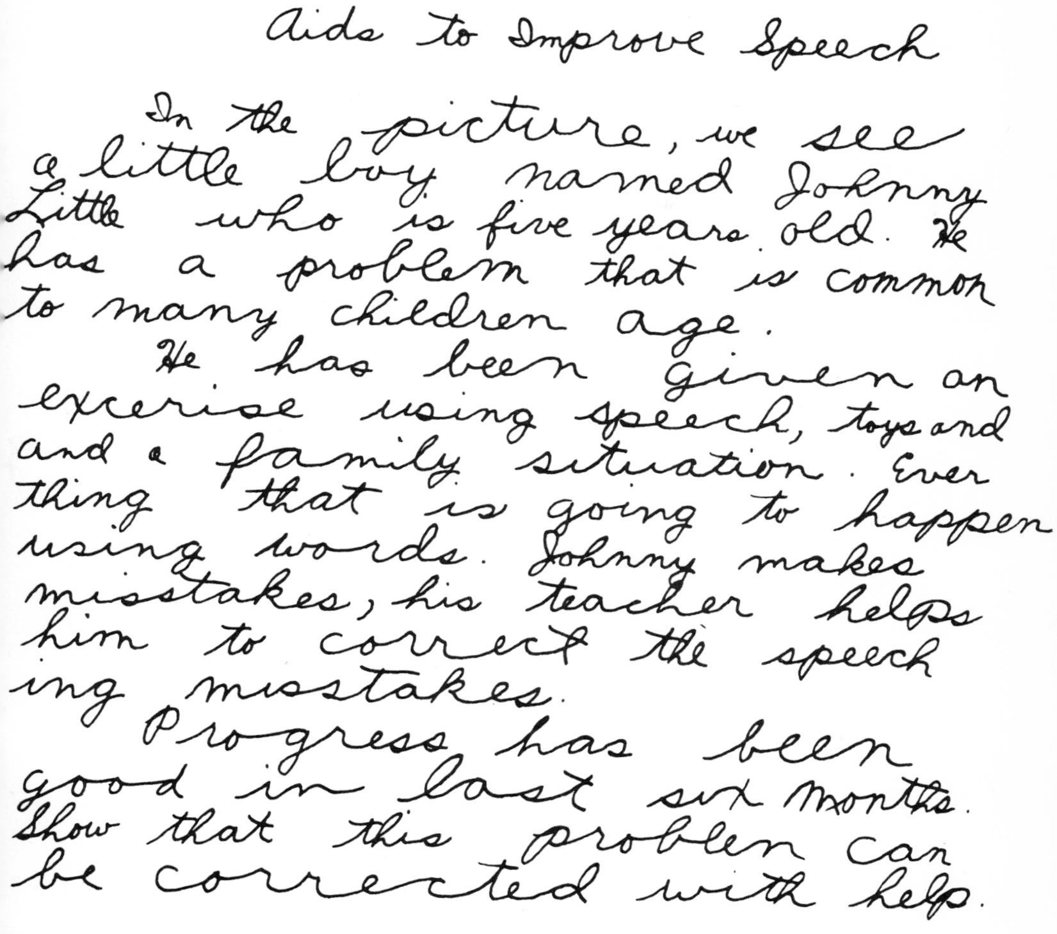

Aids to Improve Speech

In the picture, we see a little boy named Johnny Little who is five years old. He has a problem that is common to many children age.

He has been given an excerise using speech, toys and and a family situation. Ever thing that is going to happen using words. Johnny makes misstakes, his teacher helps him to correct the speech ing misstakes.

Progress has been good in last six months. Show that this problem can be corrected with help.

ILLUSTRATION 58. His progress in written language after 18 months of training.

Techniques for improving awareness of errors and for establishing auditory-visual integration are given below. The exercises are designed according to the specific types of errors present. Initially, the exercises should be structured so that the sentences do not contain different types of errors, e.g., errors of word order, word endings, word omissions, etc. Later, whole stories are written with various types of mistakes and the student is encouraged to find as many as possible.

(1) Write sentences containing one or two errors; read the sentences as they should be and ask the child to note whether the sentence he hears

is the same as the one he sees. It may be necessary to read the sentences very slowly at first in order for the student to check each word; as he progresses, they should be spoken at the normal rate. Examples are:

Written	Read
Mother went the store yesterday.	Mother went to the store yesterday.
The boy fell off him bicycle.	The boy fell off his bicycle.
The children are going to school.	The children are going to school.
Yesterday we skating in the pond.	Yesterday we went skating in the pond.

(2) Sentences such as those above can be written without grammatical errors but with words transposed for children who make errors of word order. Or the child is given a group of word cards that must be arranged according to a sentence spoken by the teacher. (She might say, "The cow went into the barn," and the student places the cards in the correct order.) Then the child reads the sentence and writes it, checking his work by looking at the arrangement of the cards.

(3) Negative practice is sometimes beneficial. The child is asked to give an oral sentence about an action picture. The teacher writes what he says, but omits a word or changes the sentence in some manner. She then shows him the sentence and asks him to find the error.

(4) Select action pictures and write two or more sentences to accompany each one. Write one sentence correctly and others with errors. Assume the picture shows a group of girls roller skating; sentences are written as follows:

> The girls am skating.
> The girls are skated.
> The girls are skating.
> The girls is skating.

Encourage the children to do the exercise silently, but if they cannot do so, ask them to read each sentence aloud.

In each of the above exercises the child is not required to write. He is required only to identify the errors. It is important to consider the basic principle of recognition before recall.

Ideation and Productivity. Often we hear a child lament, "But I can't think of anything to write." This comment is not unique to those with learning disabilities. All children, with the exception of the most creative, benefit from stimulation and encouragement before they write. Creativity does not emerge in a vacuum. Broad and varied experiences are necessary, particularly for children who seem unable to organize their thinking for written language.

Applegate (1955, p. 23) asks, "How do we turn it on?" Although he was referring principally to creative writing, this question is appropriate to our discussion. How do we get the child started? How can we stimulate written expression in those who cannot write, in those who have tried and failed, or in those who know their limitations and are hesitant to try?

First, the atmosphere, i.e., the environment of the classroom, should be accepting, lending itself to spontaneous expression. The child is permitted to talk freely about his ideas and made to feel that he has something to say. Through guidance the teacher helps the student express these same ideas in writing. A punitive, hypercritical environment does not lend itself to the type of freedom which is essential. The teacher who begins correcting a story before the child has an opportunity to complete an idea only thwarts future attempts. Perhaps the disorders of written language are difficult for teachers to understand since they see the children doing satisfactory work in other areas of learning. Nevertheless, degrading remarks written on their papers are unwarranted and psychologically harmful. Typical comments we have overheard include, "Is this supposed to be a story?" or "You can take this paper to Miss Jones in the second grade class and have her correct it. *I* can't read it!" Sarcastic remarks stifle output and carry over into other areas of work where the child performed successfully. Other teachers, rather than providing constructive criticism or remediation, operate on the assumption that the child can get along by talking. "Lots of people get by without writing; just let him get a secretary when he is old enough." Still others feel that "healthy neglect" is the answer and that he will write when he gets ready. None of these approaches is satisfactory. The teacher must let the child know that she is aware of his problem, that she understands it, and can be of assistance. Since most of the children are at least mid-elementary school age, they can be given reasons for the remediation procedures; they appreciate frank explanations.

Training begins with oral discussion of experiences, ideas, and feelings. These auditory verbal expressions are then converted into written language. Although the ultimate goal is for the student to convert thought into written language, it is essential to follow the progression of *experience* to *auditory language* to *written language*. The rationale for this progression evolves from normal development and experience with children who have learning disabilities. Previously, Myklebust (1965, p. 5) stated that "only those sophisticated in verbal behavior can 'bypass' the auditory and truly engage in silent reading or writing." Many children with writing disorders must use "auditory translations" much longer than the average. Some cannot write unless they verbalize aloud. Others learn to reauditorize or sub-vocalize. For these reasons training begins with stimulating experiences that will foster interest, discussion and writing.

Concrete to Abstract Ideas. A second basic progression to consider in the development of written language is to assist the children in going from concrete to abstract thinking. This progression is emphasized in all forms of verbal behavior but it is particularly relevant for remediation in writing. Often, educators are content when a child can write simple sentences or thank-you notes. This is insufficient for bright children with written formulation difficulties. We must provide the type of remediation that permits them to actualize their potential and to convey ideas in keeping with their mental abilities. Two bright fifth-grade boys developed ulcers, presumably because of emotional stress associated with an inability to do written work. One had a verbal intelligence quotient of 125 but wrote more nearly like a child of seven years. While his oral language contained an abundance of descriptive phrases and abstractions, his written language was concrete, limited in output, and incorrect syntactically. Note the contrast in his oral and written language in Illustrations 59 and 60.

A developmental progression from concrete to abstract language has been outlined by Myklebust (1965) and is useful both in evaluation and in planning remedial programs. The four levels of abstraction sequentially are: Concrete-Descriptive, Concrete-Imaginative, Abstract-Descriptive, and Abstract-Imaginative. In developing the Abstract-Concrete Scale, Myklebust referred to the definitions of abstraction as provided by Goldstein (1948), Hinsie and Campbell (1960), and Oléron (1953). He stated that when ideation is bound to the observable, it is considered concrete; the more it is detached from the stimulus, the more it is viewed as being abstract. Concrete expressions include descriptive words, phrases, and sentences directly related to experience. Abstract language consists of figures of speech, metaphors, allegories, and stories with a plot or moral.

When a child is severely limited in written language, we begin at the lowest level on the scale, *Concrete-Descriptive*. The emphasis is on helping the child write in a simple, descriptive manner about things he sees. He writes names of objects or simple sentences and uses a few adjectives denoting size, color, or appearance. The teacher selects objects, places them before the child and asks him to write the names of each. Next she asks him to think of a word that describes each of the objects and to

A short time ago the United States Navy sent up a moon. This moon is traveling around our earth extremely fast. Sometimes it is less than 400 miles from the earth. At other times it is more than 2,500 miles away. The Vanguard has had many failures, but one morning the pencil-shaped rocket was sent into space. The transmitters inside the moon are run by two different sources of electricity. One is powered by the sun. This is called a solar battery. The other is just an ordinary battery. The Museum of Science and Industry has put up a few new exhibits on the Vanguard. Now we may trace its flight.

ILLUSTRATION 59. Oral language of a 10-year-old.

The train ride

When we went on our vacastion we left Evaston a 130 P.M. Boraud the rain. We soon past the sulerben rea. We finly got en to open untry. After a few hours we ad to eat. We would write down he things we want end the Waiter took then. The food was very good. We arrived a 745 P.M. And aunt pick us up.

ILLUSTRATION 60. Written language by the same boy.

write it together with the name (a purple pencil, a big ball, a red dress). Later, it is helpful to illustrate how two descriptive words can be used in front of each name, e.g., a long, purple pencil; a big, green ball; etc.

Simple sentences are also introduced. Presenting the objects of the type mentioned above, the child is asked to write a sentence telling how or where each is used. The more structured the assignment, the more readily the child will write. If he is not given specific instructions, he may sit for several minutes trying to think how to use the word in a sentence. Action pictures are used but both the picture and the instructions are highly structured. For example, a typical instruction might be, "Write a sentence about each of these pictures. In each sentence tell what the person is doing or tell where the person is going." With the proper selection of pictures the child then writes: *The boy is eating. The girl is sleeping. The men are working.* For the second instruction he might write: *The boy is going to school. The lady is going to the store. The man is walking to his car.*

To develop more complex descriptive sentences it may be necessary to present a series of pictures to stimulate different types of sentences, e.g.:

The boy is walking.
The lady is walking.
The boy is walking to the store.
The lady is walking to the store.
The boy and the lady are walking to the store.

The sequence of auditory to written language is used simultaneously with the development of concrete to abstract thinking. Thus, a child might tape record his oral sentences, listen to them and then write them from his own dictation.

At the next level, *Concrete-Imaginative*, we teach the child to infer ideas from the stimulus picture or experience. If he sees a person eating something from a bowl, he no longer is to write only, *The boy is eating*, but, *The boy is eating soup*, even though he cannot see soup in the bowl. The teacher guides his thinking to imagine that which is not present or to think about the merely possible. This is a difficult step for some children with learning disabilities because of their stimulus-bound tendencies. They react only to what they see and often refuse to generalize. We were helping a nine-year-old over this barrier but his comments were, "We don't know there is soup in the bowl; maybe the boy doesn't like it." Patiently, the teacher helps the child understand, to generalize on the basis of past experience and to accept the fact that it is all right to make assumptions of this type.

Not all children with written language disabilities have problems in generalizing, but discussions are provided at this level to stimulate ideas for writing. Lead questions form a framework for stories and increase the output and productivity. (Who is in the picture? What is happening? What do you think is in the bowl?)

The third level for remediation is *Abstract-Descriptive*. Stories with more detail are developed and emphasis is given to concepts of *time* and *sequence*. Many children with learning disabilities are deficient in these aspects of behavior, so considerable effort is required. One of the most effective techniques utilizes film strips or reading readiness sequence pictures. The child is given one picture at a time and is asked to write a sentence about each. After he has completed the series, he goes over the sentences and is taught to insert appropriate transition words denoting the passage of time, e.g., later, next, afterwards. This procedure is valuable also for raising the tolerance for written work. Many children are frustrated when asked to write an entire story but can manage to do so if they first write sentences about individual pictures.

Another technique found to be beneficial for the development of time and sequence is a diary. The children are asked to keep records of their activities by writing several sentences each day. At night or in school the next day, they summarize the events. Initially, detailed summaries are written, but as the student learns to abstract, he groups events or ideas together into single sentences.

At the upper limits of the Abstract-Descriptive level, stories are written in which the characters assume roles. Often this is best handled by having the group write simple plays about an experience. Have them engage in a pretend situation, such as going to the store, tape record the conversation and then transcribe what they said. Typical stories or plays should be used, e.g., "A visit to the shoe store," with a girl in the class assuming the role of the customer and a boy the role of a salesman.

At the highest level, *Abstract-Imaginative*, the stories should consist of a plot, imaginative setting, occasional figures of speech, and some connotation of moral values. There should also be continuity from beginning to end of the story. The teacher guides the child's thinking with open-ended questions which lead him to perceive and imagine various relationships. Done well, this can be an exciting experience both for the child and the teacher. Take, for instance, the development of simple figures of speech. Beginning at a very concrete level and following a step-by-step progression, a child can be taught to relate the experience and the symbol. The teacher asks the group to think of things that are yellow. Generally, they respond with words such as *butter, gold, corn, sun*. The teacher agrees that these things usually are yellow and suggests that they write the words on the blackboard:

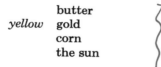

yellow   **butter**
          gold
          corn
          the sun

After the words are written, the teacher explains that we use expressions by placing the word *as* between the color word and the object (as yellow as gold). "Sometimes," she adds, "we see things that are yellow and they remind us of other things. If I say to you, 'I saw a golden tulip,' it would make you think of the color of a pretty gold bracelet or a watch, and you would have a good picture of the tulips even though I did not tell you what color they were." She explains further that we can make pictures by using words and can make our language more interesting and colorful by using these expressions.

Some children who have deficits in written language use figures of speech orally but must be encouraged to use them in writing. Through discussion they are led to develop other figures of speech and more abstract language. The exercises below are interesting and facilitate more colorful writing.

My new dress is as *blue* as the ____.
The man is as *strong* as an ____.
The candy is as *hard* as a ____.

Choices: *rock, grass, pillow, sky, ox*

Story plots are developed by teaching the children to outline their material before they begin writing. Key words, including names of characters, important places, and the sequence of events, are discussed before writing. While looking at the outline, the student tapes his story and writes it from dictation. Many high school students have used this procedure when writing themes, book reports, or other assignments. They must write what they tell. Some teachers permit the students to record their stories without writing them. This, in our opinion, does not provide experiences which facilitate written language; it only emphasizes the intact mode of expression. The purpose is to make use of auditory verbalizations as a means for improving written language.

Punctuation. "Punctuation is a system of inserting various standardized marks or signs in written or printed matter in order to clarify the meaning and separate structural units" (Webster, 1963). It is well to remember that these marks are symbols and that we are dealing with children who have symbolic disorders. Thus, they may not be able to associate the mark with its name or to learn how and when it is used. The nine-year-old girl who wrote the outline in Illustration 4 (Chapter IV) had not associated the words comma, period, or question mark with the symbols but she knew they appeared in various positions in written work.

Many children, notably those with visual-spatial disturbances, must be taught that the positions and number of marks have significance. The dot over the letter *i* is a part of the symbol but the dot at the end of a sentence has nothing to do with an individual letter; it signifies the end of a thought. The comma indicates a pause, but two figures of the same shape placed above certain letters indicate what someone has said.

The teacher should determine whether a child knows the names of the punctuation marks, whether he can differentiate them visually, whether he knows their proper location and, finally, whether he knows when to use them. Instructions, such as, "Point to the period," are useful in ascertaining if he has associated the sign with its name. When a child can point to the proper mark but cannot give its name spontaneously, it might indicate dysnomia or a reauditorization difficulty.

Grammar. In high school, grammar and English are the most difficult subjects for students with learning disabilities. Those who enroll in college also are in need of supplementary tutoring or help in grammar and English. The reasons for the difficulty are numerous, but of primary significance are the problems of memory and abstraction. Learning the parts of speech, types of phrases or clauses, and grammar rules assumes that the student can use symbols to talk about symbols. When a child learns about nouns, he not only must comprehend and remember the definition but he must understand which words in our language do, in fact, represent a person, place, or thing. This is not an easy task for many children who have symbolic disorders. Grammar books should be selected which concretize or picture the parts of speech as vividly as possible. If none are available, the student should make his own outlines with pictures and words denoting nouns, verbs, adjectives, and other parts of speech. Our students have found a small book entitled *Living Grammar* (Watson and Nolte, 1956) to be beneficial. No student should be required to memorize definitions or rules without understanding them. Thorough discussion of each principle is emphasized and the student is encouraged to verbalize that which he does not understand.

Spelling. Spelling requires more auditory and visual discrimination, memory, sequentialization, analysis and synthesis, and integration simultaneously than perhaps any other skill. Thus it is evident that the majority of children with learning disabilities have deficits in spelling. Problems in reading, in discrimination, or in memory usually are reflected in spelling. For this reason the remediation of spelling begins with isolation of the basic deficit. As reading improves, spelling also improves; as revisualization improves, spelling improves.

Too often children are required to memorize words that they cannot read. Therefore, the first step in learning to spell words is to learn to read them fluently. Secondly, the teacher should separate the words into those which are phonetic (which have a fairly consistent auditory-visual correspondence) and those for which there are no consistent spelling rules (the non-phonetic words). Generally, the phonetic words are taught according to the procedures outlined for syllabication in Chapter V. The student reads the words, says them as wholes, and then says them one syllable at a time, writing each syllable as he says it. Then he is given exercises to complete, such as those in Illustration 61. He listens to the word said by syllables and inserts the missing part. Next he writes the entire word from dictation without any visual cues. Exercises of this type are prepared for independent work on tape recorders. Often the teacher must dictate the words very slowly, drawing out each syllable and emphasizing individual sounds within words. Ultimately, the student should listen to a word spoken normally, analyze it, and write it, but until he reaches this level, the teacher must do it for him.

Most classroom teachers agree that students spell more accurately when words are dictated slowly. Those with learning disabilities can evidence as much as a two-grade discrepancy between the two presentations, depending upon the rate of dictation. Note the writing of a fifteen-year-old boy in Illustration 62. The words in *List A* were dictated one syllable at a time; the words in *List B* were dictated normally; the words in *List C* were names of objects around the room which he was asked to write without hearing any type of dictation. He performed best when the words were broken down so he could hear all of the sounds and he was the most inferior when given no auditory cues.

Non-phonetic words are taught by the procedures outlined previously, under Revisualization. Words are written as wholes, then letters are omitted in various positions throughout the word. Gradually, the student learns to spell the entire word.

Oral spelling is not emphasized since there is little demand for it in our culture. The emphasis should be on the written form so that the child can use his skills in everyday living. Many parents spend hours drilling on oral spelling at night only to find that the child fails the written test the next day. Generally this is because the child has not integrated the letter name with the visual equivalent, or because he cannot revisualize the letters. Whatever the reason, it is more beneficial to practice writing than saying the words aloud. Only when a child *must* go through an oral translation is spelling aloud advised. Occasionally, an individual can spell better orally than in writing, in which case remediation for auditory-visual integration is recommended. Until he learns to revisualize words, oral spelling is a mediating step but it should be eliminated as soon as visual memory improves.

Listen carefully to the words you heard on the tape and write the missing part.

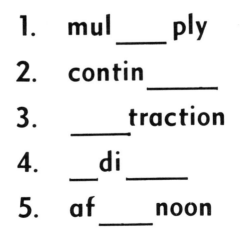

1. mul____ply

2. contin____

3. ____traction

4. __di____

5. af____noon

ILLUSTRATION 61. Exercise for improvement of syllabication and spelling.

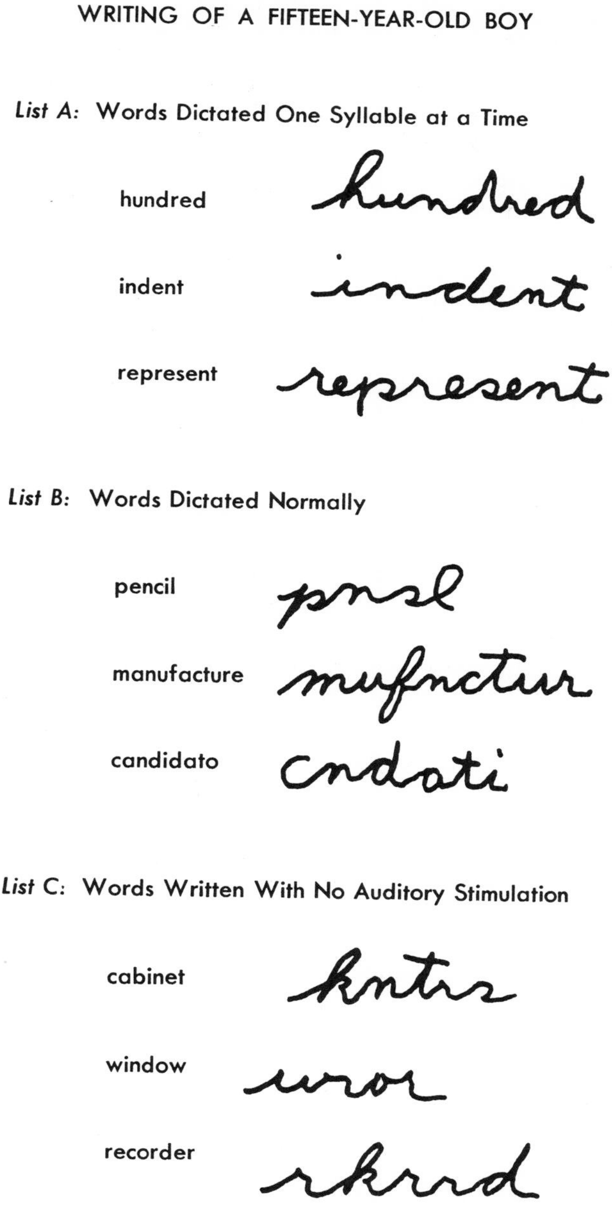

WRITING OF A FIFTEEN-YEAR-OLD BOY

List A: Words Dictated One Syllable at a Time

hundred	*hundred*
indent	*indent*
represent	*represent*

List B: Words Dictated Normally

pencil	*pnsl*
manufacture	*mufnctur*
candidato	*cndati*

List C: Words Written With No Auditory Stimulation

cabinet	*knts*
window	*wor*
recorder	*rkrrd*

ILLUSTRATION 62. Writing by a 15-year-old boy.

The role of kinesthesis in learning to spell should be considered. As indicated in the discussion on revisualization, some children are helped by relying on the "feel" of the word. Sometimes they gain clues to the correct spelling by observing the speaker's lips. We attempted to study this facet of behavior by giving a group of inferior spellers two comparable lists of words. The first list was dictated from behind so that only auditory stimulation was received. The second list was dictated so the teacher could be clearly seen when she said each word. When the results were analyzed, we found that the children fell into three distinct groups: some performed equally well on the two presentations, some performed better when only auditory stimulation was provided, and the remainder performed better when they had an opportunity to observe the lip movements of the speaker. These results suggest that it is well for the teacher to explore various presentations when she begins remediation. Only then can she understand the learning processes and plan proper educational procedures.

Typewriting. The question of typewriting is often raised when students are inferior writers. We hope to raise the child's writing to a level where he can communicate his personal and business needs by the use of pencil and paper, but beyond that point, typing is recommended. Those who cannot form the letters because of dysgraphia usually make good progress in writing but those who do not may profit from instruction in typing. It is necessary to break down the motor patterns for typing, as it is for writing, but the movements are less complex than those needed for cursive script. Electric typewriters require less pressure than manual machines.

Children with revisualization deficits also profit from typing. A fifth-grade boy who could copy but not revisualize, took a dictated spelling test and missed six words; on a comparable list the same day he missed only two words when he used a typewriter because he could see the letters on the keys. Typing also reinforces the visual images since they see letters both on the keys and on the page. Those with written language problems do not profit from typing until they gain facility with words, sentences, and syntax. The problem of these children is less related to visual-memory and visual-motor functions; the emphasis is on language.

Writing and School Assignments. Modification of school assignments must be considered for those with deficiencies in ability to write. It is not suggested that written work be eliminated completely for these children, but if society can give handicaps to golfers, it seems that the same should be granted the student with a learning disability. He is encouraged to put forth his best effort but exceptions are made when necessary. When writing is very deficient, oral questions can be given to determine whether information and concepts have been assimilated. Sometimes it is difficult to determine how much a student knows because the quality of his written work is so inferior. A college student explained to each of her professors that she knew the material, that they would be unable to read her writing, and that she would be happy to discuss the examination if they would give her the opportunity.

When writing is slow but accurate, the student can be given a greater time allotment. A common practice is to ask the individual to take the examination with his class and complete it at a later time. Those students who must auditorize while writing are placed in another room so that they do not disturb others. Additional exceptions are made depending upon the extent of the involvement. Optimum effort is encouraged and remediation is provided, but demands beyond a child's integrative capacities are avoided.

CHAPTER VII

Disorders of Arithmetic

"Mathematics may be regarded as a symbolic language whose practical function is to express quantitative and spatial relationships and whose theoretical function is to facilitate thinking" (Brown, 1953, p. 18). Man, throughout the ages, has developed symbols for expressing ideas in many ways. He talks, reads, writes, composes music, calculates, and engages in other forms of communication. He uses spoken and written language to express many thoughts and feelings, but to express particular types of ideas—ideas of quantity, size, and order—he developed mathematics. According to McSwain (1958), numbers are convenient devices used to record or communicate ideas and relationships of quantity.

The origin of mathematics has intrigued scholars for centuries. Although the phylogenetic stages of number evolution are not clearly established, it is believed that man had some number concepts long before he developed symbols for expressing abstract ideas of quantity. Dantzig (1939) feels that man, even in the lower stages of development, possessed a faculty which he called *number sense*. He states further that number sense should not be confused with counting, which seems to be of later origin. Most likely, members of early civilizations used a system of identifying animals by relating pebbles or marks for each. Even though early man had no system of counting or calculating, this so-called number sense made possible the resolution of certain practical problems in his life. Nevertheless, alone it does not explain the creation of arithmetic; primitive man had to go beyond the number sense (Stern, 1949). It is suggested that the thought process evolved first from direct contact with objects, then to mental perception, name, and number symbols (McSwain, 1958).

A similar sequence can be observed in the ontogenetic development of number concepts in children. Long before they come home from school saying, "two and two are four," they have, or should have, acquired some number sense; they should have an accumulation of meaningful experiences on which to base numerical symbols. Without integrated experiences, number and arithmetic facts are no more than nonsense words. The acquisition of a number sense is comparable to the developmental stages of inner language in other forms of verbal behavior. In relating the concept of inner language to arithmetic, we are concerned with a child's ability to understand experiences which are prerequisite to quantitative thinking, particularly those dealing with relationships of quantity, space, form, distance, order, and time.

Piaget (1953) states that it is a mistake to suppose that a child acquires the notion of numbers just from teaching and warns that when adults try to impose mathematical concepts on a child before he is ready, his learning is merely verbal. The development of numerical concepts begins as early as one year with the child's manipulation of one object after another; this is a prerequisite to counting (Gesell and Amatruda, 1947). As he plays with form boards, puzzles, boxes, pots and pans, he gains insight into pre-symbolic concepts of size, number, and form. He strings beads or puts pegs into boards and learns about sequence and order; he learns the phrases, *all gone, no more, too much,* thus adding to his ideas of quantity.

We are suggesting that there are inner, receptive, and expressive aspects of mathematical language just as there are with other forms of symbolic behavior. A child first assimilates and integrates nonverbal experiences, then he learns to associate numerical symbols with the experience, and finally expresses ideas of quantity, space, and order by using the language of mathematics. One of the important educational innovations in recent years is the development of new methods for teaching mathematics, with emphasis on meaning rather than on rote learning. Welch (1965, p. 44) feels that "when one examines critically and analytically the modern mathematics programs . . . one is struck with the emphasis placed upon *search* and *discovery.* The *search* is for patterns which grow out of the logical structure of the science of mathematics." He states further that (1965, p. 53) "a search for mathematical structure, for patterns, relationships and generalizations which can be appropriately symbolized. The *discovery* is the unfolding of the relationships as these patterns are adjusted from one quantitative situation to another." He adds that proponents of this method believe that all a teacher has to do is to present a child with a mathematical problem and say, "Discover." In reality, using this or any method, good instruction requires that the teacher act as a stimulator, an arranger, and a guide. Children cannot merely be given answers; the teacher helps them search for and discover patterns and relationships through planning, careful wording of instructions, presentation of materials, and continuous guidance.

Failure to learn mathematics may be due to various causes, including inferior teaching and limited intellectual capacity. Difficulties in learning arithmetic also can result from central nervous system dysfunctions. These disorders have been referred to as forms of *dyscalculia* (Cohn, 1961). But this term, like aphasia, must be clarified and the specific disability described if appropriate remediation is to be provided. Because of the complexity of the symbols involved, it is apparent that many types of disorders may result. Critchley (1953) points out that there may be deficiencies in identification of visual symbols, calculation, ideation, verbal or non-verbal aspects.

Dyscalculia has been included in a syndrome associated with a specific type of neurological breakdown; this is the Gerstmann syndrome (1940) which includes finger agnosia, right-left disorientation, agraphia, and acalculia. Critchley also discussed a cluster of problems sometimes designated "Leonhard's syndrome," consisting of dyscalculia, agraphia (the power of reading being intact), constructional apraxia, and temporal disorientation. Leonhard, however, cautioned others about ascribing these symptoms to a single underlying disorder since they might merely be epiphenomena.

In a study of brain-damaged children, Strauss and Werner (1938) found a relationship between arithmetic disability and finger agnosia. Recent research, however, indicates that these characteristics are not necessarily associated. Benton, Hutcheon, and Seymour (1951) reported that children with poor arithmetic ability do not invariably have poor finger localization. Benton (1959) concluded that finger localization and arithmetic ability have no specific relation to one another.

In our remedial work we have found it necessary to separate children who fail in arithmetic because of language or reading problems from those who have disturbances in quantitative thinking. Children fail arithmetic assignments not only because of a dyscalculia (in the more traditional sense), but because they cannot revisualize numbers, because they cannot form written numbers, or because they cannot remember instructions. These disturbances interfere with arithmetic learning, but the remediation must be based upon the nature of the deficit, not on the improvement of quantitative thinking.

ARITHMETIC AND RELATED LEARNING DISABILITIES

Auditory Receptive Language Disorders and Arithmetic

The child with an auditory receptive language disorder is not necessarily deficient in understanding quantitative relationships. Often arithmetic is his best subject in school and he performs written calculation with ease. The nine-year-old described in Chapter IV was at the bottom of his class in the language arts areas but second in arithmetic computation. He and others with verbal comprehension disorders have difficulty understanding the words used to describe certain processes or in grasping word meanings in story problems. Numerical symbols seem to have a more stable referent than other verbal symbols. When a child learns the numeral 5, he knows that it represents a certain quantity and that neither the symbol nor its meaning changes. In contrast, spoken words often vary in meaning and are more confusing. Many words used in describing mathematical processes (e.g., set, times, base) are unusually difficult for the receptive aphasic because he cannot shift meanings from one context to another. His problem is not one of quantitative thinking but one of word meaning. Typically, he does well in computation but is inferior in reasoning and on arithmetic vocabulary tests. The teacher should be aware of the verbal comprehension problem and clarify meanings through remediation.

Auditory Memory and Arithmetic

Two types of auditory memory problems interfere with mathematical performance. The first is a problem of reauditorization which prevents the child from quickly recalling numbers. He recognizes the correct number when he hears it but cannot always say the one he wants. When asked to read numbers aloud or to do oral calculation, he may say a number, realize it is wrong, but be unable to evoke the correct one. For him, rapid oral drills are frustrating and should be avoided until reauditorization improves.

Deficits in auditory span interfere with arithmetic in that the child cannot listen to story problems presented orally. He cannot hold and assimilate all of the facts in mind so he cannot work the problems. If, however, he is permitted to read them he has no difficulty. Oral work should be kept to a minimum when this problem is severe.

Disorders of Reading and Arithmetic

Dyslexic children do not always have a disturbance in mathematics. An inability to read does not impede acquisition of mathematical concepts. It interferes with ability to read story problems but not with the ability to calculate when the problems are read aloud. Learning numerical symbols does not require the high degree of auditory-visual analysis and synthesis essential for reading. When learning to read the word *cat*, the child must associate a visual sequence of letters with a sequence of sounds, but when learning the numerical symbol *2*, only one visual symbol is related to the spoken word. For this reason dyslexics have less difficulty learning arithmetic. However, they may not have facility to sound out the words *two* or *three*; hence they would not be able to solve problems in which the written word rather than the numerical symbol were used.

Visual perceptual disturbances resulting in confusion of letters (*m* and *n* or *b* and *d*) usually affect number work as well as reading (*3* and *8* or *6* and *9*). The inversions, rotations, and distortions should be noted and the procedures for remediation outlined in Chapter V are recommended.]

A disturbance in revisualization has a marked effect on written calculation because the child cannot remember the appearance of the numbers.

He can copy and reauditorize numbers but he cannot write them. A nine-year-old with this disability could do written assignments only while looking at the clock on which he could see the numerals. The deficiency in revisualization should be corrected, but in the meantime these children can be given charts showing numbers in sequence so they can refer to them while working problems.

Disorders of Writing and Arithmetic

Children with dysgraphia (apraxia) cannot learn the motor patterns for writing either letters or numbers; they profit from the training procedures outlined in Chapter VI. Until they learn to write numerals they are given problems with multiple-choice answers which they can encircle or underline. Or they are given a rubber stamp set containing numbers to arrange. They are not urged to write if they cannot form the numbers. Teaching of concepts continues but other modes of response are permitted until the disorder of writing is alleviated.

DISTURBANCES IN QUANTITATIVE THINKING

The problems outlined in the preceding section interfere with performance in arithmetic but they are not like those of the dyscalculic who fails to understand mathematical principles and processes. In this chapter we are concerned primarily with children who can understand and use spoken language, who can read and write, but who cannot learn to calculate. Generally, arithmetic is the system that is most affected but other problems sometimes coexist. The characteristics below are prevalent in the dyscalculic population.

(1) Many dyscalculics are deficient in visual-spatial organization and nonverbal integration (Strauss & Lehtinen, 1947). They cannot quickly distinguish differences in shapes, sizes, amounts, or lengths. They cannot look at groups of objects and tell which contains the greater amount. Some have difficulty estimating distances and making judgments related to visual-spatial organizations.

A study of the case histories of children with these disturbances reveals many nonverbal problems in early life. Parents often report that the children rarely enjoy working with puzzles, blocks, models, or construction-type toys. Some of the children find it difficult to learn to make the proper judgments for eating and dressing. Typical comments by parents include the following: "When he eats he always overestimates the amount of food he can put on his fork and as a result is always a mess at the table." "He can't dress himself completely, at even ten years of age he never lines up the buttons with the buttonholes on his shirt." "He never estimates how much milk he can pour into a glass, or the speed for pouring it. Even now, at the age of twelve, he can't always figure out how to get peanut butter out of a jar with a knife and onto a slice of bread, so he 'orders' his six-year-old brother to do it for him."

(2) In contrast to nonverbal visual deficiencies, many of these children show extraordinary auditory abilities and are early talkers. One mother wrote, "When John was twenty three months old we called him the little professor because he could carry on a conversation with any adult and he talked all of the time." Such children may spend hours listening to records or classical music and even learn foreign languages. A few of the parents, recognizing their children's auditory superiority, try to improve the mathematical deficiencies by purchasing records with multiplication tables or other arithmetic procedures. The records are of little value in establishing numerical concepts, as the children memorize the numbers without understanding them.

(3) Children with dyscalculia may excel in reading vocabulary and in syllabication skills. Even though some have visual perceptual deficits, these do not interfere with interpretation of the printed word. The visual symbol, when stabilized with an auditory symbol, is easy for them to learn. As soon as they learn the sounds of letters, they find it easy to spell or sound out words. Many, however, encounter problems at the higher levels of reading comprehension. It may be that the deficiencies in integration of certain types of nonverbal experience interfere with ability to grasp the total meanings of what is read.

A school psychologist reported the following about an eight-year-old. "His learning in the basic reading and spelling skills has progressed normally; in fact, he is such a good oral reader that one is apt to overestimate his reading ability. He has a remarkable sight vocabulary and his mechanical reading skill is excellent. A comprehension test, however, reveals some word calling. He often knows what all of the words mean but he does not grasp the thought or content of units greater than one sentence in length. He has made very little progress in numbers—his writing is neither good in form nor conventionally produced. He cannot maintain the proper sequence or organize the material meaningfully on a page." The mother of the same boy wrote, "He was a joy and constant companion as a young child; he was and still is eager to learn. He had learned to read some words before he started school and has gone to the library every week for as long as I can remember. Now—however, we know he needs help, for we realize that arithmetic seems to elude him completely."

(4) Some dyscalculics have a disturbance in body image. They seem to have incomplete or faulty knowledge of their own bodies (Kephart, 1960), and their drawings of the human figure are lacking in organization. They include details but fail to organize or structure the parts appropriately.

The eyebrow may be drawn below the eye or the nose below the mouth. Note the drawings in Illustration 63.

(5) Disturbances in visual-motor integration (apraxia), either for writing or for nonverbal motor skills, are not unusual in dyscalculics. Some can spell and formulate ideas but have deficits in forming letters and aligning them properly on the page. Others have no difficulty writing but cannot learn the nonverbal motor patterns for riding a bicycle, jumping rope, or using tools and utensils.

(6) Occasionally disorientation accompanies dyscalculia; there is neither a distinction between right and left nor a strong sense of direction. One thirteen-year-old loses orientation in his school if certain doors that normally are open happen to be closed. A high school sophomore refuses to do errands in the local supermarket for fear of getting lost. Children such as these are unable to grasp the various types of visual nonverbal cues that serve for purposes of self-orientation. Generally their reference points are verbal, i.e., numbers on doors, names of streets, or a billboard with a verbal caption. Rarely do they note the types of homes on specific corners and the nature of the landscaping, but use only the street sign as an indication of where they are. If this single type of reference point is altered, they have no other means for orienting themselves.

(7) Often the dyscalculic is poor in social perception and in making judgments. He has little conception of distance and the time that it might take by bus to reach a destination. A twelve-year-old was asked, "If you wanted to go from Evanston to the airport, would it be better to walk or take a car?" His response was, "Which airport do you mean— Midway or O'Hare?" In either case one would not walk since it is at least a forty-five minute drive by car.

Social maturity usually is low and in keeping with their nonverbal rather than verbal abilities. Because of their deficiencies in self-help, locomotion, and manipulation of utensils, they remain dependent upon adults. The mean social quotient for a group of fourteen dyscalculics was 77.3, with a range from 62 to 91. This quotient is substantially below the mean verbal intelligence quotient for these children.

(8) On standardized tests of intelligence, dyscalculic children tend to be considerably higher on verbal than nonverbal functions; we have observed a discrepancy as wide as 72 points. The mean verbal intelligence quotient for the fourteen children cited above was 109.7, with a range from 96 to 134; the mean performance intelligence quotient was 82, with a range from 62 to 104. The two children who scored above 100 on the performance scale had a significant discrepancy between their verbal and nonverbal abilities; their verbal quotient was in the superior range.

ILLUSTRATION 63. Drawing of a man by a dyscalculic.

Arithmetic Disturbances

Not all deficiencies in arithmetic are identical. The teacher must know the level of ability and also the nature of the disorder. Standardized achievement tests which yield information regarding both computation and reasoning should be used, but an item analysis is necessary, as is the investigation of many other skills. The following disabilities may be found in varying degrees.

(1) Inability to establish a one-to-one correspondence. The number of children in a room cannot be related to the number of seats, nor an estimate made of how many forks to place on a table at which four people are to eat.

(2) Inability to count meaningfully. Although numbers can be said in rote fashion, relationship between the symbol and the quantity is not established.

(3) Inability to associate the auditory and visual symbols. It is possible to count auditorially but not to identify the numerals visually.

(4) Inability to learn both the cardinal aud ordinal systems of counting.

(5) Inability to visualize clusters of objects within a larger group; each object in a group must always be counted.

(6) Inability to grasp the principle of conservation of quantity. Some dyscalculics are not able to comprehend that ten cents is the same whether it consists of two nickels, one dime, or ten pennies, or that a one-pound block of butter is the same as four one-quarter pound sticks.

(7) Inability to perform arithmetic operations.

(8) Inability to understand the meaning of the process signs. In certain instances the deficiency is related to a perceptual disturbance (inability to distinguish the difference in the plus and multiplication signs). More important is failure to grasp the meaning conveyed by the signs.

(9) Inability to understand the arrangement of the numbers on the page. Children learning to read must know that the sequence of letters within a word is significant. Those learning arithmetic must know that a specific arrangement of numbers also has meaning. Because of visual-spatial problems, this factor often interferes with computation abilities.

(10) Inability to follow and remember the sequence of steps to be used in various mathematical operations.

(11) Inability to understand the principles of measurement.

(12) Inability to read maps and graphs.

(13) Inability to choose the principles for solving problems in arithmetic reasoning. The dyscalculic can read the words and do the problems if he is given the principle (add, subtract, multiply, etc.) but without assistance he cannot determine which process to use.

EDUCATIONAL PROCEDURES

Nonverbal Concepts

The primary goal in teaching the dyscalculic child is to help him symbolize a particular type of experience—experience dealing with quantitative relationships. Because he frequently has a disturbance in visual-spatial perception or in the understanding of certain nonverbal experiences, he fails to comprehend relationships of quantity, order, size, space, and distance. He does not make the generalizations or draw the proper conclusions from experiences that ordinarily would lead to understanding concepts of number and quantity. Therefore, remediation often begins with meaningful nonverbal activities related to arithmetic.

Use concrete materials which can be manipulated and arrange experiences in a manner that will facilitate numerical thinking. Through structured presentations and minute steps, such as those prescribed for programmed instruction, the teacher assists the child in gaining insight into concepts of quantity. Only after concrete operations are clearly understood can mental perception and mental manipulation of symbols be expected. Learning numbers without consideration for the pre-symbolic aspects will result in rote learning of arithmetic facts.

A primary factor in teaching many dyscalculics is utilization of auditory verbalizations. As indicated previously, they tend to learn best through this modality, so this avenue may be the one through which to improve quantitative thinking. In contrast to the normal child, the dyscalculic cannot be given manipulative materials such as a formboard and be expected to make generalizations about quantity or size; these relationships must be learned. Auditorization as a mediating process often is the key to his understanding of numerical relationships.

Shape and Form

One cannot assume that because a child is in the elementary grades, or even in high school, he can distinguish differences in figures, shapes, or forms. Irrespective of age, abilities in these areas should be explored. A high school geometry teacher observed that one of her students had made no progress in mathematics since the third grade, and after checking his records noted that he had learned the fundamentals of addition, subtraction, and multiplication but could not employ arithmetical reasoning or handle geometric concepts. Intuitively she considered all types of problems that could prevent him from learning geometry and began with recognition of shapes and forms. She found that this boy, at the age of fifteen, could not differentiate between a circle, a hexagon, and octagon. This is not an isolated example. Many dyscalculics have spent years memorizing arithmetic facts, rules, and theories which were of little value to them because they were unable to relate them to experience.

The reasoning processes for early quantitative thinking are largely based on visual inspection; hence, the child must be able to observe general configurations, to see how things are similar, and to follow nonverbal operations. Various types of puzzles including pegboards, formboards, and jig-saw puzzles are useful.

(1) Begin with a puzzle in which only one figure can be fitted into a space. Multi-piece puzzles are used only after the child has facility with single forms. Observe him placing the figures into the spaces and note whether he systematically scans all of the pieces. Often he pays little or no attention to the shape of the piece in relation to the space and tries to insert it anywhere, turning it, pushing it, and hoping that if he pushes hard enough it will fit. As a rule, such children must be shown either through verbal explanation or taction how and why a piece fits or does not fit into a particular space. Rarely do they learn from their own trial and error methods of visual inspection.

In timing the performance of children on successive trials on a formboard, only slight improvement was made in speed and accuracy. A nine-year-old who was asked to do a formboard containing nine different figures (square, circle, triangle, etc.) used five minutes and forty seconds to complete the puzzle; on the second trial he cut his speed by ten seconds and on the third by only two seconds. The next day a similar puzzle was used but after the first trial each piece was discussed. Sometimes the child was given the name for the figure and at other times an extensive description. For example, when given the square he was told, "This is a square—feel the sides, they are smooth and straight; this is a corner—do you see how the two sides of the figure come together into a point—feel it; here is another corner," etc. "Now look at the circle. Do you see any corners or points on this figure—no, there are none; you can feel all around the edge and do not have to stop at any point. Look at the spaces, they are just like the pieces; trace around this one and see if it feels the same as the circle." After a discussion of approximately twenty minutes the boy was asked to do the puzzle again. The time required dropped from five minutes and two seconds to two minutes and fifteen seconds. This illustrates that it is the *way* in which materials are used that is critical for learning. If this boy were given puzzles to explore without the verbalizations, only minimal learning would have occurred. On the other hand, a receptive aphasic might profit more from visual inspection; bombardment with auditory descriptions would only confuse him.

(2) Two-dimensional figures are recommended in the early stages of remediation since many dyscalculics are more confused when working

with blocks, cubes, or spheres. Figures are cut from cardboard, construction paper, or felt and the child inserts them into the proper spaces. The flannelgraph is a good teaching device and can be used for either group instruction or independent work. Different shapes are cut from large pieces of felt and the child replaces them in the correct areas. He has an opportunity to trace around the figures, as well as the edge of the hole, and in this way learns about spatial relationships.

(3) Gross motor activities and kinesthesis are beneficial in establishing differences in form. Outlines of figures can be made by placing ropes on the floor. The child is asked to look at two shapes and tell whether they are the same. If he cannot do so by looking, he is asked to walk along the edge or on top of the rope and note whether the patterns feel the same.

Size and Length

Without understanding and perception of different sizes and lengths, most children have trouble in dealing with such mathematical concepts as perimeters and areas. This leads to confusion in everyday life situations. An inability to see the differences in objects of varying sizes has been observed in adult aphasics and has been designated as visual size agnosia (Wepman, 1951). Although this concept has been applied mainly to reading difficulties, it is even more critical for learning arithmetic. One boy was taught for a period of several months in an attempt to help him perceive differences in size. He could distinguish differences in shapes but could not determine which coin was a dime or which was a nickel on the basis of size; he had to read the word *nickel* or *dime* on the coin to make the proper identification. This same boy could not demonstrate with his hands the size of an average apple, or the length of his shoe, nor could he draw the approximate length of a dollar bill. It was not unusual for him to place his index fingers thirty inches apart to show the length of an average pencil. Others with this problem can memorize a formula dealing with area or perimeter but they cannot visualize the figures represented by these dimensions; therefore they have no check on the accuracy of their calculation. A thirteen-year-old boy, above average in verbal intelligence, failed to see the incongruity when asked if a house would fit on a lot which is two feet by fifty feet. When asked to draw the representative sizes of a lot fifty feet by fifty feet and one which was one hundred feet by one hundred feet, he drew the figures presented in Illustration 64. This same boy could memorize geometric theorems and other rules but never fully understood them or used mathematical language until he received remedial training to improve his abilities in nonverbal relationships.

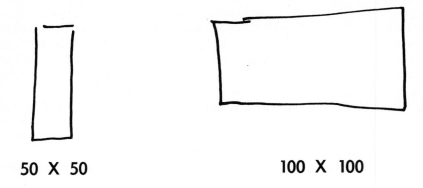

50 X 50   100 X 100

ILLUSTRATION 64. The spatial disturbance of a 13-year-old dyscalculic.

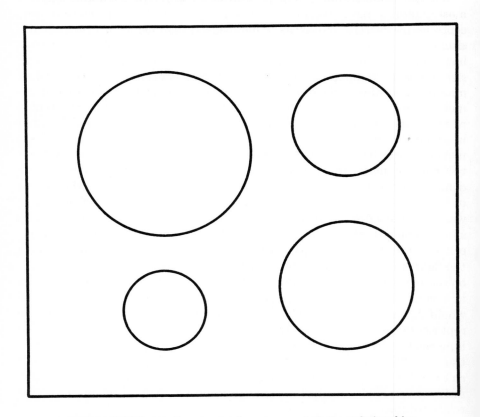

ILLUSTRATION 65. Exercise for improvement of size relationships.

Procedures similar to those suggested in the preceding section are useful in teaching children to differentiate between figures of different sizes. Color cones and other toys which have pieces of graduated size can be beneficial. Figures of identical shape and color are preferable so the child does not make the differentiation on bases other than size.

(1) Cut various size circles or squares from large pieces of felt as shown in Illustration 65 and ask the child to place the missing circles in the correct spaces. If he cannot do so, permit him to superimpose the figures so that he can feel around the edges and perceive which is larger.

These cutout figures can be used in other ways. Ask the child to arrange them in a row beginning with the smallest and working toward the largest. If he is unable to do so, provide a key, that is, a page of circles drawn in the proper order, and ask him to match the felt figures to the proper outline (see Illustration 66.)

(2) On occasion we have utilized audition to help a child visually perceive the differences in lengths of lines. Two tones of the same frequency (produced by a whistle or a pure tone audiometer) were presented and the child was asked to indicate whether the sounds were of the same duration. The dyscalculic usually can make correct distinctions auditorially. Therefore, attempts are made to integrate the auditory and visual functions. Present two tones, one long and one short, and ask the child to tell whether they are the same. Next present a tone while simultaneously drawing a line at the rate of approximately one inch per second. For example, listen to a tone of four seconds and draw a line four inches long; listen to a two-second tone and draw a line two inches long. Have the child watch and listen closely, noting the differences which he *sees*.

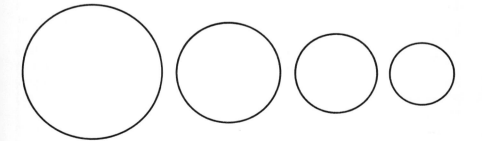

ILLUSTRATION 66. Exercise for teaching gradation of size.

(3) Often a child ruins materials, books, and garments because he tries to place them in drawers or spaces that are too small. He fails to relate the size of the object to the area in which he tries to place it. He may try to put a book in his lunch box or a large card into a small envelope, failing to foresee the results of his actions. For more successful achievement in everyday life, as well as in numerical concepts, exercises are planned in which the child must make determinations of size. Matching index cards to different sized envelopes has proved effective. The child first superimposes the card on the outside to determine whether it will fit; later he is taught to make these estimations using only visual inspection.

One-to-one Correspondence

Before a child grasps the concept of number, or before he learns to count meaningfully, he must have an understanding of one-to-one relationships. Just as the shepherd used a pebble to represent each animal in the flock, so the young child must have an understanding of "one for one." Many dyscalculics are deficient in this ability and count erratically because of it. When counting pegs they may say, "one, two," when touching the first peg, "three, four," when touching the second, and skip the third peg completely. Others fail to grasp the concept that a room with only six chairs will not seat a group of eight children, or that three ice cream bars is not enough for a group of four children if each person is to have one. The following techniques assist in developing one-to-one correspondence.

(1) Match the rows of pegs. Arrange a row of pegs in a board and give the child another set to arrange in exactly the same way with one peg opposite each of the ones in the board. Do not permit him to skip holes or put more pegs in any row than there are in the model rows.

(2) Utilize the auditory modality. Rather than working only with visual materials, ask the child to relate a number of sounds to a number of objects. Beat a drum and ask him to put a peg in a hole each time he hears the beat, or clap your hands and ask him to make a mark on a paper each time he hears a sound.

(3) Taction is effective when working with small quantities. Place five pennies in front of the child and ask him to put a finger of one hand on each penny. Explain that the number of pennies and the number of fingers is the same. Then place a sixth penny before him and explain that the number of pennies and fingers is not the same; there are too many.

(4) Prepare several pieces of flannel on which there are various numbers of buttons. Prepare a second set in which there are only button holes. Give the child the pieces of flannel and ask him to match the pieces with the same number of buttons and holes. Do not permit him to skip or misalign.

(5) Place a series of doll figures or paper dolls in a row and ask the child to draw a hat for each one, stressing the concept of one-to-one correspondence.

(6) Assign errands that will foster an understanding of numbers. Ask one child to place a sheet of paper or a pencil on each desk, explaining that every child must have one and that no child should be without.

(7) Those who know how to write numbers are given a series of circles in rows and asked to write a number in each circle. Again they are told not to forget any circles and that no circle can have two numbers inside. Of all the procedures tried with a nine-year-old, this was the most effective and was the only means by which he learned to count properly.

Counting

While babies are still in the crib, parents sing number jingles to them. Many of these same children learn to sing number songs long before they understand counting as a meaningful process. Even though the rhymes do not develop concepts of quantity, they establish the auditory sequence of numbers which is prerequisite to rational counting. Dyscalculic children learn the auditory sequence but fail to associate the numbers with the appropriate quantity. In contrast, children with deficits in auditory sequentialization cannot learn numbers in a series.

When a child learns to count, he is using a thought process to find how many in all (McSwain, 1958). Failure to count properly may result from an inability to establish a one-to-one correspondence, to maintain the auditory series of numerals, or to associate the symbol with the quantity. The objective in training is to integrate these facets of the counting process. When the child hears the auditory symbol *six* he should visualize the appropriate quantity and when he sees a number of objects he should be able to determine how many there are. In doing so he must integrate auditory, visual, and nonverbal processes.

In developing numerical concepts, Welch (1965) cautions the teacher against using the words *large* and *small* to refer to numbers. These words refer to the concepts of spatial relationships and should be used when discussing things of different *size*. The words *greater* and *less* are for comparison of quantities. (Which number in the series is less? Which number is greater?) If these terms are used synonymously with the words *larger* and *smaller*, children become confused.

Some children cannot look at a series of objects and count aloud; they cannot hold the auditory sequence while simultaneously following the visual pattern. Although achievement of such integration is a major objective, it may be necessary to reduce the task at first. Since these children tend to be more successful auditorially, we might begin by co-ordinating two factors, i.e., the auditory series and one-to-one correspondence. The following procedures are suggested for teaching children to count aloud.

(1) Have the child close his eyes and concentrate only on counting and listening to the beat of a drum. Have him listen for a series of drum beats and simultaneously count (saying the number each time he hears a beat). When he achieves success, ask him to open his eyes, listen to the drum beats, and make a mark on the paper for each sound he hears. He is not asked to write the numbers but only to make marks representing the number of drum beats. This technique helps him understand concepts of *more* or *less* because he can associate the numeral *10* with a large group of marks and the numeral *2* with a smaller group. After he has learned to listen, count, and mark correctly, have him recount his marks, this time without the aid of the drum. Encourage him to use a steady, even rate while counting. Make certain that he touches each figure as he says the numbers.

(2) Have the child count objects in a manner that requires a motor response. Strauss and Lehtinen (1947) recommend the use of a counting box in which the child places a peg in a hole as he says the number. Stringing beads while counting also is useful. The rationale derives from the fact that many of the children count erratically, skipping objects or saying two numbers for a single object. By encouraging him to say a number only when he touches a peg or when he places a bead on a string, he gains understanding of the purpose of counting and his performance improves.

(3) Somewhat less easy to establish is the concept of ordinal counting. Children usually first learn the cardinal system which tells how many (1, 3, 7). The ordinal system indicates the place of the number in a sequence (first, third, seventh). This means that a child learns not only to tell how many cars are in a line but also to tell which is the third car from the corner. The main objective is to provide help in understanding that *first* and *second* refer to positions or locations within a sequence. Meanings of the words *how many* and *where* are critical for learning the two systems of counting.

To develop the ordinal system the teacher begins by placing three or four toy cars in a line near a toy garage. She leads the child to discover the meaning of ordinal numbers by asking, "Which car is closest to the garage? Which car is farthest away? Which car is at the end of the line? Which car is at the beginning of the line?" As he responds, she explains that the car at the beginning of the line is the *first*, the next is the *second*; thus he continues to develop the concept. Objects are used as a reference point when learning this system of counting, since a discussion of position in line is not specific enough.

Visual Symbols

Soon after a child learns to count auditorially, he becomes aware of printed numerals in books, on street signs, and in stores. At the same time he hears his parents say the numbers that refer to visual symbols. When he is read to, he begins to notice that the page numbers in books always follow the same order. He listens to his parents say, "Next page, please" or "You skipped a page," and even though he may not know the names of the symbols, he begins to understand that the figures refer to quantity. This system of counting places more demands on the child with an arithmetic disturbance. Now he must hold an auditory sequence and relate it to a visual sequence; he must associate an auditory symbol with a visual symbol and must associate either or both with a given quantity. The teacher's objective is to integrate these systems so the child understands that the quantity *three* can be represented by a spoken symbol, by *3*, or by the written word *three*. Many types of breakdowns occur in children with learning disabilities. Some can match the symbol *7* with seven beads but not associate it with the correct spoken number (they may say there are five beads). Others cannot read or write numbers from dictation because they have not associated the auditory with the visual symbol. The teacher must note where the breaks occur and improve the deficits. The following procedures are suggested for teaching the proper visual sequence of numbers.

(1) The number line as shown below is a useful aid in discovering and understanding the quantitative concepts to be associated with a number and its symbol (McSwain, 1958, p. 22).

$$0 \quad 1 \quad 2 \quad 3 \quad 4 \quad 5 \quad 6 \quad 7$$

The number line shows continuous magnitude. The number *2* represents the length from 0 to 2, or $1 + 1$. The number *6* represents the distance from 0 to 6, or $1 + 1 + 1 + 1 + 1 + 1$. The number line also provides a good opportunity for the child to see the numbers in sequence. Welch (1965) suggests that prior to the actual use of the number line itself, young children should use "number stepping blocks." Blocks or cardboard sheets with painted numerals from 1 to 10 are placed on the floor and the children are asked to walk forward and back on them. A child takes one step and then three more steps and notes how many steps he took altogether (see Illustration 67). Large number lines can be painted on rolls of wrapping paper and the child steps from dot to dot, saying the number and observing the visual symbols. Although these procedures are used with normal first- and second-graders, it has been necessary to use them with older dyscalculic children in order for them to understand number processes and ideas of quantity.

ILLUSTRATION 67. Number stepping blocks.

(2) If the child has no ability to relate quantity with the visual symbol, present dot configurations such as those found on dominoes. Each numeral is represented consistently by the same arrangement of dots until he can make the proper associations; use extra-large dominoes with indented dots so the child can feel as well as see the configuration. He is asked to close his eyes and concentrate on the tactile impression. After he has the experience of feeling the configurations, he is asked to match the "feel" with the appearance. He is given one of the large dominoes, asked to feel it, carefully touching all of the indentations, and then asked to open his eyes, look at another, and tell whether it is the same as the one he felt. Next these configurations are matched with the symbols (2, 4, etc.).

As soon as the child can make the association between the quantities and the numerals, the dots are arranged in other ways since he should not be led to think that the number refers only to a specific visual configuration. It must be clearly understood that the quantity *eight* is not always represented by two groups of four dots arranged in a particular fashion but that quantities can be distributed in many ways.

Conservation of Quantity

Piaget (1953) has suggested that children must grasp the principle of conservation of quantity before they can develop the concept of number. He demonstrated this principle by having young children explore quantitative relationships and by noting their responses. The children were given two receptacles of identical shape and size, then asked to place beads in them, one at a time, using both hands simultaneously—putting a blue bead into one box with the right hand and a red bead into the other with the left hand. When finished, each child was asked how the boxes compared. Piaget found that most children were sure that there were the same number of beads in each container. He then asked them to pour the the blue beads into a receptacle of a different size and shape. The youngest children thought that the number changed if the beads filled the new receptacle to a higher level; they thought there were more beads in it than in the original container. Children near the age of seven, however, realized that the transfer had not changed the number of beads.

We have tried similar experiments with dyscalculic children and found that many are deficient in understanding the principle of conservation of quantity; they perform like the younger children in Piaget's group. Two severely dyscalculic twelve-year-olds who had above average verbal intelligence thought that the container in which the level of beads was higher contained the greater amount, even though they had placed the beads in the receptacles. One of the boys was asked to perform a similar task using water instead of beads. He was given two one-cup measures and was told to pour the water up to the line indicating one cup. He was then asked to pour one cup into a flat bowl and the other into a tall glass. When asked about the amounts in each container, his response was, "There is more water in the glass."

The same boy was told to pour equal amounts of water from a one-cup measure into two half-cup measures. He poured about one-fourth cup into the first measure and then tried to pour the remainder into the other. Without considering that he should watch the water level and relate it to the rim of the cup, he continued to empty all of the water into the second container. The result was that the water spilled onto the table since he tried to pour approximately three-fourths cup into a one-half cup measure. Preschool children make better judgments than this twelve-year-old; they learn to equalize amounts of water in bottles or sand in pails and enjoy transferring quantities from one receptacle to another.

When children do not understand this stability of quantity, much arithmetic is meaningless. They must recognize that a unit of ten things need not always be in a single group but can be arranged and divided into many different groupings with the value remaining constant. A dollar is the same whether it is in the form of a paper bill, two fifty-cent pieces, or a hundred pennies.

Procedures for developing this principle must utilize concrete, manipulative materials. Toys recommended by the Montessori schools and by Stern (1949), as well as other materials such as the Cuisinaire Rods, are useful. As with any materials, however, it is the *way* in which they are used that determines whether the child will learn. Sample techniques are given below.

(1) Cut strips of paper or posterboard into pieces about one inch wide, varying in length from one to ten inches. Leave some pieces unmarked and prepare others showing the one-inch intervals. Show the child the strips and ask him to tell which is the longest, the shortest, etc. Then take the ten-inch strip and demonstrate for him the many ways in which he can group or regroup smaller strips to make an amount that is equal to the one long strip. For example, begin with two ten-inch strips; ask him to superimpose one on the other and note whether they are the same. Then

place a nine-inch strip on top of the ten-inch strip and ask him whether they look the same. When he sees that it is shorter, explore with him, in a systematic way, the other strips to determine which one could be added to the nine-inch strip so that it would be as long as or the same as the ten-inch strip. Continue to show him how to use different combinations which equal ten. Although many normal children play with puzzles of this type and generalize the principles from observation, it is necessary to demonstrate the similarities for the dyscalculic and to use many more verbalizations with him. He does not gain insights from visual inspection; his learning requires guidance, considerable discussion, and repetition.

Inlay puzzles can also be made for this purpose. Cut ten-inch strips from a block of wood and then cut many smaller pieces varying in length from one to ten inches. The child is encouraged to recognize the different combinations which equal ten, the purpose being to demonstrate the stability of quantity.

The Cuisinaire Rods have been effective in teaching some children. The rods are of different colors and lengths (e.g., a short brown rod represents *1* and a rod twice as long of a different color represents *2*, etc.). Initially the child is not given the number symbol for each rod but he merely explores the rods visually and tactually. With his hands behind his back he is given a rod to feel and tries to match this one with one he sees. Normally a child begins by comparing rods grossly different in size; later he learns to make finer discriminations. Children are also asked to arrange staircases with the rods, going from the largest to the smallest. In addition they plan combinations of tens, as described earlier with the number strips. As they match and compare each unit, they begin to realize that a whole can be divided into many parts and in different ways.

Interesting results were obtained when these rods were used with children who have learning disorders. The school-age receptive aphasics did well in dealing with the visual-spatial relationships; they quickly noted the differences in sizes and figures. They did well until verbal symbols were presented or until they had to verbalize the relationships. In contrast, those with dyscalculia and nonverbal learning difficulties were able to verbalize more quickly than the normal but were unable to deal with the nonverbal relationships. If they were told that a red rod represented three, they had no difficulty, but until the relationships were verbalized they could not deal with the visual-spatial relationships. While working they tended to verbalize freely. A ten-year-old who was trying to build the staircase with the rods first used only trial and error methods, but when he realized there was a progression from the largest to the smallest he made comments such as, "There's a place for everything—everything has a place."

We have also developed the concept of conservation of quantity by using scales, especially balance scales. For example, place one pound of beans in a bag and ask the child to weigh them, making certain that he notes the one-pound indicator. Then ask him to pour the beans from the large bag into two or three smaller ones. He should observe that even though the beans were divided into smaller lots, the total amount is the same.

Visualizing Groups

A problem common to many dyscalculics is their inability to quickly identify the number of objects in a group. Consequently, they always must count objects one by one to determine the total. Furthermore, when they see a large number of objects they cannot visualize smaller groups within the whole. This disability impedes arithmetical operations and interferes with everyday situations in which it is helpful to have facility in visualizing a quantity. For these reasons it is necessary to teach number groupings.

(1) Tachistoscopic procedures are important in developing these skills. The teacher begins by presenting small groups of dots which are widely separated, as shown in Illustration 68. The child is given a paper on which there are similar groupings and after the figures are flashed on the screen, he circles those that are the same. Then he is asked to count the number in each group and to determine how many there are in all. Color cues may be added in the initial stages of training. For example, the group of dots on one side of the screen may be red while those on the other side are blue. Size cues also foster learning (three big dots and two small dots). These supplemental cues help the child visualize small groups within the whole. As he improves, the dots are drawn closer together and the child now "imagines" the smaller groups within the whole.

Another technique for reinforcing ability to visualize groupings is to have the child arrange objects into different units. Ask him to place ten blocks in two groups of five or eight blocks in four groups of two. As he gains practice with the parts that form a whole, he becomes more conscious of the groupings that are possible.

The Language of Arithmetic

There will be no attempt to present all of the steps used in teaching arithmetical operations, particularly in view of the current changes in terminology and methodology. Irrespective of terminology, however, the teacher should consider the inner, receptive, and expressive processes required for learning the language of quantity. No child should be expected to use arithmetic symbols until he first understands them. Specifically, the teacher should note whether the child has made the proper

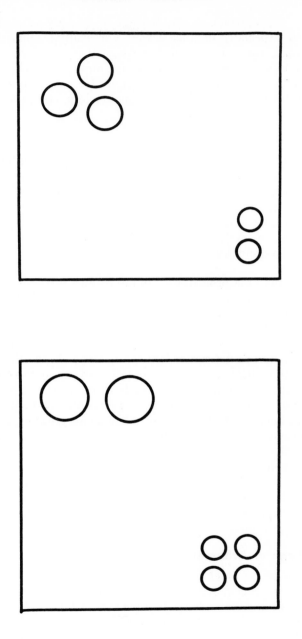

ILLUSTRATION 68. Exercise for improving visualization of groups.

associations between nonverbal experiences and auditory and visual symbols. We have observed children who could work problems visually but who did not coordinate the printed and spoken forms. One boy worked the problem $6 + 7$ correctly but, when asked to read it, said, "six from seven is thirteen." He had not associated the auditory terms with the visual process signs. One means of evaluating such lack of integration is to have the children read the problems aloud or write problems from dictation, noting whether they relate the auditory and visual forms. It is exceedingly interesting to have the children verbalize while working. This is one of the most valuable opportunities the teacher has to observe the child's thinking processes and to ascertain where he needs assistance.

Certain problems occur more frequently than others when children begin to calculate. Each of these is discussed.

Process Signs. The signs in arithmetic indicate the relationship between numbers and how they should be manipulated. Unless a child clearly perceives the signs and knows their meaning, he is helpless when trying to solve a problem. Because of visual perceptual disturbances, some children cannot differentiate between the signs, especially those denoting multiplication and addition or those indicating greater than ($>$) and less than ($<$). These figures are the same except that they are rotated. Others fail to learn that signs composed of separate figures are a single unit (e.g., the $\div$ and $=$ signs). If they fail to perceive these as whole, meaningful symbols they will confuse them with each other and with the single line denoting subtraction.

Exercises are given to make certain that the child clearly differentiates one figure from another. Write three or four signs in a row and ask him to tell whether they are the same or which one is different. If he cannot perceive them as units, draw borders around each sign until he learns to visualize them properly (see Illustration 69).

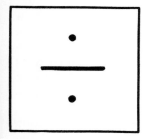 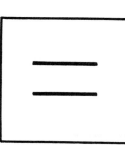 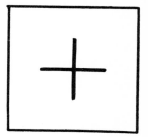

ILLUSTRATION 69. Structuring of the process signs.

Meaning of the process symbols should be explored in great detail. The child should know the name of each sign and what it means in terms of mathematical operations. Practice is given in merely reading problems without working them. Have the student read problems such as $6 + 3 = 9$ or $6 - 3 = 3$. Determine whether he associates the spoken word with the visual symbol. Synonyms for each sign should be clarified so he understands that 6 *plus* 3 means the same as 6 *and* 3. Every effort is made to use a precise, mathematical vocabulary so that he, in turn, will understand and use the correct terms.

Alignment and Arrangement of Numbers. The arrangement of numbers in an arithmetic problem is of significance. A child must learn that he cannot write the figures in any position but that they must be arranged in specific ways to be meaningful. In our discussion of dyslexia, we indicated that children must understand that the order of letters within a word is relevant. Now, in arithmetic, the arrangements are even more complex, not only with regard to left and right but from top to bottom. When a child writes numbers from dictation he moves from left to right, yet when he solves many problems he works from right to left. If he is told to write the problem "four plus five," he can arrange it in an order from left to right or with numbers in a vertical position.

Each time a new process is introduced, the teacher explains the sequence and arrangement of numbers in a problem, indicating where numerals of greater value can or cannot be placed, the position of the sign, and the arrangement of the figures. No assumptions can be made with regard to what a child does and does not understand. Instead, each minute aspect of the problem is explored to make certain that there are no deficits. Some children cannot think about how to write the numbers, arrange them, and derive an answer all at the same time; exercises must be provided to improve each deficiency. Overloading and stressing too many goals cause the entire process to break down.

To improve the visual-spatial arrangement of numbers, students are given cutout numbers and process signs to arrange, first according to a visual model and then from dictation. The teacher writes problems on the blackboard and asks the children to reproduce them in the same way. She calls attention to any inversions, reversals or misalignments, and corrects each one, pointing out the mistakes and rearranging the figures. Later the students are asked to write problems from dictation, which involves conversion of an auditory statement to the visual form.

Sequence of Steps. Memory disturbances interfere with calculation because the student cannot retain the sequence of steps used in solving problems, especially the more complex processes of multiplication and long division. Those with this disability are encouraged to verbalize each step in detail while working. If confusion persists, various types of cues

can be used to indicate the operational procedures. For example, a green
dot might be drawn above the numbers showing the starting point for
calculation; arrows may be drawn to show the direction in which to work.
Until the steps are automatic, written charts are provided containing
step-by-step procedures for each process. A twelve-year-old boy kept
detailed instructions for doing multiplication and division problems. He
knew the arithmetic facts and the meanings of the signs, but could not
remember the steps to follow. By using the chart of procedures he completed most of his assignments successfully. Gradually, cues are reduced
and the charts eliminated.

Problem Solving and Reasoning. When presenting new processes or
concepts, begin at the most concrete level; the teacher reduces the task
to a level at which the child understands. Each new concept is introduced
with concrete materials and the process is verbalized, then converted into
mathematical symbols. Inner, receptive, and expressive stages are considered at all times. For example, in teaching addition demonstrate how
an abacus is used to concretize the process, next indicate how the problem
is verbalized, and then converted into written numerals.

Teacher: (Shows three beads on an abacus) How many beads do you see?

Child: (Counts and says) Three.

Teacher: (Showing three beads on a second row) How many beads do you
         see in this row?

Child: (Counts again and says) Three.

Teacher: If I put all of these together, I will have one large group. I will
         have more than I started with. How many will I have all together?
         Count them.

Child: (Counts and says) Six.

Teacher: We have seen the beads and talked about them; let's see if we can
         say it in writing. We will use numbers instead of words. (Goes
         through the same process as above and shows the child the first
         row of beads) Write the number that tells how many.

Child: (Writes the symbol 3)

Teacher: Now I want to add some more. Please write the sign that tells me
         to add.

Child: (Writes the plus sign so he has 3 +)

Teacher: Look at the next row. Tell me how many beads I have.

Child: (Writes the symbol 3; he now has 3 + 3)

Teacher: Now I need a sign that tells me how many are in both groups.
         Write the equal sign.

Child: (Writes the sign and solves the problem)

This example illustrates how we work from inner to receptive auditory to
visual processes and how, in this way, arithmetic becomes a language.

Welch (1965, p. 55) recommends the use of number sentences for intermediate school children, but it is helpful to use them throughout. He states that "in number sentences certain symbols define mathematical relationships between two number expressions. An understanding of these relationships is essential for a meaningful approach to the operations of addition, subtraction, multiplication and division." He gives an example of problems and number sentences.

Problem: David bought a notebook for $1.00. He also bought 3 packs of notebook paper at $.25 a pack. How much money did he spend?

Number sentence: $1.00 + (3 × $.25) =

This approach helps the children begin work on arithmetic problems in a more systematic way and stresses unity of thought rather than random manipulation of figures.

The arithmetic program for dyscalculic children should be kept as practical as possible. Problems for everyday living should be stressed. Although some students are unable to achieve a high degree of mathematical skill, most can complete a basic course in high school. Goals should be considered in terms of the individual's attaining independence in society: his need for giving and receiving the correct change when making a purchase, recognition of coins and their values, paying bills, balancing a check book, determining whether he has enough money for dinner or for bus fare. The concepts of measurement are also taught. Students should learn how to use scales, rulers, and other units of measure. Students must learn to make judgments regarding time, distance, and space, to read maps, to estimate how long it will take to go from one place to another, to determine whether there is enough gas in the car to reach a specific destination. Girls are taught how to read recipes, to measure liquids and solids, how to cut recipes in half or to double them, and how to measure cloth or surfaces so they can manage household affairs. Each new concept is concretized and is presented through direct experience whenever possible. The children are encouraged to solve practical problems using the speedometer of the car so that they begin to internalize the feeling of two miles as contrasted with twenty miles.

The teacher remembers that there are many symbols and abbreviations that are difficult for children with learning disabilities. Symbols such as lb., ¢, $, and ft. should be clarified. Throughout the training period emphasis is placed on logic and rational thought rather than on rote memorization.

Examples shown in Illustration 70 are exercises for this purpose.

CIRCLE THE **T** IF THE ANSWER IS TRUE. CIRCLE THE **F** IF IT IS NOT TRUE.

1. If I am paid every two weeks I will receive about 40 checks each year.   T   F

2. Two pieces of wood 4 feet long will fit exactly on a wall which is 140 inches long.   T   F

3. A light bulb that is supposed to last 100 hours will be good for about one year if it is burned about four hours each night.   T   F

4. A man coming to Chicago from Detroit will have a longer drive than the man who comes from San Francisco.   T   F

5. Several dozen people can sit in a room with 26 chairs.   T   F

ILLUSTRATION 70. Exercise for improvement of quantitative reasoning.

CHAPTER VIII

Nonverbal Disorders of Learning

The behavioral concomitants of brain dysfunction are best understood in both children and adults in terms of verbal disabilities. In adults this is revealed through the area of study referred to as Language Pathology and in children by the designation of Learning Disabilities, usually interpreted as a deficiency in verbal acquisition or in academic achievement. It is interesting, however, that some pediatric neurologists describe the "typical" child with a learning disability as being high in verbal but low in nonverbal functions. The educator tends to describe this child in a reverse manner, identifying him as inferior in factors related to school success, not in aspects of learning that entail daily routines. Both of these learning disabilities can be attributed to involvements of the neurology of behavior.

In this chapter we give attention to the child whose deficits are not verbal, not academic in the usual sense but who is unable to comprehend the significance of many aspects of his environment. An example is the child who fails to learn the meaning of the actions of others, so he cannot grasp the game of "cowboy"; he cannot *pretend* and *anticipate*, as do his playmates. He fails to learn the implications of many other actions, e.g., gestures, facial expressions, and caresses, as well as other manifestations of attitude. He is unable to understand the relevance of time, space, size, direction, and various aspects of person and self-perception (Allport and Vernon, 1933; Fisher and Cleveland, 1958; Hécaen, H. & Ajuriaguerra, J., 1964; Hall, 1959; Heider, 1958). We categorize this child as having a deficiency in *social perception*, meaning that he has an inability which precludes acquiring the significance of basic nonverbal aspects of daily living, though his verbal level of intelligence falls within or above the average. There are many such children but they are largely unrecognized since test procedures for identifying them, as well as procedures for educational remediation, have been slow in developing.

In our experience with children having learning disabilities, we have encountered this type of child over and over again. This led to the theoretical formulation of behavioral concomitants of brain dysfunctions as described in Chapters I and II. It was clear that a disturbance of brain processes could affect essentially verbal *or* nonverbal aspects of behavior, or both. The fact that one of these can be affected, while for practical purposes the other remains basically intact, led to the premise that the brain categorizes experience on the basis of whether it is verbal or non-verbal. The next inference was that, in terms of brain function, information can be classified as Nonsocial-Nonverbal, Social-Nonverbal, and Verbal. Since arriving at this classification, we have developed automated procedures for evaluating each of these levels of function (Myklebust, 1967). Moreover, data that support these postulations have been collected (Boshes and Myklebust, 1964; Hughes, 1967; Lawson, 1967; Zigmond, 1966).

The intricate nature of nonverbal learning disabilities remains to be explored, but certain general characteristics have emerged. Before considering these we must recognize that the most basic experiences are nonverbal. When a hierarchy of experience is developed (Myklebust, 1964), we find that the lowest, most primitive level is sensation. By gradation it evolves to perception, imagery, symbolization, and lastly to conceptualization. As discussed in Chapter I, verbal learning disabilities fall at the level of symbolization, thus often affect conceptualization. On the other hand, the nonverbal disabilities fall at the levels of perception and imagery and therefore constitute a more fundamental distortion of total experience. It is for this reason that children having nonverbal deficits usually fall significantly below their chronological age in social maturity (Doll, 1953) as well as below their level of mental ability as measured by verbal tests. Also, this may be the reason that the social quotient, more than most other measures, correlates with the diagnostic findings of the neurologist (Boshes and Myklebust, 1964).

Perhaps the most consequential factor, in terms of special education, is that it is experience itself which is distorted, not ability to use spoken language or to read and write. The astute, observing teacher recognizes that the ways in which words are used provide a clue to the problem. The words have an "emptiness" that belies superficial facility. In normal learning every word assumes a learned referent, a unit of nonverbal experience which it symbolizes. The child with a nonverbal learning disability is like the child who lacks color vision. He has no difficulty in learning the *word* red, but cannot acquire the *experience* red, so he cannot distinguish it from the experience green or yellow. When he uses the *word* red, as required by daily activities, it connotes only a vague, conglomerate impression often unrelated to the actual circumstances. The manifestations nonverbally are distortions of perception and of mental imagery.

The development of procedures for remediation has only just begun. Currently this problem is one of the most challenging for special education. Throughout the remainder of this chapter we present suggestions for remediation as they have been evolved up to the present time.

LEARNING THROUGH PICTURES

Pictures portray visual nonverbal aspects of experience. Especially in early life, much learning is through this two-dimensional type of representation of objects, persons, ideas, and situations. Failure to gain meaning from pictures can be due to an inability to comprehend that they represent something in the environment. We worked for several days with a four-year-old to help him understand that the picture of a spoon represented the object he used for eating and that the picture of a chair stood for the object on which he was sitting. After several training sessions, he finally grasped this principle and became so excited with his discovery that he spent the remainder of the day looking at pictures and running to the objects they represented.

Some children are aware that pictures represent objects, but because of figure-ground disturbances cannot interpret them correctly. They do not recognize objects that are only partially pictured and respond to the detail rather than to the whole. Strauss and Lehtinen (1947) described similar disorders and developed tests and methods for remediation. They stress that in order for a figure to be recognized, the individual must attend to both the whole and its parts, that is, to the general configuration as well as to detail. Persons with perceptual disorders may rely only on detail and not relate the parts to the whole. For example, a five-year-old looked at the picture of a rural mailbox and said, "It's a piece of toast"; he looked only at the door of the box, not seeing the total configuration. Another child of the same age looked at a picture of a knife and called it a banana; he looked only at the general configuration and did not notice the lines separating the handle from the blade. Accurate picture interpretation requires both analysis and synthesis.

In another instance we worked with a young man from whom a brain tumor had been removed. He was able to see but could not interpret what he saw. When looking at a black and white outline drawing of a coat, he traced the edges saying, "I see lines, I see lines . . . what is it?" After tracing it four or five times, he suddenly realized that the dots represented buttons and said, "Ah, ah . . . it's a robe." Later he was given a black and white drawing of a face with two lines below to represent the neck. These two lines disturbed integration of the whole so he could not interpret the meaning of the picture. The following transpired between the man and the teacher while he was examining the drawing.

Man: Why . . . I . . . don't know . . . I see two ears (points to them) . . . What are these? (pointing to the lines representing the neck)

Teacher: Can you tell me what the whole picture is?

Man: I don't know . . . two ears . . . but these . . . (still bothered by the lines of the neck)

Teacher: What are these? (pointing to the eyes)

Man: Eyes.

Teacher: Yes, and this? (pointing to the mouth)

Man: Mouth.

Teacher: Now, look at the picture and tell me what you see.

Man: I don't know.

Teacher: (Covering the two lines of the neck) Now can you tell me?

Man: Oh yes, a face; it is a face.

Drawings often reveal an inability to perceive significant detail, as shown by Illustrations 71 and 72. These drawings were made by a twelve-year-old who was unable to identify details or to organize visually without assistance. The first drawing was made spontaneously without instruction. The second was made after only twenty minutes of discussion, in which he was taught to observe details while looking at himself in a mirror.

Educational Procedures

Pictures are used to identify visual nonverbal deficits in learning and they also constitute a fundamental resource for the development of remedial procedures. Realistic pictures or photographs are most beneficial since actual representations facilitate learning. Moreover, at the outset it is suggested that flat objects (e.g., comb, key) be selected for picture-object matching, eliminating as much as possible the problem of relating a three dimensional object with a two dimensional representation of it. In practice, the child is encouraged to handle the object, trace the edges, and then place it on the proper picture.

Many considerations go into the selection of the pictures to be used in remediation.

(1) *Size.* Most children work comfortably with pictures that vary from approximately four by six to eight by ten inches. If the pictures are too large they fail to comprehend the whole and when too small they cannot identify the details.

(2) *Color.* For motivation and ease of interpretation, realistic colored pictures provide the best stimulation. Many children use color cues as a means of identification.

(3) *Background.* Pictures that are free from background shadings and clutter are most suitable because of the ease with which they can be recognized; also, they prevent responses to irrelevant lines rather than to the picture. A typical remark from a five-year-old when he saw the shading on a window was "broken window." A first grade girl looked at the picture of a blue stocking which was pasted on a large white card and could not tell what it was; yet we knew she had identified stockings in other situa-

tions. The teacher tried to ascertain whether a reduction in background would alter her response, so she drew a border around the picture about one-half inch from the edge of the card. The child immediately responded with the word *sock*.

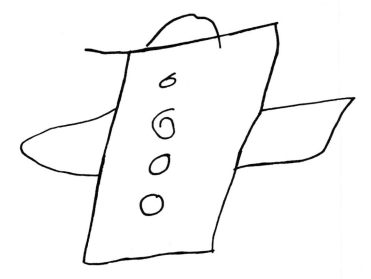

ILLUSTRATION 71. First drawing of a shirt by a 12-year-old.

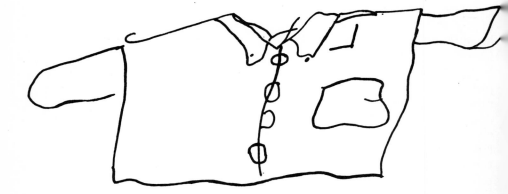

ILLUSTRATION 72. Progress in drawing a shirt after 20 minutes of training.

ILLUSTRATION 73. Exercise for improving visual synthesis.

Mountings for the pictures should be dark, subdued colors; black, dull brown, or gray-green have been used with success. Bright reds and yellows detract from the picture.

Matching to Outlines. Some children attend to the detail without noting general configuration. They look at a picture of a dress and respond to the flowered pattern of the material rather than to the shape of the garment. These children are given pictures to be matched with their outlines. Realistic pictures of houses, balls, dresses, hammers, etc., which have a definite, identifiable shape, are selected and outlines are drawn to go with each. The child traces the edge of the figure, observes the general configuration, and superimposes it on the outline.

Analysis and Synthesis. Many techniques can be devised to improve ability to analyze and synthesize. For example, prepare pictures of a house, a telephone, and a coat, omitting some internal detail (window, telephone dial, button.). Then give the child a picture of the missing part and ask him to place it in its proper position. In other instances, prepare pictures from which an external detail is missing (handle of a cup, stem of an apple, chimney from a house) and ask him to place it on the correct figure.

Jig-saw puzzles are useful but at the lower age levels only simple ones should be presented, that is, pictures that are cut into only two parts. The purpose is to help the child recognize an object even though he may see only a part of it. First he is shown the picture of a common object. Then the teacher cuts the picture in half and places two parts next to each other. Gradually she moves the parts away from each other and then together again. One kindergarten boy could identify the halves as long as they were no more than two inches apart; when the space between the parts was increased or when he saw only one half, he no longer could recognize it. With training he learned to relate the parts to the whole and identified objects even though the figures were incomplete.

After the child learns to work with picture cards, he is given work sheets (Illustration 73) and asked to draw a line between the parts that make a whole figure. Not only is he asked to determine which parts go together but he must identify the picture. Some children correctly draw lines between the two halves of the picture but cannot recognize it. A nine-year-old thought that the lamp was a skirt and that the mouth was a valentine.

General Significance

Interpretation of a complex action picture requires considerable integrity. It involves more than ability to identify objects or persons inasmuch as it assumes understanding of relationships and general meanings.

Just as comprehension of spoken language and reading involves more than single word meanings, so the interpretation of a complex picture requires awareness of the total experience.

Certain children with nonverbal learning disorders do not perceive the interrelationships in nonverbal situations; hence, they give inadequate responses when asked to describe what is happening in an action picture. They also behave inappropriately when they must rely on nonverbal experiences for meaning. In contrast, the child with a language disorder may grasp the meaning but cannot express his ideas because of his verbal deficit. The differences in ability between those with verbal and nonverbal problems often are reflected in tests which require arranging pictures so that they tell a story. Children with nonverbal disabilities generally are inferior because they are unable to ascertain which picture should precede or follow another.

To study this problem, we selected action pictures and asked the children to tell a story about them. The first picture was a simple one showing a boy eating soup. The second portrayed a scene in a railway station; in the foreground a little girl was running to her father with outstretched arms, and in the background the train conductor was helping the mother down the steps of the railway car. The third picture was more complex. A man was kneeling by the wheel of his station wagon, looking very unhappy about a flat tire; his wife was standing on the opposite side of the car and a little girl was looking out of the car window. The fourth picture was the most difficult because of the humor and subtleties it expressed. In the foreground a boy, looking very apprehensive, was hiding in a woodshed and putting a book in the seat of his trousers to protect himself from an angry man coming out of the house with a belt in his hand. In the background was a house with a broken window and a baseball bat was on the ground.

We showed these pictures to children aged five to fifteen years and asked them to tell what was happening; their responses were recorded. Nearly all, including the preschoolers, were able to describe the first picture.

The second picture, the mother and daughter getting off the train, was difficult for some of the children. They thought that the mother was going away rather than coming home; they failed to observe the bag being placed on the platform, did not identify the mother's position and the placement of her feet on the steps of the train. Two children with disabilities in the interpretation of facial expressions did not recognize the expression of joy on the little girl's face as she greeted her father; one even thought she was crying because the mother was going away.

The third picture, a man looking at his flat tire, was misinterpreted by many of the children. An eight-year-old boy with both visual nonverbal problems and dyslexia said, "The man is kneeling down to see the line on

the road." A young aphasic who clearly understood the picture said, "Oh
. . . oh! Dada . . . got . . . fat." (Daddy has a flat.)

We did not expect very young children to interpret the fourth picture,
the boy in the woodshed protecting himself from a spanking, but many
ten- and eleven-year-old dyslexics got the point and found the picture
humorous. Some thirteen-year-olds, however, who had high verbal and
low performance abilities, missed the point completely. The following
illustrate the responses given by the group and reveal the markedly
distorted impressions of those with visual nonverbal learning deficiencies.
Typically the seven- and eight-year-olds gave a simple description of what
they saw.

Seven-year-old dyslexic:

This boy's holding a book in his pants and this man's going to whip him
with a tie and a dog's behind the door and a mother's looking out and he's
hiding in the tool shed, and there's a baseball glove, a watering can and a
book in there.

Eight-year-old dysgraphic with visual involvement:

My name is Tom. I was throwing the ball against the wall of my house and
the ball had hit the window. Suddenly I saw my Dad come out with his
belt. I knew that was trouble, so I took my English book and put it in the
seat of my pants. Then I think you will know the ending if I say I could
not sit down for a week.

Twelve-year-old, formerly a receptive aphasic and now in training for reading comprehension:

One day Bobby was playing catch with his friends. Then one of his friends
threw the ball to Bobby and then Bobby threw the ball towards the
window. When the ball got to the window, the window broke. Then his
father came outside with a belt and then Bobby's friends ran home and
then Bobby hid in the shack. His father was so angry that he was going
to hit Bobby, but while Bobby was in the shack, he put his English book
in his pants so his father won't hit him too hard.

In contrast note the stories by two boys with visual nonverbal problems. Both were good readers, had excellent spoken language, but were
dyscalculic.

Nine-year-old, above average in verbal intelligence:

A poor kid hid in a tool shed and tried to read a book. Then he heard
footsteps. A man was coming so he ran away with the book.

Thirteen-year-old, superior in verbal and below average in nonverbal performance:

A boy who lives on a farm is trying to hide his books so that the man
will not know with what he did the damage to his house. He is hiding in a
shack which will do him no good.

One of the highest levels of meaning to be gained from pictures is humor in the form of cartoons. Children with nonverbal disorders often grasp the meaning of jokes that have verbal captions but not those based solely on pictures. Others fail to grasp any humorous situation because of their inability to acquire subtle meanings. An adult aphasic remarked as she looked at the cartoons in her favorite humor magazine, "Used to be funny . . . no more."

A teen-ager with a severe visual nonverbal disturbance and deficiencies in social perception remarked, after working on several pictures and cartoons, "They are so much easier when you talk to me about what is going on. I just don't get what they're about otherwise." To illustrate, she was presented with a cartoon showing a man seated on a stool and talking. He was surrounded by six men, four in police uniforms and two in detective-type plain clothes. The caption below the picture was, "Well, that's enough about me. How's everything with you boys?" The girl's first response was, "Well, the boss of the company was on vacation and came back and kept talking about himself making his workers wish he'd stop. He decided that he is through and asks how is everything with his workers?" The teacher then explained that this was not really the meaning of the picture and that the clue to the joke was the clothes worn by the men who were standing. Immediately she responded with, "The man is being questioned by a bunch of cops about a murder or something; he is through telling them and then asks them how is everything with them." More detailed explanations were necessary to help her appreciate the humor. These examples illustrate the ways in which children and young adults might misinterpret social situations and thus behave inappropriately.

GESTURE

Gesture is a nonverbal form of communication. It has both receptive and expressive components. Understanding gestures assumes ability to associate meaning with a visual-movement pattern. A waving movement of the hand means that a person is departing. Some movements indicate "come" or "go away"; others reflect feelings and attitudes, e.g., pounding the fist in anger. Verbal communication is enhanced by gesture; some gestures have universal meaning and others are unique to a particular culture.

Learning the meaning of gestures is relatively simple in comparison to learning verbal systems, but when children fail to understand them we realize their importance and complexity. Some do not respond appropriately to the outstretched arms indicating "come," or the shaking of the forefinger meaning "no-no." Some imitate the movements but they do not know what they signify; they are like echolalic children who repeat words without understanding them. Or, they might have an expressive disorder; they comprehend the gesture and respond appropriately, but cannot imitate the movement or use it spontaneously.

To teach the meaning of gestures the teacher assists the child in associating the proper movement with the experience it connotes. Simultaneity, repetition, and meaningful settings are essential. Gestures cannot always be learned from pictures because the sequence of movements cannot be observed. Neither can meaning be established only by imitation. As implied previously, some children can imitate but not comprehend. A few simple gestures (bye-bye and come) are used in a highly structured manner so the child experiences the feeling of going away when he sees a hand waving, or the feeling of going toward someone when he sees a gesture indicating "come." Several times each day the teacher arranges situations in which the experience can be associated with the gesture.

Children who comprehend gestures but who cannot use them expressively do not need assistance with meaning but must be taught the necessary motor patterns to convey the intended meaning. They know what they want to do but cannot relate the movements to their motor system. The same remediation procedures used for deficits in motor learning are recommended (see Chapters IV and VI). Because most children in this group cannot look and imitate, their hands and arms are placed in the appropriate position and guided through the sequence of movements. Sometimes they are asked to close their eyes and concentrate on the feel of the movement; at other times, they are asked to watch themselves in the mirror and to observe their performance, comparing their movements with those of the teacher.

NONVERBAL MOTOR LEARNING

Earlier we discussed deficiencies which result from an inability to learn motor patterns (Chapters IV and VI). These can occur in the auditory-motor system and affect ability to speak or in the visual-motor system and interfere with writing. Still others affect the learning of nonverbal motor patterns; if so, a mild writing disorder usually is present, but this is not the chief concern. The parents of an eight-year-old girl stated that what they wanted most for their daughter was to help her learn to perform everyday routines. At the age of eight she had not learned to cut with scissors, comb her hair, skip, or jump rope.

Deficits in learning nonverbal motor patterns are frustrating to children. They become embarrassed in many situations because they cannot perform as well as their friends. They are inferior on the playground, in creative activities, in getting from one place to another, and in completing a task, all because they cannot learn the motor patterns required for tying shoes, opening a milk carton, using a hammer, climbing, or riding a bike. These children know what they should do and they have no paralysis but they cannot relate the motor patterns that they see to their motor systems.

Disturbances of this type, sometimes referred to as nonverbal apraxias, have been recognized in adults for many years. After brain disease the adult cannot hold a cup, strike a match, or blow out a candle. His attempts to perform show confusion and bizarreness. We observed a man who tried to drink from a cup and kept putting his thumb into his mouth. A woman tried to blow out a match but protruded the tongue between the lips. Although the actions of children appear less bizarre, they show the same confusions. When trying to jump over a rope they may try to pick up their feet with their hands. A teen-age girl with whom we worked had serious nonverbal motor problems in addition to a disturbance in social perception, yet she was average in verbal abilities. At eighteen she did not know how to open a coke bottle, to throw a ball, or to cut smoothly with scissors.

One of the most vivid descriptions of a disturbance in learning new motor patterns was given by a twenty-eight-year-old woman, referred by a psychiatrist who felt that her symptoms were not indicative of mental illness. We found that she had always had difficulty in learning new motor patterns, time concepts, and mathematics. When asked whether she liked to dance or swim, she commented, "Every time I go to learn something new I have a terrible time. I went wild trying to learn to dance, but once I learned I became one of the best in my group. Learning any sport is the same way—it takes me a lot longer to learn these things—sometimes I forget what I am supposed to do next and get all mixed up. Other times I know what I am supposed to do but I just can't seem to get my feet to do what I'm telling them." When asked how she learned to do these things she said, "It took absolute concentration on the movements—I still can't talk or look around when I dance—I can't talk to my partner and lots of times I have to close my eyes and just think about where my feet are and where they are going."

Educational Procedures

Because disturbance of nonverbal motor integration is a learning disorder, remediation should be provided through special education. It is not a paralysis of the type treated by the physical therapist, but rather it is a type of deficiency to be resolved by the educator. The physical education instructors can be of great assistance when the deficiencies are explained to them. In teaching skills such as buttoning, tying, cutting, or bike riding, we break the complex act into simple movement patterns, as was suggested for writing (Chapter VI). After each movement is performed without undue effort it is blended with the others into a smooth pattern. Often it is necessary to have the child form a kinesthetic image of the sequence of movements but for others verbal instructions are emphasized.

In teaching a child to skip we begin by having him stand on one foot for a few moments. Occasionally even this is difficult, not because of poor balance but because he cannot imitate from simple observation. Therefore, we hold on to his finger tips and ask another instructor to lift the child's foot so he gains the kinesthetic impression of standing in this position. While supported in this way, he is asked to close his eyes momentarily and to concentrate on the "feel." Then he is asked to observe himself in a large mirror to see the position of his body. Since skipping is a variation of a hopping movement the child is next taught to hop. The teacher faces the child, holds on to his finger tips, and encourages him to hop toward her while she moves backwards in time with his hopping. Sometimes it is necessary to have a second instructor take hold of the child at the waistline and lift him. Generally, after he has experienced the feel he is able to perform successfully by himself. To establish the rhythm for skipping the child is asked to listen to the auditory pattern made by the feet of another person skipping around the room. This should result in a sound such as *"hop—a—hop—a—hop."* Next he is asked to watch the feet of another person skipping, noting the number of times he comes down on one foot and then the other. Finally, he is encouraged to try the total pattern himself. It is important to provide ample space for skipping so he can have an opportunity to feel the entire rhythmic pattern.

In a similar manner we have taught children to jump rope, breaking the motor pattern into simple movements, making each automatic, then blending them together. First we have the child swing the rope over his head from back to front, concentrating on this movement. Next, without a rope in his hands he is taught to jump to a rhythmic pattern such as "1—2—3—jump; 1—2—3—jump."Then he is taught to jump over the rope while it is being held (still, not swinging) or while it is lying on the floor. Finally by combining these movements he learns to coordinate them into the total action. Through these techniques it is sometimes possible to teach a child to jump rope in less than a half hour.

Learning to use scissors requires similar procedures. We begin by asking the child to touch his thumb and forefinger together several times as required when cutting with a scissors; he holds neither a paper nor a scissors but merely concentrates on the opening and closing movements. If he cannot imitate this act the teacher guides his fingers, simultaneously saying "open—shut." Next the child is given a scissors and continues to perform the same movement. The teacher must be explicit in telling him which fingers go into the holes of the scissors. Often a verbal cue, such as "thumbs up," will serve as a reminder for those who forget or who tend to hold the scissors in an awkward position. As the child opens and closes his fingers, call his attention to the blades of the scissors and to the way they open and close as he moves his fingers. It is important that he see this entire operation because while he is engaged in cutting paper he sees only the top blade and cannot perceive the total pattern. After he performs the opening and closing movement with ease, we have him make short snips (or cuts) along the edge of the paper. The teacher holds the paper for him so he can concentrate on the cutting movement. Fairly heavy paper which is easily cut is used since light weight paper requires more tension in the blades of the scissors and in the cutting movement. While the teacher continues to hold the paper, the child is asked to make three or four cuts across the paper, no longer making the single snips along the edge. When he achieves success, he performs the same operation but is required to hold the paper himself, the teacher again using the verbal cue "thumbs up" so he does not assume awkward positions that interfere with more complex cutting. Finally he is asked to cut along folds, along straight lines, and to perform more difficult tasks.

It is helpful to have some children verbalize what they are doing while performing a motor act (e.g., I am putting my thumb in one hole of the scissors; I put the third finger in the second hole; I move my fingers apart and bring them together again). However, some who cannot verbalize while engaged in the motor act were aided by verbal discussions before or afterwards. To ascertain whether the kinesthetic image has been internalized we ask the children to tell us how they make or do something. Many parents, particularly fathers, intuitively have used these techniques for teaching their children to ride bikes, use tools, etc. The father of a twelve-year-old did so in teaching his son to use a hammer and a screwdriver. He said, "Jim never learned anything just from watching me and he never seemed to know how to go about practicing on his own; after we talked through each movement he learned quickly."

BODY IMAGE

As the child develops year by year, he becomes conscious of his own body, internalizes his perceptions of it and acquires what is commonly referred to as *body image*. Self-perception and person-perception (Heider, 1958) are not synonymous. On the other hand, it is not easy to define precisely what is meant by body image. For our purposes, because we are concerned with the learning disabilities that result from brain dysfunctions, we will be guided mainly by the point of view expressed in neurology (Critchley, 1953; Hécaen and Ajuriaguerra, 1964; Nielsen, 1946; Schilder,

1950). Through work with adults who have sustained damage from brain disease, much has been learned regarding the relationships between brain functions and perception of one's own body. Most of what has been learned is relevant also to children, though differences must be assumed.

A predominant difference affecting the study of body image in children concerns development factors. Binet (Terman and Merrill, 1937) recognized that ability to identify body parts on oneself was acquired and as he originally measured it, the average child could do so only after he was three years of age. Ilg and Ames (1965) have made a noteworthy contribution through determining the age at which the average child learns the names of various parts of his body. Goodenough (1926) showed that, as measured through drawings, body image awareness continues to mature until early adolescence. Other psychologists have contributed to the understanding of this concept (Benton, 1959; Fisher and Cleveland, 1958). It is acknowledged that many conditions are influential in determining body image, including emotional disturbance, mental retardation, and deafness (Myklebust, 1964), in addition to dysfunctions in the brain. Our concern is with the distortions associated with neurogenic involvements in children.

In terms of the functional specialization in the brain, it is of interest that Critchley, Hécaen and Ajuriaguerra, and Nielsen attribute deficiencies in body image to disturbances of the non-dominant hemisphere, which in the average right-handed person is on the right. This being the case, it is the left half of the body scheme that most often is distorted. For example, in the "denial syndrome," in which the patient denies that there is anything wrong with him, the hemiplegia is on the left side (Weinstein and Kahn, 1955).

Person- and self-perception, including body image, appear to be highly meaningful aspects of nonverbal experience. Guilford (1959) refers to interpersonal relationships as being largely nonverbal. Disturbances of self-perception as well as of interpersonal relationships are common in children with nonverbal deficits in learning. Gerstmann (1940) has shown that body image deficits can occur for any body part, whether or not paralysis is present; this is particularly relevant to children. Nielsen's designations which include visual agnosia for laterality and for the fingers, as well as loss of revisualization of one's own body and body parts, also are revealing. Hécaen and Ajuriaguerra, from an extensive review, conclude that the formation of concepts and verbal formulation are especially altered by left-sided lesions, and that the manipulation of corporeal and extracorporeal space and the recognition of human features are disturbed when the lesion is on the right hemisphere.

An intriguing type of body image disturbance is that designated as finger agnosia (Benton, 1959; Gerstmann, 1940; Schilder, 1931; Strauss and Werner, 1938). In this condition the individual is characterized by a specific disturbance of ability to identify his fingers. A considerable number of children with learning disabilities manifest this inability, usually in association with other deficits. The child who drew the figure in Illustration 74 is an example. He was six years of age and had high average intelligence as measured verbally, but was encountering difficulty in learning arithmetic. He made the drawing after being instructed to draw a picture of himself and quickly drew all of the figure except the fingers. When he came to the point of wanting to put on fingers, he became confused, looked at the examiner's hands and then at his own mittens in an attempt to adapt them to the situation. Finally, in a mood of desperation, he placed his hand on the paper in the appropriate position and traced around two of his own fingers; he repeated this procedure on the other side, thus putting fingers at the end of both arms. From this performance and on the basis of other evidence, we concluded that this boy had a finger agnosia. He was unable, except by highly devious routes, to visualize his own fingers. Because he could not get the image of his fingers in mind, he could not draw them, except in the manner described.

These observations, and the research and clinical evidence on which they are based, is highly pertinent to consideration of learning disabilities. A number of children, though competent verbally, have marked deficits in nonverbal learning, including perception of their own body and its relation to the external world. Much has been learned about the neurology of these deficits which characterize a certain group of children with neurogenic learning disabilities. It is in these terms that we discuss this nonverbal deficiency and indicate remediation procedures that have been beneficial.

Many types of disturbances are seen. Some children are unable to identify body parts on command, others cannot recognize their own faces in a mirror. Still others cannot make spatial judgments, and some cannot construct models of the human figure or produce organized drawings of it. When these problems are present, the psychologist and special educator must determine whether they are due to faulty body image or whether they result from other types of learning disabilities. An inability to identify body parts may indicate a disorder of auditory comprehension rather than one of body image. Many receptive aphasics cannot point to body parts on command, nor can they identify simple objects because of the deficit in understanding the meaning of words. Other children, however, can point to objects but not to body parts. When asked, "Show me your nose," they know that the word refers to a part of the body but in trying to find it they look questioningly at their own bodies and "search" their faces with their hands, apparently looking for the nose, but they are

ILLUSTRATION 74. Drawing by a six-year-old boy with finger agnosia.

unable to point to it. Some can point to the nose on a doll or on a picture of a person but not on themselves.

To determine the nature of the disability we ask each child to point to parts of the body on himself, on a doll, and on a figure in a picture, noting whether there are discrepancies. Although wide discrepancies are rare, even minor differences provide further insight into the disorder. For example, a five-year-old boy could point to an eyebrow, finger, and heel on himself but not to these parts on a picture of a boy. It was our impression that his failure was due to other disturbances rather than to one of body image since other test information showed that he also incorrectly interpreted pictures of activities not involving people. In contrast, another boy of the same age pointed to the thumb, the shoulder, the elbow, the wrist, and the foot in pictures but could not do so on himself. In this case, performance on other tests and clinical observations were indicative of body image distortions.

As with all learning disabilities, no single diagnostic instrument invariably differentiates faulty body image from other conditions. Various aspects of behavior must be explored. Although drawings of the human figure may show poor body organization, they also reflect deficits in visual perceptual abilities and in visual memory for detail, as well as apraxias which interfere with drawing. When the child does not have the proper image of body organization, of the body parts as they relate to the whole, and of the ways in which he uses his body in space, remediation should be provided. The following procedures are useful.

Educational Procedures

Life-size pictures of the children are drawn on large sheets of brown wrapping paper. The child is asked to lie down on the paper while an outline is drawn around him. Later he draws in parts of his face, clothing, and details such as fingernails. Although the average child quickly recognizes body parts from the outline and perceives the relationships of the parts to the whole, many with learning disabilities do not. Therefore, each body part is named and identified on the picture. Then the child is asked to close his eyes and the teacher touches him. Next he opens his eyes and points to the spot that was touched, first on his body and then on the picture. Attention is drawn to the ways in which the body parts are connected, i.e., what is below the arm, above the neck, which parts of the body bend and which do not.

Some children must be made aware of the appearance of the body and its parts from different angles and in different positions. They are asked to look at the foot from the side, from the bottom, and as it appears when they look down at it. Pictures as well as direct experience are used. At other times we ask the child to stand on a piece of paper, first drawing around the sole of his foot. Similar procedures are used with drawings of the hand. He is asked to trace around his hand twice, once with his palm down and once with it up. While looking carefully at his own hand, he puts in details such as the lines over the knuckles and the fingernails.

Work is also done in front of large mirrors, but it is critical to first determine whether the child recognizes himself in the mirror. Some with body image disturbance do not recognize themselves either in pictures or in the mirror. A three-year-old aphasic looked at pictures of her family, named all of the people, but upon seeing herself she said quizzically, "Who dat?" Until the child is aware of the fact that it is *he* that he sees in the mirror, there is little point in using this technique. When he recognizes himself, however, many activities can be stressed to make him aware of different body positions and the body's general organization. For example, he is shown silhouettes of children standing in different positions, waving, or standing on one foot. He is to look at the picture and try to imitate the position, then check himself by looking in the mirror. In other words, he uses the mirror as a visual monitoring system when he is not sure of where his hands or feet are. Games such as Simon Says are played in front of the mirror and the child is told, "Put your hands on your head," or "Put your hands under your chin."

Puzzles also are used as a training technique. These are simple, clear pictures of paper dolls cut into pieces. The training begins with the figures on a flannelgraph in an upright position. Many children with learning disabilities cannot organize body parts when they are on a table, on a horizontal plane; they can visualize the body only in an upright, standing position. When working on a table they will hold the parts in a vertical position because they are more easily perceived. As they improve, they learn to complete the puzzles in any position. To begin with, the puzzle is cut into only two parts, the head and the body. Next it is cut into three parts, the head, trunk, and legs, and gradually into several pieces. Initially many children need a completed model. Later they are encouraged to revisualize the whole and construct the puzzles without a model. Picture completion exercises are also beneficial; the children are given pictures in which a finger or a foot, etc., is missing and they are to tell or draw what has been omitted.

SPATIAL ORIENTATION

Disturbances in spatial orientation are closely allied to disturbances of body image. Because of faulty body image, or because of an inability to relate themselves to the spatial world, some children with learning disabilities bump into things, cannot estimate distance, and lose their way enroute to a destination. An informative discussion on this deficiency is provided by Goody (1952, p. 472) who described the process of maintaining orientation in space as follows.

> Orientation in space is a term describing the faculty normally possessed by humans which permits them to have at all times precise knowledge of their position in relation to the outside world as it is perceived by them. This faculty is not a specific or an isolated one, but is dependent upon a variety of psychological and physiological processes. In order to be correctly oriented a man must be aware of the position in space, from moment to moment, of the parts of his body in their relation one to another, as well as of their relation to the outside world as perceived by him; he must also recognize their relation to objects in the outside world to one another and to himself. This faculty depends upon the integration of all sensory stimuli arising from within and from outside the body.
>
> Orientation implies the ability of the individual to relate himself to a fixed point. This point may be part of his own body, or it may be perceived by him in space outside his body. Human orientation depends upon the complete integration and harmonious balance of the sensorimotor system, and all the senses contribute towards its achievement.

Both Binet (Terman and Merrill, 1960) and Kent (1946) include items concerning orientation and direction in their tests of intelligence. Common observation, as well as these measures, attests to the fact that directional ability shows maturation with age and covers a wide range of mental capacity. On the Binet the items extend into the superior adult level. Like the concept of time (Buck, 1946), capacities for orientation and direction are viewed as factors of intelligence. On the other hand, experience with children having neurogenic involvements of learning clearly indicates that deficits in these abilities occur without major intellectual impairment. Children with such deficiencies often fall at the average or above average level on verbal measures of intelligence. As Goody suggests, orientation ability perhaps is not a specific faculty but develops through integration of all sensory information. However, there is reason to presume that deficiencies of this function occur mainly through dysfunctions in the right hemisphere of the brain.

Ilg and Ames (1965) have shown that self-perception and body image are closely related to the development of normal function in orientation. One should expect, therefore, that children having various types of learning disabilities might also have deficiencies in this nonverbal aspect of behavior. Indeed, this is the circumstance in children with learning disabilities. The auditory agnosic, for instance, fails to recognize the sound of a car or a fire engine because he cannot locate the source of the sound and relate it to his spatial world. Likewise, those with visual perceptual disturbance do not interpret visual experiences normally and must use cues from other modalities to stabilize their spatial world.

In training we emphasize work on body image, teaching the child to use reference points for orientation. We verbalize the relationships. These children, because of deficits in social perception, require that the non-verbal, spatial world be translated into verbal experience. In addition, we stress development of a systematic means for scanning the environment. Only when they can do so successfully can they appropriately integrate the information they receive from it. To improve spatial orientation further we have the older children draw blue prints of their homes, maps of their routes from home to school, etc.

RIGHT-LEFT ORIENTATION

Perhaps no psychoneurological facet of behavior has attracted more attention than that of laterality. Early in the investigation of verbal disorders, Orton (1937) and Travis (1931) implicated the lack of cerebral dominance, with resultant ambidexterity, as being associated with stuttering. Even earlier, neurologists had recognized relationships between right- and left-sidedness and brain disorders. For decades research workers have been exploring the interconnections between dominant hand and cerebral dominance for language (Hécaen and Ajuriguerra, 1964; Head, 1926; Penfield and Roberts, 1959; Wepman, 1951). Though the same hemisphere usually carries major responsibility for both language and the "lead" hand, it is now generally agreed that this is artifactual and does not mean that language and handedness are inextricably associated.

A basic characteristic of the human being, however, is his "two-sidedness," his development of a dominant side. The implications, personal and social, are phenomenal. We need only to think about the innumerable ways in which the concept of right and left influences our daily lives to recognize that no aspect of our person contributes more to our orientation in space. Moreover, though authorities to some extent disagree, this feature of our development seems to be unique to the human being. It is one of the specializations of the brain which makes it possible for Man to be Man. Unless such specialization occurs within the nervous system, it appears the organism remains at a sub-human level. It is in these terms that we consider the disorders of sidedness, and ability to orient oneself accordingly. When such orientation does not develop normally, the problem which results is of considerable consequence. In children, even when concomitant learning disabilities are not severe, it constitutes an involvement which justifies their being considered handicapped and in need of special education.

Gerstmann (1940), when he clinically observed the *behavioral* deficiencies associated with certain brain dysfunctions, made a contribution of great consequence; these behavioral concomitants make up the *Gerstmann*

Syndrome. It was he who recognized that right-left orientation was lost in adults who had a type of brain damage as a result of illness or accident; he found that these same individuals were deficient in recognition of their own fingers (finger agnosia) and that they had dyscalculia and dysgraphia. These observations led to many investigations and, though exceptions occur, generally his observations have been substantiated.

Right-left disorientation and disturbances in the development of a dominant side should not be viewed as synonymous deviations. These frequently occur in the same child; nevertheless, each must be examined, diagnosed, and treated separately. A disturbance in this ability rarely occurs in isolation but rather in association with other learning disabilities, as shown by Hécaen and Ajuriaguerra, and Myklebust and Johnson. It seems to be most prevalent in children with dyslexia or dyscalculia.

Developmentally, the ability to understand right-left in relation to the spatial world is closely related to body image. In association with one's own body, Werner (1942) found that this aspect of orientation was acquired by the average child by the age of six or seven years. The judgment of right-left in relation to others was not acquired until eight years, and so far as inanimate objects are concerned, not until eleven years. However, highly specific evidence on the maturation of right-left orientation was not available until Ilg and Ames (1965) reported their studies. An important aspect of their work is the revelation that ability to identify one's own right or left does not mean that one can also indicate the right eye, or the left ear, etc.; there are hierarchies of difficulty in establishing this facility. These workers found that about two-thirds of the six-year-olds correctly identified the hand on others and by eight years, essentially all normal children could do so. These findings are noteworthy because developmental factors are involved both in diagnosis and training of children.

Various workers have emphasized that right-left orientation is deficient in children with learning disabilities (Dearborn, 1931; Hécaen and Ajuriaguerra, 1964; Monroe, 1932; Orton, 1937; Zangwill, 1960). When present, this ability usually is pervasive and not restricted to the child's own body. He shows limitations in awareness of right-left in general, the deficit often including other aspects of orientation and directionality. He cannot properly follow directions in regard to pencil and paper routines, in physical education, or in everyday activities. These inabilities cause frustration and embarrassment.

Educational Procedures

One of the first steps in training is to make the child more aware of both sides of his body and to relate them to direction in space. In describing right-left disorientation as a part of the Gerstmann syndrome, Critchley

(1953) suggests that this is a "disorder of directional selection." According to Kephart (1960), a directional sense begins within the body and is developed or projected outward into objective space. Hence, we begin with activities involving the child's own body. The child is asked to close his eyes, then the teacher touches his left or right hand, and the child raises the one that was touched. On other occasions, after the teacher has touched the child's arm or hand, he opens his eyes and points to the part that was touched.

Although the directional sense is often associated with visual-kinesthetic impressions, audition plays a valuable role in certain aspects of training, especially since many children with this disturbance are more competent auditorially than visually. We ask the child to close his eyes, listen for the sound of a drum or a bell, and turn his head toward the source of the sound. Then he is asked to open his eyes to determine whether his observations were correct.

Another procedure in remediation is to provide a cue to right-left on the child himself, particularly if he is confused when given directions. This is easily done by having him wear a watch on the left arm or a ring on the right hand to serve as a reminder. Then he is given simple directions: *Put your right hand up—keep your left hand down. Put your left hand in front of you— put your right hand behind you.* As soon as he can follow directions of this type, he is given more complex ones, involving total movement in space: *Walk two steps forward—turn to the right; walk half way across the room—turn left and take three more steps.*

The child learns to coordinate visual and kinesthetic impressions by observing himself in a mirror, noting the position of the hand that is up, down, over his head, etc. Through verbal discussions and by watching himself in the mirror he is taught to perceive right and left on others. Considerable practice is done with directional orientation as it relates to inanimate objects, since this is where many of the children fail in school. They become confused when told to put something on the right side of the shelf or when asked to write their names in a certain position on the paper. In addition to a cue, such as a watch on the left arm, a number of techniques can be used to help them with assignments. A green X can be placed on the left side of the paper to indicate the starting position for reading and writing and a red dot placed in the upper right hand corner of the paper to show where a child should write his name.

Games can be used to reinforce right-left concepts. Children enjoy activities in which they must imagine what they would see if they turned in a certain direction. For example, *If I turn to the right I will be facing the* _____ (door); *if I turn to the left I will be facing the* _____ (bookshelf). Having the children verbalize directions also stabilizes their perceptions.

The teacher has one child be the leader and tell the others how to go to the playground, or how to go to the cafeteria, by giving exact directions: *go through the first door, turn right and go to the next hallway, turn left, etc.*

SOCIAL IMPERCEPTION

One of the more intriguing problems associated with neurogenic learning disorders is that of a deficiency in *social perception*. English (1958) uses this terminology to mean awareness of the actions of another person that reveal his attitudes, feelings, or intentions. We use it more broadly to include the perception of the total social field, perception of oneself in relation to the behavior of others as well as to events and circumstances that involve others.

The problem of social imperception referred to here should not be confused with severely abnormal behavior as seen in autistic children (Goldfarb, 1961; Kanner, 1957; Myklebust, 1954). The child who has a learning disability and who is deficient in social perception is not bizarre and makes every effort to conform. He wants to participate with others, to engage in play activities and the routines of his family. But because of his deficiency, he does not comprehend his social world to the extent that he can do so. It is in this sense that he is different, not in the fundamental aspects of his personality. When he happens to understand a social situation adequately, he shows elation and enthusiasm. This child is seriously misjudged, often being considered emotionally disturbed or as a disciplinary problem and therefore punished.

The neurology of this type of learning disability is not well defined. However, it can be assumed to be related to the involvements that impede other nonverbal learning, that is, with dysfunctions principally on the right hemisphere. Moreover, some authorities implicate the parietal lobe (Cohn, 1960; Critchley, 1953). In any event, for purposes of special education we must be concerned with this child who has deficits in social perception. Though these deficits usually are associated with other deficiencies in learning, his special needs warrant attention diagnostically and in terms of remediation. There is little question but that some of these children, if not given proper opportunities for training, inadvertently become delinquent.

Ability to make social judgments, like many other aspects of adjustment, must be acquired through maturation and learning. The normal child naturally, without direct training, learns to perceive the feelings of others, the significance of physical contacts, the meanings conveyed by the tone of voice and by overt actions. He "sizes up" the situation and adapts to it. Gradually he acquires tact and manners and learns to anticipate the consequences of his own behavior. He is guided by his observations and acquires ability to empathize on a nonverbal basis. Though he engages in verbal discussions and receives instructions from his parents, most of this aspect of growth and adjustment seems dependent on nonverbal perception and abstraction.

It is precisely in these aspects of learning that some children are deficient. They can speak, read, and write, but the nonverbal world of experience does not develop and stabilize; the printed word, when stabilized with the auditory, is acquired easily. They do not perceive the relationships among nonverbal experiences unless they are appropriately taught and verbalized for them. They cannot interpret the behavior of others from observation, failing to learn the meanings of facial expressions, actions, and gestures. As a result they are described as being tactless and stupid.

Mothers sense that something is wrong, even at an early age. A mother of a five-year-old said, "Bobby has always seemed different. Even as a baby he did not cuddle and coo as other children. He watched our two-year-old come running for a hug after he had fallen or when he wanted affection, but Bobby seemed not to know how to react in the same way. He has now learned how to hug, even though he is a bit stiff—I guess you would have to say that we had to teach him to show affection."

Disturbances of social perception often are among the most debilitating of the learning disorders because they impede acquisition of basic adaptive patterns of behavior. Verbal facility is of little value if one cannot perform day to day nonverbal routines. Social maturity remains deficient despite average to above average verbal ability. The test performances of these children often show 20 to 30 points discrepancy between verbal and performance abilities, the nonverbal being lower. Their test profiles may be similar to children with dyscalculia with the exception that those with dyscalculia usually are lowest on object assembly and block design, whereas those with deficits in social perception are lowest in picture arrangement; they do not comprehend the experiences shown in one picture in order to determine which should precede or follow the others.

In addition to the symptoms already described, many of these children fail to grasp the significance of hazards. They do not perceive danger and hence do not relate immediate behavior to the future. Rarely do they understand the rules and sequences of games unless these are verbalized for them.

Educational Procedures

Training in social perception requires verbalization and interpretation of the nonverbal world. It seems that children with impaired social perception cannot understand visual nonverbal experiences until they are translated into verbal symbols. As indicated earlier, they cannot look and comprehend, but through verbalization they learn to understand. Therefore, we capitalize on their verbal facility and arrange meaningful experiences. It is impossible to anticipate all of the events in the child's world, but the training is geared toward helping him establish a frame of reference; its purpose is to give him a means of scanning the environment systematically, while noting relationships and internally verbalizing what he observes.

One of the most significant areas to be dealt with is the meaning of facial expressions. Before these children are able to interpret complex social situations, they need practice in observing a single person. They cannot tell from appearance how an individual feels because they have not related the upturned mouth with a happy feeling or the raised eyebrows with a feeling of surprise. By utilizing direct experience and carefully selected pictures, we have taught them to relate feelings to facial expressions. Since these children do not grasp experience vicariously, it is important to emphasize direct learning whenever possible. The teacher catches the child in an excited or an unhappy mood, draws his attention to the reaction and the concomitant facial expression. A Polaroid camera in the training room can be advantageous in assisting the child to remember the experience, including the expression on his face and its relation to the situation.

After the child has gained facility in simple interpretations of feelings and expressions, more difficult exercises are introduced. He is presented with a picture of a situation and must interpret how the person feels. For example, he sees a man stooping to look at his flat tire; then he is given three pictures of men with different facial expressions (smiling, angry, sleepy) and is asked to select the one that shows the way the man feels. Social studies charts are excellent for such training. Each picture portrays a family situation, e.g., the mother looking disgusted after the children and a dog run across the clean kitchen floor. The child is asked to describe what has happened and how each of the people in the situation feels.

Picture stories and film strips are used to improve visual nonverbal sequentialization, i.e., to develop ability to follow and integrate a sequence of events. Through verbalizations and by structuring each picture (as suggested in the discussion on general significance) the teacher leads the child to see all aspects of the situation and how they are related.

Some children cannot simultaneously integrate all the various aspects of a situation. We develop visual integration by preparing sets of pictures mounted on plastic overlays, as found in anatomy books. We construct a complex environmental scene by placing single pictures on a sheet of plastic and superimposing the sheets, one on top of the other. The first might be a picture of an empty room, the next shows a sofa, then a lamp by the sofa, then a coffee table in front of the sofa, then a woman sitting on the sofa, and finally a second woman carrying a tray of tea cups. As each picture is presented, the child is asked to tell what he sees; by the time he sees the final picture his response should be, "A lady serving a cup of tea to her friend." Through this type of training the child learns to respond appropriately to similar experiences in everyday life.

Another approach which benefits many children is charades. The children do both the pretending and the interpreting of actions. During the early stages of training usually it is necessary to tell them what to act out: bat a ball, mow the lawn, brush your teeth, pound a nail, etc.; without suggestions they cannot think of something to do. The more pretending they do without verbalizing, the more they must think about activities that they observe and the meanings which they connote.

Working with practical situations and teaching manners are imperative. Although this type of training is done largely by the parents, they too need assistance to understand this unique learning problem. The normal child abstracts certain patterns of behavior after he has made several observations and has had verbal instructions, but those with social perception disturbances must be told time after time how to behave in each situation. They do not abstract the common characteristics from one setting to another and hence do not generalize the appropriate behavior. They must be repeatedly instructed as to how or how not to behave. On the other hand, some who are given verbal instructions become rigid and cannot make social judgments. A thirteen-year-old with superior verbal intelligence had been told to rise when an adult entered the room. He learned the rule and used it without exception. Whenever an adult stepped into the classroom, he stood up and held out his hand to shake with the adult. This was done even though the room was crowded and the child was seated near the back of the room. Often he had to be told to be seated, that he did not need to follow this procedure in all situations. He had not learned to judge when such behavior was indicated.

Progress usually is slow with this group of children and measurement of improvement is difficult. However, as we learn more about the nature of this learning disability, new techniques are being devised. The basic significant factors in training are utilization of structured meaningful experiences and auditory verbalization.

DISTRACTIBILITY, PERSEVERATION, AND DISINHIBITION

During the past few decades much attention has been given to children with brain dysfunctions who exhibit certain behavioral characteristics. This syndrome ingeniously recognized and described by Doll (1951) and by Strauss and Lehtinen (1947) is characterized by distractibility, perseveration, and disinhibition. Strauss and Lehtinen attributed this behavioral pattern to disturbances of perception. A number of workers continue to do so even though experimental evidence demonstrating an association between perceptual disorders and this type of behavior is exceedingly meager. Though such an association may exist, in view of the progress made in understanding brain function, it is pertinent to consider other possibilities.

For purposes of diagnosis and remedial training it is advantageous to regard distractibility, perseveration, and disinhibition, all three, as representing a breakdown in attention. If the child is *distractible*, he is unable to give normal attention to the events and circumstances that surround him. Instead of attending to the consequential for a proper period of time, various events and objects are attended to fleetingly, irrespective of their relevance to immediate circumstances.

If the child *perseverates,* he unduly attends to an isolated phenomenon without regard to its importance, its pertinence, or its suitability. Rather than ceasing to attend after an experience is no longer of consequence, and possibly detrimental, attention continues inflexibly, hence the perseveration. This perseveration may entail either external or internal aspects of experience. For example, he may attend unduly (beyond the time of its having relevance) to any object in the immediate environment (visual perseveration). Or he may perseverate on a particular sound instead of diverting attention to sounds in the environment that are more meaningful as well as purposeful (auditory perseveration). On the other hand, perseverative attention may be given to a past experience, or to an internal aspect of experience. Instead of shifting attention in a normal, fluid manner from external to internal aspects of experience, the child attends abnormally to an isolated sound or to a scene, usually from the recent past. In some children internal perseverations are severe and exceedingly disturbing to them as well as to their parents. We have found it especially difficult to shift attention in children who have auditory perseverations.

Disinhibition likewise represents a type of attentional abnormality. In this instance the child is characterized by being unable to control ideation processes. Normal attention to internal experience is impossible because not only is that which is relevant brought into mind but *any* past experience, despite its inappropriateness, comes in to interrupt and disturb the process. Unlike perseverations on internal experience, in disinhibition the attention to any idea is only fleeting, with the mind shifting randomly from one internal event to another. This condition can be highly debilitating.

Distractibility, perseveration, and disinhibition may be analyzed in terms of deficits in monitoring systems. In distractibility there is a lack of normal feedback so the child is unaware of his giving attention to irrelevancies, or if he is aware of it, he cannot monitor (scan and select) that which is of consequence. In perseveration we have a similar circumstance in that normal monitoring of attention fails so it persists in a given direction without interruption. The concept of monitoring also can be applied to the problem of disinhibition. The processes involved in scanning and in the selection of past experience are deficient in terms of meeting immediate needs; the child is unable to scan, select, and *hold* internal events in a manner consistent with his circumstances.

More generally, these three behavioral characteristics can be analyzed according to patterns of disintegration. Previously we stressed the concept of overloading. In certain respects each of these characteristics, distractibility, perseveration, and disinhibition, is a manifestation of the child's inability to successfully integrate sensory information. Each characteristic is simply a warning that the nervous system is unable to comply with its demands; the system is overloaded. This type of analysis, stressing that "breaks" and dysfunctions are occurring in the nervous system, makes it possible to apply new findings from psychoneurology and psychophysiology. Moreover, the works of Lindsley (1960), Magoun (1963), McCleary and Moore (1965) and Young (1964), among others, indicate that when attention is disturbed, the dysfunction may be in the sub-cortex, in that area of the brain commonly referred to as the reticular formation. We anticipate that our studies of electro-cortical functions while the child is in the act of learning might provide further evidence on the nature of these highly significant learning disabilities. Using the techniques of biomedical engineering, it may be possible to relate attentional disturbances to specific learning deficits in given children (Myklebust, 1967).

Educational Procedures

Distractibility. The distractible child finds the average school room overly stimulating and therefore is unable to perform to the best of his ability. The environment should be arranged so that he can work most successfully. The room should be free from excessive visual stimulation, with the walls painted a plain, soft color and exhibits or pictures kept to a minimum. Cupboards for toys and shelves are covered so as to be less distracting. Likewise, auditory distractions should be reduced since these children tend to respond to extraneous sounds. The slightest click of heels down the hall or the sound of steam from a radiator distracts their attention and ability to listen. In our setting on Lake Michigan, it is not unusual for one of the five-year-olds to suddenly jump up while listening to a story and say, "Lake, lake, lake," when he hears the lapping of the waves. With maturation, the average child learns to inhibit background noises, to select those that are most pertinent, but this boy is unable to do so.

Although it is not always possible to alter the physical location of a classroom, a room that is away from the street and playground noises should be selected. Myklebust (1955) indicates that soundproof rooms are not desirable, however, because the child must learn to structure the auditory field in an environment containing both foreground and background sounds. On the other hand, noisy rooms make it difficult for the child to learn. Floors can be covered with rugs or tile and rubber tips put on the legs of furniture to lower the noise levels.

Auditory training materials, such as phonograph records, are carefully selected. The most suitable records for rhythm work are those having clearly defined patterns, without language or stories. Those intended for development of listening ability should not have background music. All records must be free from scratches and other distortions since even these sounds may become foreground to these children. Toys which produce irrelevant noises or squeaks are avoided so the child does not become engrossed in listening to these sounds rather than in playing and learning appropriately.

Myklebust also suggests that proximity be controlled since distance or space sometimes is distracting. Therefore, small rooms or work areas are most satisfactory. Screens which surround the child free him from distraction and assist him in learning to work independently. Many children voluntarily go to small work areas when they find they cannot work well in a group. In some instances proximity is controlled even more closely by having the teacher sit behind the child with an arm on the back of his chair or over his head, thus providing a boundary within which he can function more comfortably. The degree to which the environment is structured varies with the degree of distractibility. The purpose is not to punish but rather to facilitate learning. As the child establishes inner controls, external adjustments are gradually modified; until these controls are established, little learning takes place.

In addition to modification of the environment, distractibility is reduced by altering the presentation of assignments. Materials for the day's work are kept in a closed cupboard and only one thing is presented at a time. When the child has finished with an activity, it is removed and the next task is introduced. Toys with several pieces (puzzles, color cones, etc.) are presented carefully. If the child sees pieces of a puzzle scattered about, he becomes overly stimulated and his performance deteriorates. Instead, the pieces are kept out of sight and he is given only one at a time.

The daily routine is planned to alternate auditory and non-auditory activities. Periods of quiet follow language work and other stimulating auditory activities. For these children listening and concentration require a great deal of effort. A nine-year-old expressed this by saying, "I wish I didn't have to work so hard just to listen." Adult aphasics as well as children have commented on the difference in conversing in a one-to-one situation and in a group; many cannot tolerate group conversation.

Specific procedures are necessary to develop foreground listening. When giving instructions a small portable binaural amplifying unit is beneficial because it provides a means for structuring sound. The child is provided with a sheet of paper with pictures or words and the instructions are given through the head phones with the volume slightly increased. When he has learned to follow directions in this manner, faint background sounds are introduced and he is asked to continue listening only to the instructions; the background sounds may be faint drum beats or soft music.

Throughout the training sessions the teacher is alert for signs of fatigue and "overloading." Distractible children often cover their ears or walk away when they can no longer tolerate listening. When signs of frustration are apparent, the teacher reduces the auditory activities, including her own verbalizations. Eventually children learn to maintain attention. Although some residuals of the disability remain, they learn to structure themselves and select seats in a quiet part of the room or turn themselves away from noises. Parents must be made aware of the ways in which they can modify the home environment by providing an area to which the child can go when his problem of maintaining attention becomes overwhelming.

Perseveration. Perseverations are manifested in a number of ways. Some children perseverate on a type of toy. Initially they might have played appropriately with a little car but they cannot shift so they tend to "over-use" it. Or they cannot stop running, laughing, or giggling. They literally need help in interrupting these actions or they disintegrate. This inability to shift also is seen during play time when they are unable to shift from running to jumping or from rolling the clay to patting it. Or when asked to draw a circle they cannot stop but continue to draw more and more circles. Subtle perseverations are sometimes seen in older students. A twelve-year-old boy when asked to write the alphabet wrote the letters in proper sequence but with three *f*'s. When asked why he had written them, he replied, "I got started and couldn't stop." This boy often wrote the words *see* or *three* with either three or four *e*'s instead of two.

Verbal perseverations are seen in both children and adults. They may name an object correctly, then continue saying the same word when trying to name others. One boy looked at the picture of a squirrel and named it correctly but called all the other animals squirrels because he could not shift his response pattern. Adult aphasics in particular are aware of such errors and become frustrated when they cannot voluntarily alter what they are saying. Though more severe, their experience is like that of the individual who gets a tune in mind and continues to hum it hour after hour.

Remediation for perseverations begins with an analysis of the situations in which they occur. Often they increase as the child fatigues; therefore, the routine should provide for quiet rest periods. When the perseveration is on particular toys, the objects are removed. When the toy has been disposed of and the child persists in asking about it, the teacher does not reinforce the perseveration by saying, "No, you can't have the little red car, I put the little red car in another room." Instead she calmly but firmly says "no" and goes on with other activities. Parents should be advised not to purchase toys that cause the child to perseverate.

When the perseveration pertains to a certain type of action, the teacher frequently uses the single word "stop." For example, if a child persists in making circular movements, watch his drawing and when he has completed the circle say "stop." This verbal signal may be reinforced with either a tactual or visual cue. Sometimes it is necessary to physically stop him by holding his hand; at other times it is sufficient to raise a finger. A visual cue, such as a red dot, can be drawn at the end of a line or at the top of the circle to help him see the position for stopping. To reduce verbal perseverations, it is necessary to help the individual "out of the groove" by introducing an activity which requires a completely different type of response. If an aphasic persists in saying the same word, he is asked to read or write for a few minutes, after which work on spoken language is resumed.

Disinhibition. The disinhibited child appears apathetic and spends a good part of the school day gazing around the room or looking out of the window. Usually he presents less of an overt behavior problem in the classroom than the distractible child, but he *is* a problem inasmuch as he does not complete his work. He must be reminded time after time to continue with his assignments because he cannot sustain attention for more than a few minutes.

Some disinhibited children, due to their inability to control their ideation, make irrelevant remarks. They think of something and cannot wait, thus the unusual remarks. A nine-year-old made comments in class discussion such as, "What kind of soup did you have for lunch?" Because of these irrelevant and inappropriately timed comments, the disinhibited child is judged to be silly or odd. Learning to postpone reactions is a part of maturation but many children with learning disabilities find this a difficult behavior pattern to establish. Sometimes the problem is so great that parents are advised not to bring their child to school until time for class to begin. Others, who cannot wait, "plunge" into an assignment, and make errors because they cannot listen and thereby postpone an immediate response.

We have found that disinhibition can be reduced by establishing routines both at school and at home. When the child knows the general pattern and sequence of events to be expected, his behavior is less impulsive and better organized. Before each school day the activities are outlined verbally or on the blackboard so the child has ample opportunity to know what will happen next. It is beneficial to have him help make the outline and to judge the approximate length of time he feels it will take to complete various assignments. Although we emphasize use of a daily plan, both teachers and parents should avoid setting up anticipatory situations. The child should not be told far in advance about things he or his family will do. Being told about a dinner party or the arrival of guests several days before the event only creates undue questioning and anxiety. He persists in asking questions because he cannot mentally inhibit the anticipated event, though he should be attending to other work. If the daily routine is to be altered or if guests are coming to the home, the child might be given a rather detailed explanation of these events just prior to the occasion. Rather than saying, "Mr. and Mrs. Jones are coming for dinner tonight," the mother pre-structures the child so he will know what will happen and what he is to do when the guests arrive. She may say, "Mr. and Mrs. Jones are coming after Daddy gets home from work. First we will sit in the living room and talk; then we will go into the dining room and eat. You will sit in this place, I will sit beside you, Daddy will sit here, etc. After dinner Mr. and Mrs. Jones, Daddy and I will go into the living room. You may play with the toys in your room. I will watch the clock and come to your room when it is time for you to go to bed." The amount of detail in the description depends upon the individual child and his ability to understand verbal instructions.

Various techniques improve ability to wait. Tape recorded instructions with timed delays between items have been used successfully. The child is given a page of pictures or words and listens to instructions on tape which are worded so that he must slow down his impulsive actions and learn to wait. Typical instructions are as follows:

> Listen, I am going to tell you to mark some pictures. Do not pick up your pencil yet; just wait and listen. Mark only the pictures that I name; do not mark any others. Wait . . . (pause two or three seconds) Pick up your pencil . . . wait . . . Mark the kitten. That's nice . . . wait . . . Mark the dog.

As the child improves the time delay is increased and more complex directions are given:

Listen . . . Pick up the red pencil. Mark the dog. Wait . . . Put the pencil on the table. Wait . . . Pick up the blue pencil . . . Wait . . . Mark the house. Wait . . . Put the pencil on your desk.

Older disinhibited children who cannot complete assignments independently are given alarm clocks and told to work until the bell rings. Initially the timer may be set for only two or three minutes, then gradually the delay period is extended.

Hyperactivity. Hyperkinetic children are always on the move, shifting feet, tilting chairs, tapping pencils, or rustling papers. Some are unaware of their excessive movements and must be made to realize the disturbance they create. They should be given sturdy, immovable desks and chairs which are not easily overturned. The amount of material in their desks is reduced to a minimum to avoid manipulation of extra pencils, crayons, or paper. We also recommend that simple clothing be worn. Girls who wear fancy dresses with ruffles, belts, and necklaces tend to fumble with these accessories to an extent that interferes with their learning.

Techniques are devised to help the child control his random movements. A seven-year-old learned to walk down the school halls with his hands in his pockets to control his tendency to touch everything along the way. Another who darted in and out of the classrooms while walking from one place to another learned to follow a block pattern in the tile floor. Once he had established the correct habit of going directly from one room to another, he no longer looked at the tiles but walked casually down the hall with the other children. A teacher may sit or stand behind the hyperactive child and place a hand, or only a finger, on his shoulder as a cue to stop the movement. Eventually he internalizes the "feel" of this hand on his back and gains the essential inner control.

Overstimulation. Certain children with learning disabilities lose control of themselves when confronted with unfamiliar or overstimulating activities. They run wild, burst into euphoric laughter, or suddenly begin tipping over tables and chairs. This type of reaction is known as _catastrophic behavior_ and occurs when the child faces situations requiring greater integrative capacities than he possesses (Myklebust, 1954). Activities which create overstimulation are visits to supermarkets, parties, gym classes, and the less structured classes in school. Gross motor activities also tend to cause loss of control; the child starts to jump or run and finds it difficult to stop.

When a catastrophic reaction occurs, the teacher helps the child regain his equilibrium. The best procedure is to remove him from the situation by placing him in a small, quiet environment, without toys or activity.

Often he is exhausted after the episode and needs a period of rest. The child is removed, not for punishment but so he can regain self-organization and control. Sometimes the teacher sits near him for reassurance.

Some children are overstimulated by excessive praise; they become excited and disintegrated. Only moderate praise and encouragement should be given. A simple "that's nice," or an approving smile is more beneficial than exuberant praise. Excessive verbalizations and auditory stimulation of any type can be disturbing. If the level of frustration appears to be increasing, the teacher must reduce stimulation and try to prevent the catastrophic reaction.

In summary it should be emphasized that not all children with psychoneurological learning disabilities exhibit the behavioral symptoms discussed above. Many organize sensory experiences successfully and enjoy normal stimulation in the classroom. Controls are necessary only for those who cannot. Initially, the environment is structured to provide a setting in which they can work and learn.

Kaliski (1959, p. 688) says that the "world around the child may be perceived in a diffused, chaotic, structureless conglomeration of visual, auditory and kinesthetic impressions; the child needs help to bring order into that chaos." She suggests that the teacher provide a structure—a framework in which a child can function spatially (a limited area), temporally (clearly defined and sufficiently brief periods of time for each activity), contextually (plan and outline the program of the day), emotionally (setting reasonable limits), and socially (working with small groups, selective groupings, working toward integration into larger groups).

When ability to integrate and respond appropriately improves, external controls are reduced. The environment must be flexible. The children should not become dependent upon the structured setting but gain ability to function in a more normal environment. We do not wish to produce rigidity; we do not want children without spontaneity, without a range of freedom. Sears, Maccoby, and Levin (1957) state that it is not sufficient that a child be kept from doing damage—he must develop standards of conduct that will not require constant policing in order to maintain acceptable kinds of behavior. Ultimately the control and organization should come from the child himself.

CHAPTER IX

Implications and Outlook

The concentration of effort on children with learning disabilities has far-reaching implications for the development of better programs of education for all children. A number of professional groups, in a manner never previously realized, are deeply concerned about how children learn and why they do not learn. We are searching for new ways in which to view children and their problems.

The diagnostician no longer can ask only whether the child is emotionally disturbed, mentally retarded, or impaired in vision or hearing because consideration must be given to the possibility that learning processes have been altered by a dysfunction in the brain. As indicated throughout this volume, the dysfunction may be subtle, affecting only a certain process of learning without reducing or modifying intellectual capacity. There are many implications for the training of diagnosticians. It is incumbent upon training centers to recognize this new demand—their changing role—in the training of specialized personnel. Though it is not easy to single out disciplines, perhaps this is particularly true in the training of clinical child psychologists, school psychologists, and pediatricians.

The impact of the child with a learning disability on special education can be expected to be profound. In a real sense this child's problem presents a new challenge in that he compels the educator to learn more about learning (Bruner, 1966). No other child has presented this challenge in this way. The imposition is not on mental ability, not on sensory capacities, not on emotional development, but on learning per se. As an indication of the educational programs that are needed and the results to be anticipated when remediation is provided, we briefly consider the progress made by some of the children with whom we have had the pleasure of working.

PROGRESS WITH REMEDIATION

Evaluation is an integral part of the educational program. Through use of objective measures and through observations, teachers and administrators can appraise the effectiveness of the remedial work. They also can measure the degree of progress made by each child and determine whether changes in procedure are indicated. Appraising progress requires more than a single measure; it should parallel the multi-dimensional criteria outlined in Chapter III. We ascertain progress academically but also in areas of specific deficit, e.g., perception, memory, etc., as well as in

307

total behavior. In other words, we assess progress in reading but we also study whether a child can learn more effectively through debilitated modalities and if he can transfer newly learned skills into everyday life.

Although much remains to be accomplished by way of controlled studies in remediation, our experience and our results from longitudinal studies suggest that progress can be made at all levels and that the outlook is favorable. Progress is dependent, however, on careful long range planning and repeated evaluation of each child.

Preschool Children

Most preschool children are referred because of disturbances in auditory learning. Although other disabilities may be present, it is the inability to communicate that causes most concern. In Chapter IV we discussed the subgroups within this population; for our purposes now, we divide them into two major categories: those who cannot understand the spoken word and those who understand but cannot use spoken language expressively. There are significant differences to be considered in these populations in terms of educational planning and the progress to be expected.

Children with disorders of auditory input are more debilitated in total learning (McGrady, 1964). One of the measures by which this more generalized involvement can be revealed is the Vineland Social Maturity Scale (Doll, 1953). This scale is especially useful because it includes areas of behavior affected by the learning disability, i.e., communication, socialization, self-help, occupation, locomotion, and self-direction. In order to determine the effect of auditory disorders on total social maturity, the scale was used with 40 preschool children in our training program, 20 with primarily receptive disorders and 20 with primarily expressive disorders. The mean social quotient for the receptive group was 68.3 and for those with expressive deficits, 78.6. From these results it is evident that a disturbance of auditory learning affects total social maturity and that receptive disorders are the more debilitating.

After the children had been in our program of remediation for approximately two years, the Social Maturity Scale was administered a second time. The mean social quotient for the receptive group had increased to 79.8 and for the expressive group to 90.2, a gain of approximately ten points for each. Progress also can be demonstrated in the areas of specific deficit. For example, in an analysis of 10 four-year-old receptive aphasics, the mean verbal comprehension age prior to initiation of remedial training was 2 years and 11 months. After 11 months of remediation the mean comprehension age was 4 years and 6 months, an average gain of 1 year and 6 months. Similarly studies of children having deficits primarily in expressive language manifest a favorable outlook. For example, vocabulary growth was studied in a group of 12 children, with a mean age of 38 months. When remedial training was inaugurated the mean size of vocabulary was 6 words, a range of from 2 to 8 words. After 6 months of training the average vocabulary ranged between 150 and 200 words.

Individual longitudinal studies likewise are valuable indicators of progress. A four-year-old with formulation difficulties used only 1 word sentences prior to initiation of training. Within 3 months after remediation was begun the average length was 3 words; after 6 months it was 4, and after 9 months it had increased to an average of 5½ words.

Progress made by children who began training during preschool years has been studied more broadly. Eighty-five children enrolled in our training program and in the local schools were evaluated to determine the need for special education to be continued. Some were dismissed after kindergarten because they required no further help; others were placed in special programs as follows:

15 remained in the regular class—no further remediation necessary
41 remained in the regular class but required supplemental assistance
18 required special class placement
11 required placement in a special school

It was the children who had mild expressive disorders and mild auditory receptive deficits that remained in regular classes without supplemental education; occasionally conferences were held with the classroom teachers. With minor modifications in classroom seating, in wording of instructions, and in presentation of assignments, this group was able to do average work.

The type of special education for the others depended upon the severity of the problem and multiplicity of involvements. Those with deficiencies in auditory motor integration needed the least amount of remediation in areas of academic learning. Language training usually was necessary for two or three years but the majority learned to read, write, spell, and calculate from instruction in the regular classroom. Many had difficulty reading aloud until they learned the motor patterns for speaking, but even those who could not utter intelligible words learned to read silently. While over-compensation in reading is not encouraged, reading instruction should not be delayed for school-age children who have expressive aphasia. As shown in Chapter IV, some learn to speak by associating a movement pattern with the written word. A few found it hard to write because they could not learn either auditory-motor or visual-motor patterns.

Children with reauditorization disturbances often had difficulty with oral reading and phonics because they could not remember letter sounds, names, phonograms, or words. Some, but not all, of those with deficiencies in formulation or syntax found the auditory aspects of reading trouble-some. It appeared that the disability which interfered with holding a sentence plan in mind interfered with ability to blend sounds and syllables into words. About 50 per cent of the group with expressive disorders had problems in reading, writing, or spelling. Relatively few had difficulty with subject matter. They understood classroom discussions and the basic concepts in social studies, science, etc., but as long as the expressive disorders were present, verbalizing in the classroom was limited.

In contrast, children with receptive impairments had more pervasive learning disabilities. They tended to have deficits in most aspects of learning in relation to the language arts and with the other areas of study. Because auditory comprehension was inferior, they could not progress to higher levels of read and written language. A few excelled in phonics, in learning to read, but could not understand what they read. Some did well in spelling; however, they could not always use the words meaningfully. Many were good in penmanship but their written expression, grammar, and punctuation were deficient.

Children with deficits in auditory comprehension often achieve more successfully in science than in social studies because the emphasis is on demonstration rather than on verbal discussion; even preschoolers show good problem-solving ability. A severe receptive aphasic was "experimenting" at the age of seven. He spent his free hours watching repairmen or visiting a radio station, learning from observation. By the age of nine he had constructed ingenious devices and could work with complex electrical circuits, yet at the same time his language was almost unintelligible to the casual listener. The science curriculum, with its emphasis on direct experience, serves as a basis for language development.

Children of School Age

The school-age population with learning disabilities is composed of those who have various types of deficits and integrities. Behrens (1963) studied 40 children of school age to determine the psychological and behavioral changes following a period of remediation. His sample included dyslexics, aphasics, dysgraphics, and some who were primarily dyscalculic. He found that the greatest improvement was in verbal learning. Social maturity did not show the expected gain, indicating that more emphasis should have been given to this important facet of everyday living.

In a study of a more homogeneous population, comprised of 60 dyslexics, we found the social quotient to be 86.1. The mean intelligence quotient was 101.3, the mean oral reading quotient, 77.6, and the reading vocabulary quotient, 80.3. Of these 60 children, 16 were evaluated again after one year of remedial education. The average gain in reading vocabulary was 1.9 grades and in spelling, 1.3 grades. The social quotient rose from 83.1 to 88.2 (Johnson and Myklebust, 1965).

In the dyslexic population as a whole, the overall learning disability is less pervasive than that of receptive aphasics. Yet because of their reading disability, school subjects are difficult. They understand discussions and concepts presented orally in class but they cannot read their textbooks or do homework assignments unless the material is read to them. Classroom teachers have commented that the dyslexic children have a good grasp of content. A third grade teacher who asked her class to write a short story about Memorial Day wrote the following about Bill, a dyslexic boy who read at a first grade level: "I could not read Bill's story because the words were composed of nothing more than a series of letters in random order, but when he read his story back to me I realized that he had grasped the meaning of this holiday better than any other student in the class. I could give him 100 per cent for content, but the story itself could not be graded."

Children with written language disorders are not deficient in acquisition of content from either classroom discussions or from reading their assignments. Hence, they rarely need special class placement. However, they require training for a considerable length of time since the demand for written work increases with advancement in school. On the average, those who have only written language disorders have the highest social quotient of any group with learning disabilities. A study of ten children in our training program yielded a mean quotient of 90.1. The only functions falling below average were those involving written communication. Of those with disorders of written language, dysgraphics require the shortest period of remedial education. After the motor patterns for all of the letters are acquired, these children have only slight difficulty with school learning.

IMPLICATIONS FOR SCHOOL PLANNING

There are many implications for school planning. There is a need for identification of children with learning disabilities and for establishment of remedial programs. However, as our discussion suggests, there is considerable variability in the extent and type of remediation required. It should not be assumed that all children with learning disabilities require special class placement. Many profit from instruction within the regular class and are removed only for remediation in the areas of learning that are disturbed.

In a review of 350 children for whom we have provided special training and whom we have followed for several years, only 46 needed a special class. Although we do not know that ours was a representative sample, these findings suggest that self-contained classrooms are necessary for about 15 per cent of the group. Ultimately, however, most school systems must have two, and possibly three, types of programs for children with learning disabilities. The following are suggested.

The Self-contained Classroom

Children who cannot profit from regular educational experiences require special class placement. This includes the hyperactive children and those whose disability is so severe that they cannot be taught in the average setting. Arbitrary decisions regarding the number of children per class only detracts from the objective of individualized planning; nevertheless, guide-lines are helpful. If the learning problems warrant special class placement, no more than ten children should be assigned to one teacher; eight is preferable. In some instances even eight is more than one teacher can teach properly. When the group is hard to manage, teacher aids or semi-trained assistants can be used. The task of the assistant is to help with assignments and with independent effort while the teacher is free to work with children individually or in small groups.

When warranted by the size of the group, classes should be arranged according to the major learning deficit, thus achieving greater homogeneity. Preferably, the age span of the children within the group should not exceed three years.

The Resource Room

Resource rooms are especially adaptable for children with mild to moderate learning involvements; they are highly effective at the junior and senior high school levels. Students attend the special room for as many as three class hours per day, depending upon individual needs. They remain in the regular room for the periods from which they profit from normal instruction. This plan is based on the evaluation of integrities and deficits for each of the children.

The teaching within the resource room is individual or in small groups, four being the maximum size of the group. Every attempt is made to keep the groups as homogeneous as possible in terms of age, grade levels, and types of disabilities. In this setting the maximum case load for teachers is approximately twenty; some school districts restrict the number to ten because they want all of the children to be seen individually. In many instances, however, well-planned group activities are more effective than individual instruction.

The resource room occasionally consists of a suite of small rooms, some of which are free for students to work on assignments, specially prepared tapes, or other activities. High school students learn to operate tape recorders and can go over assignments orally, take their own dictation for book reports, themes, etc. Initially students may spend two or three hours per day in the resource room but as they improve, the time is reduced. They are encouraged to seek additional help when new and complex subject matter is introduced.

The Itinerant Program

Some school districts plan for teachers to work in two or possibly three different schools. Usually the teacher then works both with individuals and with small groups. Each session, however, should cover a period of from 40 to 60 minutes. Any child whose learning problem warrants special education should not be seen for less time. With varied activities and with proper management, the well-trained teacher can work an hour with the most hyperactive child. She begins with an hour of individual work each day; later she adds another child so that he learns to tolerate additional stimulation, and then gradually integrates him into classroom activities. The *how* and *when* of integration require careful study of the child, his behavior and patterns of learning. The first classroom experience is not necessarily in nonacademic activities, as art or physical education. For some, especially distractible children, this is the most troublesome. Many do well when they are first integrated into a reading group or a social studies discussion. The first group experience should be pleasurable and related to something that the child can do well.

The itinerant teacher also works with children who have mild learning problems, with specific deficits, and she frequently consults with the classroom teacher. Normally she deals with fewer children than the teacher in the resource room since time is spent in transportation from one school to another. The children should receive daily instruction so that they will make as much progress as possible in the shortest period of time.

PLANNING WITHIN THE PROGRAM

Educational planning within the program varies, depending upon whether the teacher is in a self-contained classroom, in a resource room, or is assigned as an itinerant teacher. Yet, fundamentally the objectives and procedures are the same. Irrespective of the setting, the teacher views the disabilities in all dimensions, from the specific deficits to the affected areas of academic achievement, to the overall affects on social maturity and adjustment. Then and only then can the needs of children with learning disabilities be met.

The primary differences in programming pertain to the amount of comprehensive education for which the teacher is responsible. In a special class, the teacher is responsible for most of the child's education, for the development of skills, and for all other information he should acquire. Although emphasis is given to tool subjects, the plan should be broad enough to include all aspects of the curriculum as well as extracurricular activities; every classroom, from kindergarten through high school, should include work in the language arts, mathematics, social studies, science, art, music, health and physical education, each at the optimum level of the child's ability.

Encompassed in the total plan is individualized instruction adapted to the learning disability. With careful planning the teacher, while covering areas of the curriculum, can bring about the improvement of deficits and provide for the acquisition of knowledge. A science lesson emphasizing non-verbal problem solving may be the base for language stimulation but it also can be an excellent opportunity to teach students with nonverbal disorders how to perceive subtle changes in the effects of light and heat on plant growth. In the same manner art, music, or physical education provide unique opportunities for teaching specific skills, such as auditory sequencing, visual-motor patterns, and left-right orientation.

The lesson plan for children within special classes is developed according to subject matter, e.g., reading, social studies, etc., or according to broad unit plans. In the latter instance, a topic such as "The Post Office" or "The Bakery" is selected and all subject matter woven into the daily or weekly program. The advantage of the unit plan is that it can be set up according to a developmental sequence, starting with the experience (a visit, field trip, or film) and progressing through oral discussions, reading, and written language. Arithmetic is brought into the lessons whenever appropriate. Social studies with discussions around the importance of community helpers, personal and civic responsibilities also can be used. Art, music, or creative activities are woven into the program, especially for younger children. Whatever the plan, it is critical that the specific deficits be considered. The teaching cannot stop with acquisition of information; it must go to deeper levels of learning to make certain that disturbances in perception, memory, and sequentialization are given proper remediation.

Planning within the resource room or in the itinerant program varies from that of the self-contained classroom because the teacher is less responsible for all aspects of the child's education. Yet she must know the total educational plan, be familiar with the course work and the textbooks. In these settings the teacher works with the areas of disability, but she also analyzes the child's school program to determine how and where the disability might interfere with learning. While the objective is not to tutor the child in school subjects, support is given when possible. Throughout the programming, the teacher uses a double plan, looking at the deficits and relating them to broad areas of learning and behavior.

The teacher is always *curriculum conscious* but never *curriculum bound*. She works with the child's deficits but incorporates newly acquired skills into academic learning. It is important that the child not feel the work done by the special teacher is separate from the rest of his school program. No child is more in need of an integrated program than one with a learning disability. Whether in a self-contained class or in a resource room, the teacher first considers the disturbances in learning and gradually raises the level of function so that the child can relate more normally with others.

ON-GOING DEVELOPMENTS

The outlook for the child with learning disabilities is optimistic because of the remarkable interest in the problems which he presents. The approach, however, varies from state to state, from one geographic area to another, and from nation to nation. We will not attempt to review these trends. Instead, to illustrate the ways in which the future is promising, we discuss only certain developments with which we are involved.

Criteria for Diagnosis and Classification

As indicated in Chapter I, there is an urgent need for further evidence on reliable criteria for diagnosis and classification in education, psychology, and medicine. With support from federal, state, and local agencies we are conducting research designed to provide such criteria. This investigation involves an entire community, several school districts, highly trained psychologists, language pathologists, teachers of learning disabilities, ophthalmologists, pediatricians, neurologists, otolaryngologists, electroencephalographers, data processors, and computer programmers. Several thousand school children and their families are participating to make the study possible.

The investigation began with evolving a battery of screening tests to be administered to entire school populations, the purpose being to identify those who are underachieving. As stressed in Chapter I, underachievement is defined, not in terms of grade placement alone, but in terms of a quotient based on potential for learning (mental capacity), chronological age (maturational level of the nervous system), and on grade placement (opportunity for being taught and for school experience).

The areas of learning measured by the screening tests include receptive (input) and expressive (output) processes, verbal and nonverbal: verbal intelligence, nonverbal intelligence, reading, written language, spelling, arithmetical processes, emotional growth and maturation, and the teacher's judgment of learning and adjustment. Any child failing to attain a quotient of 90 on any area of learning is considered to be an underachiever; he fails the screening test and must be seen for an intensive diagnostic study.

The screening tests simply identify underachieving children, while the purpose of the intensive study is to determine the cause of the underachievement. The areas of behavior and learning covered are essentially the same as those included in the screening battery, but each area of function is investigated in greater detail; group techniques are not applied. In addition, each child is studied pediatrically, ophthalmologically, neurologically, and electroencephalographically. The findings from all aspects of the study are coded for extensive statistical analysis using computer methods.

The plan is to identify clusters of disturbed processes that impede learning—disturbances that are mainly auditory, visual, verbal, nonverbal, that entail memory, that are reflected in learning to read, in learning to use the written word, to calculate, to spatialize, to develop orientation, to acquire social perception, to learn motor patterns, and to acquire other functions of the type discussed throughout this volume. These clusters of deficits then will serve as a guide for diagnosis of learning disabilities in education and psychology. There are implications also for programming of remediation.

Similarly, it is assumed that clusters of characteristics will emerge from the findings of the evaluation in pediatrics, neurology, ophthalmology, and electroencephalography. These in turn will constitute guides for diagnosis and classification of learning disabilities in each of these areas of medicine.

Finally, it is intended that the interrelationships among all of the findings will be determined, as shown by the Schema below. The ultimate

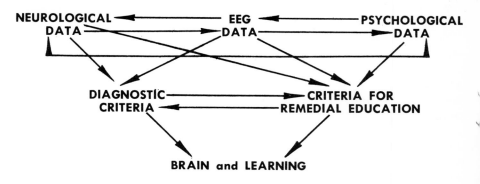

goal is to "learn more about learning" so that all children will be benefitted to the greatest extent possible.

Brain Dysfunctions and Learning

One of the most urgent needs is for research on the relationships between
brain dysfunctions and types of learning disabilities. That relationships
exist between electro-cortical patterns and types of sensory stimulation in
normal persons has been shown, especially by Cohen and Walter (1966).
The work of Hughes (1967) also is pertinent. Using standard EEG
techniques he has shown associations between classifications on the basis
of the patterns of the electroencephalogram and certain types of learning
disabilities.

Another approach to more precisely determine the ways in which given
brain dysfunctions alter patterns of learning is to obtain electroencephalographic recordings while the child is in the act of learning. Using automated
biomedical engineering techniques, we have been engaged in such studies
during the past few years and the results are promising. A fundamental
aspect of the hypothesis is that to demonstrate certain dysfunctions, the
brain must be working, in the act of learning. In other words, to show that
a system, such as the auditory or the visual, is not functioning normally,
it may be necessary to activate it by placing demands on it for learning.
Moreover, it may be possible to reveal dysfunctioning only when a given
system is required to operate in a given manner. For example, the auditory
system may function normally when the demand is intra-auditory (auditory
for both input and output), but not when the function requires interneurosensory processes (auditory to visual or visual to auditory).

This research is based on such presumptions and a number of learning
tasks have been prepared and preprogrammed for automatic presentation.
Both intra- and inter-problems have been included and cover the range
of nonverbal-nonsocial, social-nonverbal, and verbal. Previously we indicated that the brain codes and classifies, not only on the basis of whether
the information is auditory, visual, etc., but also on the basis of whether
it is meaningful or meaningless. The learning tasks have been designed
accordingly.

It is not our intention to discuss results; they still are preliminary. However, it appears that much can be gained from this approach. The findings
for Paul, who when evaluated was 10 years of age, are illustrative. He had
a marked deficiency in learning to read but was of normal intelligence.
Four types of auditory learning tasks were given to him: (a) nonverbal-
nonsocial (tonal patterns); (b) social-nonverbal (common everyday
sounds); (c) verbal (spoken word); (d) verbal-nonsocial (nonsense syllables). All tasks were intra-auditory in nature. While he was making

judgments about these tasks, EEG recordings were made and the results averaged by an analog computer.

On the basis of these findings it appears that in Paul's case the auditory system functions normally when the information entails tasks which are nonverbal-nonsocial, social-nonverbal, and verbal-nonsocial, but not when the task is verbal and *meaningful*. In other words, when the demand is for coding and classifying meaningful words that sound alike, the brain shows evidence of a dysfunction. Such evidence is not elicited unless the brain is activated in a certain manner and unless the results are averaged by computer techniques.

Over a period of time, when many more results are available, it may be possible to be much more precise in the diagnosis of brain dysfunctions that disturb learning processes and, hence, vastly more specific in regard to the type of remediation that may be most successful. In this, and in many other ways, the outlook is both promising and challenging.

A PSYCHONEUROLOGICAL CONCEPT OF LEARNING AND LEARNING DISABILITIES

Through study of learning disabilities insights will be gained which lead to a more complete understanding of all learning. Work accomplished during the past century is highly relevant, but more specific to current definition and effort are the contributions of Birch (1964), deHirsh (1966), Kirk (1963), Orton (1937), Cohen and Walter (1966), and Young (1964). Of special importance to the concept discussed here are studies made by Boshes and Myklebust (1964), Hughes (1967), Lawson (1967), McGrady (1964), and Zigmond (1966). These investigations make it possible to formulate a psychoneurological concept of learning. It is expected that this formulation will be modified and enlarged as further evidence is forthcoming.

McGrady investigated verbal and nonverbal functions in normal, speech defective, and aphasic children. His findings are noteworthy in showing how deficiencies in receptive processes bring about a greater imposition on learning than those affecting expressive functions.

Zigmond's research is particularly revealing in terms of the psychoneurological implications of learning disabilities. She studied a population of dyslexic school children, comparing them with the normal on a number of criteria, including rate of learning auditorially, visually, and intersensorially (auditory to visual and visual to auditory). She also obtained evidence on neurological status. Her findings manifest that, in dyslexics, an imposition on auditory learning brings about a greater deficiency than impositions on the visual, irrespective of whether the deficit is in intra- or inter-learning processes. Significant too is her finding that the intercorrelation of abilities varies greatly in dyslexics as compared with the normal. Though functions such as auditory memory were deficient in the dyslexics, these functions did not correlate with reading. In contrast, for the normal, such intercorrelations were highly positive. These results are in agreement with our experience in remediation. Certain abilities may not be deficient or can be raised by training, but unless special stress is placed on integration of functions, these abilities develop in isolation. As shown by the Schema below, these findings are critical to theoretical formulations as well as for educational planning.

Still another type of evidence is provided by the investigations of Hughes, Lawson, and Boshes and Myklebust. Lawson classified children with learning disabilities on the basis of ophthalmological findings, then compared the intercorrelations of abilities by group. Statistically significant differences were noted; the interrelationships of behavioral functions varied according to diagnostic classification. He concluded that this variation might be attributed to factors other than visual impairment, such as to the disease processes causing the deficit in vision as well as the disturbance of learning. Significant for this discussion is the fact that when classified on the basis of physiological findings, the intercorrelation of abilities varied.

Hughes studied a similar group using electroencephalographic techniques. He too classified the children into groups on the basis of physical findings: the type and pattern of the EEG. Using multiple regression statistical procedures, he showed that the clusters of abilities varied significantly on the basis of the brain dysfunction present, measured by the electroencephalogram. According to these results, to some extent the type of imposition on learning can be predicted from the EEG findings.

In another investigation Boshes and Myklebust used findings from the neurological examination as the basis for classification: negative, suspect, and positive. The three groups, each varying in neurological status, were compared on 21 behavioral variables: oral reading, auditory blending, spelling, etc. Though there were no differences among the groups in levels of achievement, as shown by the means and standard deviations, the type and the extent of the intercorrelation of abilities varied significantly. They were equal in levels of function but dissimilar in the manner in which each function was related to the other. In other words, though equivalent in degree of ability, the manner in which the abilities were used varied according to neurological status. The study concluded that the psychology by which each group learned and compensated for their deficiencies was determined partially by the pattern of the neurological dysfunctions.

From these studies, covering educational and clinical experience, as well as intensive statistical analyses, a psychoneurological concept of learning and learning disabilities may be formulated (see Schemas below). Learning occurs intra- and intersensorially, verbally and nonverbally, in terms of meaningful and meaningless information, as well as in terms of input and output processes. In normal children essentially all functions and processes are interrelated. Information and learning of one type is spontaneously converted or translated into other types, without training. Therefore, studies of normal children using the intercorrelation technique reveal associations among functions and relationships, as shown by the Schema for normal learning (below).

Schema illustrating a psychoneurological concept of normal learning

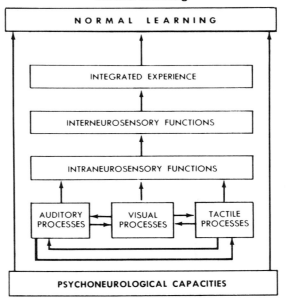

In contrast, a dysfunction in the brain causes an imposition which affects one or more of these processes. This in turn brings about a modification, characterized by a pattern of learning in which abilities and processes develop in isolation, shown in the schema for children with learning disabilities. Though a given ability such as auditory or visual memory may not be deficient, or is raised to the average level through remediation, this ability is not spontaneously converted into other types of function (represented by arrows with broken lines). Hence, the ability is not available to the child for learning in manners which typify the psychological processes in normal children.

The implications for remedial education are numerous; different assumptions must be made in relation to children with learning disabilities. In comparison with the normal, they must be viewed as having deficits and integrities but neither of these necessarily is interrelated psychologically in the manner characteristic of normal children. Accordingly, the educator faces a challenging task, but also an opportunity. He must provide a circumstance for learning that not only provides for development of deficit areas of function but one that fosters normal association of experience. He must educate in a manner that makes it possible for a disintegrated child to become a wholesome, integrated individual. The child with a learning disability presents this challenge in a new and urgent manner.

Schema illustrating a psychoneurological concept of learning disabilities

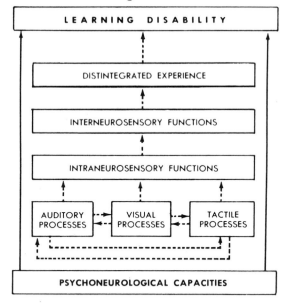

References

Agranowitz, A. and McKeown, M. *Aphasia handbook for adults and children.* Ann Arbor: Edward Brothers, 1959.

Allport, G. and Vernon, P. *Studies in expressive movement.* New York: Macmillan, 1933.

Anderson, H. (ed). *Creativity and its cultivation.* New York: Harper & Bros., 1959.

Applegate, M. *After all, Mrs. Murphy.* In C. Carr (ed). When children write. Washington: Association for Childhood Education International, 1955, *95*, 23–29.

Babinski, J. Anosognosie. *Rev. Neurol.*, 1918, *I*, 845–848.

Badal, J. Contribution a l'étude des cécités psychiques: Alexie, agraphie, hémianopsie inférieure, trouble du sens se l'espace. *Arch. d'ophthal.*, 1888, *8*, 97–117.

Baker, H. and Leland, B. *Detroit tests of learning aptitude.* Indianapolis: Test Division of Bobbs-Merrill, 1935.

Bax, M. and MacKeith, R. (eds). *Minimal cerebral dysfunction.* Little Club Clinics, #10, London: Heineman, 1963.

Bayley, N. The development of motor abilities during the first three years. *Soc. Research Child. Develop.*, #1, 1935.

Beach, F. et al. (eds). *The neuropsychology of Lashley.* New York: McGraw-Hill, 1960.

Behrens, T. A study of psychological and electroencephalographic changes in children with learning disorders. *Unpublished doctoral dissertation*, Northwestern University, 1963.

Bender, L. *Problems in conceptualization and communication in children with developmental alexia. Psychopathology and communication.* New York: Grune & Stratton, 1958.

Benton, A. *Right-left discrimination and finger localization.* New York: Paul B. Hoeber, 1959.

———, Hutcheon, J., and Seymour, E. Arithmetic ability, finger-localization capacity and right-left discrimination in normal and defective children. *Am. J. Orthopsychiat.*, 1951, *21*, 756–766.

Berg, P. *Reading in relation to listening.* In O. Causey, (ed). The reading teacher's reader. New York: The Ronald Press, 1958.

Binet, A. and Simon, Th. *The intelligence of the feebleminded.* Baltimore: Williams & Wilkins, 1916.

Birch, H. (ed). *Brain damage in children—the biological and social aspects.* Baltimore: Williams & Wilkins, 1964.

——— and Belmont, L. Auditory-visual integration in normal and retarded readers. *Am. J. Orthopsychiat.*, 1964, *34*, 851–61.

——— and Lefford, A. *Two strategies for studying perception in "brain-damaged" children.* In H. Birch (ed). Brain damage in children. Baltimore: Williams & Wilkins, 1964.

Boshes, B. and Myklebust, H. A neurological and behavioral study of children with learning disorders. *Neurology*, 1964, *14*, 1.

Brain, R. *The nature of experience.* London: Oxford University Press, 1959.

Brown, C. *The teaching of secondary mathematics.* New York: Harper & Bros., 1953.

Brown, R. and Bellugi, U. *Three processes in the child's acquistion of syntax.* In E. Lenneberg (ed). New direction in the study of language. Cambridge: The MIT Press, 1964.

Bruner, J. *The process of education.* New York: Vintage Books, Knopf, Random House, 1963.

———. *Toward a theory of instruction.* Cambridge: Harvard University Press, 1966.

Bryant, N. Characteristics of dyslexia and their remedial implication. *Exceptional Children*, 1963, *31*, 4, 195–199.

Buck, J. *Time appreciation test.* Los Angeles: Western Psychological Service, 1946.

322

Cassirer, E. *The philosophy of symbolic form. Vol. I.* New Haven: Yale University Press, 1953.

Chomsky, N. *Syntactic structures.* The Hague: Mouton, 1957.

Cobb, S. *Borderlands of psychiatry.* Cambridge: Harvard University Press, 1948.

Cohen, J. and Grey Walter, W. The interaction of responses in the ' ain to semantic stimuli. *Psychophys logy,* 1966, *2,* 187–196.

Cohn, R. Dyscalculia. *Archives of Neurology,* 1961, *4,* 301–7.

———. *The person symbol in clinical medicine.* Springfield, Illinois: Charles C Thomas, 1960.

Creak, M. and Ini, S. Families of psychotic children. *J. Child Psychol. Psychiat.,* 1960, 1, 156–175.

Critchley, M. *The parietal lobes.* London: Edward Arnold, 1953.

———. *Developmental dyslexia.* Springfield, Illinois: Charles C Thomas, 1964.

Cruikshank, W. *A training method for hyperactive children.* Syracuse: Syracuse University Press, 1961.

Dantzig, T. *Number—the language of science.* New York: Macmillan, 1939.

Davitz, J. (ed). *The communication of emotional meaning.* New York: McGraw-Hill, 1964.

Dearborn, W. Ocular and manual dominance in dyslexia. *Psychol. Bull.,* 1931, 28:704.

de Hirsch, K., Jansky, J. and Langford, Q. *Predicting reading failure.* New York: Harper Row, 1966.

de Quiros, B. Research in dysphasia in school children. *La Revista Fonoaudiologica,* 1962, *8,* 1, 22–68.

Doll, E. Neurophrenia. *Am. J. Psychiat.,* 1951, *108,* 50.

———. *The measurement of social competence: A manual for the Vineland Social Maturity Scale.* Minneapolis: Ed. Test Bureau, 1953.

Durrell, D. *Improving reading instruction.* New York: World Book Company, 1956.

Eames, T. Some neural and glandular bases of learning. *J. of Ed.,* Boston University School of Ed., 1960, *142,* 4, 1–34.

Eisenson, J. *Aphasia in adults.* In L. Travis (ed). *Handbook of speech pathology.* New York: Appleton-Century-Crofts, 1957.

English, H. B. and English, A. *A comprehensive dictionary of psychological and psychoanalytical terms.* New York: Longmans, Green, 1958.

Ernhart, C. et al. Brain injury in the preschool child: Some developmental considerations: Comparison of brain injured and normal children. *Psychol. Monog., General and Applied,* 1963, *77,* 10.

Ervin, S. *Imitation and structural change in children's language.* In E. Lenneberg (ed). *New direction in the study of language.* Cambridge: MIT Press, 1964.

Fernald, G. *Remedial techniques in basic school subjects.* New York: McGraw-Hill, 1943.

Fisher, S. and Cleveland, S. *Body image and personality.* New York: D. Van Nostrand, 1958.

Freud, S. *On aphasia.* New York: International Universities Press, Inc., 1953.

Frostig, M. and Horne, D. *The Frostig program for the development of visual perception.* Chicago: Follett Publishing Company, 1964.

Gates, A. *The improvement of reading: A program of diagnostic and remedial methods.* (3rd ed). New York: Macmillan, 1947.

Gerstmann, J. Syndrome of finger agnosia, disorientation for right and left, agraphia and acalculia. *Archives of Neurology and Psychiatry,* 1940, *44,* 389.

Geschwind, N. *Neurological foundations of language.* In H. Myklebust (ed.) *Progress in learning disabilities.* New York: Grune & Stratton, 1967.

Gesell, A. and Amatruda, C. *Developmental diagnosis.* (2nd ed). New York: Paul B. Hoeber, 1947.

Gibson, E. Learning to read. *Science,* May, 1965, 148.

Gillingham, A. and Stillman, B. *Remedial training for children with specific disability in reading, spelling and penmanship.* New York: Sackett & Wilhelms, 1940.

Goldfarb, W. *Childhood schizophrenia.* Cambridge: Harvard University Press, 1961.

Goldring, S., Sugaya, E. and O'Leary, J. *Maturation of evoked cortical responses in animal and man.* In P. Kellaway and I. Petersen (eds). Neurological and electroencephalographic correlative studies in infancy. New York: Grune & Stratton, 1964.

Goldstein, K. Language and language disturbances. New York: Grune & Stratton, 1948.

—— and Scheerer, M. Abstract and concrete behavior. *Psychol. Monog.,* 53, 1941.

Goodenough, F. *Measurement of intelligence by drawings.* Yonkers-on-Hudson: World Book Company, 1926.

Goodglass, H. Application of psycholinguistic research to clinical diagnosis in aphasia. *Paper read at the 12th Annual V.A. Med. Res. Conf.,* Cincinnati, 1961.

Goody, W. Time and the nervous system: The brain as a clock. *Lancet,* 1958, 1139–44.

—— and Reinhold, M. Some aspects of human orientation in space. *Brain,* 1952, *75,* 472.

Graham, F. et al. Brain injury in the preschool child: Some developmental considerations: Performance of normal children. *Psychol. Monog. General and Applied,* 1963, *77,* 10.

Guilford, J. Three faces of intellect. *Am. Psychologist,* 1959, *14,* 469.

Hall, E. *The silent language.* New York: Doubleday, 1959.

Hallgren, B. Specific dyslexia (congenital word blindness): Clinical and genetic study. *Acta Psychiat. Neurol.* (Supp. 65), 1950, 1–287.

Hardy, W. G. *Problems of audition, perception and understanding.* Washington: The Volta Bureau (reprint), 1956.

Head, H. *Aphasia and kindred disorders of speech.* New York: Macmillan, 1926.

Hebb, D. The semi-autonomous process: Its nature and nurture. *Am. Psychol.,* 1963, *18,* 1, 16–27.

Hécaen, H. and Ajuriaguerra, J. *Left-handedness.* New York: Grune & Stratton, 1964.

Heider, F. *The psychology of interpersonal relations.* New York: John Wiley and Sons, 1958.

Hermann, K. *Reading disability.* Springfield, Illinois: Charles C Thomas, 1959.

Hinshelwood, J. Congenital word blindness. *Lancet,* 1900, 1, 1506–8.

——. *Congenital word-blindness.* London: H. K. Lewis, 1917.

Hinsie, L. and Campbell, R. *Psychiatric dictionary.* (3rd ed). New York: Oxford University Press, 1960.

Hiskey, M. *Nebraska test of learning aptitude for young deaf children.* Lincoln: University of Nebraska, 1955.

Hughes, J. *A review of electroencephalography in learning disabilities.* In H. Myklebust (ed). Progress in learning disabilities. New York: Grune & Stratton, 1967.

Hughes, M. *Relationship of Maturation to Writing.* In C. Carr (ed). When Children Write. Washington: Association for Childhood Education International, 1955, 7–15.

Ilg, F. and Ames, L. *School readiness.* New York: Harper & Row, 1965.

Ingram, T. Perceptual disorders causing dyslexia and dysgraphia in cerebral palsy. Oxford: *Child neurology and cerebral palsy.* Second National Spastics Society study group, 1960, 97–104.

John, E. High nervous functions: Brain functions and learning. *Ann. Rev. Physiol.,* 1961, *13,* 451–484.

Johnson, D. and Myklebust, H. *Dyslexia in Childhood.* In J. Hellmuth (ed). Learning Disorders. Vol. 1. Seattle: Special Child Publications, 1965.

Johnson, M. Reading problems: Diagnosis and treatment—a summary. *Paper read at Reading Institute,* Temple University, 1961.

Kaliski, L. The brain-injured child: Learning by living in a structured setting. *Am. J. of Mental Deficiency,* 1959, *63,* 4, 688–96.

Kanner, L. *Child psychiatry.* (2nd ed). Springfield, Illinois: Charles C Thomas, 1957.

Kaplan, G. (ed). *Emotional problems in early childhood.* New York: Basic Books, 1955.

Kastein, S. *An analysis of the development of language in children with special reference to dysacusis.* In J. Hellmuth (ed). The Special Child in Century 21. Seattle: Special Child Publications, 1964.

Kent, G. *E-G-Y Scales.* New York: The Psychological Corporation, 1946.

Kephart, N. *The slow learner in the classroom.* Columbus: Charles E. Merrill, 1960.

Kirk, S. A behavioral approach to learning disabilities. In *Conference on children with minimal brain impairment.* Chicago: Easter Seal Foundation Research, 1963, 40–51.

Klausmeier, H., Dresden, K., Davis, H. and Wittich, W. *Teaching in the elementary school.* New York: Harper & Bros., 1956.

Knoblock, H. and Pasamanick, B. Syndrome of minimal cerebral damage in infancy. *J.A.M.A.,* 1959, *170,* 12 1384–1387.

Langer, S. *Philosophy in a new key.* Cambridge: Harvard University Press, 1957.

Lawson, L. *Ophthalmological factors in learning disabilities.* In H. Myklebust (ed). Progress in learning disabilities. New York: Grune & Stratton, 1967.

Lenneberg, E. (ed). *New directions in the study of language.* Cambridge: MIT Press, 1964.

Lindsley, D. *Attention, consciousness, sleep and wakefulness.* In J. Field, H. Magoun, and V. Hall (eds). Handbook of physiology, Section I: Neurophysiology, Vol. III, 1960. Washington, D. C.: Am. Physiol. Society.

Lowenfield, V. *Creative and mental growth.* New York: Macmillan, 1952.

Luria, A. *The role of speech in the regulation of normal and abnormal behavior.* New York: Liveright Publishing Corp., 1961.

McCleary, R. and Moore, R. *Subcortical mechanisms of behavior.* New York: Basic Books, 1965.

McGinnis, M. *Aphasic children.* Washington, D. C.: Alexander Graham Bell Association for the Deaf, Inc., 1963.

McGrady, H. Verbal and nonverbal functions in school children with speech and language disorders. *Unpublished doctoral dissertation.* Northwestern University, 1964.

McSwain, E. and Cooke, R. *Understanding and teaching arithmetic in the elementary school.* New York: Holt, Rinehart & Winston, 1958.

Magoun, H. *The waking brain.* (2nd ed). Springfield, Illinois; Charles C Thomas, 1963.

Miller, G., Galanter, E. and Pribram, K. *Plans and the structure of behavior.* New York: Henry Holt & Co., 1960.

Miller, J. *Adjusting to overloads in information.* In D. Rioch and E. Weinstein (eds). Disorders of communication. Baltimore: Williams & Wilkins, 1964.

Milner, B. Intellectual function of the temporal lobes. *Psychol. Bulletin,* 1954, *51,* 42.

Money, J. (ed). *Reading disability: Progress and research needs in dyslexia.* Baltimore: Johns Hopkins Press, 1962.

Monroe, M. *Children who cannot read.* Chicago: University of Chicago Press, 1932.

Morgan, W. A case of congenital word-blindness. *Brit. Med. J.,* 1896, *2,* 1378–9.

Mowrer, O. *Learning theory and the symbolic processes.* New York: John Wiley & Sons, 1960.

Myklebust, H. *Auditory disorders in children: A manual for differential diagnosis.* New York: Grune & Stratton, 1954.

———. *Development and disorders of written language. Vol. I, Picture Story Language Test.* New York: Grune & Stratton, 1965.

———. *Development and disorders of written language. Vol. II.* New York: Grune & Stratton, 1967.

————. *Learning disabilities in psychoneu-rologically disturbed children: Behavioral correlates of brain dysfunctions.* In P. Hoch and J. Zubin (eds). Psychopathology of mental development. New York: Grune & Stratton, 1967.

————(ed). *Progress in learning disabilities.* New York: Grune & Stratton, 1967.

————. *The psychology of deafness: Sensory deprivation, learning and adjustment.* (2nd ed). New York: Grune & Stratton, 1964.

————. Training aphasic children. *Volta Review*, 1955, *57*, 149.

————. *Aphasia in Children.* In L. Travis (ed). Handbook of Speech Pathology. New York: Appleton-Century-Crofts, 1957.

———— and Boshes, B. Psychoneurological learning disorders in children. *Arch. Pediat.*, 1960, *77*, 6, 247–256.

———— and Johnson, D. Dyslexia in children. *Exceptional children*, 1962, *29*, 1, 14–25.

Neff, W. and Diamond, I. *The neural basis of auditory discrimination.* In H. Harlow and C. Woolsey (eds). Biological and biochemical bases of behavior. Madison: University of Wisconsin Press, 1958.

Nemoy, E. and Davis, S. *The correction of defective consonant sounds.* Boston: Expression Co., 1937.

Nielsen, J. *Agnosia, apraxia, aphasia: Their value in cerebral localization.* New York: Paul B. Hoeber, 1948.

Nissen, H. *Axes of behavioral comparison.* In A. Roe and G. Simpson (eds). Behavior and evolution. New Haven: Yale University Press, 1958.

O'Connor, N. and Hermelin, B. *Speech and thought in severe subnormality.* New York: Macmillan, 1963.

Oléron, P. Conceptual thinking of the deaf. *Amer. Ann. Deaf*, 1953, *98*, 304.

Olson, W. *Child development.* Boston: D. C. Heath, 1949.

Orton, S. *Reading, writing and speech problems in children.* New York: W. W. Norton, 1937.

Oseretsky, N. Psychomotorik: Methoden zur untersuchung der motoric. Beih,

Zeitschrift Angewandte, Psychol., 1931, *17*, 162.

Penfield, W. and Roberts, L. *Speech and brain mechanisms.* Princeton: Princeton University Press, 1959.

Piaget, J. *Play, dreams, and imitation in childhood.* New York: W. W. Norton, 1951.

————. How children form mathematical concepts. *Scientific American* (reprint), 1953.

Pimsleur, P. and Bonkowski, R. Transfer of verbal material across sense modalities. *J. Ed. Psych.*, 1961, *52*, 104–107.

Porter, R. and Cattell, R. *IPAT—CPQ, Form A.* Champaign, Illinois: Institute for Personality and Ability Testing, 1963.

Rabinovitch, R. et al. A research approach to reading retardation. *Research Publications, Assoc. for Nervous and Mental Diseases*, 1954, *34*, 363–96.

Revesz, G. *Psychology and art of the blind.* New York: Longmans, Green, & Co., 1950.

Rimland, B. *Infantile autism.* New York: Appleton-Century-Crofts, 1964.

Robinson, H. *Why pupils fail in reading.* Chicago: University of Chicago Press, 1946.

Russell, D. *Children's thinking.* Chicago: Ginn, 1956.

Russell, W. *Brain, memory and learning: A neurologist's view.* London: Oxford University Press, 1959.

———— and Espir, M. *Traumatic aphasia.* London: Oxford University Press, 1961.

Schilder, P. *Image and appearance of the human body.* New York: International Universities Press, 1950.

————. Fingeragnosie, fingerapraxie, fingeraphasie. *Nervenarzt*, 1921, 4, 625–629.

Schuell, H., Jenkins, J. and Jimenez-Pabon, E. *Aphasia in adults.* New York: Paul B. Hoeber, 1964.

Sears, R., Maccoby, E., and Levin, H. *Patterns of child rearing.* White Plains: Row Peterson, 1957.

Shneidman, E. A manual for the MAPS test. *Proj. tech. monog.*, 1951, *1*, 2.

Simon, C. *The development of speech*. In L. Travis (ed). Handbook of speech pathology. New York: Appleton-Century-Crofts, 1957.

Skinner, B. Teaching Machines. *Scientific American* (reprint), 1961.

Smith, H. and Dechant, E. *Psychology in teaching reading*. Englewood Cliffs, N. J.: Prentice-Hall, 1961.

Smith, J. and Kellaway, P. *The natural history and clinical correlates of occipital foci in children*. In P. Kellaway and I. Peterson (eds). Neurological and electroencephalographic correlative studies in infancy. New York: Grune & Stratton, 1964.

Stern, C. *Children discover arithmetic*. New York: Harper & Bros., 1949.

Stevens, G. and Birch, J. A proposal for classification for the terminology used to describe brain-injured children. *Exceptional Children*, 1957, *23*, 346-349.

Strauss, A. and Lehtinen, L. *Psychopathology and education of the brain-injured child. Vol. 1*. New York: Grune & Stratton, 1947.

―――― and Werner, H. Deficiency in the finger schema in relation to arithmetic (finger agnosia and acalculia). *Am. J. Orthopsychiat.*, 1938, *8*, 719-725.

Taylor, I. *Neurological mechanisms of hearing and speech in children*. Manchester: Manchester University Press, 1964.

Taylor, J. (ed). *Selected writings of John Hughlings Jackson. Vols. I and II*. New York: Basic Books, 1958.

Templin, M. *Certain language skills in children*. Minneapolis: The University of Minnesota Press, 1957.

Terman, L. and Merrill, M. *Measuring intelligence*. New York: Houghton Mifflin, 1937.

―――― and ――――. *Stanford-Binet Intelligence Scale*. Manual for 3rd revision. Boston: Houghton Mifflin, 1960.

Travis, L. *Speech pathology*. New York: Appleton-Century Co., 1931.

Van Riper, C. *Speech correction: Principles and methods*. (2nd ed). New York: Prentice-Hall, 1947.

Vygotsky, L. S. *Thought and language*. Cambridge: MIT Press, 1962.

Watson, W. and Nolte, J. *A living grammar*. New York: Sterling Co., 1956.

Webster's Third New International Dictionary. Springfield: G & C Merriam Co., 1963.

Wechsler, D. *Wechsler Intelligence Scale for Children*. New York: Psychological Corporation, 1949.

Weinstein, E. and Kahn, R. *Denial of illness: Symbolic and physiological aspects. Vol. 1*. Springfield, Illinois: Charles C Thomas, 1955.

Welch, R. *New Mathematics in the primary grades*. In. E. Weber (ed). Primary education: Changing dimensions. Washington, D.C.: Association for Childhood Education International, 1965, 44-55.

――――. *Developing rational power in intermediate-grade mathematics*. In E. Weber (ed). Intermediate education: Changing dimensions. Washington, D.C.: Association for Childhood Education International, 1965, 53-63.

Wepman, J. *Recovery from aphasia*. New York: W. W. Norton, 1951.

――――. Auditory discrimination, speech, and reading. *Elementary School Journal*, 1960, 325-33.

――――. *Auditory Discrimination Test*. Chicago: The Language Research Associates, 1958.

―――― and Jones, L. *Studies in aphasia: An approach to testing*. Chicago: Education-Industry Service, 1961.

Werner, H. and Carrison, D. Measurement and development of the finger schema in mentally retarded children: Relation of arithmetic achievement to performance on the Finger Schema Test. *J. Educ. Pyschol.*, 1942, *33*, 252-264.

―――― and Kaplan, B. *Symbol formation*. New York: John Wiley & Sons, 1963.

Whitehead, A. *The aims of education*. New York: Macmillan, 1929.

Young, J. *A model of the brain—An interdisciplincary approach to the study of brain function*. Oxford: Claredon Press, 1964.

Zahl, P. (ed). *Blindness; Modern approaches to the unseen environment.* Princeton: Princeton University Press, 1950.

Zangwill, O. *Cerebral dominance and its relation to psychological function.* London: Henderson Trust, 1960.

Zigmond, N. Intrasensory and intersensory processes in normal and dyslexic children. *Unpublished doctoral dissertation,* Northwestern University, 1966.

Zirbes, L. *Why Write?* In C. Carr (ed). When Children Write. Washington, D.C.: Association for Childhood Education International, 1955, 2–15.

Author Index

Agranowitz, A., 122, 128
Ajuriaguerra, J., 44, 272, 285, 292, 293
Allport, G., 34, 272
Amatruda, C., 15, 67, 245
Ames, L., 286, 291, 293
Anderson, H., 42
Applegate, M., 232

Babinski, J., 47
Badal, J., 47
Baker, H., 132
Bax, M., 7
Bayley, N., 15
Beach, F., 60
Behrens, T., 55, 63
Bellugi, U., 2, 130, 134, 135
Bender, L., 148, 150, 151
Benton, A., 8, 150, 246, 286
Berg, P., 180
Binet, A., 39, 286, 291
Birch, H., 5, 12, 21, 26, 28, 55, 318
Birch, J., 6
Bonkowski, R., 26, 28
Boshes, B., 8, 23, 24, 40, 55, 61, 63, 273, 318
Brain, R., 33
Brown, C., 244
Brown, R., 2, 130, 134, 135
Bruner, J., 136, 307
Bryant, N., 148
Buck, J., 291

Campbell, R., 234
Cassirer, E., 42
Cattell, P., 16
Chomsky, N., 130, 132
Cleveland, S., 272, 286
Cobb, S., 42, 203
Cohen, J., 316, 318
Cohn, R., 47, 245, 295
Creak, M., 46
Critchley, M., 89, 147, 148, 150, 151, 207, 245, 285, 293, 295
Cruikshank, W., 51

Dantzig, T., 244
Davis, S., 128
Davitz, J., 34
Dearborn, W., 293
Dechant, E., 190
deHirsch, K., 21, 318
deQuiros, B., 148
Diamond, I., 27
Doll, E., 6, 15, 16, 273, 298, 308
Dresden, K., 179
Durrell, D., 181

Eames, T., 147
Eisenson, J., 114, 122
English, A., 295
Ernhart, C., 11
Ervin, S., 130
Espir, M., 29, 36, 37

Fernald, G., 17, 56, 189
Fisher, S., 272, 286
Freud, S., 28, 66
Frostig, M., 57

Galanter, E., 29, 33, 35
Gates, A., 17, 147, 180, 183, 184
Gerstmann, J., 246, 286, 292
Geschwind, N., 26, 29, 36
Gesell, A., 15, 67, 245
Gibson, E., 26, 28
Gillingham, A., 148, 151, 158
Goldfarb, W., 1, 46, 295
Goldstein, K., 22, 30, 31, 42, 43, 74, 129, 234
Goodenough, F., 286
Goodglass, H., 131
Goody, W., 291
Graham, F., 11
Grey, Walter W., 316, 318
Guilford, J., 44, 286

Hall, E., 272
Hallgren, B., 148
Hardy, W., 66
Head, H., 122, 124, 292
Hebb, D., 26

Subject Index

Agnosia, 28f, 286ff
  auditory, 66
  auditory imperception, 66
  finger, 32, 47, 289f
  perception and, 32
Anomia, 114ff
Anosagnosia, 47
Aphasia, 35, 62
  auditory-motor integration and, 122ff
  central, 30
  educational procedures for 68ff, 82ff
  expressive, 28, 114ff
  receptive, 74ff, 99
  speech reading, 47
  syntactical, 130ff
Apraxia, 15, 41f, 114, 122ff, 125ff, 200ff
  expressive aphasia, 28
  nonverbal, 282f
  See also Dysgraphia, Motor Abilities
Ataxia, 15, 42, 45
  See also Motor Abilities
Auditory Language
  arithmetic and, 246ff
  auditory dyslexia, 170ff
  comprehension and, 78ff
  disorders of, 66ff, 74ff
  educational procedures for, 68ff, 82ff
  expressive, 114ff, 196ff
  learning disabilities and, 78ff
  memory span and, 111ff
  written language and, 195

Brain, the
  auditory learning and, 66
  cerebral dominance and, 45f
  conceptualization and, 42ff
  dysfunction, 23ff, 316ff
  expressive language and, 44ff
  inner language and, 36f
  language and, 36ff
  learning and, 26ff, 316
  nonverbal abilities and, 11f, 300
  overloading and, 30ff, 60, 64
  receptive language and, 37ff
  semi-autonomous systems concept, 26f, 44, 45, 64, 75
  underloading and, 30

verbal abilities and, 11f
verbal functions and, 35ff

Central nervous system
  brain dysfunction, 23ff
  functions, 4
  integrity of, 4
  See also Brain
Clinical teaching, 54, 63ff
  definition of, 63ff
  See also Educational procedures, Special education
Conceptualization, 42ff, 87ff, 97
  abstract ability and, 42ff

Dysarthria, 42
Dysgraphia, 40f, 62, 199ff
  spacing and, 213
  See also Apraxia, Teaching techniques
Dyslexia, 22, 28f, 62, 36, 48
  auditory, 173ff
  body image and, 151
  developmental, 147
  left-right orientation and, 150f, 292f
  letter orientation, 165ff
  perceiving detail, 165
  rate of discrimination, 169f
  remediation for, 147ff
  strephosymbolia, 147ff
  time orientation and, 151
  visual, 152ff
  word blindness, 147
  word form and configuration, 163ff

Educational procedures, 68ff, 82ff, 111ff, 156ff, 206ff, 253ff, 275ff
  auditory receptive language, 74ff
  dyslexia, 152ff
  See also Special education
Emotional adjustment, 15f, 55
  definition of, 15f
  learning disabilities and, 15f

Imagery, 58, 272ff
  as a process, 33f
  auditorization, 33f, 114ff, 180, 185ff
  ideation and productivity, 232